I Peed on Fellini

I Peed on Fellini

Recollections of a life in film

David Stratton

WILLIAM HEINEMANN

A William Heinemann book
Published by Random House Australia Pty Ltd
Level 3, 100 Pacific Highway, North Sydney, NSW 2060
www.randomhouse.com.au

First published by William Heinemann in 2008

Addresses for companies within the Random House Group can be found at www.randomhouse.com.au/offices.

National Library of Australia
Cataloguing-in-Publication Entry

Stratton, David, 1939–.
I peed on Fellini.

ISBN 978 1 74166 619 9 (pbk.).

Stratton, David 1939–.
Stratton, David 1939– – Contemporaries.
Film critics – Australia – Biography.
Film festivals.
Motion picture industry.

791.4309

Cover photograph by Jacky Ghossein / Fairfaxphotos
Cover design by Taryn Miller, Marlin Communications
Typeset in Garamond by Midland Typesetters, Australia
Printed and bound by Griffin Press

This book is dedicated to my children,
grandchildren, nieces and nephews;
and, indeed, to all young people
passionate about cinema.

Acknowledgements

I am extremely grateful to the following for their help and encouragement: Tom Ryan, the estimable film critic of *The Sunday Age*, was the first person who urged me to write a book based on my life in film. I hope he won't regret it. Gil Appleton was kind enough to read the early drafts and to make invaluable and supportive comments. I would also like to thank others who read earlier versions of the manuscript, or sections of it, and who offered essential advice and support: my niece, Helen Ensor, who undertook some research in the UK; Beverley and John Burke, who helped fill in some of the background to the Sydney Film Festival; Ross Tzannes, President of the SFF for so many years; and my friend and colleague Margaret Pomeranz, who provided her viewpoint on the early days of SBS and the genesis of *The Movie Show*. John Martin, Gerry Bartlett and Stig Björkman supplied photographs, and Alexandra Lamas also helped with her recollections. Errol Simper was kind enough to allow me to quote from 'A Certain Scribe'. I would also like to offer my thanks to Peter Weir and his daughter, Ingrid.

Tom Keneally, the grandfather of my god-daughter, introduced me to Fiona Inglis, the managing director of Curtis Brown (Australia), who became my greatly valued agent. I would also like to acknowledge the enthusiasm, support and encouragement of everyone at Random House Australia, especially Jeanne Ryckmans; Ali Urquhart; Julian Welch, my erudite editor; Lisa Shillan; Kelly Fagan; Amanda Mobbs; and Judy Jamieson-Green.

I am also grateful to Maxine McKew, who has been an inspiration to so many of us.

Finally, I would like to thank my wife, Susie, for her patience and support.

David Stratton
Leura, November 2007

Contents

Foreword
by Peter Weir

David Stratton, as Director of the Sydney Film Festival from the mid 1960s to the early 1980s, curated a set of programmes which had a strong influence on an emerging generation of Australian filmmakers. Sydney shared the programme with Melbourne. The Melbourne Festival Director, Erwin Rado, having passed on his contacts, left it to David to do the extensive travelling required to put a programme together. These festivals, together with the arthouse cinemas we haunted, served as film schools in a way, and, along with hands-on experience, this was how many young directors like me learnt the trade.

I submitted my first picture to the Sydney Film Festival in 1968 – a 16-mm black-and-white short which had taken a year of weekends to shoot. David's letter of rejection was tactful. While not feeling the film 'suitable', he looked forward to seeing my 'next film'. I wasn't all that disappointed, as I had thought it a long shot – the film having been made for the Christmas Revue at the television station where I worked as a stagehand. What was significant to me was the part about wanting to see my *next* film. That he even presumed there would be a *next*, and that he wanted to see it, was encouraging. As it happened, I was at work on a more ambitious short film for the station's next Christmas Revue. I did submit that film to the 1969 SFF and David accepted it.

From his first Festival onwards, David set out to establish strong personal connections with established and emerging filmmakers in Europe, Asia and the United States. At the time, very few prints were made of arthouse films, and they were generally earmarked for what were seen as the established and prestigious festivals. A print was an expensive and precious artefact, each screening risked potential damage. Many filmmakers had to be convinced that sending a print all the way to Australia was worth it. David understood this and worked hard to build a rapport with the directors; despite the title of this book, his was usually a conventional approach! He spent time with them, ate and drank and watched movies with them, both at festivals and in their homes. He knew their work and they came to trust him, and some began to factor a screening in the Antipodes into their release planning. Many came as guests, which further made local filmmakers feel connected to the wider film world.

Giants like Kurosawa, Ray and Fellini were still active at this time, but their movies were only the highlights of programmes that put audiences in touch with little-known and soon-to-be-known directors from across the world. Films like theirs were never seen on television, and of course there was no video or DVD. There were the arthouses but they tended to show films by well-known directors, at least until the Festivals began to broaden the taste of the audience.

Looking back at those programmes, which are included at the close of this book, the titles can still evoke an echo of the excitement they created in me at the time – films which sent me home with my head spinning, back to my own screenplays, to destroy yesterday's awful dialogue and banal plotting; to begin again with the inspiration of a particular film still buzzing in my head.

From the start, David encouraged young Australian filmmakers to screen their work at the SFF. He set up a competition – which was often how you came to know who else was out there. There's hardly a name amongst directors prominent in the 1970s and 80s who didn't screen at the Festival.

There were few venues for short films – television occasionally bought a short, and the commercial cinema still programmed them, but these tended to be 35-mm prestige offerings from government agencies like the Commonwealth Film Unit, or from equivalent bodies in other countries. So a director with a scruffy 16-mm short looked to UBU Films in Sydney – they ran a couple of excellent short film festivals – or to the Sydney and Melbourne Festivals. Looking back, it fascinates me that one screening at a festival was enough to justify the effort of a year of weekend work. Today a short film might keep a filmmaker travelling the world's festivals for a couple of years, but there was no such possibility then.

However, a festival screening could go awfully wrong – the audience could be vocal and turn the stalls into the Colosseum, with thumbs down to the filmmaker who displeased them. I saw this in 1969 with Tim Burstall's first feature, *2,000 Weeks*, when a section of the crowd began laughing at the dialogue and, finally, booing during the end credits, all in the presence of the director and his leading lady. It happened to me in Melbourne at the 1974 Festival with my first feature. Towards the end of the film, booing from one part of the audience was answered with cheers from another. An unnerving experience, but the late 1960s and early 70s was a period of extremes – a picture was declared 'ratshit' or 'brilliant', with little in between. Festival-goers took their films very seriously, especially in Melbourne. As I entered the foyer in 1974, I was greeted by a prominent handwritten sign: 'Owing to the death-threats to the projectionist, Antonioni's *China* will not be screened.'

As I graduated to feature films, David was a frequent visitor to my sets, and we stayed in contact over the years, always talking films and filmmakers – I remember one particularly excited call in the 1980s when he told me about a new young director whose work I just *had* to see: Jane Campion.

After several hours of pleasure with this book, of the many images I take with me perhaps the strongest is of the ten-year-old David, coming out of the Savoy Cinema in Andover, writing up his screening notes to be read late at night to his fellow boarders at Chafyn Grove School. Somehow, in my mind's eye he already has hints of that signature beard, and on the end of his nose a pair of spectacles – a sort of film-buff Harry Potter – and he has his young audience held captive by his ability to distil the mystery and wonder of a powerful motion picture. And he hasn't stopped since.

Preface

My only encounter with Federico Fellini occurred in a toilet. This was in 1966, when he was one of the most celebrated and admired film directors in the world. I'd seen and loved *I Vitelloni* (1953), Fellini's autobiographical film about life in his home town of Rimini; it was, and still is, one of my favourite movies. Also high on my list would be Fellini's *La Strada* (1954), *Le Notti di Cabiria* (1957, a film which celebrates a sublime, Chaplinesque performance from the director's wife, Giulietta Masina), *La Dolce Vita* (1960), *8½* (1963) and *Giuletta degli Spiriti* (*Juliet of the Spirits*, 1965). Fellini was something of an idol for me and though I liked his later films – from *Satyricon* (1969) onwards – less than his earlier ones, I remained an admirer even after our meeting, which occurred in Venice one hot summer night.

I was twenty-six years old and had recently directed my first Sydney Film Festival, one of eighteen I would direct and programme between 1966 and 1983. I was on my first visit to one of the legendary European festivals. Venice was, in fact, the oldest of all the film festivals, having been founded in 1933, during the era of Mussolini and Fascism. I had written to the Biennale, the arts organisation that runs the festival, explaining that, as Director of the Sydney Film Festival, I was seeking an invitation to Venice, and I had received the most cordial reply inviting me to attend as an honoured guest and offering me fourteen days of full board at the famous Hotel des Bains, on the Lido (the hotel later immortalised by Luchino Visconti in his film *Death in Venice*). The Lido is a long, narrow island located in the Venetian lagoon, about half an hour by boat from the city itself. Famous for its beaches and elegant hotels, the Lido is one of the most expensive resorts in Europe and it hosts the Film Festival every August–September.

In 1966 the Festival was directed by Luigi Chiarini, who had obviously decided to create some kind of controversy with his selection for the Opening Night. *The Wild Angels* was the latest production from the prolific Roger Corman, a director known, and in some quarters admired, for his prodigious output of C-grade shlockers (among them *Swamp Women*, *Naked Paradise*, *It Conquered the World* and *A Bucket of Blood*). Since the beginning of the 1960s Corman had become equally celebrated for his cycle of films based on stories by Edgar Allan Poe, but his latest film, *The Wild Angels*, which had opened in America a month earlier, was by far his most extreme work to date. Taking as his basis the Marlon Brando bikie film *The Wild One*, made twelve years earlier, Corman cast Peter Fonda in the Brando role as the leader of a biker gang which terrorises small California communities. Nancy Sinatra played his girl, Bruce Dern his mate, and the film was a polemic full of violence, pot-smoking and a pervasive attitude of anti-Establishmentism. The climax took place in a church: Fonda and the gang invade the funeral of the Dern character, oust the ineffectual preacher from his pulpit and turn the solemn ceremony into an orgy. It was certainly a sensationalist piece of work and, though I didn't know it at the time, it had just been banned in Australia.

The Palazzo del Cinema was packed that evening, and, since many of the seats appeared to be double-booked, there was a certain amount of confusion and even hostility. Despite the efforts of a large and angry woman to evict me, I clung doggedly to the seat to which I'd been assigned, which was just in front of the VIP party – Corman, Fonda, his sister, Jane, and her husband at the time, the French director Roger Vadim. When the audience finally settled down a short film commenced; 'short', that is, in the sense that it wasn't a feature film. It was, in fact, interminably long and consisted of nothing more than a pair of talking heads. There was no translation, so I had no idea what they were talking about. But I did learn one Italian word during that endless half-hour: '*Basta!*' ('Enough!') was the cry taken up by first one or two and then, it seemed, half the audience.

Finally *The Wild Angels* began. The audience was quiet, for a while, until the enormity of the film's anarchy and blasphemy became apparent, whereupon the noise erupted again. It was, indeed, a stimulating evening.

After the conclusion of the film the somewhat stunned guests were guided to boats located at the pier behind the Casino and transported, across choppy water, to the Piazza San Marco. The opening night party was to take place at the Palazzo Ducale, the Doge's Palace, which is to the right of the beautiful old Basilica of Saint Mark, and adjacent to the Bridge of Sighs. When you pass through the main entrance to the palace there is a vast courtyard surrounded by pillars, and this was where the party was taking place.

This being the first international film festival I'd attended, I knew nobody. The friends I would make in the future were unknown to me then; I was a babe in the woods, a novice at the game. But waiters offered glasses of champagne and I drank a few, realising, as I did so, that I was drinking on an empty stomach, not having had time for dinner that evening. And as I drank I observed my fellow party-goers.

I was certain that Corman and the Fondas were there somewhere, but I couldn't see them. I could, however, see other celebrities of the film world. There, for instance, was Julie Christie. And could that be François Truffaut with her? (It was; one of the films competing in Venice that year was *Fahrenheit 451*, directed by Truffaut and starring Christie.) And there was Dana Andrews, leaning against a wall, sipping whisky and looking bleary-eyed.

After about an hour of such 'star-gazing', several glasses of champagne, a few canapés and the occasional desultory conversation, I felt an urgent need to find a toilet. This did not prove to be all that easy. With an increasing sense of urgency I sought a 'cabinet' and, when I finally located one, the urge had become close to desperate. There I was at last, standing up against the porcelain, feeling a sense of relief. A man was standing next to me, a big man who looked vaguely familiar. I stole a glance at him. Could it be? It was.

Urinating next to me was none other than Federico Fellini. I can only excuse what happened next because of the excitement of the occasion, the champagne and my youthful naivety. I turned towards the great man.

'Mr Fellini,' I began. And I peed all over his shoes.

One result of this brief, unfortunate, encounter was that I learnt another Italian word: '*Stronzo!*' It means 'Asshole.' It was well deserved.

Chapter One

I have loved the cinema for as long as I can remember. I used to love the *smell* of cinemas in the old pre-multiplex, pre-popcorn days. I loved the moment when the lights started to dim and the curtains parted, I loved the trailers of coming attractions, the bold lettering of the opening credits, the stirring music. From an early age I decided that the director was the most important person involved in the making of a film because his was the last name to fill the screen before the movie proper began. I loved the five-minute *Tom and Jerry* and *Bugs Bunny* cartoons. I loved cartoon features, Technicolored musicals, westerns, swashbuckling adventures. Later on I learnt to love romantic films as well, and, indeed, almost any genre of film. I don't know why I developed this passion for the medium some called the Seventh Art, the medium that, more than any other, defined the twentieth century. But develop it I did.

In later years I have pondered on the fact that cinema, unlike the theatre, or television in its early days, has a permanence about it. Even when I was young it was possible, sometimes, to see revivals of old films; now, with the DVD revolution and the availability of feature films for downloading, it's relatively easy to see films from many different eras and even from many different countries whenever you choose. So we will always be able to see and enjoy the young Greta Garbo or the young Laurence Olivier. The latter's stage performances live on only in the memories of those who witnessed them, and when they die they're lost forever. But his film appearances will, I think, always survive. That's one of the reasons I love cinema.

One of my earliest memories involves making a film about myself. I don't know how old I was at the time – perhaps three or four – but I must have been sufficiently impressed by a visit to the cinema to attempt this experiment. I borrowed my mother's make-up mirror from her purse and used it to reflect an image of myself, deciding I would 'film' every minute of my life from then on, except, of course, when I was asleep. I was filled with regret for all the events I'd already missed in my life so far, but no matter; from now on everything I did would be 'recorded' in the mirror. This ambitious plan probably lasted all of half an hour, but somehow I never forgot it.

We're all fascinated by how we are formed, what makes us what we become, why we take this direction and not that. Why did I become passionate about the cinema? There was certainly no family background that could possibly have foreshadowed such an obsession. I was born into a world of bacon, cheese, tea and coffee. Stratton Sons & Mead Ltd was a well-respected wholesale and retail grocery company which, from its headquarters in the modest Wiltshire market town of Melksham (twelve miles south-east of Bath and about thirty-five miles north of Salisbury), served small retail stores in four counties. In the 1931 census (the last that would be taken for the next twenty years) the population of Melksham 'within' (that is, discounting the surrounding villages) was 3881, but the Avon Rubber company was based there, and so was Wiltshire Dairy Farmers, along with smaller companies like Maggs' Rope and Hemp, and Hurn Bros. Timber Yards, so it was quite a prosperous little place. The Strattons and the Maggs had intermarried over the years and my father's best friend was Dick Hurn, so the families that owned the town's businesses were a close-knit group.

My great-great-grandfather, James Stratton, had founded Strattons (as it was usually known) in 1824. It was originally called James Stratton & Son, but James's son, my great-grandfather, who inherited the business on his father's death, had taken a partner, a Mr Mead, and his name had been incorporated into the business. By the time I arrived on the scene Mr Mead was long gone, but his name was still used by the company.

The Stratton family had lived in Wiltshire for centuries; one branch of the family had always been farmers, though the members of our branch were 'gentlemen', according to the records in St Michael's Anglican Church where the death of an earlier James Stratton of Melksham, 'Gentleman', was recorded in 1580. My great-grandfather James was still alive when I was born, and still, nominally, managing director of the company; a photograph showing him, my grandfather and my proud father, with me, a small baby in his arms, had pride of place on the mantelpiece in our home when I was growing up. My grandfather, Arthur Duncan, always known as Bob, was a director of the company, but although he lived in Melksham he managed the Devizes branch, seven miles away. My father, Wilfred James, who was never called anything but Jim, grew up in a comfortable, modern two-storey house called Canewdon, located on Sandridge Road at the edge of the town. His brother, John, was seven years younger.

In addition to the establishments in Melksham and Devizes, Stratton Sons & Mead had branches in Marlborough and Newbury, which was in the neighbouring county of Berkshire. The firm had also acquired a hardware business in the town of Shaftesbury, in Dorset.

Strattons operated high-class retail establishments, but, as wholesalers, also supplied smaller retailers all over Wiltshire, northern Somerset, western Berkshire and parts of Gloucestershire. In 1938 my father, having served his apprenticeship working in the retail business for a company called Wrensons in Birmingham, was back home working as a salesman for the family business, based in Melksham.

The Strattons were strict Methodists; my grandfather, the gentlest and kindest of men, was passionate in his opposition to the Demon Drink. My father's younger brother, my Uncle John, followed in his father's footsteps in this regard, but my father was a rebel. He'd tried alcohol as a teenager, and as an adult he enjoyed his Scotch and his beer and, in later years, there was always a bottle of wine on the dinner table. In other respects he was pretty sheltered, by today's standards. At the time he married my mother, he had never been out of Britain and even a trip to London – about 100 miles away – was something of an expedition, rarely undertaken.

My mother, Mary, was altogether more sophisticated. Her parents came from Somerset. Frank Wells and Jessie Crocker were both born in Street, the town where the Clarks Shoe Company was founded. As a young man Frank had started working for Clarks; he was so successful that, soon after his marriage, he was sent to London to open the company's first West End retail outlet. Jessie was none too happy about leaving behind her family and friends, and she hated life in the capital.

Matters weren't helped by the fact that Frank was, according to my mother, neglectful of his wife. He bought a house in the suburbs but he often stayed at his club in the city at night, and Jessie, lonely and frustrated, turned to drink. Many of my mother's early memories were of coping with her mother when she had consumed a drop too much. As Clarks grew and expanded, Frank Wells prospered. He enjoyed the good life – meals in expensive restaurants, smart clothes, the best of everything. He often took his wife and daughter on summer holidays to Switzerland. He became a Mason and, in keeping with the rules of that society, was extremely secretive about his activities.

After leaving school my mother obtained a job as a demonstrator at an electricity showroom in London's West End. Her best friend during her teenage years was Frieda Taylor, whose father had been involved in the design of a section of the London Underground system. The two girls enjoyed an active social life in the city and, for his daughter's twenty-first birthday party, Frank Wells hosted a dinner at the exclusive Café Royal in Piccadilly; he hired an immensely popular comedian, Arthur Askey, to be the MC for the evening.

Jim Stratton and Mary Wells could not have come from more different backgrounds; indeed, it was quite by chance that they met. A married couple in their thirties had moved into a house near Canewdon and had befriended Jim; they offered to take him on a trip to London one weekend, which must have been a rare treat, and they stopped off to visit Frank and Jessie Wells, who were old friends of their family. My mother always said that, at this initial meeting, she wasn't impressed by the tall man with the deep blue eyes who accompanied her friends, but Mary soon accepted an invitation to spend a weekend in Melksham. Before long, Mary and Jim were seeing each other whenever possible. They quickly fell in love and I think they loved each other for the rest of their lives.

Jim's straitlaced parents were horrified when they discovered that the parents of the young woman their elder son planned to marry were consumers of alcohol! Frank Wells wasn't even a religious man; he used to describe himself as a 'non-fogian', and when asked what that meant explained that he cared more for his guts than for religion. His ample girth testified to his appetites.

Soon after the engagement was announced, Frank Wells decided to retire from Clarks. Instead of returning to Somerset, which would have pleased his wife, he bought a house in Andover, in Hampshire, probably because it was closer to London, which would enable him to keep his ties with friends in the city.

My parents' wedding took place on 27 August 1938 at All Saints Church in the quaintly named village of Upper Clatford, near Andover. The wedding breakfast was, apparently, a strange affair with the non-drinking, slightly disapproving Strattons on one side of the room and the more ebullient Wellses on the other.

My great-grandfather James lived, at the time, in one of the largest homes in Melksham, a seventeenth-century dwelling called Giffords. As a child I remember exploring the house, which seemed vast; but even more enormous was the garden, which had a large croquet court, stables and an apple orchard. As a wedding present, the old man gave his grandson a part of the orchard, and my father built a small bungalow on the land; he called the house Speedwell, and this became the young couple's first home. A few years ago I made a pilgrimage back to Melksham and found that both Canewdon and Speedwell were still standing.

I was born in Trowbridge, the county town of Wiltshire (and thus the headquarters of the local council), at 6.45 pm on 10 September 1939, exactly a week after Britain declared war on Germany. My mother, who kept a diary for the first few weeks of motherhood, reported that I weighed 8 pounds and 4 ounces and was 20 inches long. I was also rather sickly, having been born with a hernia. My mother seems to have found feeding me a painful process, and after a few days I alarmed the family doctor by losing weight. I was promptly weaned, which seemed to solve the problem.

Not long after my arrival on the scene my father was visiting clients in Salisbury and had taken Frank, his father-in-law, along for the ride. After a rather boozy lunch, the men noticed a recruiting office and my father decided that, rather than wait to be conscripted into the army, he would volunteer for the navy or the air force. Both these branches of the service showed little interest him, however, and when he returned home to Melksham that evening he told my mother that he'd enlisted in the army.

Within a few weeks he was dispatched to an army camp at Ripon, in the North of England, for basic training, and then he was shipped overseas, eventually winding up in Burma. It must have been an astonishing experience for such an unworldly man to find himself facing Japanese forces in far-off Asia. He survived the fighting but succumbed to malaria and other jungle sicknesses. He was sent to India to recuperate, and I remember being shown photographs of this handsome but emaciated man I was told was my father.

My mother, unwilling to stay on in Speedwell under the eye of her disapproving in-laws, rented the bungalow to an RAF officer who was stationed at a nearby air force base and took me to Andover to spend the war with her parents. Here she performed volunteer work for the Red Cross and was, as I recall, almost never at home. Unable to obtain enough petrol to drive her car, she acquired a bicycle and rode around the town, sometimes carrying me in a specially made basket.

On one of the rare occasions that I recall spending time with my mother I unwittingly experienced my first brush with the cinema. She had taken me to a Red Cross fundraising fete in the town and she was, as I learnt later, very excited because the guest of honour was to be the celebrated actor, Laurence Olivier. Crowds awaited the arrival of the great man, and my mother managed to get into the front row, holding me by the hand. Just as Olivier arrived I slipped away and toddled into the path of the actor, who knocked me over. I, naturally, raised the roof, whereupon Olivier picked me up, planted a kiss on the top of my head and handed me back to my mother. The incident caused a minor sensation, and my mother talked about it for years.

With my father away and my mother occupied, I spent most of the war with my grandparents. My grandfather spent every morning reading the *Daily Express* and the *Daily Telegraph* from cover to cover. As far as I could tell, the news was entirely concerned with the war, and I recall that when I heard one of the adults say that the war was coming to an end I expressed a childish concern that, if there was no more war, then there would be no need to publish any newspapers and my grandfather would have nothing to read in the mornings. Everyone thought this remark was very funny. After lunch my grandfather would play patience, using two packs of cards in a complicated system all his own. Occasionally, he would take me with him when he went shooting rabbits. I remember a day when a farmer was using a thresher to cut a field of wheat; as the area of wheat got smaller the rabbits hiding there were forced to flee and became easy victims for the bullets of my grandfather and his friends. I was both horrified and thrilled at the spectacle.

There were constant reminders that the war wasn't all that far away. The iron from gates and railings at the entrances of imposing buildings was crudely cut away for scrap to make guns. I remember hearing about the bombing of cities, and towards the end of the war everyone was fearful of the V1 and V2 rockets which we could hear flying over our heads; if the sound of them stopped suddenly, that meant they were coming down with their explosive load and, indeed, one fell on a pub in a nearby village one weekend, killing Londoners who were spending a few quiet days in the countryside. From time to time there would be an air-raid warning, and I would have to put on my Mickey Mouse gas mask (I will never forget the rubbery smell) and go with my mother and grandparents to the nearest shelter, which was situated a few doors away.

Church bells were not rung during the war; they would only peal in the case of an enemy invasion. If I encountered someone with a funny accent, I was told, I had to find a policeman quickly. Would an invading German – or, for that matter, an Irish spy (I later learned that they were the real worry) – ask advice of a five-year-old child? Well, maybe, because all the road and street signs had been removed. I, at least, knew that I lived at 76 Winchester Road, Andover, Hants. The address was drilled into me.

Rationing was a depressing fact of life, but my grandfather was often able to augment our food supply with rabbits he'd shot and even an occasional (and probably illegal) pheasant. These delights would be cooked by my grandmother or, if he'd been unusually lucky, they would be taken surreptitiously to the local butcher to be exchanged for difficult-to-obtain items like bacon, or even the occasional small piece of mutton, without the formality of 'points', the rationing coupons usually required for such things.

On most days my grandmother would take me shopping and, more importantly, to the cinema. She was a keen filmgoer (which her husband most certainly was not) and though my mother disapproved of that fact that I was taken to quite unsuitable films from an early age, my grandmother blithely ignored her daughter's protestations.

The wartime population of Andover was 8996, and the town boasted three cinemas at the time: the Odeon, which was owned by the Rank Organisation, the brand-new Savoy, completed in 1938, which was part of the Associated British chain, and the independently owned Rex, which changed its programme midweek. Most weeks, then, my grandmother and I would make four trips to the cinema, walking down Winchester Road into the town and back up the hill afterwards. My young mind was filled with images and stories I couldn't really comprehend. And I loved it. Recently I visited Andover for the first time in more than fifty years; the Odeon and the Rex had disappeared, but the Savoy was still there, exactly as I remembered it, standing back from the road. It had, however, been transformed into a trendy-looking pub.

Like most children of my generation, the first films I was taken to see were Walt Disney animated features. I have no recollection of it, but my mother told me that the first time I was taken to the cinema was to see *Dumbo*, which was released in 1941, so I was probably only three years old. I have more vivid memories of later Disney films: *Snow White and the Seven Dwarfs* (which I must have seen in revival, because this pioneering film – the first animated feature – dates from 1937), *Pinocchio*, *The Three Caballeros* and *Bambi*. The latter film had a tremendous impact on me, mainly for the scene in which Bambi's mother is killed by a hunter; but most of these films contained 'scary' scenes (the Witch in *Snow White* is a wonderfully malevolent creation). I think the first non-animated film I was taken to see was a Bob Hope comedy, *The Princess and the Pirate* (1944), a Technicolor extravaganza full of slapstick and jokes I couldn't possibly have understood. I have a strong recollection of this occasion because towards the end of the film I needed to go to the toilet; I told my grandmother, who – presumably not wanting to miss the climax of the movie – told me to just go where I sat. I still remember struggling to comprehend this strange order, but I duly peed in my pants, and felt highly uncomfortable for the rest of the film. I'm sure the theatre cleaning staff were very unimpressed.

During the war we only made a couple of visits to Melksham to see my other grandparents. My mother had no particular feelings for Bob and Winnie Stratton, but I suppose she felt obliged to make the effort once or twice. Since there was no petrol for the car this meant a somewhat tortuous bus journey, first from Andover to Ludgershall, and then a longish wait until another bus took us on to Devizes. There my grandfather would meet us, and we'd drive to Melksham.

I loved my paternal grandparents, but not as much as my maternal ones, probably because I didn't know them as well. My grandmother used to make sickly sweet fudge, to which I became quite addicted, and my grandfather smoked a smelly pipe. But they didn't listen to the radio, apart from the news, and visits to the cinema were as off-limits as the consumption of alcohol.

It was on these brief trips to Melksham that I first made acquaintance with the family business. My earliest memories were the smells. Bacon was cured and cheese stored at both the Melksham and Devizes branches of Strattons, and I loved my visits to these old-fashioned establishments with their wooden counters and devices for measuring ground coffee and specially blended tea into half-pound packets. I also loved the cats which prowled the warehouses and which were tolerated, even encouraged, to keep the rodent population under control. The big green delivery vans, with the firm's name in yellow lettering on them, were a familiar sight in the district.

In 1942, when I was still only three years old, I was enrolled in Miss Nello Pegum's nursery school. At the end of my first term Miss Pegum reported to my mother that 'David's progress has been oral . . . I have not even been able to teach him 'D' for David or OXO (never known to fail) – he just wasn't interested. He is quick at picking up other things – rhymes, songs, stories – [but] he is too impatient to persevere with learning to write.' Six months later, she reported that 'When [David] is in the mood, he can work surprisingly well . . . [but] he becomes very impatient with anything at all that is slow. His inattention prevents his making steady progress, but he certainly knows as much as he should, and a whole lot more.' These are interesting comments because, I must admit, I always have been rather impatient; I tend to make quick decisions, and to chafe when my time is wasted. However, I have no problem with slow-moving films.

My mother's car had been garaged at Winchester Road from the time that petrol rationing had been introduced, but by 1944 she had saved enough coupons for a trip to see her old friend Frieda, who had married George Woodfine, manager of the Boots chemists branch at Bexhill-on-Sea in Sussex. Although my mother had driven down to Bexhill from Andover a couple of times before the war, it was now five years since she'd made the journey, and I well remember how nervous she was about it, partly because she only had just enough petrol for the trip there and back and partly because of the wartime lack of signposts and street signs. We frequently had to stop to ask for directions, and on one occasion we took a wrong turn and found ourselves driving in a restricted area leading towards a military base, which was quite scary; my mother did a quick U-turn and, fortunately, managed to find her way out of the area.

Frieda and George had a daughter, Rosemary, a couple of years younger than me. We stayed with them for about a week, but I was very disappointed by my first view of the sea. The beach was covered with barbed wire and it was impossible to paddle in the water. After our stay in Bexhill we made the journey back to Andover without incident, although my mother's concern that we might run out of petrol before we made it home was vividly communicated to her five-year-old son.

Because of wartime shortages and rationing, luxuries were few. There was little fruit to be obtained and almost nothing in the way of confectionary. Ice-cream was unknown. With the approach of D-day, American convoys started rolling down Winchester Road, and I would stand outside the house watching the enormous tanks and armoured vehicles with fascination. Often the American soldiers would throw oranges and chewing gum in my direction, but catching was never something I was very good at and as a result the fruit was invariably bruised. Incidentally, rationing didn't come to an end with the cessation of hostilities; sweets and confectionary remained rationed until 1954, and I was fourteen before I was able to go to a shop and order a packet of sherbert lemons without the need for coupons.

During the war the tradition of having a bonfire and fireworks to celebrate Guy Fawkes Day on 5 November every year was understandably discontinued; my first experience of a celebratory bonfire was, in fact, on 8 May 1945, when I was five years old. A nearby street was closed off for a huge bonfire, atop of which an effigy of Hitler was consigned to the flames; this was VE (Victory in Europe) Day. VJ Day followed in August and I knew my father would be coming home soon but, in fact, it was months before he actually did.

By the time I was six years old, I was beginning to follow the storylines of the films we went to see. I vividly remember many elements from the films I saw then: the tragic conclusion to *Piccadilly Incident*, a doomed love story set in London during the blitz and starring Anna Neagle and Michael Wilding; the sultry sensuality of Jane Russell in *The Outlaw*; and the shocking revelation at the end of the hospital whodunit *Green for Danger.*

My grandmother had a strange habit, not uncommon at the time, of arriving at the cinema midway through the presentation of the feature film. Screenings were continuous in those days, and she seemed to be unable – or unwilling – to arrive at the start of a session. We would invariably see the last reels of the 'big picture' first; then we'd sit through the ads, the newsreel, trailers and a supporting feature (I especially liked the *Andy Hardy* and the far more adult *Crime Doctor* series) before the main feature started again and, when we got to the bit where we came in, we'd 'see it round'. Even as a child I thought this was rather odd, but that's the way it always was.

One of the films that affected me most of all was the luridly shocking, highly sensational David O. Selznick super-production *Duel in the Sun*, a western with Jennifer Jones as a half-caste girl who is seduced by charming villain Gregory Peck. Selznick's film, directed by King Vidor (among others) was, in 1946, notorious for its sex and violence. Dubbed 'lust in the dust' by the popular press, it was definitely adults-only fare. I'd seen enough Roy Rogers and Gene Autry cowboy movies to know that the good guy always wins at the end, but at the climax of *Duel in the Sun* bad guy Gregory Peck shoots his saintly brother, Joseph Cotten, and then goes on to a fateful rendezvous in the red sandstone mountains with his mistress (Jones), whereupon they pump each other full of bullets and die in the sun together.

This film caused a major row between my mother and my grandmother. I had loved every minute of it but when my mother discovered that I had been exposed to such unsuitable fare she exploded in fury. I well remember the scene, which took place in the garden behind the house in Winchester Road and which culminated with my poor grandmother sitting down rather too heavily on a deckchair which collapsed under her weight, bruising her terribly.

Oddly enough, it wasn't these 'unsuitable' film that gave me nightmares; it was the trailer to a film I've never seen and can't identify. I saw it twice, a black-and-white trailer for what was presumably a horror film. The moment I have always remembered involved a little girl coming into a room, quaking with obvious fear, and telling her mother: 'The man next door hasn't got a head!' I turned that ominous line of dialogue over and over in my mind. What did it mean? What would happen to the little girl and her mother? Ever since then I've tried to find out the title of the film; I thought it might be one of the *Invisible Man* series, but I've seen them all and that scene doesn't appear in any of them. In recent years I even sought the advice of Australia's leading expert on Hollywood cinema, Bill Collins, but he wasn't able to help me either. I'd still dearly love to know the title of the film whose trailer gave me the most alarming nightmares.

There were more suitable films too. Danny Kaye's debut, *Up in Arms* (which was double-billed with *Bambi*), *Lassie Come Home*, *Sinbad the Sailor*, *The Bandit of Sherwood Forest* and more Disneys – *Song of the South*, *Melody Time* and *Make Mine Music*. I don't know why I was taken to see Laurence Olivier's *Henry V* at the tender age of six, but it was probably because Olivier was so revered by both my mother and grandmother.

It was thanks to Granny Wells, then, that I caught the cinema bug. And it wasn't just *seeing* films; I remember the day I discovered, in the garage, a pile of old newspapers. The place smelled of the apples that were stored there and of the rarely used car. I went through the papers, initially looking at the cartoons and comic strips they contained, but what I found utterly fascinating were the movie ads. I'd always enjoyed seeing movie posters, displayed outside cinemas or on street hoardings. Here were black-and-white replicas of those posters, ones that I could cut out and keep. And keep them I did, for many years.

Apart from the cinema my other passion as a child was music. My grandparents had a large electric radio-gramophone, and I used to spend hours standing on top of a chair putting records on the turntable. I especially liked the recordings of the Disney films – *Snow White* and *Pinocchio* were particular favourites, records with bright yellow or blue labels illustrated with the characters from the films. I also played my mother's records, which included the music from the show *Chu Chin Chow* ('When a pullet is plump she's tender, when she's scraggy no teeth can rend her. 'Tis so even with a wife, if she's fat you're blessed for life; but if she's skin and bone, she'll ever nag and moan . . .') and, in more sombre mood, *Finlandia* by Sibelius. My family marvelled at the fact that, at the age of three, I was able tell which record was which. These were, of course, 78 rpm bakelite discs and you were supposed to insert a new needle into the arm of the player before each record was played (this was before the arrival of a diamond stylus long-playing needle). The needles were sold in little tin boxes containing fifty or a hundred and we often had to go to the local music shop in Andover to replenish our supply, always hoping that they'd be available given the shortages. I loved that shop, with its displays of sheet music and the shelves filled with records.

I also enjoyed listening to the radio. To begin with there was 'Children's Hour', broadcast every day at five pm on the BBC Light Programme. Uncle Mac was the avuncular host. But I soon tired of this and started to listen to more grown-up fare. At lunchtime there was 'Workers' Playtime', a variety show which always ended with a comedian. And there was 'ITMA', a half-hour comedy show with Tommy Handley, which I loved. I was devastated when I heard on the news that Handley had died suddenly and that there would be no more 'ITMA's. Later on, at 6.45 pm, there was 'Dick Barton – Special Agent', a fifteen-minute serial which had me glued to my seat. There were also the 'Paul Temple' mysteries, written by Francis Durbridge, which began each episode with the most evocative and thrilling musical theme.

Because of my father's frail health, he didn't return from Asia until the middle of 1946. I had left Miss Pegum's establishment behind by then, and I came out of school one afternoon to be met not by my mother or grandmother, but by a vaguely familiar stranger, very suntanned, very thin, wearing an army uniform. I wish I could say that I was pleased to see him, but even at that age I could tell that his return would mean a significant change to my life.

He had brought me a present, which dramatically symbolised how little he knew me. It was a balsa-wood plane which had to be assembled; I've never had any ability with such things, and I'm afraid I must have expressed my lack of enthusiasm at receiving from my long-lost father a present which didn't appeal to me at all. How disappointed he must have been at this awkward reunion.

Soon afterwards we left Andover and returned to Melksham. Abruptly, my visits to the cinema with my grandmother came to an end. I was unhappy and resentful, and undoubtedly I behaved like a truly horrible child. I missed my grandmother, I missed the house on Winchester Road, and above all I missed those cherished visits to the Odeon, the Rex and the Savoy. There was a cinema in Melksham, the Maxime, but my parents seemed not in the least bit interested in taking me there. Why would they? They were busy picking up the pieces of their lives.

My father returned to work at Stratton Sons & Mead, and soon was promoted from salesman to manager of the Devizes branch. Grandfather Stratton, nearing retirement, ran the whole company from Melksham. Uncle John, who had survived the war without seeing any action, returned home to marry Mary, his sweetheart. I remember visiting him at my grandfather's house as he was sorting out his things prior to leaving home and starting his new life. He offered me one of his records and told me I could choose any one I wanted; I was terribly tempted to take one I liked very much, a comic song entitled 'Does Santa Claus Sleep With His Whiskers Over Or Under The Sheet?' (I can still recall the record's red label). But for some strange reason I felt I should take a record that my father would like and I remembered that he was often talking about his admiration for Bing Crosby. In what I saw as a major act of self-sacrifice, the record I took from my uncle was not the cherished Santa Claus number but Crosby singing 'Sam's Song'. I took it home in triumph to my father, who accepted it without enthusiasm and, as far as I know, never played it. More disappointment! Even at this early age I realised that I would much rather my Uncle John were my father than my real father.

I was a pageboy at the wedding of John and Mary, who soon moved to Marlborough, where John was placed in charge of the local branch of Strattons. Marlborough was only about twenty miles from Melksham but we rarely, if ever, visited each other; my father seemed completely detached from his teetotal brother. Nor did I get to know my father's cousin, Jo Webb, at this time, because she was working in London; Jo was about the same age as Uncle John and had grown up in Canewdon. Her father, a Canadian, had married Granny Stratton's sister, Marjorie, after she had nursed the wounds he received during World War I, but he had died soon after and my ever-generous grandfather had invited the widow and her child to live with his family. I don't think my father was as close to Jo as Uncle John was. Towards the end of 1946 Jo decided to go to Canada to seek out her father's family and she never returned to live in England. I well remember, over the next few years, the excitement of her visits home and the vivid stories she told about life in Canada and, especially, going to the movies there.

I was enrolled in a local school at Melksham but I don't remember making any friends. I spent most of my time trying, in vain, to persuade my parents to take me to the cinema. They had both been quite regular movie-goers when they were younger (my father used to talk about the time when he was apprenticed in Birmingham and he had gone to see an early talkie, *The King of Jazz*, several times in one week). A rare occasion when I was successful in my mission was when my mother took me to Devizes to see a revival of *The Wizard of Oz*; I had read about the film, because I remember excitedly telling Granny Stratton and Great-aunt Marjorie what it was about. 'I really don't know why you want to see it, if you know so much about it,' was Marjorie's rather waspish response.

It wasn't long before my mother became pregnant and, in March 1947, she gave birth to my brother, Roger. Now, I think, I was more of a nuisance than ever. I was, in fact, desperately unhappy; jealous of my baby brother and deprived of the one thing I wanted to do in life, which was to go to the cinema as often as possible. I was seven now and I spent much of my time in my bedroom reading. My father made a few efforts to entertain me. He took me to see Melksham Town play soccer, but I was bored out of my mind by the game and showed it. He never tried to interest me in sport again.

It's strange how very different brothers can be. From the very beginning Roger was closer to my father's ideal than I ever was. From the time he could crawl he was fascinated by cars, and the fascination almost killed him. One afternoon Grandfather Stratton visited Speedwell and parked his car at the end of the long, winding drive that led to the front door. Roger, unseen by the adults, crawled up to the car and gripped the bumper bar. When Grandfather drove off down the drive I was horrified to see Roger still clinging to the car, being dragged over the gravel. No-one else had seen what was happening. I cried out and ran after the car. Luckily there was traffic in Lowbourne, the main road at the end of the drive, and my grandfather was forced to stop before pulling out onto the road, so I was able to tell him what had happened. If I hadn't been able to stop him, my brother would have been dragged out into the busy road, with possibly fatal consequences. As it was, his knees were very badly scraped.

On another occasion, when Roger and I were sitting in the back of my father's car – there were no seatbelts in those days – he managed to open the door. We were travelling through the countryside, quite fast, as I recall, and I only just managed to save him as he almost fell out onto the road. My brother's fascination for cars has stayed with him all his life. I still don't know anything about them except for the fact that you fill them with petrol or diesel and off you go. I can't tell a Volvo from a Holden. Roger, from the earliest age, could name every model and make. He watched father at the wheel and learnt from him. One day my father had left his car in gear in front of the garage. Roger managed to get into the driver's seat and start the engine; the car lurched forward and crashed through the garage doors, where it jammed. Apart from the damage to the car and the garage, there were no other ill-effects.

On a couple of occasions after Roger was born I was sent to Andover for a holiday. One such trip was in the summer of 1947, when the films to which Granny Wells took me included *The Secret Life of Walter Mitty* (a Danny Kaye comedy) and the Daphne Du Maurier family saga *Hungry Hill*. Oddly enough, the moment I remember from this film was a scene in which Margaret Lockwood, sitting in front of a mirror, says to her maid, 'Haven't I got beautiful shoulders?' I thought she was obnoxiously vain. There was also a British film produced on location in Australia, *The Overlanders*. This made a great impression on me – I'd seen enough westerns to sense that there was something very different about this film about a cattle drive across inhospitable Australian landscapes. This was my first vision of the country I would later make my home. I also remember a minor western called *The Red Stallion* and was alert enough to notice that there was something unusual about the colour. Examining the poster for the film in the cinema lobby I noticed that it was in Cinecolor, not the usual Technicolor, and (with Granny Wells's encouragement) I asked the cinema manager why this obviously inferior colour system had been used for the film. He, of course, had no idea.

On another visit to Andover, in 1948, I was taken to see George Sidney's lavish version of *The Three Musketeers*, with Gene Kelly as D'Artagnan, which I enjoyed immensely, and also to see Bob Hope and Jane Russell in the comedy western *The Paleface*, and Alan Ladd in a superior western *Whispering Smith*. ('What's the matter, Smitty?' demands the evil villain of our hero. 'Losing your touch?') These were very happy times and I revelled in all the indulgence Granny Wells would lavish on me. But it was not to last. Jessie Wells died, very suddenly, one day in April 1949. My greatest ally had gone.

Before that devastating event, however, I'd been packed off to boarding school.

Chapter Two

My parents deposited me at Chafyn Grove School, Salisbury, on 8 September 1948, a couple of days before my ninth birthday. The school was housed in an ugly red-brick building at the end of a suburban street; behind the building the school grounds, including the sports fields, ended with a railway embankment, across which express trains sped towards the south coast. My father didn't want to send me to the same school he'd attended because the experience had been a bad one for him. He heard about Chafyn Grove from a friend, and was attracted by the fact that the recently appointed headmaster, Malcolm Galloway, was a relatively young man with a young family.

My first night there was the most miserable I ever spent in my life. Against my mother's wise advice I'd insisted on bringing my beloved teddy bear with me, a ragged, faded creature with blue fur which had been my bedtime companion for as long as I could remember. This naturally caused derision among my fellow boarders, who snatched Teddy away from me and tore the wretched thing into thousands of pieces, to my great distress.

I was, I think, young for my age and quite unprepared for boarding school. Children, as we know, can be very cruel, and to begin with I felt utterly alone and friendless. The only preparation my father had given to me before the fateful day I entered the school was to sit me down one afternoon and attempt to tell me the Facts of Life. I really didn't have a clue as to what he was talking about and he seemed inarticulate and deeply embarrassed, in the end getting no further than explaining that the real name for that 'thing' was 'penis'; after revealing that nugget of information, he seemed to decide enough was enough and ended the conversation, leaving me none the wiser.

Despite this bad start, I look back on the five years I boarded at Chafyn Grove with a certain amount of nostalgia. The school prided itself in its cricket team so, because I was not at all interested in sport, I was never among the upper echelons. When teams for cricket, soccer or even rounders were selected I was always the last one chosen; no team captain wanted to pick a liability like me. At first this upset me; later I accepted it as natural. I didn't want to play their sports so it was reasonable of them not to want me.

Miss Mills, a kindly woman with a round, ruddy face, taught the first year pupils. In subsequent years, every subject was taught by a different teacher. Mr Letchworth, a small, elderly man with a balding head and precise manners, was the Deputy Headmaster and also taught Geography. He was nicknamed 'Slush' (I never discovered why) and had spent a great deal of his youth travelling in the colonies – South Africa, Canada, Australia and New Zealand. His teaching consisted entirely of recounting anecdotes from his travels to these far-flung parts of the world, but somehow he managed to make them sound very uninteresting and, as a result, my marks in Geography were extremely low. Mr Dowson (stern and humourless) taught Maths. Miss Benson, who had spent many years in China and who was eager to teach mahjong to anyone willing to learn, was in charge of English. The Headmaster, Mr Galloway, taught both French and Scripture. Mr Mills, an old boy of the school and a pilot in the RAF during the war, taught Latin and was also the cricket coach; he was immensely popular. Mr Steadman taught History, and I was one of the few boys who liked him. Mr Collett was the PT instructor until he emigrated, with his family, to Australia; he was replaced by an obnoxious martinet whose name I've forgotten.

I began to enjoy classes, especially English, History and Latin. I was never any good at Maths – figures baffled me, Algebra and Geometry were a mystery I was never able to solve, and Mr Dowson's icy manner frightened me. But I loved reading and I loved learning about the English language. I came to appreciate poetry. At night, after lights out, I would continue to read under the sheets with the aid of a torch and I was regularly punished for this. I've never forgotten the lessons I learnt at Chafyn Grove. I still shudder when I hear someone say that so-and-so is different *to* something – Miss Benson instilled in me the fact that you cannot differ *to* anything, you have to differ *from* it. Equally, split infinitives drive me crazy. I'm assured that English is a living language and is changing all the time, and of course that's true. But the rules I learnt when I was nine years old are impossible for me to break.

Despite my lack of interest in sports I made a number of good friends. Prominent among them were John Newman, whose father owned a printing establishment in Swindon, and John Martin, whose father was in the RAF and based overseas. Because of this, my parents frequently took Martin (we were obliged to refer to one another by surnames and first names were never used) out with me on the allocated parents' days and he sometimes came to Melksham to spend part of the holidays with us.

I finally learnt about sex from a dayboy called Richard Moody, who assured me, just before French class one day, that women had a hole and men stuck their 'wig' (the Chafyn Grove term for penis) in it, and it was called 'fucking' and that's how women had babies. I didn't believe my parents could do any such thing, but he was pretty convincing and assured me that animals and even insects did it too. A few days later, out in the school grounds, I attempted to embarrass Miss Mills, by asking what a couple of intimately entwined ladybirds were up to. 'Mating,' she told me. 'Oh no!' I replied, full of confidence. 'They're fucking.'

During my years (1948–1953) at Chafyn Grove I saw few movies. Just outside the school gates was an advertising hoarding where the films screening in the city that week were featured on dramatic-looking posters. I used to study them eagerly and yearn to see them. The dramatic images used, the bold lettering, the names of the actors – already familiar to me – were more tempting than any forbidden fruit; I stored away memories of the film posters but it was years before I was able to actually see most of the films themselves.

During the holidays I begged and pleaded with my parents to let me go to see films, and sometimes, when they refused, I would quietly sneak off to the local cinema. If the film which was playing had an 'A' certificate (for 'adults') I would have to ask a grown-up to take me in, a potentially risky procedure, but one which, fortunately, never backfired on me. I was cautious enough to wait until a friendly-looking woman came along, ask her if she'd take me in, and then give her the money for my ticket. I'm sure that many young British film buffs of my generation were forced to do the same thing.

One memorable film I saw in this way was *The Window*, which was released in Britain the late spring of 1949 and which I probably managed to see during the summer holidays that year. *The Window* is a B-grade *film noir*, directed by Ted Tetzlaff and released by RKO; I was particularly impressed by it because I was nine years old when I saw it and the hero, played by Bobby Driscoll, is the same age. Tommy lives on the fourth floor of a

New York tenement with his hardworking parents (Barbara Hale and Arthur Kennedy) and, like me, he has a vivid imagination. He tells tall stories, which often get him into trouble. It's summer and very hot, so one night Tommy sleeps on the fire-escape, and, still unable to sleep, climbs one floor higher where the air is cooler. Hearing noises from the fifth-floor apartment located above his parents' place, he sees Mr and Mrs Kellerson (Paul Stewart and Ruth Roman) struggling with a man they appear to be robbing; Mrs Kellerson stabs him with a pair of scissors. The horrified Tommy creeps downstairs to tell his mother (his father works at night) and, of course, she doesn't believe him; the Kellersons are nice people, she assures him, and she assumes that this is just his latest tall story. Next day, as punishment, he's confined to his room, but he climbs out of the window and runs to the local police station to report the murder. The police don't believe him either and return him to his angry parents, who take him upstairs to apologise to the Kellersons. So now the Kellersons know that he knows that they're killers, and, to top it all, his parents leave him alone that night . . .

The film is pretty scary – and even scarier if you're the same age as the protagonist. And *The Window* became important in my life because, back at school, I found myself, one night in the dormitory after lights out, telling the story of the film. I remembered everything, including the names of the characters, and I described every incident in grim detail. Probably several of the other boys had nightmares that night but, at any rate, the incident established me as a night-time storyteller, a reputation that stayed with me throughout my days at Chafyn Grove. I would tell the stories of every film I saw, and of every book I read (then, as now, I favoured crime novels), and when I ran out of stories I made them up.

I now realise that this compulsion to tell the story of a film I'd seen – in effect, to recommend the film to my peers – set a pattern for my life which is still in place today. Whether running a film society, programming a film festival, hosting films on television, lecturing on film history or even reviewing films, my need to tell the story of *The Window* that night in 1949 to a dormitory full of shivering little boys is essentially the same.

Unfortunately, talking after lights out was strictly forbidden and from time to time a teacher or the matron would hear me and I would be in serious trouble. Sometimes this involved writing out lines, but as time went by it usually meant a trip to the headmaster's study and a caning. Galloway usually started off with the 'this will hurt me more than it will hurt you' routine, but what I remember most about these painful experiences was the presence of the school dog, a very friendly golden labrador, who would invariably lick my hand even as his master laid into me with six of the best.

Once in a blue moon the entire school was taken to the cinema to see a film which was considered 'suitable' for us. This was always a British film and it was far from a regular occurrence; in the five years I was at Chafyn Grove we went only three times: to see *Scott of the Antarctic*, in which John Mills played the noble and heroic leader of a doomed expedition to the South Pole; *Where No Vultures Fly*, a film about British colonialists in a game park in Africa; and *A Queen Is Crowned*, a documentary which covered, at inordinate length, the coronation of Elizabeth II in 1953.

But strangely enough, it was during the years I spent at Chafyn Grove that I started to find out more about the movies I loved so much. The school subscribed to a couple of magazines, *Punch* and *The Illustrated London News*, both of which contained film reviews. I read these avidly and made notes from them – mental notes at first, but soon I started writing them down. More importantly, I started 'reviewing' the limited number of films I was able to see. I still have these childishly written reviews.

One summer, on holiday from school and with nothing much to do that day, I explored the garage at Speedwell and, to my amazement, discovered there, neatly folded, a flag of the USSR.

There was no mistaking it, and I'd been sufficiently indoctrinated to know that this flag belonged to our country's number-one enemy. Why did my parents have a Soviet flag hidden in the garage? My imagination began to run riot. Were they, perhaps, Communists? Fellow travellers? *Spies?* Should I say anything to them? If I did and they *were* spies, would they attempt to indoctrinate me in the Communist cause or, perhaps, murder me? My film-going had already given me plenty of far-fetched ideas but, in the end, I decided the simplest thing was to ask my mother, who explained that during the war we were allied to the Russians and that's why she had the offending flag – somewhere, she thought, there was probably an American flag, too, which proved to be the case. I was still a bit dubious, so we had a ceremonial burning of the flag in the back yard, which finally put my agile mind to rest.

After Granny Wells died I only spent one brief holiday in Andover with my grandfather. Although Grandpa Wells was not a cinemagoer, I did manage to coerce him into taking me to see Raoul Walsh's *The World in his Arms*, a seafaring yarn with Gregory Peck and Ann Blyth; naturally, I enjoyed it a lot more than he did. At around the same time we made a rare family visit to London, and Grandpa Wells joined us. He insisted on taking us all to lunch at The Trocadero, just off Piccadilly Circus, which was one of his favourite restaurants from his pre-war days in the city. This was the first time I'd been to a smart restaurant (we rarely ate out) and I was very impressed with the experience. The head waiter obviously remembered my grandfather and welcomed him warmly. Perhaps buoyed by this return to one of his former haunts, Grandpa Wells was in the very best of moods and helped me choose from the large menu. Chicken vol-au-vent was the entrée he recommended and I consumed it with relish.

In November 1951 my paternal grandfather, Bob, retired from the position of Managing Director of Stratton Sons & Mead. The company gave a farewell dinner for him, which was attended by all the staff and took place at Melksham Assembly Hall. The compere was a local entertainer, Bert Fluck, who was well known in the area for his abilities as a pianist, conjurer and comedian; he was also the father of Britain's answer to Marilyn Monroe, Diana Fluck, who had wisely changed her name to Diana Dors before hitting the big time. On that autumn night, staff members who had served for more than twenty years were presented with small gifts, and I was given the task of presenting my grandfather with a television set, which was the first one I'd ever seen. The screen was tiny by today's standards but it looked very exotic to me.

The menu, which was strictly teetotal, consisted of cream of tomato soup, cold roast beef with peas and potatoes, peach Melba, and cheddar cheese and biscuits. The entertainment provided included not only the versatile Mr Fluck but also Dulcie Dunn (soprano), Alfred Salter (baritone) and Stock Wynn (impressionist).

My father now assumed his role as head of the company and I saw even less of him as his work consumed more and more of his time. On weekends he liked to play golf and my mother and I would often meet him at the golf club for a drink (lemonade for me) after his game. There was a poker machine in the clubhouse which I found very fascinating.

Nineteen fifty-one was the year of the Festival of Britain and the country was transformed with the final replacement of all street signs that had been missing since the war. The bombed-out South Bank of the Thames in London was given over to a display of futuristic exhibits and, to my great excitement, my mother took me there during the summer holidays. I was thrilled to see such 'wonders' as the Skylon and the Dome of Discovery but only later did I discover that one of the attractions we sadly didn't explore was an exhibition of 3D movies in a temporary cinema on the site of what is now Britain's National Film Theatre.

Apart from the cinema I had a couple of other interests, both indoor activities. One was photography; for a while, I developed and printed my own photographs, with mixed success. The other was conjuring, and I used the trip to London to spend all my meagre savings on buying new tricks from a professional shop for magicians. I practised these wonders for hours in front of a mirror and became reasonably adept at deceiving indulgent audiences of adults. Changing water into red wine was one miracle I achieved, though you wouldn't have wanted to drink the result; I also succeeded in transforming silk handkerchiefs of several different colours into one which was multi-coloured, and in revealing that a playing card a member of the audience had taken from the pack had been magically relocated into the centre of a balloon which had just burst. My 'magic' was achieved more by mechanical effects than by the far more difficult sleight of hand practised by the best magicians, but the hobby, while it lasted, gave me confidence to face audiences and entertain them. I even won first prize at a local talent contest.

It continued to be difficult to persuade my parents to take me to the cinema. My mother was usually more willing than my father, though I did get him to take me to see the occasional film; one was *Appointment with Danger* (1951), starring Alan Ladd. Having seen Alan Ladd in *Whispering Smith* a couple of years earlier, I assumed that he, like Roy Rogers and Gene Autry, always appeared in westerns so I was rather surprised to discover that in *Appointment with Danger* he played an undercover agent who infiltrates a gang of mail thieves. I also persuaded my father to take me to see a Dean Martin and Jerry Lewis vehicle, *The Caddy* – I talked him into this by telling him it was about his favourite sport, golf, but he was pretty unimpressed and I think that this was the last occasion during my childhood that I managed to get him to take me to a movie.

On what proved to be my final visit to Andover to stay with my grandfather, I took a photograph of him standing in his garden; after his death early in 1953, my photo was used by his old employer, Clarks Shoes, to accompany his obituary in their in-house magazine.

On two occasions, during the Easter holidays, my mother took me to Bournemouth for a few days, presumably so that we could (as they say today) bond. We stayed at a small hotel and would usually go to the local theatre to see a play and also to at least one film. During this period I spent whatever was left of my pocket money (after buying the latest magic trick I'd set my heart on) on books and records. I loved these very special trips with my mother; the hotel seemed terribly glamorous (in fact, it was a modest guest house of the type immortalised in *Separate Tables*) and the few days we spent indulging ourselves were filled with the happiest memories.

My paternal grandparents never took me to see a film but I do remember Grandpa Bob arriving at home one day with a present for me – quite unexpected, because it wasn't my birthday. It was a Frank Sinatra album, *Come Fly With Me*, which became one of the first long-playing records I ever owned. I was amazed that this conservative old man would give me such a gift, but I was very touched at the time and I'm still touched all these years later thinking about it. He must have known that I had recently 'discovered' Sinatra, whose vocal performances, along with those of Nat 'King' Cole and Ella Fitzgerald, I much preferred to the popular songs of the time.

To this day, I'm not quite sure why my parents decided that I should join the local pony club, but I think it was probably a desperate attempt to find me an interest other than the cinema and my 'indoor' activities, like photography and conjuring, of which they disapproved so much. My father's best friend, Richard Hurn, and his wife, Betty, had two daughters, both of them horse lovers. The elder daughter, Sue, was just ten days younger than I was and had her own pony. During one summer holiday I was presented with a pony myself, a grey called Pippin. Though small in size, Pippin was able to make it very clear that he disliked me; I was told he hadn't been broken in properly. Whatever the reason, he used to ignore all the instructions I'd been taught to give him, via kicks and pulls of the reins, and would head for the lowest trees in the orchard. After being knocked to the ground for the umpteenth time by low branches, I protested in no uncertain terms. Pippin was sold and was replaced by Bambi, a sweet-natured New Forest pony, black in colour and serene in nature.

Bambi lived in the orchard behind Speedwell, but she seemed to know instinctively that she could escape at any time just by leaning on the fence. One summer afternoon, when my mother was expecting guests for tea, Bambi pushed down the fence and entered the dining room via the open French windows; my mother came in with her guests just in time to see an entire chocolate cake disappear down the pony's throat. The whole point of having a pony was, of course, to encourage me to take part in social activities with other riders but, once again, I wasn't very enthusiastic. An attempt to get me interested in fox-hunting was even less successful; I only went hunting once but it was a disastrous experience I never wanted to repeat. Bambi became so excited at being in the company of so many other, mostly bigger, horses that she became as uncontrollable as Pippin had. There was no stopping her as she galloped ahead. To my horror we overtook the Master of Hounds, which is Not Done in fox-hunting etiquette, and seemed about to overtake the hounds themselves until we were confronted by a dry-stone wall, whereupon Bambi stopped dead. I, on the other hand, did not. I was both humiliated and covered in bruises.

During those years my parents, my brother and I would spend our two weeks' summer holiday by the sea. The first post-war holiday I remember was in Cornwall, at the same farm, Chimber, near Helston, where my parents had honeymooned in 1938. I loved the farm and spent a lot of time with the pigs, which fascinated me. I also fell in love with a puppy recently born to the farmer's sheepdog and, on the last day, offered the farmer all the money I had – ten shillings – for the little creature. To my joy, he accepted; my parents were less enthusiastic. We already had a dog, a fox terrier that had belonged to my mother when she was still single. It was called Don and I never liked it much; it took an instant dislike to Chimber, as we called the newcomer, but died quite soon after the puppy's arrival. Sadly, Chimber wasn't around much longer than that; a few months later, she fell victim to a speeding motorist. Eventually she was replaced by a golden spaniel we called Sugar, who became my closest companion when I was at home for the holidays.

After that first holiday in Cornwall, our holiday destination for the next few years was the Devonshire seaside town of Teignmouth, where we stayed at a small seafront hotel called Courtney House. We spent our days on the beach but I longed for the days when it rained (they were not infrequent) and I had a legitimate reason to propose a visit to one of Teignmouth's two cinemas. This is how I came to see, at the age of nine, the sophisticated Max Ophuls melodrama *The Reckless Moment*, which gave me nightmares (the scene in which the daughter's caddish seducer is killed by falling onto an anchor haunted me for years afterwards). Later, despite the increasingly congested roads to the West in the summer season, we returned to Cornwall and we stayed in a small hotel close to the sea at St Merryn, near the fishing port of Padstow. Though it was August the weather tended to be cold and wet almost every year but we went to the cinema in Padstow occasionally – that's where I saw Jacques Tati's *Monsieur Hulot's Holiday* for the first time.

During our 1952 summer holidays in Cornwall I made a new discovery about the cinema. I heard from one of the locals that a movie was being shot on location in Padstow; it was a Hollywood production called *Never Let Me Go* and it featured a couple of big-name stars – Clark Gable and Gene Tierney. I never managed to catch a glimpse of either of them, but one evening I was able to see a scene from the film being shot. A car, presumably driven by a stunt man, took off at high speed along the pier and plunged into the harbour. More than one camera was filming the shot because, quite obviously, only one take was possible. I watched this stunt being performed, utterly fascinated.

It was several months before I saw the trailer for *Never Let Me Go* and, a little later, the film itself. I was immediately struck by the fact that the scene I had watched being filmed appeared in both trailer and film – but the shots were entirely different. In the trailer, the car driving off the pier into the water was filmed from the water (presumably by a camera located on a boat) at a low angle with the car driving *towards* the camera; in the film itself, though, the shot used depicted the car travelling sideways from right to left and then tipping over the pier. I thought it was a less dramatic shot than the one used in the trailer.

To add to my fascination, the entire sequence wasn't supposed to be taking place in Cornwall at all. The scene was set in Tallinn in Soviet-controlled Estonia; Clark Gable plays an American who falls for Russian ballerina Gene Tierney, marries her, and then is refused permission to leave with her. He conceives a reckless plan to rescue her – quite ridiculous, in fact, but this kind of Cold War thriller, though efficiently directed by Delmer Daves, wasn't overly concerned with reality. In the scene in question, Gable and Tierney are both in the car – except that, during filming, they weren't; a stunt driver and a dummy dressed in women's clothes were the only occupants. This insight into the art of movie-making made a big impression on me, but I still can't see *Never Let Me Go* without thinking that the back streets of Tallinn look remarkably like the main street of Padstow. I have since visited Tallinn, and it goes without saying that the similarities are nonexistent.

I was born with a couple of medical problems which I barely understood. In 1952 my doctor decided it was time to correct them and I went into hospital at the end of the summer holidays for surgery, which proved to be extremely painful. I woke up in the early morning of my thirteenth birthday in agony and thought I was going to die. I must have spent quite a long time in hospital because I remember hearing on the radio that Eisenhower had been elected President of the United States, and that didn't occur until 5 November, almost two months later. During this unhappy period I listened to the radio a great deal and also consumed books at a tremendous rate. When I finally returned to school I was still in a weak state and was barred from playing sports (which suited me down to the ground) or even taking part in gymnastics (another plus).

The coronation of Queen Elizabeth II occurred during my final term at Chafyn Grove and the school closed for a few days to celebrate. As I was now thirteen I was allowed to travel home from Salisbury to Melksham alone, by public transport, and I felt very grown-up. It was a time of great change. My parents had sold Speedwell and had purchased Place House, a large, two-storey modern home in the middle of the town, close to St Michael's church. They also celebrated the coronation by acquiring their first television set, though the small black-and-white image was frequently interrupted by an apologetic message: 'Normal Service Will Be Resumed As Soon As Possible'.

My parents were not religious. My father had rejected his Methodist upbringing and my mother's parents were not church-goers. However, now that they lived so close to Melksham's main Anglican church, they befriended their neighbour, the vicar, and started attending the occasional service. They always referred to the vicar, to his face, as 'Bish', because he had aspirations – never fulfilled, as far as I know – for higher office. During the school holidays I was persuaded to serve as an altar boy, but this was not a success. On the two occasions I donned the appropriate vestments to serve at early morning communion, I fainted in the middle of the service – probably because I was not permitted to eat or drink anything before heading for the church. The second time, I hit my head painfully on one of the stone steps leading to the altar and my fall caused Bish to spill the communion wine. I wasn't asked to serve again.

It's fair to say that I didn't get on all that well with my parents. In truth, we lived in a kind of perpetual stalemate. They never understood my passion for the cinema, and I'm not sure I understood it myself. My father tried hard to wean me away from it by coming up with other diversions. He must have been disappointed that nothing really succeeded. My mother was more sympathetic, but not sympathetic enough to give in to me when I begged to be taken to this or that movie. After the death of Granny Wells, my greatest ally in this regard was Uncle John. Although John was both a Methodist and a teetotaller, he was charming and amusing and enjoyed a trip to the movies.

An adult whom I admired even more was my Aunt Jo; she had never returned permanently to England after leaving for Canada in 1946, but had found work in different parts of that vast country in what sounded to me, from her letters, to be most exotic places. From time to time she'd return and I would look forward to her visits. She treated me like a grown-up and would tell me about all the movies she'd seen. In 1951 I was very impressed by the fact that she'd seen the sci-fi thriller *The Thing*, because I'd desperately wanted to see it myself but had been prevented by the X-rating it received in Britain. In the summer of 1953 Jo was working at the Banff Springs Hotel in British Columbia when two Hollywood production companies used it as a base for films that were being shot on the nearby river. One film was *Saskatchewan*, with Alan Ladd and Shelley Winters, under the direction of Raoul Walsh, and the other was *River of No Return*, directed by Otto Preminger and starring Robert Mitchum and the ultra-glamorous Marilyn Monroe. Jo met Marilyn on many occasions and found her to be a very sweet person. I was entranced by her stories.

Two other major events impacted on my final year at prep school. One involved the most popular master at Chafyn Grove, David Mills. Mr Mills was exceptionally charming and easy-going – except when he was in a black mood, and then everyone knew about it; he always wore the same scarlet sweater on those 'wuzz' days, as we called them. Usually, however, he was an exemplary teacher, a great raconteur and full of fun. We always loved that he would devote his last Latin lesson of every term to reading us ghost stories. Mills was also homosexual, though I didn't know it at the time. After complaints from at least one member of the cricket team in the summer of 1953, it was announced, to the astonishment of those not in the know, that Mr Mills would be leaving at the end of the term. A few days later we were told that he was dead. He had apparently gassed himself in his room at the school.

The boarders gleaned little of this but the dayboys, with access to the local newspaper *The Salisbury Times*, were mines of information. I found the fate of Mr Mills incomprehensible; I had no inkling about homosexuality and for a long time I couldn't begin to understand what he had done that was so bad, what crime could have led to his suicide. A few days before his death he had signed my autograph book for me, and I remember still the mischievous sense of humour he displayed that day.

Another of my best friends at this time was Richard Bateman, a dayboy who lived with his parents and older sister, Bridget, in Salisbury. Richard's father was a scientist, an enormously impressive and kindly man who came to the school occasionally to give lectures on a variety of subjects. Because Richard and I were friends I was allowed to go out with the Batemans occasionally at weekends; the favourite destination was the Cadena Café for a meal of bacon and eggs.

A further tragedy impacted on our young lives when Mr Bateman was killed, along with everyone else on board, when a British Overseas Airways Company (BOAC) passenger plane, the newly designed Comet, crashed while taking off from Calcutta airport. Richard was, needless to say, devastated at his father's death, and so was I, because I'd found Mr Bateman to be a far more sympathetic role model than my own father. I discovered later that he had been employed at a top-secret facility, Porton Down, near Salisbury, and my active imagination and fondness for conspiracy theories led me to wonder if the work he had been doing had been in any way the cause of his death.

Despite these gloomy events in my final year, I was very happy at Chafyn Grove. Malcolm Galloway, the headmaster, was a stern but very fair man and I liked most members of the staff. Thanks to the persistence of the Maths master, Mr Dowson, I did very well in my O-levels at arithmetic, algebra and geometry, subjects I detested, and academically I showed plenty of promise. Although my antipathy towards sports increased during this time, I learnt to swim at school and thoroughly enjoyed this pastime.

I was never made a school prefect but that didn't really bother me. A greater disappointment was the fact that I was never given a starring role in the annual school play, which was performed every December. Mr Letchworth was in charge of producing the play, which was always a musical, and he decided early on that I didn't have a suitable singing voice. The first play during my time at Chafyn Grove was *The Pied Piper of Hamelin*, which was staged in December 1948, and I was cast as the Fourth Rat, but every year after that I was passed over for better singers. This made me terribly unhappy, because from an early age I had a keen sense of drama. So I was delighted when, for my final year, I was cast in *The Willow Pattern Plate* as a comic character who didn't have to sing. I started rehearsals with great enthusiasm and was really getting into the role when disaster struck: Mr Letchworth was taken ill and the play was cancelled. I was destined never to make my mark in a school play!

By now I was writing notes on all the films I saw and listing the dates and places where I saw them. I still write such notes today and they form the basis of the reviews I write. I've saved all the notes I've ever written, and it's often fascinating to look back to see what I wrote about a film at the age of thirteen or fourteen and how much, if at all, my opinion has changed over the years.

My passion for the cinema had, in fact, become something of an obsession. This obsession was increased by an unwitting Bridget Bateman, the seventeen-year-old sister of my friend Richard. A few months after I left Chafyn Grove, in December 1953, I accepted an invitation from Mrs Bateman to stay for a few days at their home in Salisbury. I was now fourteen and I developed a bit of a crush on Bridget, who seemed to me to be very glamorous. One aspect of her glamour, as far as I was concerned, was her knowledge about new films, a knowledge derived from her weekly purchase of a film magazine called *Picturegoer*, which she read avidly. I had never come across this magazine before; among other things it reviewed every new film using a one- to four-star system (with the occasional *Picturegoer* Seal of Merit for exceptional films), and I decided that, from then on, I too would buy the magazine every week and try to see all the three- and four-star films. During the few days I spent with the Batemans, Richard and I accompanied Bridget to Salisbury's ornate Gaumont Cinema to see a double-bill of *Back to God's Country* (Rock Hudson) and *Veils of Bagdad* (Victor Mature). I felt very sophisticated to be in such company but Bridget, I'm sure, never gave her younger brother's friend a second thought.

However, this visit entrenched my interest in film even more. Thanks to Bridget I had now discovered a magazine devoted entirely to film, and from that moment on I bought *Picturegoer* every week until it ceased publication a few years later. It was in the pages of *Picturegoer* that I first read about the new wide screens which were, in 1953, revolutionising the cinema experience. I devoured every word written about 20th Century-Fox's anamorphic widescreen system, CinemaScope, and its first production, *The Robe*.

I was terribly disappointed to discover that the British release of the film was delayed because of a dispute between Fox and the Rank Organisation, whose cinemas had traditionally shown all the Fox films. Fox, it seemed, was demanding that cinemas must not only install the huge wide screen essential for CinemaScope but also a six-track stereophonic sound system. Rank accepted the inevitability of the massive screen but baulked at the huge extra cost of a new sound system. Fox retaliated by refusing to allow Rank to screen its films which, after *The Robe*, were all made in the Scope system.

In the end, Fox did a deal with independent cinemas on a one-by-one basis. They guaranteed these independents exclusive rights to Fox's product in their areas for a period of three years, provided they install screen and sound equipment which came up to Fox's high standards. The closest independent cinema to Melksham which participated in this arrangement was the Astoria at Chippenham, seven miles away, and I was full of anticipation when it was announced that *The Robe* would be given a special two-week engagement there during the summer. Imagine, then, my horror to discover that those two weeks *exactly* coincided with our 1954 summer holiday. I begged to be left behind – I was, after all, fifteen years old now – but my parents wouldn't hear of it. Never was there a more reluctant holiday-goer; every day I was away I imagined that I could be at the Astoria witnessing this new miracle of the cinema, and it was no real consolation when my mother accompanied me to see the second CinemaScope film, *How to Marry a Millionaire*, the week after we returned. It was years before I finally caught up with *The Robe*, which turned out to be a turgid religious spectacle despite the presence of Richard Burton and Jean Simmons in the cast. By that time CinemaScope was old hat; the magical moment had passed.

Despite my initial misgivings, I can look back on the years I spent at Chafyn Grove with affection. I can't pretend that my school days were the happiest in my life, but I made at least one lasting friendship (I'm still in touch with John Martin today) and my love for cinema, despite being denied access to films for much of my time in Salisbury, increased. My next school experience wasn't nearly as pleasant.

Chapter Three

During the five years I spent at Chafyn Grove I only saw my parents during the holidays and on the occasional open day, but my father had made it very clear to me that I was expected to follow family tradition and work for Stratton Sons & Mead. He was, I think, concerned that, despite my reasonably good O-levels results, especially – and surprisingly – in Maths, I might not be cut out to be a good businessman. I think he saw me as a dreamer like his brother, John, whom he tolerated without much enthusiasm as manager of the Marlborough branch of the company – and a hushed-up scandal involving Uncle John and one of his female staff certainly didn't help matters as far as my father was concerned. At any rate, it was decided for the meantime that my education should continue at what the British call a public school but which Australians would rightly refer to as a private school.

I presume that Malcolm Galloway had informed my parents that I wasn't academically bright enough to be accepted at one of the famous public schools – Eton, Winchester, Harrow or Westminster. Instead they sent me to Bradfield College, which was situated in Berkshire, in the countryside between Newbury to the west and Reading to the east. It was about six times bigger than Chafyn Grove (which had only 100 pupils) and it prided itself in a tradition of teaching classical Greek and Latin – the school play was pretentiously performed in ancient Greek in a custom-built amphitheatre.

I was assigned to Army House, one of – I think – six houses that made up the school, and from the very first day I hated it. Although probably not as snobbish as Eton or Westminster, Bradfield venerated the old traditions of privileges and 'fagging'. Every new boy was presented with a list of rules, which were laid down by the school itself, and privileges, which were handed down by the senior boys to the juniors. For example, a boy wasn't allowed to walk around with his jacket unbuttoned until he'd been at the school for a year; there were hundreds of other equally absurd regulations. Also, for the first year, every junior was a 'fag'. Each House had about eight prefects and each prefect had his own study where he slept, prepared his own food and did his prep. Whenever a prefect yelled 'Fag!' the junior boys were expected to come running, and the last one to reach him (usually me – I was never very quick off the mark) would have to do whatever the prefect wanted – clean his study, make his bed, cook his dinner, get something from the tuckshop, even prepare his prep for him. If you've seen the Lindsay Anderson film *If . . .* (1968), you've got a pretty good idea of what life at Bradfield was like.

I think it was my experience at this august establishment that began, in a small way, to radicalise me. Although my parents were conservative and, I'm quite sure, always voted Tory, I found myself quite unable to cope with the kind of perverted traditions that Bradfield celebrated. As a result, I lost interest in school and withdrew into myself. I'd made many friends at Chafyn Grove but I made none at Bradfield. I remember, with mixed degrees of fondness, all the teachers at Chafyn, but I would be hard put now to attach a name or a face to any of the teachers at Bradfield. I turned into a loner, ostracised because of my lack of interest in sport, and constantly punished because my academic performance began to suffer.

The one bright spot on my horizon was that, in the summer, cycling was listed as an optional sport and was unsupervised. If you elected to cycle rather than play cricket, which was the sport of choice for most of the other boys, you were allowed to go off to ride in the lanes around the school. However, it was strictly forbidden – on pain of expulsion – to venture into Reading, which was seven miles away and which was the nearest big town. There were several cinemas in Reading, as I knew from Parents' Days (I persuaded my parents to take me to see William Wellman's lengthy airliner-in-trouble melodrama *The High and the Mighty* on the occasion of my first outing, and to see Danny Kaye in perhaps his funniest comedy, *Knock on Wood*, in which his co-star was the delectable Swedish actress Mai Zetterling, on another). However, I wasn't game to defy the ban on entering the town of Reading; it was too close to Bradfield and the likelihood that I'd be seen and recognised was too great. But there was no specific edict against cycling to Newbury, probably because it was fourteen miles away and thus considered too far. Newbury boasted two cinemas so Newbury was where I went.

I would conceal 'civilian' clothes in my cycle-bag and change out of my school uniform behind a hedge a mile from the school. I would then cycle like mad into Newbury without even being aware what films were actually playing. It really didn't matter what was screening; any film would do. There were continuous performances at most cinemas and I found that, as luck would have it, I would usually arrive at one or other of the cinemas just as the main feature was ending. This was simply a repeat of the pattern of film-going I'd learnt from Granny Wells. But in this case, I'd see 15 or 20 minutes of the second half of the feature film and then have to sit through the ads, a newsreel, a trailer or two, and a supporting feature before the main feature started again. By that time I would only have time to see the first ten or fifteen minutes before I had to head back to Bradfield before my absence was noticed. It was a frustrating routine, but in spite of that I did it often and enjoyed what I saw of films like *The Glenn Miller Story*, *The Runaway Bus* and *Saskatchewan* (retitled *O'Rourke of the Royal Mounted* in Britain), which was one of the films shot at Banff the previous summer and which my Aunt Jo had told me about.

Once in a while a film was screened in the Great Hall at Bradfield thanks to a donation made by John Davis, a senior executive of the Rank Organisation whose son was a pupil at the school. Davis had donated a pair of 35-mm projectors and also loaned the occasional 'suitable' film, but I usually found I'd seen them before. More exciting for me was the fact that Davis's second wife, the actress Diana Sheridan, would usually accompany him on Parents' Days. Sheridan, the talented blonde who had appeared in British films like *Where No Vultures Fly* and *Genevieve*, a funny comedy about vintage cars, had retired from acting when she married Davis. It was quite exciting to catch the occasional glimpse of her in the school grounds.

I was becoming aware of censorship. Every film screened in Britain was preceded by an impressive-looking certificate, issued by the British Board of Film Censors, which rated films 'U' (universal), 'A' (adults) or, after 1951, 'H' (horror). The H certificate was quickly replaced by the 'X', and no children under the age of sixteen were admitted to X-rated films, whether or not they were accompanied by adults. As I had found, children couldn't get into A-rated films unless an adult accompanied them, which very often led to children like me, who couldn't persuade their parents to take them to the cinema, approaching total strangers and asking them to take them into the cinema to see A-films.

In a way, it was the A certificate that originally introduced me, quite by chance, to a more sophisticated kind of movie. It was

3 April 1954, during the Easter holidays, and I was fourteen. I had decided to take the bus to Trowbridge to see an action film called *Hell Below Zero*, with Alan Ladd, which was playing at the Gaumont; at the time, I favoured this kind of film – westerns, swashbucklers, anything which centred on action – above any other genre. But when I arrived at the Gaumont I discovered that *Hell Below Zero*, rated U, was accompanied by a supporting film rated A. 'How old are you?' asked the woman at the box office suspiciously, and when, somewhat taken aback, I boldly replied 'Sixteen', it was clear she didn't believe me. At any rate, I was denied admission.

In order not to waste the afternoon completely I went around the block to the Regal Theatre. There the main feature was a musical comedy, the kind of film which, at the time, I wasn't so very keen to see. *Gentlemen Prefer Blondes* was rated A, but, thank goodness, the woman at the Regal box office wasn't as concerned for youthful morals as her counterpart at the Gaumont; she sold me a ticket. And that's how I got to see Howard Hawks's exuberant comedy starring the delectable Marilyn Monroe. I was completely entranced and I vowed after that experience that I would keep an open mind for any kind of cinema entertainment on offer.

The BBFC ratings were advisory only, and could be overruled by local councils. I was aware that the pioneering Walt Disney animation feature *Snow White and the Seven Dwarfs*, made in 1937, was given different ratings by different councils. In some parts of the country it was rated U, but in other areas the machinations of the Wicked Witch were deemed scary enough to merit an A-rating. What I didn't realise at the time was that, despite these ratings, films were often being cut by the censors. I could never understand the ending of John Sturges's exciting modern western *Bad Day at Black Rock* (1955); one moment, the villain Robert Ryan, armed with a rifle, had the one-armed, unarmed hero Spencer Tracy pinned down in a canyon; a quick cut, and then there was some kind of fire and the Ryan character was dead.

What had happened? Well, as I discovered when I saw the film again years later in Australia (where it wasn't cut), Tracy uses an empty beer bottle, petrol from his jeep and a handkerchief to make a Molotov cocktail, which he hurls at Ryan. The British censors deleted this handy lesson in how to create a weapon out of everyday ingredients but, in the process, they ruined the film.

Similarly, the climax of Richard Fleischer's superior thriller *Violent Saturday* (also 1955) was deleted by the censors. In that film, the hero Victor Mature and members of a Quaker family are trapped inside a barn by bank robbers led by Lee Marvin; the barn has been set on fire and Mature attempts a break-out, and he is about to be shot by Marvin when – CUT! Again, the uncut Australian version showed what happened; Mature was saved by Ernest Borgnine's pacifist Quaker farmer, who impales Marvin in the back with a pitchfork. A rather nasty moment which the British censors simply eliminated but, once again, in the process they left the film with a conclusion that made no sense.

Even more serious was the total ban the British censors imposed on the Marlon Brando bikie film *The Wild One*, made in 1953. The censors were apparently so concerned that British bikers might emulate the film and take over an entire town that they refused it a certificate. Only one council, Cambridge, was willing to give the film an X-rating. If you couldn't get to Cambridge, however, there was another way of seeing Brando in one of his most compelling early roles: film societies were permitted to show films without censorship for their members. As a result, societies around the country programmed the film and attracted larger audiences than ever before, but I was unaware of this at the time.

Every time I saw my parents I complained about life at Bradfield, and my low marks and bad reports must have convinced them I was not suited to that particular environment. After four terms (a year and a quarter) they withdrew me from the school. I had absolutely no regrets about leaving.

Instead of the refined atmosphere of a public school I completed my education at the Technical College in Melksham. It was now February 1955, and I was fifteen and living at home for the first time (apart from school holidays) since 1948. I was also attending a coeducational school for the first time since I was seven, and this proved to be both exhilarating and frustrating. We were taught skills necessary for business – maths, book-keeping, typing and shorthand – and though the latter was of little use to me I found it interesting. To learn typing was very advantageous and is something I've never regretted.

For the first time in my life I was able to keep up with most of the films being released and from then on I rarely missed a movie. My parents despaired of me as I spent all my spare time in the cinema. If I'd already seen the film playing at the Maxime in Melksham I'd take a bus to Trowbridge or Chippenham or, even farther afield, to Bath to indulge my passion. I wrote notes about every film I saw and my taste was already pretty refined.

At the time, the final film session of the day ended with the national anthem; the young Queen Elizabeth II, on horseback and dressed for the Trooping of the Colour, appeared on the screen as the stirring music played. Patrons were expected to stand to attention during this procedure, but most of them seemed to be not all that keen to express loyalty to the monarch at the end of an evening at the pictures. Accordingly, a significant proportion of the audience would make for the exits the moment it seemed as though the feature might be coming to an end. Because I always wanted to see the end of the film, I stayed put. From time to time the national anthem-avoiders also succeeded in missing the surprise ending of a film; this was the case in 1956 with *The Fastest Gun Alive*, a western in which Glenn Ford played the titular character, who is confronted by rival sharpshooter Broderick Crawford. The inevitable gun duel takes place in the main street of the town but we don't see what happens – there's a cut to two graves, indicating that both the goodie and the baddie had perished. While the stampede for the exits started the more relaxed members of the audience discovered that it was all a ruse: the grave supposedly containing the corpse of Glenn Ford was empty and he was free to lead a peaceful life with Jeanne Crain. For me, this was a lesson in the perils of second-guessing how a movie was going to end, and so I always stay to the end of the credits – which, these days, often seem to be endless. But the patient viewer is sometimes rewarded with a final scene, such as the resonant moment at the very end of the credit crawl of *The Mission*, a short vignette which very few people have seen.

After my sixteenth birthday, in September 1955, I was legally able to see X-rated films, and I was very impressed by such controversial movies as *Blackboard Jungle* and *The Man with the Golden Arm*, which I saw on the same day – 16 April 1956 – the former in Melksham, the latter in Trowbridge.

I spent a year at Technical College and during that period I fell in love for the first time. Her name was Angela, and she was a tall blonde who wore her hair in a ponytail like Shirley Jones in *April Love*. We never got past the stage of kissing, however, partly because we were both so shy and partly because teenagers back then were far more restrained and cautious than they are today. I was very smitten by Angela's freshness and beauty, but there were a couple of seemingly insurmountable problems to any kind of long-lasting relationship. One was her Best Friend, a rather plain girl who usually tagged along on dates. The other complication was one which today's teenagers would find impossible to conceive: Angela lived with her parents in a small village and they didn't have a telephone. I could only communicate with her by writing a letter or, on occasion, just turning up at her house. Neither solution was very satisfactory and so my first love ended without consummation.

After I completed my business course at Melksham College my father arranged for the next step in my training to assume an executive role at Stratton Sons & Mead. When he was seventeen he had been sent by his father to Birmingham, in the Midlands, to work in a retail store called Wrenson's, a company which operated a chain of high-class grocery stores throughout the Birmingham area. He'd enjoyed the experience and thought it would be important for me to have similar retail experience in a part of Britain far removed from Strattons' sphere of influence. As a teenager he'd befriended the man who now ran Wrenson's and he arranged for me to be employed at the same store where he'd been apprenticed twenty-five years earlier, which was located in the suburb of Edgbaston, at a junction known as Five Ways; it was very close to the famous cricket ground, though that connection never meant anything much to me.

Just before leaving for Birmingham I went with my family for one last holiday in Cornwall. For some reason my father could only get away for a week so I accompanied my mother and Roger without him. It had been decided to break the journey with an overnight stay in Exeter and, as we arrived at the hotel where we'd made reservations, I couldn't help noticing that, around the corner, a cinema was showing *23 Paces to Baker Street*, a Henry Hathaway thriller starring Van Johnson as a blind detective. While my mother was putting Roger to bed, I offered to take Sugar, my golden spaniel, for a walk without, of course, telling her my plans (she'd have said no). Without giving the matter a second thought, I tied the unfortunate animal to a lamppost and rushed to see the film. By the time I emerged some time after eleven pm Sugar was gone, and back at the hotel I discovered that my distraught mother had called the police. She had gone looking for me, had found the dog and had gone into hysterics. It was a very long time before I was forgiven.

I needed somewhere to stay in Birmingham and my father settled on Toc H, a Christian values-based charitable organisation founded in World War I to provide basic comforts for young men on their way to and from the Western Front. I don't know where my father had heard about this organisation but it was, in effect, a chain of youth hostels for men of all ages; the Birmingham branch was located in Wake Green Road, Moseley Village, a short bus ride away from Edgbaston. I had my own room, which was small but comfortable, and breakfast and dinner were provided. Typically, I suppose, I made no friends among the other residents; they had different interests from mine and my interests were becoming increasingly single-minded.

I moved to Birmingham in September 1956, and stayed there for a year and a half, working a five-and-a-half-day week – Wednesday was my half-day – learning the practical side of the retail business. I was instructed in the art of boning and slicing bacon and skinning and cutting cheese. The bacon cuts were different in Birmingham from the cuts in Wiltshire and the inhabitants of the Midlands liked their bacon 'green' (unsmoked) rather than the smoked bacon we preferred at home. The Birmingham accent was a strong one and some basic words were completely different. When a customer asked for 'pikelets' I had no idea what she meant; in the south of England we called them crumpets.

Outside working hours I found myself more than ever before immersed in movie-going. I would go to the cinema every night of the week, twice on Wednesdays and three times on Sundays. I used to travel by bus all over the city area, tracking down revivals of older films as well as seeing every one of the new releases. In the days before video, opportunities to see films were fleeting. If you missed the initial release of a particular movie, you wouldn't have many chances to catch up with it later on. In 1956 there were probably more than a hundred cinemas in central Birmingham and the suburbs and many of the smaller halls, which didn't belong to one of the two big cinema chains, were able to play revivals on a regular basis. This was a great opportunity for me to catch up with films.

Here's a typical record of my cinematic activities over a period of just over a week in 1956. On Tuesday 16 October, after work,

I went to the Imperial Cinema in Moseley to see a double-bill of two revivals, William Wyler's version of the play *Detective Story* (1951), plus the 1953 version of H. G. Wells's *War of the Worlds*. The following day, my half-day, I went first to the Moseley Picture House (a rather rundown 'fleapit') to see a double-bill of two 1953 horror films, *House of Wax* and *The Beast from 20,000 Fathoms*. After that I walked across the road to the Alhambra to see Doris Day in a revival of her 1948 debut film *Romance on the High Seas*, which was titled *It's Magic* in Britain, after its most popular song. The next day, Thursday, I was again at the Imperial, this time to see Bette Davis and Ernest Borgnine in Richard Brooks's *The Catered Affair* (retitled *Wedding Breakfast* in Britain), and on the Friday night I went to see a very funny British comedy, *The Green Man*, with Alastair Sim and George Cole, at the Odeon in New Street in the city centre. On Saturday evening after work I went to the Bristol to see George Cukor's *Bhowani Junction*, with Ava Gardner and Stewart Granger, and on Sunday 21 October I managed to pack in three visits to the cinema: to the Futurist to see a double-bill of the French thriller *Les Diaboliques* coupled with a British horror film, *X the Unknown*, then to the Kingsway at King's Heath to see Jack Hawkins in a British cop movie called *The Long Arm*, after which I finished the day at the Edgbaston Cinema with John Ford's great western *The Searchers*. I should emphasise that I was seeing all these films for the first time and the rather formidable list is indicative of just what was available to cinemagoers then. Looking over my notes of the period, I can assure you that this was a very typical week.

At almost exactly the same time I was wallowing in the experience of seeing for the first time some seminal movies in Birmingham, Central Europe was in turmoil. The people of Hungary rose up in a counter-revolution against Soviet domination and the Red Army invaded the country. I was only dimly aware of these events, mainly because my mother, in her capacity as a senior member of the Wiltshire Red Cross, became actively involved in helping the wounded refugees who managed to escape and to arrive in the UK. A camp was set up for them, and my mother was one of many volunteers who worked tirelessly on their behalf. She phoned me in Birmingham one day to tell me about the men, women and children she had bandaged and counselled. I've often wondered since if friends and colleagues I got to know in later years were treated by my mother: the Australian film director Carl Schultz and the movie presenter and critic Andrew Urban both fled Hungary in 1956, though they were only children at the time.

I was profoundly influenced by the films I saw. After enduring Susan Hayward suffering from the extreme alcoholism that ruins the life of her character, actress/singer Lillian Roth, in *I'll Cry Tomorrow* (1956) I made a quiet vow not to drink hard liquor. And to this day I don't drink whisky or gin (Ms Roth's beverages of choice) – wine and the occasional glass of brandy are another matter. *The Man with the Golden Arm*, in which Frank Sinatra memorably played a heroin addict, convinced me never to try drugs and I never have, except for the occasional joint during the 1970s.

I enjoyed working at Wrenson's. I learnt stock and order control and customer relations. But life wasn't always perfect. On one occasion, while opening a large can of luncheon meat for a customer, I almost cut off my right thumb on the jagged edge of the can; there was blood everywhere and I was rushed off to hospital to have several stitches in the wound. I still have the scar.

During my time in Birmingham I developed a bad case of facial acne, which was perhaps not surprising because my diet was terrible. Toc H supplied a hot meal every night but, by the time I got back from the cinema, my meal had been congealing in the cold oven for several hours. Because I spent all my money on cinema tickets, buses and the weekly copy of *Picturegoer*, I had no money for lunch and I used to survive on bars of chocolate. No wonder my face reacted in protest!

Of course, what I was really doing during this period was preparing myself for my future profession. I saw literally hundreds of films during the eighteen months I was in Birmingham and I wrote detailed 'reviews' about all of them. I became extremely knowledgeable about the cinema, though at this stage I had no idea how I would put this knowledge to any practical use. I also bought a pocket-sized book about film history and started reading about films of the silent era and the great classics of the distant past. I was determined to see all these films as soon as possible. I suppose an objective observer would have thought I was living a very lonely life, immersed in my fantasy world of the cinema. I had no friends and I never dated a girl during the entire time I lived in Birmingham.

It was during my period in Birmingham that I discovered the film society movement. One day I realised, after reading the cinema ads in the local paper, that I'd seen every film playing in the city. But a small notice caught my eye: the Cadbury chocolate company, which was based in the suburb of Bournville, was advertising a film society organised by its social club. Non-employees of Cadbury's were welcome to enrol, but you had to pay for a subscription for six months. The opening film of the new season was Billy Wilder's 1944 film noir *Double Indemnity*, which I'd read about in my film history book. I needed no further encouragement. I made the long trip from Moseley to Bournville, a unique area of the city where the entire suburb smelled of chocolate, and signed up for the society. I found it all very impressive; there was a well-equipped cinema/theatre, with 35-mm projection, and programme notes were supplied to everyone. The audience consisted of about a hundred people. I loved the film with its crisp dialogue and the witty performances by Barbara Stanwyck, Fred MacMurray and Edward G. Robinson, and I journeyed back to Moseley very elated. A month later I returned to see something very different – Ingmar Bergman's elegant, sweetly sexy comedy *Smiles of a Summer*

Night. This wasn't my first foreign-language film – I'd previously seen the French thrillers *The Wages of Fear* and *Les Diaboliques* among others – but it was my first Swedish film and I was very impressed. A month later I saw my first silent feature at Bournville, the Harry Langdon comedy *Long Pants*, a charmingly funny piece of slapstick that featured one of cinema's forgotten entertainers. My eyes were well and truly opened; there was a vast world of cinema out there quite apart from the Hollywood and British films I saw in the local cinemas. There was even more to see than I ever dreamed!

On a few occasions I decided to go home for a weekend, but I didn't have enough money for a bus or train ticket and my father was adamant that he would not augment my modest wages. So I took a bus to the southern extremity of Birmingham and then hitchhiked. I usually had no trouble getting as far as Bristol, but getting from there to Melksham was far more problematic. I usually had to phone my father and beg him to come and get me; he always did.

At the end of 1957, now aged eighteen, I was given a new assignment by my father. He decided that I would spend the next year in London working for two different importers, six months at each. One of these companies imported New Zealand butter, and the other Australian canned and dried fruit, and Strattons did business with both of them. However, the managers of the two companies concerned weren't as welcoming as the people at Wrenson's had been. They seemed to have no notion of apprenticeship and I was given little or nothing to do. I quickly grasped what was involved in importation but I was never given an opportunity to actually *do* anything – except for one occasion when there was a dock strike and all the white-collar employees, including me, were coerced into breaking the strike by removing perishable goods from one of the ships at the centre of the dispute. I was so ignorant about work practices that I was only dimly aware that I was involved in something unethical.

In London I stayed at another branch of Toc H, in Fitzroy Square, near the Warren Street tube station on the Northern Line. The Odeon, on Tottenham Court Road, was just a few steps away and it was there that I saw David Lean's great war film *The Bridge on the River Kwai* for the first time. But more important to me was the Classic chain of repertory cinemas. There were several Classics in Central London – the Baker Street, Chelsea and Notting Hill cinemas were easily accessible. Here I saw the celebrated MGM musicals for the first time, including my all-time favourite, *Singin' in the Rain*, as well as the films of the Marx Brothers, Greta Garbo and many more. On one occasion I was making notes as I watched one of these films and an elderly lady admonished me, warning me that what I was doing was bad for my eyesight!

I saw hundreds of classic films during my time in London and all the new foreign-language films released as well. In addition, I discovered that, in the second-hand shops in Tottenham Court Road, it was possible to purchase very cheaply 78 rpm records of movie soundtracks. I bought a great many of them, including the soundtrack recordings of *Singin' in the Rain*, *The Band Wagon* and other favourite musicals.

I had always had a taste for drama but, up until then, it had been frustrated. When I discovered that some of the young men at Toc H had formed a dramatic club, I was immediately interested. They were planning to stage a production of the British farce *Reluctant Heroes* in the crypt at St Martin-in-the-Fields in Trafalgar Square. I immediately volunteered but, to my intense disappointment, I wasn't offered an acting role. The company did, however, need a stage manager and, in lieu of any better offer, I accepted the position. One of my tasks was to supervise the explosion that ends the play, when one of the characters drops a lighted cigarette into a pile of gunpowder. At the dress rehearsal the explosion was, I thought, very disappointing. It was achieved by some harmless flash powder, into which the cigarette was thrown, while at the same time a switch was thrown which caused a loud bang. The bang was fine but the flash and smoke caused by the ignited powder seemed pathetically insubstantial; accordingly, for the opening night, I placed about four times as much powder as before. The result was beyond my expectations; there was an enormous flash and not only the stage but the entire auditorium filled with smoke. The hall was quickly evacuated and the actors were denied a curtain call. The blame for this debacle quite understandably fell on me, and I was dismissed from the production. This ignominious embarrassment was my last brush with the world of live theatre.

During my time in London I also discovered the British Film Institute, and I began to subscribe to the BFI magazines *Sight & Sound* and *Monthly Film Bulletin*, which provided more rigorous assessments of new films than the reviews contained in *Picturegoer* or most of the daily papers. However, I never went to the National Film Theatre, London's *cinematheque*; I think that at the time I was unaware of its existence, or perhaps screenings there were beyond my limited budget.

In the summer of 1958 I went abroad for the first time. My parents – my father especially – had become fed up with driving through the increasingly chaotic traffic to holiday in Devon or Cornwall and so had decided to go farther afield. They booked a package holiday on the Spanish island of Majorca; included in the package were the air tickets and ten days in a hotel by the sea with three meals a day included. Roger came too, and it was a holiday to remember – not least because I travelled by plane for the first time, but also because I was thrilled to be in a foreign country. I revelled in the sights, sounds and, especially, the smells of somewhere so completely different. The Majorcan capital, Palma, was beginning to cater for the newly affluent British tourist, but I saw everything through rose-coloured spectacles. We stayed at the ornate Principe Alfonso Hotel, which was perched on a cliff above an azure sea. For two weeks we enjoyed hitherto unimagined luxury, including the 'roast duckee and green peas' the head waiter so enthusiastically recommended. We spent most of the day swimming but I was able to sneak into Palma one night to the cinema, though the Mexican comedy on offer – untranslated, of course – was impossible to understand. The second film on the programme was Stanley Kramer's anti-racism drama *The Defiant Ones*, dubbed into Spanish. We went back to Majorca again the following year and that holiday, in 1959, turned out to be the last vacation I enjoyed as a family with my parents and my brother.

Chapter Four

By the time I ended my year in London I was nineteen, and still without a regular girlfriend. Sue Hurn, the daughter of my father's best friend, had also been living in the capital while I was there, and I'd dated her a few times but without anything serious happening. I think I just felt too awkward around girls; I never knew how to approach them, and I was self-conscious and clumsy. I knew all about romance in theory from the movies I'd seen, but in practice I was a virgin.

It was time for me to start work at Strattons, so I returned to live with my parents for what proved to be a fairly short period. During my absence they had left Melksham and moved into The Coppice, a handsome four-bedroom house located at the top of Bowden Hill just outside the National Trust village of Lacock. The Coppice had formerly belonged to a distant aunt of my father's and he had always admired it; it was, I believe, his dream house. After moving in, my parents arranged for the construction of a swimming pool in the garden, where a tennis court had been, and they revelled in the beauty and tranquillity of their surroundings; on a clear day you could see as far as Wales.

In the summer of 1960 I went on a trip to Germany with my old Chafyn Grove headmaster, Malcolm Galloway, one or two other old boys and a couple of female friends of the Galloways. I was rather surprised, but quite pleased, to be invited to take part in what proved to be a camping trip with the object of seeing the Passion Play, which is staged once every ten years by the inhabitants of the Bavarian mountain village of Oberammergau. I wasn't very interested in the play but I leapt at the chance to travel; I'd been dying to see other parts of Europe.

We set out in four cars – one of them the Galloways' ancient Rolls-Royce, on which he had bestowed the whimsical name of Rupert. We took the overnight Channel ferry from Dover to Ostend – a very rough passage – and breakfasted next morning in the beautiful Belgian canal town of Bruges. We drove to Bavaria via Cologne, the Rhine Valley, Heidelberg and the old Romantische Strasse, with its ancient walled towns, Rothenberg and Nordlingen. The weather was great and I was in the highest of spirits. Oberammergau was beautiful; the play was interesting, but very long (it lasted all day). After spending two nights in the village, we drove on into Austria, stopping at Innsbruck, and then we headed for home via the Black Forest and the sites of World War I battles, including Ypres.

On the film-going front things were a little *too* quiet for me. I had passed my driving test at the age of seventeen, and my mother would lend me her car in which I would travel to Bath or even further, to Bristol, to see films. Nevertheless, the range of choice was still small compared to what I'd experienced in Birmingham and London and I missed all those repertory and revival cinemas. One compensation was the fact that old films were beginning to appear on television, which was not the ideal way to see them but was better than nothing. The BBC had purchased the RKO Radio library, and ITV, the Beeb's commercial rival, had acquired both the Warner Bros catalogue and the Alexander Korda films, a selection of prestige British productions. I saw Frank Capra's exhilarating *It's a Wonderful Life* for the first time on BBC television on Christmas Eve 1957, and my first viewing of Orson Welles's masterpiece *Citizen Kane* was also on the BBC, in March 1960. I've seen both films countless times since, in cinemas as well as on DVD. Less successful was my first viewing of John Huston's powerful *The Treasure of the Sierra Madre*, which aired on ITV in March 1958. This 124-minute film had been allocated a two-hour timeslot, including commercials, by the television programmers and so the geniuses at ITV had simply eliminated the first twenty minutes or so of the movie, cutting out all the establishing scenes with Humphrey Bogart down and out in Mexico City which give this tragic story its essential depth.

Inspired by the activities of the Bournville Film Society and the nearby Bath Film Society, which I attended whenever possible, I decided to start a film society in Melksham. I took an advertisement in *The Wiltshire Times* to see if there was any interest in such an idea and was gratified by the instant response. I had calls from several people including Diana Denney, an artist and single mother of two beautiful twin daughters about my age. A committee was formed of what would be known as The Melksham & District Film Society and Uncle John agreed to serve as President. I was Treasurer/Secretary but in fact I did just about everything. We registered with the British Federation of Film Societies, and we arranged to book – free of charge – the main hall at the Technical College where I'd studied three years before. We also obtained the use (free) of two 16-mm projectors, one from the College and the other from the social club attached to St Michael's church. Uncle John, who was adept with constructing things in a way I never was, built a portable projection booth to house both machines and cut down on the noise they made. We quickly put together a programme of seven films for our first season, starting with *Monsieur Hulot's Holiday*, and including Akira Kurosawa's epic *Seven Samurai*, H. G. Clouzot's *Les Diaboliques*, Frank Capra's *Mr Deeds Goes to Town* and Robert Hamer's sophisticated Ealing comedy of murder, *Kind Hearts and Coronets*. We circulated brochures around the district. Membership (15 shillings) was essential, and I was thrilled at the positive response. The first screening was held on 20 September 1959, ten days after my twentieth birthday, and despite the fact that the seating was uncomfortable the response of the audience was very positive. The Film Society survived and even flourished until I left Melksham some four years later. My parents were reluctant subscribers, and for years afterwards my father complained bitterly about having to sit through the admittedly lengthy Kurosawa film; the experience in no way changed their minds about my hobby.

After quite a short time spent at the Melksham office my father sent me to work at the Newbury branch of Strattons. Since it was too far to commute to Newbury, I needed a car of my own, and – with my father's help – acquired a second-hand vehicle. As I've already mentioned, my knowledge of cars is minimal and I don't recall its make or model, only that it was grey and that the gear stick was on the steering wheel. I think most people recall the registration number of the first car they owned and I'm no exception: it was MGK 333.

I needed somewhere to stay in Newbury and moved into what used to be called 'digs': a room in the house of an elderly woman with a Middle European accent. She provided breakfast and dinner, and most weekends I went home to Lacock. The only other lodger was an Indian, Jagdish Anand, who came from New Delhi and whose father managed a prestige car dealership there. Jagdish – who, for some reason, preferred to be called Bill – became a good friend and we often went to the cinema together. Bill was a girl-hunter and always had many salacious stories about his conquests. I remained celibate – not because I wanted to be, but because I still felt awkward around girls.

But now, egged on by Bill, I'd decided that it was high time I had a girlfriend. I very much liked the Denney twins, whom I saw most weekends when I went home, but I couldn't make up my mind which one of them to ask out. I was in an agony of indecision; the girls weren't identical but each was very pretty in her own way. I was sure that if I asked one of them out the other would be upset so, in the end, I simply did nothing. The Lovin' Spoonful performed a great song on this very subject – *Did You Ever Have to Make up Your Mind?* – and whenever I hear it I think of the Denney sisters.

In the spring of 1960 the entire family went to Bexhill-on-Sea to see the Woodfine family; I drove separately from Newbury. This visit reunited me with Rosemary, who was now seventeen, and a brief, and again very chaste, romance resulted. We went for drives in my car and parked on the beach for hours. She was delightful and I was smitten – but Bexhill was a long way from Newbury and the romance was doomed by geography.

In June 1960 a third lodger arrived at the house where Bill and I were living; and his arrival changed my life. Gerry Bartlett was an Australian from Sydney who had completed his training as a dentist and was working – and earning generous sums of money – doing locum work in Britain. He'd been to several different parts of the country, and Newbury was his last stop before going home. He was an exuberant character, unlike anyone I'd met before, and we became instant friends.

During Gerry's stay our landlady took two weeks' holiday, leaving us to cook for ourselves. This proved to be a lot of fun. Gerry was a great cook and Bill was able to provide some spicy Indian cuisine. The experience gave Bill and me the idea, encouraged by Gerry, to find a flat of our own. We duly found one on the first floor of a building in a quiet square. And so, just a couple of months before my twenty-first birthday, I finally became more independent.

In July 1960, Grandpa Stratton, who had been suffering from cancer, died. I went to Melksham for the funeral, and it seemed as though half the town was at the cemetery for the burial. I always knew he was a popular man, but now I realised that he was much loved. He was certainly one of the kindest and warmest people I ever met. The rain poured down as he was buried; my grandmother was too upset to attend.

Two months later I celebrated my twenty-first birthday. My parents hosted a dinner at a restaurant in Bath, and close friends and family were in attendance. The most exciting present I received was an 8-mm cine-camera from Uncle John. I was thrilled at what I saw as a very generous gift and I'm sad to say that I can't remember now what my parents gave me. Many years later my father told me (somewhat bitterly) that the camera had been given to my uncle by a soap powder manufacturer as a reward for placing a particularly large order of detergent. It hadn't cost him anything, and I don't blame my father for feeling resentful. Not for the first time, I was guilty of rejecting a gift from my father and favouring my uncle. It wasn't one of my finest moments.

During the two years I was based in Newbury changes were taking place at Stratton Sons & Mead. My father had decided to build one enormous warehouse and office complex to cover the activities of all the branches. This was constructed at Calne, near Melksham, and when it was completed the other branches were closed down, one by one. Melksham itself was the first to go, the old shopfront demolished to make way for a new development. The narrow street next to the site of the old shop is still called Stratton's Lane.

With the closure of the Newbury branch, I was brought back to the new head office in Calne. Other major changes were taking place in the company. My father had become convinced that, with the advent of American-style supermarkets, the days of the small grocery retailer were numbered, even in rural areas. Accordingly, he had made Strattons a founder member of the British offshoot of SPAR, an association of independent wholesale and retail grocers which had started in the Netherlands and had quickly spread across Western Europe. In a nutshell, the idea behind SPAR was that the wholesaler (such as Strattons, and other companies like it located in different parts of the country) would encourage its retail customers to buy *exclusively* from it and not (as most retailers did) deal with two or three wholesalers in the area. For this exclusivity, the wholesaler would offer better rates and would also offer the SPAR corporate identity; the individual retailer would no longer be John Smith & Co, but a SPAR shop. Weekly special offers would be prepared (my Uncle John was responsible for buying stock at very keen rates for these offers) and the SPAR members would thus be competitive, in theory, with the bigger companies.

In practice, it was often difficult to get independently minded retailers to surrender completely to the ideas promulgated by SPAR, and this was quite understandable because, although the arrangement did indeed offer them the chance to compete with the growing number of supermarkets and, equally importantly, to *belong* to a bigger chain of other retailers, it also undoubtedly took away their individuality. For the retailer who had traded under his own name for years (as, very often, his father had before him) in a village store, it was asking a lot to get him surrender his identity to the SPAR image.

That's where I came in. Along with two other 'fieldmen', as we were called, I was assigned to visit SPAR retailers every week, take their orders, iron out any problems, convey news of policy and future developments to them, advise on shop modernisation, conversion to self-service and so on, and, when time permitted, to go out in search of new recruits in villages and towns where Strattons was not so well known. I was given a car (a green Austin Mini Minor) and I spent a couple of nights each week away from home, staying in cities like Cheltenham, Gloucester or Oxford, all of which were in my assigned area and, not coincidentally, had excellent cinemas.

Although I was a pretty good driver I was soon involved in an embarrassing accident. Driving home too fast in the rain along narrow country lanes, I skidded on a sharp corner and hit a tree. I wasn't hurt, but the car – the company's car – was badly damaged and my father wasn't at all amused. On another occasion I was driving home in one of those very thick fogs which often blanketed England in those days. You could hardly see anything, and although I knew the road well I drove off it, very slowly, into a ditch. Again the car was hurt more than I was and, again, my father made no secret of his disapproval.

While Bill and I were sharing the flat in Newbury I met Margaret, a schoolteacher who shared a flat nearby with a girlfriend. We actually met at a discussion which involved films, and I soon discovered that, although she was not as obsessed about cinema as me (few people were), we did have common interests. We started dating: at last I had a girlfriend. We spent many happy times together and, in the summer of 1961, we drove up to the Highlands of Scotland, a part of the world for which I still have great affection. It was at around this time that Margaret and I became engaged to be married, an engagement that lasted two years.

I was also keeping busy with film society matters. I'd been elected onto the western regional committee of the Federation of Film Societies, and there were meetings to attend. One of these took place in June 1962 at Knuston Hall, near the village of Irchester in Northamptonshire. One of the topics for discussion was the new approach to film criticism, promulgated by the French, which was beginning to make its way across the Channel. In essence, the theory of 'auteur' cinema – pioneered by writers for the famous magazine *Cahiers du Cinema*, among them François Truffaut, Jean-Luc Godard, Eric Rohmer and Claude Chabrol – was that the director of a film – even a Hollywood film – was the author of the film. They contended that strong directors, like Hitchcock, Ford, Hawks, Samuel Fuller, Otto Preminger, Nicholas Ray, Vincente Minnelli and others, stamped their personality on their films.

This was a radical theory for most British critics, who were generally more interested in the script of a film or the acting rather than the direction (*mise en scène*, the French called it). The chief speaker at the conference was Ian Cameron, a persuasive, opinionated young man who had just launched a new magazine, *Movie*, which promulgated these theories. Also present that weekend were V. F. (Victor) Perkins and Mark Shivas (later an important producer at the BBC and elsewhere), both of whom were contributors to the new magazine.

There was another interesting new film magazine around at the time: *Motion* only lasted a few issues, but during that period it produced special editions on the French New Wave and on horror films that provided invaluable reading for me. Much of the latter edition was written by Barrie Pattison, who was also writing for *Films and Filming* at the time; I was very impressed with his enthusiastic, knowledgeable and distinctly different approach to the films he wrote about. I didn't know at the time that he was Australian and that our paths would eventually cross. Meanwhile, I avidly devoured all these magazines, which affected my own approach to films in no small way.

But by this time a new idea was forming in my mind. Gerry Bartlett had returned to Australia and had written frequent letters urging me to take advantage of the 'ten pound' scheme to come and visit him. Under this program, the Australian Government invited approved would-be migrants to commit to a minimum two-year stay in Australia, in return for which they (the Government) would pay the cost of travel to the country, minus £10. It sounded exciting to me and I talked it over with Margaret. We decided to make the trip to Australia our honeymoon. At the time, British migrants were invariably assigned berths on one of several ocean liners which travelled regularly between Southampton and Australia, which sounded like a great holiday. On a chilly day during the bitingly cold winter weather we experienced in January 1963, I drove on icy roads to the Australian consulate in Bristol to complete the forms and undergo an interview.

I explained to my father, who was none too happy about the plan, that the Australian trip would be no more than a two-year departure from Britain; that I'd return after that time to take up my position – my destiny – at Stratton Sons & Mead.

The winter of 1962–3 was one of the coldest on record. It snowed hard on New Year's Eve. Roger and I had been to a party near St Albans, and the drive back to Lacock was extremely difficult. The snow continued and we were virtually cut off for several days, as were many of the small village shops that Strattons serviced. Every Strattons staff member, including me, took part in assisting the team of delivery trucks to take much-needed supplies to shops which had, in some cases, been cut off for a month. After weeks of snow came the thaw and, inevitably, floods. The River Avon at Lacock broke its banks and once more it was difficult to get out and about. My last winter in England was one I have never forgotten.

When I told Margaret Hancock, Secretary of the Federation of Film Societies, that I was going to Australia she advised me very seriously not to go to Sydney which was, in her view, a cultural desert. Melbourne was where the film society movement was strongest, she assured me, and she also waxed lyrical about the Melbourne Film Festival. However, as Gerry was based in Sydney, and since he had agreed to be our sponsor, there was no other option.

Just before my wedding in the summer of 1963, I spent a few days in London catching up with all the latest films; the last film I saw in a British cinema was David Lean's magnificent epic, *Lawrence of Arabia*. Since it had opened at the Dominion at the end of the previous year, the running time had been reduced from the original 222 minutes, but the screening I saw (at the Metropole, Victoria, on 18 June) was still a magnificent experience.

On 24 June 1963, Margaret and I sailed from Southampton on the *Castel Felice*. (Much later, I learned that the director Paul Cox had migrated to Australia from his native Holland and had travelled on the same ship on its previous voyage.) I expected that after two years in Australia we would have saved up enough money to travel home via Asia or the United States and that then I would resume my career as a grocer. Little did I realise on that warm June day that I would never live in Britain again; and that my destiny would prove to be a completely different one.

Chapter Five

When I look back at the events leading up to my departure from Britain in 1963 I can see with a kind of grim clarity that the David Stratton who sailed from England with his young wife was a strange, and probably quite boring, character. Despite a relatively comfortable middle-class upbringing – affected, it's true, by the war – I was undereducated; I had received no tertiary education at all and had only passed my A-levels in a couple of minor (business-oriented) subjects. I wasn't interested in anything much outside the cinema.

Politically, I voted Tory because my parents did and it seemed the right thing to do. Socially, I wasn't very confident; I loved to watch singing-and-dancing musicals on the screen but I had no sense of rhythm and was a hopeless dancer; I couldn't sing very well either, though that didn't stop me trying – painfully, I suspect, on occasion. I disliked the taste of English beer so I had never spent any time in the pubs where people of my age had tended to congregate (though my limited experience of

Australian pubs, where at least the beer was drinkable, instilled in me a feeling of deep nostalgia for the English watering hole; Australian bars, it seemed to me, had much of the charm of toilets – they were strictly for drinking, not socialising). I had no head for the practicalities of life; I wasn't artistic, I couldn't draw or make things, or repair anything. I knew nothing about mechanics; I could change a car tyre, but otherwise I had no idea how the machine worked. I had no head for figures.

I suppose I lived in a kind of dream world, a world in which film – not just the Hollywood variety, but film in all its manifestations – was my chief and over-riding obsession. I was ill-equipped, it seems to me now, to be a husband – and I was hardly equipped at all for the great adventure on which I was setting out.

The five-week voyage proved to be less of a great adventure than I'd imagined in my dreams. The cabin was small and cramped and the facilities on board were limited if you weren't interested in deck sports or in drinking at the bar. The food was moderately good and Margaret and I made friends with fellow passengers who were embarking on a similar adventure, but mostly we read books and relaxed. For much of the voyage, Margaret was feeling unwell; at first we thought it was a case of seasickness, but later the real reason became evident; she was pregnant. This was clearly going to impact considerably on our plans, but the implications didn't sink in just yet.

Meanwhile, there was a film screening every night, which naturally interested me. I'd seen most of the films before, of course, and those that I hadn't (*Carry on Cruising* was one) weren't of paramount importance. I had to wait until the very end of the voyage, between Melbourne and Sydney, before a film of interest which was new to me was screened – John Huston's *The List of Adrian Messenger*, a strange thriller in which several 'guest stars', among them Frank Sinatra, Tony Curtis, Burt Lancaster and Robert Mitchum, as well as the nominal star, Kirk Douglas, appeared in elaborate disguises. With nothing much else to do at night I saw several films for the second time.

One of these was *Cape Fear*, a taut thriller in which Mitchum plays an ex-con who threatens the lawyer (Gregory Peck) he blames for his conviction and terrorises the man's wife and teenage daughter. When *Cape Fear* had opened in Britain a few weeks earlier there had been something of a scandal surrounding it. The director, J. Lee Thompson, had angrily revealed that the British censors had demanded 161 cuts in his film; I had seen that cut version and it quickly became clear that the version screening on the *Castel Felice* was completely uncut. I made a few enquiries and discovered that this (16-mm) copy had come from Australian sources. This surprised me; I hadn't really thought about the way censorship might differ from country to country, but I was pleased to think Australia might be more progressive than Britain. I was soon to be disabused on that score.

For someone like me who had always longed to travel, the voyage was full of interest, especially when the big liner passed through the Suez Canal and, a few days later, when we docked at the port of Aden. I went ashore and was thrilled with this bustling city with its intriguing smells and activities. *This*, I thought, was what travelling was all about. I joined a few others on a short trip inland to visit an oasis, and returned to the ship satisfied that everything was going to be fine – that the adventure really would live up to my expectations.

After Aden the next stop was Fremantle. The voyage across the Indian Ocean took two weeks and seemed interminable. There were traditional festivities when we 'crossed the line', but by the time we docked in Western Australia we were desperate to get ashore. There was an overnight stop in Fremantle and all the 'ten-pounders' were immediately contacted by members of a very enthusiastic association of local people which made a point of welcoming Brits to Australia. Representatives of this group, who seemed dedicated to populating the country from Britain rather than from any country they saw as less salubrious, drove us into Perth and showed us round the city. One member of the group invited us to her house for afternoon tea.

My first impression of Australia was that it was far from what I had imagined. Britain in the Pacific it was not. The light was different, and the people talked differently (I don't mean the accent, which of course I had expected, but rather the choice of some words). The awnings which were a feature of every shopfront were unfamiliar and the grass was so much thicker and tougher than English grass. The colours were less vibrant than the rich hues of the Wiltshire countryside; the red-tiled rooftops of the one-storey houses were an improvement on the grey conformity of the suburbs of the big English cities, but I'd expected something a little livelier.

The next stop was Melbourne and, again, there was an overnight stay. We went into the city to do some sightseeing but after looking at the Botanical Gardens, Captain Cook's Cottage and the Parliament Buildings, I was determined to see my first movie in Australia. I'd already seen everything that was playing in the main cinemas but the little Australia Cinema, in Collins Street, was screening an Italian film, *This Crazy Urge* (*La Voglia Matta*), of which I knew nothing. So, on 26 July 1963, my first experience of going to the movies in Australia was to see what proved to be a mediocre Italian film.

Three days later, on 29 July, just as dawn was breaking on a beautiful winter's morning, we sailed through the heads into Sydney Harbour. It was a breathtaking sight – the boats on the blue water, the red-roofed houses, the famous Harbour Bridge. Construction had only just started on the Opera House, which today shares dominance of the harbour with the Bridge; there was still a gaping hole where the old tram terminus had been; and the old Customs House dominated the buildings on Circular Quay instead of the glass and steel skyscrapers of today. We docked at Woolloomooloo and, after routine immigration and customs procedures, went ashore. Gerry Bartlett was there to meet us.

It had been three years since I'd seen Gerry and in the meantime his circumstances, like mine, had changed dramatically. He had acquired a dental practice in the NSW country town of Gunnedah and, more importantly, he had acquired a fiancée, Gwenda. We were, he assured me, welcome to stay at his parents' home in Willoughby, under the shadow of the TCN Nine television tower, but the implication was that we should find somewhere else to stay in the not-too-distant future.

Gerry was full of plans for us. He wanted us to see Gunnedah, and proposed driving there the next day. In the meantime, he insisted that we should see the sights – Bondi Beach, Taronga Park Zoo (where I was amused to see that the bird cages were plastered with posters for the new Alfred Hitchcock film: '*The Birds* is coming!', they proclaimed). That evening I expressed a wish to do something I'd never done before – go to a screening at a drive-in. So we piled into Gerry's Citroen and headed for the Skyline at North Ryde, where *Waltz of the Toreadors*, a Peter Sellers comedy I'd seen months earlier in England, was playing.

Gerry had also planned a great holiday before he settled down to hard work in his new practice and he wanted us to join him; we were to embark on a drive through the centre of Australia. It sounded very exciting. Gwenda stayed in Sydney the next day while Gerry drove us to Gunnedah. There were no freeways then to speed traffic out of the city, and it was an exhaustingly long drive. We arrived in the early evening and were given a quick tour of the town, which was, of course, unlike any small town in England. My first impression of the Australian bush was a fairly negative one; I immediately missed the lush greenness of the English countryside, the picturesque villages, the dry-stone walls and hedgerows. This arid Australian landscape, with its dead trees, patches of Paterson's curse and ubiquitous galahs, had a sameness about it which, to begin with, quickly became boring.

It took me a long time to appreciate the beauty of the Australian landscape.

Gerry had decided that Margaret and I should take the train back to Sydney. It departed very late in the evening, so first we had dinner at the RSL Club, which was an experience in itself. I learnt the difference between a 'schooner' and a 'middy' and was informed by one cheerful local that the letters NSW actually stood for 'Newcastle, Sydney and Wollongong'. 'Those bludgers don't care about anywhere else in the state,' he assured me. The train was heated by metal containers apparently filled with hot coal. They made the compartment cosy at first but they very soon got cold and when they did it was freezing. The train seemed to stop at every station on the journey south, and I had never been so cold – not even in an English winter. It was a great relief when we finally alighted at Hornsby, as instructed, to take the suburban train to Willoughby.

We had a couple of weeks to sort ourselves out before we were to take the train to Brisbane for a rendezvous with Gerry and the start of our hectic three-week outback trip. Obviously, a major consideration was to find somewhere to stay. Gwenda suggested that the area around Double Bay was an attractive one; indeed it was, but rental apartments proved to be very expensive. I'd saved up a certain amount of money but was relying on both Margaret and myself quickly to find work – to enable us to live, but also to save up for the trip home in two years' time. Despite those considerations, we settled on a flat above a shop on the corner of New South Head Road and Bellevue Road in the middle of Double Bay.

We spent the next few days exploring Sydney. We were restricted to public transport, of course, but that proved more than adequate to get around. How can I describe the Sydney of 1963? It seemed a big city – there were always a lot of people about – yet it was very modest compared to the Sydney of today. To give just some idea of how much the city has changed since then, I can best describe the cinemas. The only cinemas operating in central Sydney in 1963 which still exist today are the State, a magnificent art deco building constructed in 1929, and the Capitol, which is equally grand and even older – but neither of these places runs films on a regular basis any more. In addition to the State and the Capitol, there were several Hoyts cinemas in the city centre: the Plaza, opposite the site of the present George Street cinema complex, screened all the Cinerama films on a roadshow (extended run) basis; nearby, on the same side of the street, was the Century; the Paris (in what is now Whitlam Square) was also a roadshow cinema; the Regent, a beautiful old cinema adjacent to the present cinema complex site on George Street; and the Esquire, near the corner of Pitt and William Streets, a pokey second-run cinema. Greater Union controlled the Rapallo, next to the Regent, the Barclay, a 70-mm cinema on George Street at Haymarket and the nearby Forum, also capable of running films in 70-mm. GU also booked the Lyceum, on Pitt Street, opposite what is now the Hilton Hotel (the building was owned by one of the churches, and only family fare was screened there). The Prince Edward, on the corner of Castlereagh Street and Martin Place, showed Paramount productions exclusively, and featured Noreen Hennessey on the organ between sessions. The St James on Elizabeth Street between Market and King, and the Liberty, near the Lyceum on Pitt Street, as well as the Metro in Orwell Street, Kings Cross, were owned by MGM. Then there were the small 'art' cinemas, notably the Gala in Pitt Street (near William), the Savoy in Bligh Street (next to the censors' office) and the Lido on George Street between Market and King. None of these survive today.

On 3 August I made my first visit to the State Theatre, which proved to be a quite magnificent, classically designed, picture palace resplendent in marble and bronze, with intricate statues dotted all over the place and amazingly elaborate toilets. This opulent venue would play such an important part in my life in years to come and the film that took me there for the first time was *The Birds*. It had opened in Australia at about the same time it was opening in Britain – a rare occurrence in those days, as I later found.

My father had prepared letters of introduction for me to take to the chief executives of a number of prominent companies in the retail or food supply trade who were based in Sydney. He had written personally to the CEOs of David Jones, Coles, Woolworths, Peter's Ice Cream and others. I called up the offices of the various companies but I was given short shrift; perhaps not surprisingly because, of course, Stratton Sons & Mead Ltd didn't mean anything at all in Australia. The CEO of David Jones never called me back but I was given appointments to meet with the personnel managers of Coles, Woolworths and Peter's, and went to see each of them in search of a job. Nothing came of this, perhaps because they expected me to seek some kind of executive employment. The man from Peter's was particularly scathing: 'We don't like lotus eaters in Australia,' he told me. I'd never heard the expression before but the meaning was plain enough.

We left for Brisbane on 18 August and Gerry and Gwenda met us at the Roma Street station. We spent a few hours exploring the city, which in those days had the feeling of a big country town and lacked the relative sophistication of Sydney and Melbourne. Soon after lunch, we headed west. Gerry, ever the organiser, had decided that, for maximum economy of fuel, we should average a certain speed (I forget just what it was) and that we had to travel about 500 miles every day. Soon after we left Toowoomba the sealed road came to an end, and from then on until we reached the northern suburbs of Adelaide many days later we were travelling on dirt roads. I had never experienced anything remotely like this. The roads were rutted and uneven, the dry creek beds which regularly bisected them had to be carefully negotiated, and the road trains – gigantic trailer-trucks which barrelled along these tracks at high speed – were intimidating. We drove north-west through Dalby, Roma, Longreach, Winton, Cloncurry and Mount

Isa. At night we pitched tents and cooked food on a campfire; Gerry taught us how to boil a billy in the traditional Aussie style.

My vivid memory of this trip, which was carried out at a lightning-fast pace, is of the dust and the flies. The red dust got into everything – it filled the car and seeped into the food and water. And the flies were relentless; they covered every exposed bit of flesh whenever you emerged from the confines of the car. Though the journey into Central Australia was a once-in-a-lifetime experience (or so I thought at the time), it had its nightmarish qualities too.

We hit the main north–south highway at Tennant Creek and headed south through tiny communities like Barrow Creek and Ti Tree until we reached Alice Springs, which, although the biggest town in the centre, was still pretty small. Then it was on to Ayers Rock, which today is known as Uluru. The giant monolith in the centre of the country, where the colour of the rock changes according to the time of the day and the day of the year, is rightly considered one of the wonders of the world. This was an awe-inspiring experience. There was hardly anyone around and we pitched our tents close to the rock, which would never be permitted today. Nor were there any inhibitions then about climbing to the top (a practice frowned on today) and so we duly made the steep climb and surveyed the spectacular views of the desert landscape from the top. After this unforgettable experience we drove south to the opal-mining community of Coober Pedy and then on past the prohibited area of Woomera, which had been used by the British for testing nuclear bombs.

We stopped short of Adelaide, because Gerry wanted to visit Seppelts Winery in the Barossa Valley where he had a contact. We then took the Sturt Highway east and drove along the Murray River through Renmark and Mildura. Gerry wanted to visit some close friends who farmed a property near Harden, and we stopped there for a night before making the final drive to Sydney.

We drove back into Sydney on the Monday evening of a long weekend through extremely heavy traffic. From Liverpool onwards we were found ourselves in a jam such as I'd never before experienced, not even around London. We were tired and grumpy by the time we got back to Double Bay. In retrospect, this was indeed a wonderful trip, and I will never regret that I had the opportunity to make it so soon after arriving in Australia. But at the time, it was exhausting, dusty and frequently monotonous. Also, I was beginning to get nervous about what the immediate future had in store.

A few weeks later Gerry and Gwenda were married in Sydney, after which they left permanently for Gunnedah. I hardly saw anything of them for very many years. There were a couple of fleeting visits and we seemed able to pick up pretty much where we left off, but the friends who were our main incentive for coming to Australia in the first place were now living hundreds of miles away. In fact, things generally weren't turning out at all the way I'd planned. I suddenly experienced a deep depression. Why had we made this trip? We had no friends in Sydney now that Gerry and Gwenda had left the city. I was certain that there must be some like-minded film buffs somewhere, but the advertisements in the entertainment section of *The Sydney Morning Herald* didn't list any significant film society activity as far as I could see. Our money was beginning to run out, thanks to the alarmingly high rent we were paying for the Double Bay flat. I couldn't seek help from my father, so I gritted my teeth and sold my still camera as well as the cine-camera Uncle John had given me. The income from these sacrifices provided only temporary relief. I was getting desperate.

It never occurred to me to try to find work in the film distribution business. I'd been trained to be a grocer, and every day I scoured the job ads in *The Sydney Morning Herald* looking for something which would involve my experience in the grocery trade. There was nothing, however, except for the most basic handling of goods, and eventually I swallowed what was left of my pride and applied for a job working on the floor of a warehouse owned by the G&G retail grocery company. I started work on 1 October. The warehouse was in Botany, and work commenced at seven am, so I had a long journey to get there by bus from Double Bay to Central and then via another bus to Botany.

The work consisted of assembling cartons of canned and packaged goods for delivery to the hundreds of retail stores the G&G chain operated around the suburbs of Sydney and in major towns across the state. It was boring but at least the wages were reasonably good. After a week my boss – a tall, thin, bespectacled man whose name I'm afraid I've forgotten – called me into his office and quizzed me about my background. When he heard about my English training he assured me that the company had better jobs to offer for someone with my experience than working in the warehouse. On learning that I was married with a baby on the way and that we were living in Double Bay, he offered accommodation in one of the apartments located above suburban G&G stores. There was, he said, one such apartment available immediately in Petersham, on the corner of New Canterbury Road and Crystal Street, and though it was in poor condition it would only be a temporary solution; a newly renovated flat would be available in neighbouring Summer Hill before the end of the year. I was extremely grateful to this man for his kindness and accepted immediately.

The Petersham flat was, indeed, extremely run-down, with the most basic amenities and an outside downstairs toilet shared by the staff of the shop. Still, it was bearable for two or three months, and it was easier to get to Botany from there. At last I had solved the problems of employment and accommodation. The next step was to locate some fellow film people to befriend.

Chapter Six

On the first weekend in October 1963 an advertisement in *The Sydney Morning Herald* promised a full two days of films by the great Soviet director Sergei Eisenstein, to be held at the WEA in Sydney. I'd already seen several Eisenstein films, including *Battleship Potemkin*, *Alexander Nevsky* and both parts of *Ivan the Terrible*, but two films I hadn't seen were being screened – *October* and *The Old and the New*, aka *The General Line*.

The weekend was moderated by John Flaus, a thin, eager, intense man with a sharp sense of humour. It was obvious from the start that he knew what he was talking about, and also that his love of film extended beyond Eisenstein and the Soviet masters. It was a pleasure to listen to his introductions to the films and, of course, I was eager to ask questions and to contribute to the discussions. At the first break in proceedings I was approached by other members of the small but enthusiastic audience, and that's how I met Ian McPherson, John Connell and Dorothy Shoemark, three people who would play major roles in my life.

Ian, an owlish, good-natured man with the demeanour of a large, friendly dog, was, like Flaus, a little older than me; John, who was ruddy-cheeked, opinionated and somewhat more reserved at first, was about my age; and Dorothy, who reminded me very much of the Rosalind Russell character in *Picnic*, was a kind and generous but, I thought, perhaps a rather lonely woman. All three of them became firm friends, and it was through them that I became involved in the Sydney Film Festival. Ian, a foundation Committee-member of the festival, was at that time Convenor of its Publicity Sub-committee, and Dorothy had recently been co-opted as Honorary Secretary; John would join them on the Committee soon afterwards. It must have been obvious to them all that I was a film buff after their own hearts. All three were also active film society supporters and they were keen to know more about me. This was exactly the kind of contact I'd been looking for since my arrival.

I was well aware of the concept of a film festival. Film magazines like *Sight & Sound* and *Films and Filming* reported every year on the handful of festivals which were held in Europe. Venice, founded under the Fascist regime of Mussolini in 1933, was the original film festival, and the second, planned to be held in the Riviera resort of Cannes in September 1939, had been postponed because of the outbreak of war and was eventually launched in 1946. The third, the Berlin Film Festival, was a product of the Cold War. These, the three main international events, were heavily subsidised by their governments and tourist boards; they screened only world premieres, with directors and actors in attendance, and they were supported by the American studios, which saw them as a way of launching their product in Europe, as well as by every film-making country – even those behind the so-called 'Iron Curtain'. However, in 1947, in the city of Edinburgh in Scotland, a different kind of film festival had been launched, not by major film producers or the tourist board but by members of the local film society movement; they established a cultural film event designed to be held alongside the Edinburgh Arts Festival.

I soon discovered from my new friends that film enthusiasts in post-war Australia, although hampered by the non-availability of many films which they could read about in the British film magazines but which were never distributed, had followed the example of their British counterparts in establishing film societies. Occasionally, they would save up enough money to import a 16-mm print of a film which had never been available before. Although, as Margaret Hancock had warned me, the film society movement was far more organised in Victoria than it was in NSW, there proved to be a large number of film buffs in Sydney. The activities of the Melbourne University Film Society (MUFS) and the Melbourne Film Society (MFS) were legendary, and film societies were also flourishing in the suburbs of Melbourne and in some larger country areas, such as Geelong. In Sydney, there were the Sydney University Film Group (SUFG), the Sydney Film Society (SFS) and a small leftist group, the Realist Film Association, which generally showed films from the USSR and Eastern Europe. There was also the WEA Film Study Group, which had organised the Eisenstein weekend.

In February 1951 the Australian Council of Film Societies (ACOFS) – the equivalent of the British Federation of Film Societies – had, in association with the NSW Federation of Film Societies, organised a weekend of screenings and discussions at Newport, a beach suburb north of Sydney. Ed Schefferle, who had visited from Victoria, was rather unimpressed by the affair (as he reported back to his associates in Melbourne), but a significant decision was taken to hold a national film festival in conjunction with the 1952 ACOFS meeting. The location chosen was Olinda, outside Melbourne, and the event had been attended by several film enthusiasts from Sydney, including Stanley Hawes, Producer-in-Chief of the Australian Commonwealth Film Unit (CFU), the independent filmmaker John Kingsford-Smith and, as delegates of SUFG, Ian McPherson (the Hon. Secretary) and his close friend David Donaldson (the President).

The Olinda programme was a very serious one; there were sessions on Scientific Film, Art and Film, and Film and Religion. With the help of various embassies and consulates and some distributors, including MGM and British Empire Films (BEF), films were screened from several countries, including France, the USSR and China. Prime Minister Robert Menzies had sent a message of greeting ('I would like to congratulate all who have helped to organise this splendid festival . . .'), although the trade magazine *Film Weekly* later complained about 'heated attacks, mostly communist inspired, on the commercial picture industry' made during the weekend.

The Sydney contingent, who had returned full of enthusiasm about the Olinda event, became the nucleus of the Sydney Film Festival and were active in forming a committee, which was chaired by Alan Stout, Professor of Philosophy at Sydney University. The inaugural Committee included John Heyer, director of the magnificent documentary, *The Back of Beyond* (which I had screened at the Melksham and District Film Society), and members of the Australian Amateur Cine Society (AACS), who made their films on 8-mm, 9.5-mm and sometimes even 16-mm, and film society enthusiasts. In Britain, amateur filmmakers, such as members of the AACS, were not usually involved in film society activities but celebrated their interests in separate groups.

In Melbourne it seems to have been decided that the 1952 weekend in Olinda would be, in effect, the first Melbourne Film Festival. The organising committee held a Melbourne Film Festival, in June, every year after that, until recently, when it moved to July. The first Sydney Film Festival (SFF) was held at Sydney University over the long weekend of 11–14 June 1954, with a programme that included mostly classic films of another era – Rene Clair's *Sous les Toits de Paris* (1929), Buster Keaton's *The General* (1927) and Carl Dreyer's *The Passion of Joan of Arc*

(1928) – fine films, unquestionably, but more suitable for a film society than a film festival. The exceptions were the often international award-winning amateur films. Indeed, a film society – an especially ambitious and well-organised one – was basically what the SFF was at this early stage in its history. Over the next ten years the festivals in both Melbourne and Sydney flourished. From the very beginning the Melbourne event was run by Erwin Rado, who had left his native Hungary just before the war and had settled in Melbourne, where he ran a photography business. Rado was also secretary of the Melbourne Film Society, the Australian Film Institute (AFI), which, at a time when there were virtually no locally made feature films, presented awards for the best documentaries, short, and advertising films each year, and the Victorian Federation of Film Societies.

The 1963 Sydney Film Festival (the tenth) had taken place a couple of months before I arrived; it was obviously now the city's major film event, and I was looking forward to meeting its director, Ian Klava, who was a close friend of my new acquaintances. In contrast to Melbourne, the SFF had been run by several different directors since its inception. The first was David Donaldson (1954–57), who was followed by Valwyn Edwards (1958), Robert Connell and Sylvia Lawson (joint directors for one year in 1959), Lois Hunter (1960) and Patricia Moore (1961). Klava had been appointed in 1962 as the first full-time director, and he worked from home for most of the year, establishing an office in the city only a few weeks before the Festival was due to commence.

My new friends told me that the Sydney Film Society had recently collapsed, apparently because its funds had been poorly managed. The Sydney University Film Group was now the main venue where the keen filmgoer was able to see a wide variety of films for most of the year in Sydney, and I was advised to join as soon as possible, which I did.

To my very great surprise, Ian McPherson soon invited me to join the Publicity Sub-committee of the Sydney Film Festival.

I knew absolutely nothing about publicity and I thought, frankly, that it was very strange to be invited to join such a committee, but it seemed to be a foot in the door, so I accepted. We met at Ian's Northbridge home once a month, and his wife, Trish, always invited me to dinner beforehand. Ian Klava was also invited, which is how we met for the first time. Klava lived with his Latvian-born mother in the beachside suburb of Maroubra and, like the others, he was very friendly and welcoming. Joan Long, who would eventually become a feature film producer (*Caddie*, *The Picture Show Man*) and media journalist Heather Chapman were also members of this committee. I felt rather out of my depth but it was certainly an interesting experience.

It was during conversations with the Ians, John and Dorothy that I became aware for the first time of the draconian level of film censorship that existed in Australia. In the UK, the British Board of Film Censors (BBFC) was an autonomous body, independent of government. I knew that there was no government censorship in the US. But censorship in Australia, although strictly speaking the prerogative of the states, was in practice administered by the federal government through the Department of Customs. Every imported book, magazine, television programme and film was technically impounded by Customs and declared a prohibited import until cleared by the Censorship Board, which was based in Sydney.

My own observations had suggested to me that Australian censors were more lenient on scenes of violence than their British counterparts (there were not only the examples already mentioned of *Cape Fear*, *Bad Day at Black Rock* and *Violent Saturday*, but the Marlon Brando biker film, *The Wild One*, banned in Britain, had always screened freely in Australia). However, in matters of sex and religion, things were very different. I was amazed to discover that three films I admired greatly were banned in Australia. Luis Buñuel's scathing satire on religion, *Viridiana*, had been a controversial entry at Cannes in

1961, where it won the Palme D'Or. Buñuel, Spanish by birth, had been associated with the surrealists in Paris in the late 1920s and early 1930s, and had worked with Salvador Dali on *Un Chien Andalou*, which had contained some scenes that were notorious in 1929, and *L'Age d'Or*. An opponent of the Franco regime which seized power in 1936 and consolidated control after the Republicans lost in the bitter civil war that followed, Buñuel had gone into exile first in America and then in Mexico. There he had made a number of films of all kinds, including a blistering attack on poverty, *Los Olvidados* (1953), which was one of the films I'd shown at the Melksham and District Film Society. Following the success in Cannes of *Viridiana*, this scabrous tale about the corruption of a young novice had been screened to great critical acclaim in Britain, where I had seen it in 1962. I was amazed to hear that it was banned in Australia on the grounds of blasphemy.

Also banned for blasphemy was another film I regarded very highly, Charles Laughton's gothic masterpiece *The Night of the Hunter* (1955), in which Robert Mitchum played a serial killer masquerading as a preacher. Although not a commercial success, and misunderstood by many on its first release, Laughton's film, which takes place in small towns during the Depression, had impressed me enormously when I saw it. Laughton, an Oscar-winning actor, only ever directed this one film, but it was an unforgettable one. Had the censors misunderstood the film, I wondered? Had they not realised that Mitchum's switchblade-wielding killer was not, in fact, a preacher but was *pretending* to be a preacher? How then could this ultimately very moral film be banned for blasphemy? The fact that such a fine film was banned in Australia seemed incomprehensible. But worse was to come.

Banned too, I discovered, on the grounds of immorality, was Jean-Luc Godard's amazing first feature, *A bout de souffle* (*Breathless*, 1960), which I've always considered to be the most innovative debut feature film since *Citizen Kane*. *Breathless*, which I'd also seen in London, was one of the key films of the French *nouvelle vague* and was essential viewing for anyone remotely interested in cinema at the time.

In addition to these outright bans, I was told, numerous films I admired had been cut because of their sexual content, including *Room at the Top*, *Saturday Night and Sunday Morning* and François Truffaut's *Shoot the Pianist*, which had screened in a cut version at the Sydney Film Festival earlier in the year. It came as a great surprise to me to learn that even the Film Festival was not immune from censorship, in contrast to the British regulations which allowed film societies, and the recently established London Film Festival, to screen uncensored films. I was both astonished and depressed by these revelations.

I became somewhat obsessed with the phenomenon of censorship, and often speculated as to why the Australian authorities were so touchy when it came to sexual and religious themes. I eventually came to the conclusion that at least part of the answer lay in the fact that the Department of Customs seemed largely to be staffed by Irish-Catholic bureaucrats.

Meanwhile, the weather grew warmer and then it became hot. In November I was shocked, along with the rest of the world, by the news of the assassination of President Kennedy in Dallas, and by the subsequent murder of his alleged killer, Lee Harvey Oswald. I hadn't heard the news that Saturday morning, and was shopping in Petersham when I stopped to listen to a politician addressing a crowd (a federal election was imminent); I was startled to hear him say that his party had conveyed its condolences to Jacqueline Kennedy. I didn't know what he was talking about until later when I returned to the flat and Margaret told me the grim news.

These were depressing times. I hated the work at the warehouse and the Petersham flat was pretty wretched. I desperately needed to save enough money for our passage home.

On the brighter side, my beautiful daughter, Mary, was born on 14 March 1964 and soon afterwards G&G moved us into a new flat above their shop in Summer Hill. It was a major improvement over the Petersham flat; it had been freshly decorated and there was more space, so it was comparatively luxurious. Only later did we find that it was infested with bedbugs, which attacked the baby during the night. I'd never come across such sickening things before.

The birth of their first grandchild prompted my parents to take a holiday in Australia to see how we were going. We met them at Sydney Airport and they stayed in the flat for a couple of weeks. I think they were impressed with Sydney and they liked my new friends, especially Dorothy Shoemark, who made them very welcome. I assured them that I was on track to return to England, if not by mid-1965, as originally planned, then definitely by early 1966. I sincerely believed this to be so.

In June 1964 I attended my first Sydney Film Festival. Unable to afford a ticket, I applied to do voluntary work as an usher so that I could see some of the films. The very first session I attended was a Brazilian film titled *O Pagador de Promessas* (*The Given Word*). This film was preceded by a locally made short film – not *that* short, actually, since it ran for an interminable twenty-nine minutes. It was called *Music in the Making*, and it had been produced by the federally funded Commonwealth Film Unit (CFU).

The CFU had come into being before World War II, at about the same time that the higher profile National Film Board of Canada was established under the aegis of the famous Scottish documentary pioneer John Grierson. Grierson, who seemed to have become the Commonwealth's leading advisor on how to establish propaganda documentary film units, had visited Australia to advise on the establishment of a production house in this country. He had arranged for a colleague from the legendary British Crown Film Unit, the somewhat dour Stanley Hawes, to take over this new documentary film unit as producer-in-chief. Unfortunately, the CFU, one of the very few production companies in the country at the time, was forever hamstrung by the fact that it was established within a government department. In contrast, by the 1960s Canada's NFB had become celebrated for its innovative and challenging documentaries and its animated films, several of which were screening at the SFF in 1964; compared to them, the product of the CFU was strikingly inferior. *Music in the Making* took an interesting theme – literally the creation of music – but handled it in an inept, old-fashioned style, and featured a monotonous narration which consistently talked down to the audience.

I was surprised that such a film was given a prominent screening at the festival and I decided to write to the Festival Committee expressing my opinions. In writing this letter, I was only dimly aware of how many people I would be upsetting. One of the executive producers of *Music in the Making*, Frank Bagnall, had been one of the founders of the SFF, and had only recently resigned from the Committee. Stanley Hawes, the other executive producer, had been another founder and was still a member of the SFF Committee, as were the film's producer, Malcolm Otton, its scriptwriter, co-director and editor, Robert Parker, and its music co-ordinator, Elaine Fallon. What I saw as valid criticism of an inferior film was undoubtedly seen by others as a charge of nepotism, though that wasn't my intention. I think that Ian Klava may have been under pressure to screen *Music in the Making* and other CFU films like it, and so welcomed my letter as a tool to strengthen his own position. At any rate, the result was that I was invited by Ian to join the Festival's Film Selection Sub-committee and also encouraged to stand for membership of the Committee itself. I was duly elected at the Annual General Meeting which was held late in 1964.

My excitement at becoming a member of the Festival Committee, as well as serving on two of its sub-committees, was somewhat tempered by the growing realisation that I had inadvertently made quite a few enemies who were currently serving on that same committee.

The small community of film enthusiasts in Sydney was boosted at about this time by the return from overseas of Barrie Pattison, whose writing on film in the magazines *Motion* and *Films and Filming* I had admired back in Britain. He was an original thinker with an agreeably racy style and he opened my eyes to qualities in films I might not otherwise have taken seriously. I hadn't realised then that he was Australian, and now he was back and full of stories about recent films he'd seen and encounters he'd had. For a while we became friends and he would invite me to his home in Epping on weekends to watch rare films on 16-mm.

Meanwhile, things had improved a little on the work front. After labouring in the Botany warehouse for a year, I was offered the position of manager of one of G&G's smaller Sydney retail outlets in the suburb of Ashfield, close to where we were living at Summer Hill. There was only one other staff member at the shop, a teenage girl who devoted much more time to planning sexy weekends 'up The Entrance' than she did to her work. I enjoyed the challenge of running the place even though the figures showed that we had a major shoplifting problem. I was determined to stop this thievery and began to suspect an elderly man who came often to the shop but hardly ever bought anything. I rigged up a way of observing the shop floor from the storeroom at the back (there were no closed-circuit security cameras in those days) and, sure enough, my suspicions proved to be correct. But when he broke down in tears after being confronted, I didn't have the heart to call the police, a decision which didn't impress Head Office when I reported the matter to them.

I didn't mind this too much because I was now earning enough money to save up for our passages home. Our original plan to return to Britain by way of Asia or the US had been abandoned. All I could do now was get myself, Margaret and Mary home by the quickest and cheapest route. I booked a cabin on a ship scheduled to sail back to Southampton in February 1966.

I had also become involved in other film activities. Robert Gowland, who was secretary of the NSW Federation of Film Societies, invited me to assist in preparing a database, which I was happy to do, although in the days before computers were available it was a very long and arduous task. I also gave some help to John Connell, who had decided to start a new film society in Sydney after the demise of the previous one. His Sydney Cinema Society held screenings at Anzac House in Sydney for two or three years before it, too, collapsed in very unfortunate circumstances.

In the aftermath of the 1965 SFF, I became more active on the Committee. There were things wrong with the event, in my view, and, since I wasn't going to be around long, I might as well express my misgivings as speedily and as forcefully as possible. In addition to the questionable selection of poor quality films made by people closely connected with the Festival, my other concern was with censorship. I had been truly shocked, on the opening night of the 1965 Festival, to meet Joel Greenberg, who I knew to be, like myself, a lover of classical American cinema. In collaboration with Charles Higham, a British-born, Sydney-based writer, who was also a great film enthusiast, Greenberg had written a couple of excellent books on Hollywood in its golden era. My pleasure in meeting him was diminished when I discovered that he worked in an administrative position at the Censorship Office and that he supported censorship of the Festival. He was also quick to tell me that he had recently very much enjoyed the new Robert Aldrich film *Hush, Hush, Sweet Charlotte* but that 'of course' the censors had been obliged to cut it. I was quite staggered by this admission, and by what I saw as Greenberg's double standards; it was all right for him to see and enjoy Aldrich's film, but not, it seemed, for anyone else.

Thinking back on that encounter with Greenberg all those years ago, it seems to me that it was another defining moment in my life. I'd never before met someone who actually worked in a censorship office and I could not – and still cannot – comprehend how anyone who professed to love cinema could condone, indeed actively support, what I saw as the mutilation of films. I can remember the encounter vividly; I was on crutches, having stupidly trodden on a wine glass in bare feet at home a few nights before, and the stitches in the sole of my foot were throbbing painfully. I'm sure that for Greenberg the encounter was of absolutely no importance, some chance remarks no sooner said than forgotten. Yet what he said to me that night still resonates over the years. How often, I wonder, have I done the same thing myself? How often have I said or done something which was of no particular importance to me yet which profoundly affected somebody else?

It seemed to me absurd that the SFF was subjected to the harsh commercial censorship of the time, especially since many of the prints used were imported especially from overseas and therefore the property of the film's producers, not of the Festival. And yet Ian Klava didn't seem at all concerned; on the contrary, he confided in me that he thought censorship was quite a good idea, and that the cutting of a 1964 festival entry, Fons Rademakers's *Als twee druppels water* (*The Spitting Image*), from the Netherlands, had actually improved the film because it made it less violent. I couldn't accept this point of view at all. To make matters worse, censorship was carried out in complete secrecy; the public, even the Festival audience, were completely unaware of the extent of this interference in their viewing. I discovered that it was not, in fact, illegal to publicise the censorship decisions; it was just that, traditionally, the film distributors had never done so (why would they?) and the Festivals, both Melbourne and Sydney, had unthinkingly followed in their footsteps, saying nothing when their film entries were cut or, in extreme cases, banned altogether.

I sounded out my friends and allies on the SFF Committee and they all seemed to share my view, especially Ian McPherson, who became quite agitated when I pointed out to him instances of censorship. For example, the fine Japanese film *Suna no Onna*

(*Woman of the Dunes*), by Hiroshi Teshigahara, was very obviously censored when it screened at the 1965 Festival. With the support of Ian McPherson, John and Beverley Burke and John Connell, I drafted the following motion to be presented to the Committee at the October meeting.

1. That the Sydney Film Festival would, from now on, publicise all censorship of festival films by way of press releases;
2. That the SFF would apply to the Film Censorship Department, and to the Federal Government, via the Department of Customs, for complete exemption from censorship;
3. That the SFF would lobby in favour of an Adults Only (18 and over) classification, similar to the British 'X' classification, for commercial film screenings; and
4. That the SFF would announce its new policy by way of a letter addressed to the editor of *The Bulletin* magazine.

At this stage I did not go so far as to suggest that the Festival should refuse to screen any censored film; that would come later. But the motion as it stood was threatening enough. Ian Klava was implacably opposed to it, arguing that, since the SFF invited films in collaboration with the Melbourne Film Festival, Melbourne would have to agree as well (I hadn't thought of this) and that Erwin Rado would certainly oppose such action. Klava claimed the Censorship Board would react negatively if the SFF started publicising their decisions (he was proved right about that) and could retaliate by taking even more conservative decisions on festival films (again, he was proved right). Nevertheless, my motion was passed by a large majority of the Committee although I could tell that the President, Frank Bellingham, a prominent Sydney gynaecologist, was unhappy with the turn of events.

I had expected that the occasion on which I presented the censorship motion would have been my penultimate Committee meeting. I arrived at the November 1965 meeting prepared to resign on the grounds that I was leaving Australia to return to

Britain early in the New Year, but before I could speak Ian Klava dropped a bombshell. He announced his resignation as director, after four years in the position, stating that the anti-censorship policy adopted at the previous meeting would be impossible to implement and that he preferred to step down rather than to attempt it. I was sitting next to John Connell when this announcement was made and I could feel the tension in the room. Several people looked at me and my immediate thought was: 'It's my fault.' This was followed by: 'Why don't I take over from Ian? I can do it. I'm *destined* to do it.' But how long would the Festival survive, I wondered, and was it sensible to stay on in Australia and burn my bridges with my father, who had a job waiting for me at Stratton Sons & Mead, if the Festival went into freefall? I whispered as much to John and he whispered something encouraging back. After the meeting I approached Dr Bellingham and told him I was interested in the job. We arranged to meet in a couple of days.

When I met with Bellingham at his Macquarie Street surgery he seemed resigned to the situation. He told me he'd spoken to most of the Committee members, the majority of whom were in favour of my appointment to the job. As far as I know, no other possible applicants were canvassed. He then told me that, subject to ratification at the next Committee meeting (in February, after the ship on which I had booked to return to England had sailed), the job was mine.

Under these rather special circumstances I thought I might as well go for broke. Until this time the Festival had been run on a semi-amateur basis with no permanent office or secretarial assistant. Volunteers had carried out a lot of the work, as they still do to a certain extent today. This was something that had to be rectified. From the moment I left the employ of G&G, I would be homeless, so there was no question of working from home as Klava had done. It seemed essential that I be allocated enough funds to rent a permanent office and to pay for a full-time assistant as well. There was little debate about this. Somewhat more controversial was my proposal that a budget be found for international travel for the Festival Director. Klava had never been overseas; I think he didn't like the idea of travel very much. The Festival had, until then, partly been programmed by Melbourne's Erwin Rado, who travelled quite regularly, and partly by a process in which Klava and members of his Film Sub-committee pored over recent copies of magazines like *Sight & Sound* and *Monthly Film Bulletin* looking for titles that sounded interesting. I felt that it was essential that the Festival Director be given the right to select films personally by visiting, as far as possible, the countries where they were made, and that this would also be important for making vital personal contacts.

My wife and daughter took the boat back to England in February as arranged. I was very sad to see them go, and suddenly I felt very alone. A few days later, the SFF Committee confirmed my appointment as Director and agreed to a travel allowance for me. As soon as the 1966 Festival was over I planned to travel back to England by a circuitous route, selecting films along the way, and then return to Australia by the end of the year. In the meantime, I found for myself a one room flat in Palmer Street, Woolloomooloo – not the most fashionable part of Sydney, but within walking distance of the new Festival office, which was on the top floor of a building on the corner of King and Sussex Streets.

Emotionally, I was in turmoil: events had moved very fast and I knew I had a huge task ahead of me, but I was excited by the challenge. All my new Australian friends would, I knew, be totally supportive and indeed they were. But, nevertheless, I was well aware that I had done a momentous thing. I had let down my father and ruined his plans for me; I had abandoned the country of my birth; and I had accepted a challenge with no way of knowing that I could succeed.

I was twenty-six years old, the same age as my father when he joined the army to fight in World War II.

Chapter Seven

The office which became the headquarters of the Festival for the next few years was a musty, windowless, airless space on the top floor of a six-storey King Street building, accessed by a rickety lift. Our donated furniture, sparse and fairly primitive, consisted of a couple of old-fashioned desks, two or three filing cabinets, a standard manual typewriter and a pair of rather uncomfortable swivel chairs. The first thing to do was to purchase another second-hand manual typewriter for Modesta Gentile, my newly-appointed full-time secretary. The second was to adjust to decimal currency, which was introduced on 14 February 1966.

The office was divided into two sections, one for me and one for Modesta. Her father was Italian and she had been born in Italy but had lived after the war with her brother and her Australian mother in Canada and the UK. In London she'd studied drama and ballet (with Marie Rambert, who also taught Audrey Hepburn and Geraldine Chaplin) and she had acted in regional repertory and danced in a British musical film, *Tommy the*

Toreador, with Tommy Steele; but more importantly, as far as I was concerned, she had recently been employed by the London Film Festival and she was by far the best of the candidates for the new position.

As I sat at my desk that first morning I made a number of plans. The first priority, of course, was to win the censorship battle but I was ambitious to achieve far more: I wanted to turn the Sydney Film Festival into a genuinely professional organisation, similar to the overseas events I'd read about but had not as yet experienced. In my view, that meant cutting the Festival's ties to the University of Sydney.

The SFF had, until then, been focused very much on the University: the Vice-Chancellor was the titular honorary vice-president of the Committee and most screenings took place on the University campus. Until replaced in 1962 by the 620-seat Union Theatre (now the Footbridge Theatre), the main University venue for 35-mm films (then and now the standard gauge for commercial movies) had been the mid-nineteenth-century Union Hall, where generally good quality film projection was provided by the student members of the commercially oriented Sydney University Film Society. In addition, there was the main hall of the Sydney Teachers College, which was not equipped for 35-mm projection so that every year the SFF Technical Sub-committee had to make a temporary installation of a pair of second-hand projectors, together with sound equipment, which had been purchased from a doomed suburban cinema. Before the advent of the recently completed Stephen Roberts Theatre, which traded convenience for comfort, the Festival's main venue for 16-mm films had always been the well-equipped Wallace Theatre, supplemented by various lecture theatres including, in its early years, the atmospheric Great Hall. It was the closing of the Union Hall for rebuilding that had forced the Festival to move some of its 35-mm screenings off-campus to Anzac House in College Street, thus beginning the splitting of locations which continued with the use of Sydney Technical College's Turner Hall, near Broadway, and, later on, the Hub Cinema in Newtown. From the very start of my association with the Festival there had been argument and controversy over the quality of projection in some of the marginal screening venues.

However, the SFF had ambitious long-term plans. The Sydney Opera House, with its award-winning design by the Danish architect Jørn Utzon, was now under construction at Circular Quay on the site of the old tram terminus, and from its inception the Festival had expressed interest in making the Opera House its main venue. The advantages were obvious because the main hall, as designed by Utzon, would have seated 2000 people, which was the maximum number of patrons the Festival was allowed under the regulations laid down by the Federation Internationale des Associations de Producteurs du Films (FIAPF), the international body, based in Paris, which approved and recognised 'official' film festivals.

It was, then, essential that top-quality projection equipment (35-mm, 16-mm and even 70-mm if possible) and a state-of-the-art sound system be installed in the main hall of the Opera House and that the control room, or bio-box, be designed so that it was large enough to accommodate this kind of equipment. The Festival had been assured by the Opera House Trust that this would be so but the big question facing the Festival Committee was: How much would the Trust charge the SFF to rent the venue?

From the very first Festival, it had never had been possible for members of the public to purchase tickets to individual screenings. In the early days, only subscription tickets could be sold because of Customs regulations; later, the purchase of full Festival subscriptions became a non-negotiable condition of FIAPF recognition of both the Sydney and Melbourne Film Festivals.

But whatever the reasons for not selling tickets to individual sessions, the policy gave the impression, in my view, that the SFF, for all the unquestionable enthusiasm and dedication of its organisers, was at heart a glorified film society. As I knew from my experience in Britain, film societies bypassed any number of regulations by offering only subscription tickets. Most significantly, they avoided censorship thanks to their members-only policy, but this system of course did not operate in Australia.

Subscription tickets certainly made things simpler from an administrative point of view. In those days the Festival screened about thirty feature films and 130 short films. A Gold subscription ticket would allow you to see every film and to obtain a free copy of the informative catalogue, which contained synopses and the main credits of all the films in the programme. It was good value, and by 1965 the Festival was managing to sell every subscription ticket well before the event began. In fact, there was quite a rush to buy tickets as soon as the subscription mailing went out.

Under this system a Festival budget could be readily calculated. Assuming all tickets were sold, and once the price of the tickets was agreed upon, the year's likely total income was known in advance. The Treasurer, John Burke, in consultation with the Director and the various sub-committee convenors, would establish what funds were available to each for the running of the event. Theoretically, it was simple. But there was no margin for error and there were no government subsidies or sponsorships either, although the catalogue had always included paid advertisements to offset the cost of its publication.

The Festival had only recently begun to accrue a small financial surplus and I had now made a number of proposals – a permanent office, overseas travel for the Director, a full-time assistant – which had significant cost implications. The ticket prices would have to be raised to cover them, although since the tickets had always been priced so reasonably this didn't seem to be a problem.

Many of the Festival's concerns in those days centered on FIAPF, which represented the major film producing companies and associations in the non-Communist world, including the Motion Pictures Producers of America (MPPA), the mouthpiece of the Hollywood majors. One of the aims of the organisation, whose Secretary-General was a rather surly Frenchman named Alphonse Brisson, was to attempt to control the spread of international film festivals in the interests of member producers. FIAPF recognised two kinds of film festivals; A-list events, like Cannes, Venice, Berlin, Karlovy Vary (Czechoslovakia), Moscow and San Sebastian (Spain) and B-list festivals, like London, Edinburgh, Melbourne and Sydney. The A-listers were, as we have seen, competitive events, obliged to screen world premieres (though some films were allowed to have been previously seen in their country of origin), and usually heavily sponsored by their national governments; they were also required to include a festival market for the benefit of buyers and sellers (although Venice, the oldest festival, steadfastly refused to do this). B-list festivals could present feature films without a competition; entries did not have to be world premieres and there didn't have to be a formal market, though the festivals were expected to help producers sell the films they screened to distributors in their countries.

In the mid-1960s it was, generally speaking, FIAPF's policy to recognise only one festival of each type in any country, and that was the rub in Australia. On a previous trip to Paris, Erwin had managed to persuade Brisson that both Melbourne and Sydney deserved B-list recognition, arguing that the distance between the cities (comparable to the distance between London and Rome) ensured the fact that the audiences wouldn't overlap. More problematic, though, in the eyes of FIAPF, was the fact that the two Australian festivals wanted to *share* films. From our point of view this was essential to keep freight costs down, but you could see Brisson's point of view. If, individually, the Australian festivals couldn't afford to operate without sharing films, then perhaps they didn't deserve to exist, and wouldn't it be better, in the strictest commercial terms, if films seeking distribution weren't shown to festival audiences in *both* cities?

These were battles we would have to fight regularly over the next several years but, in the meantime, FIAPF had – grudgingly, I was told – recognised both festivals for 1966, in return for fairly hefty membership fees. This recognition gave us, in principle, the backing of key organisations like Unifrance, the company which co-ordinated the participation of French cinema in international events, and ANICA, which similarly represented Italian cinema. Without FIAPF recognition, we were told, we would not be able to obtain French or Italian films or, indeed, films from many other countries. FIAPF membership placed many restrictions on us, including the maximum number of people attending any one screening. Many of our decisions were made in the shadow of these constant threats that FIAPF might at any time cancel our international recognition.

If we had enjoyed the complete support of local film distributors FIAPF recognition might not have been so vital, but this was not the case. In addition, the endorsement of an imposing sounding international body like FIAPF could, we felt, be of help in our battle against censorship. FIAPF was opposed to censorship, and this was surely a weapon we could use in our appeals to the government. FIAPF membership proved that, to use one of Erwin Rado's favourite expressions, we were not some fly-by-night group; we were an internationally endorsed film festival. That status would surely do us no harm.

Ian Klava, who had typed all his own letters, had been meticulous in filing copies of his correspondence, so the main international sources of films were well documented. He had also drawn up, with the help of members of the Film Sub-committee (which had included myself) and with some advice from Erwin Rado, a list of titles of interest for the 1966 Festival together with their sources where possible. Rado had not been overseas to select films in 1965 so both Sydney and Melbourne Festivals were programming 'blind', relying on overseas reports and reviews, or sometimes suggestions from returning travellers and friends abroad, to assemble their programmes.

My first task was to have an official Festival Entry Form printed, and to write to the producers of the films on the list to invite them to participate. This was, of course, long before telexes, faxes and email. There was no money in the budget for overseas phone calls. Everything had to be done by what is now known as 'snail mail'. It was laborious work, yet I rather enjoyed composing letters to people all over the world and there was always a thrill of excitement when a letter arrived, usually bearing colourful foreign stamps, confirming the entry of an invited film.

Dorothy Holt, one of the Committee's Vice-Presidents, was married to Edgar Holt, a cousin of Harold Holt, who had just succeeded Robert Menzies as Prime Minister. The previous year, in his capacity as Federal Treasurer, Holt had attended the Festival's opening night, so I held the hope that he might be sympathetic to our anti-censorship cause. Dorothy pledged to do whatever she could to interest the PM. In the meantime, she insisted that I should be introduced to key members of the media. Accordingly, she arranged a series of lunches to be held at one of the better restaurants in Sydney's CBD, the Fjord Room at the Menzies Hotel. Media people who were considered to be potentially helpful were invited, and in due course small stories, with photograph attached, appeared in the social pages of some of the papers. More important to me was making contact with the main film critics of the time – Josephine O'Neill, the veteran reviewer of *The Sydney Morning Herald*, Billie Burke of *The Daily Telegraph* and Charles Higham of *The Bulletin*.

My most important meeting, however, was to take place a couple of weeks after I started work officially at the King Street office: Erwin Rado was coming to Sydney to see me. This was an encounter I was rather dreading. I knew that Rado disapproved of me, that he thought my stand on censorship was sheer folly and that he saw me as a kind of upstart out to cause trouble. It was agreed that he would spend a couple of days in Sydney and that I would accompany him for my initial meetings with our Customs Agent, John Stephenson, and with the Chief Film Censor, Richard Prowse, to discuss the tricky matters of importation and censorship. Rado would also meet with some members of the SFF Committee.

I expected a stern, humourless man and was quite unprepared for the reality. Erwin was aged fifty-one at the time, about the same age as my father. He was tall and handsome, with wavy grey hair and a charming Hungarian accent. He was impeccably groomed, extremely courteous and blessed with a dazzling smile. As I anticipated, however, our first meeting was fraught with tension. He told me, in no uncertain terms, that he believed the course I had embarked on was doomed to fail. He predicted that the Customs Department and the Government would react by making things more difficult for us. He feared they might even deny us the privilege we now enjoyed, which allowed us to import films on a temporary basis without paying customs duty. He was arguing, as he made it clear, not from a moralistic point of view but from a practical one.

I poured out my heart to him and told him how passionately I believed that the festivals were wrong to accept censorship without protest. I predicted that, as films became more sophisticated, more cutting edge, our problems would become worse; that we had to act now. I pointed out that Sydney could not do it alone, that Melbourne had to go along with us. The argument went back and forth but I could feel that my sincerity and my passion were having an effect. He decided to sleep on it and to discuss the matter further the next day, and I think that was when he made up his mind that I had made a convincing argument and that, despite all the problems in store for us, this *was* a battle worth fighting. The next morning we shook hands on it, and from that moment – subject to his own committee's approval, which was, I sensed, a foregone conclusion – he became as passionate an opponent of censorship as I was.

More than that; I had made a firm and loyal friend. Over the subsequent years we often had differences, and occasionally there were heated arguments; but these upsets were few and they never lasted long. The better I got to know Erwin the more I liked, admired and respected him. We exchanged letters almost every day for the next fifteen years or so, letters in which we both wrote frankly and without inhibition about our problems, frustrations, dreams and nightmares. Some of these letters, now in the archives of the two festivals, make interesting reading.

Having now agreed on a course of action, we went together to meet with Stephenson (who clearly thought we were crazy to confront the Customs Department but who was professional enough not to say so) and the Chief Censor, Richard Prowse. Prowse was a short, dapper man with only one arm, apparently the result of a war wound; he met us in his office in Bligh Street in the city and introduced us to Lyn Kirkwood, his deputy, a bluff, hearty man, and to John McAleer, his plump and jovial administrative officer.

It was immediately obvious to me that Prowse and his colleagues genuinely had no idea what we were talking about when we put to them the need for the festivals to be allowed to screen uncensored films. This, they pointed out, was quite impossible because it was against the law. Nor could they see any reason *why* these films should receive special treatment. We tried to argue on the grounds of practicality. We pointed out that we were not the *distributors* of the films we screened, that we didn't *own* them; we borrowed them from the people in various countries who made them. So when frames were removed from a 35-mm print (which, of course, is what happens when a film is cut) the damage was being done to property which belonged to companies and individuals overseas. In addition, English-subtitled prints of foreign films were in such demand around the world that they often arrived late for festival screenings. What would happen, we asked, if a film arrived late and the Board had no time to view it before its scheduled festival screening? That would be just too bad, we were told. 'You must tell your suppliers to get the films here in time,' Prowse said. He couldn't understand that this might not always be practicable.

Although we realised from this encounter that our battle wouldn't easily be won, we laid out our policy. From now on, we told Prowse, we would publicise all cuts demanded in festival films and protest against them. 'We can't stop you,' he told us. 'But we advise against such a policy.' We told him that we intended to lobby the Minister for Customs, but I could see by his scarcely concealed smile what he thought about that. The Customs Minister was Ken Anderson, a Country Party Senator not noted for his liberality.

After the meeting Erwin and I had lunch. Our meeting with Prowse had been a sobering, depressing experience. I had never thought that the fight against censorship would be easy, but I was beginning to understand just how difficult it was going to be. Still, we had to begin somewhere. Erwin invited me to come to Melbourne to meet with members of his committee, which I agreed to do as soon as possible. There was an allowance in the budget for one such trip, and this seemed the best time to do it.

I soon discovered that Erwin had a great many enemies. Some members of the SFF Committee found him arrogant and patronising. There was resentment over the fact that the Victorian Government had traditionally supported film culture and that the NSW Government had not. The Victorian State Film Centre was a source of envy around the country, and film appreciation (later 'film study') had been on the Victorian high school curriculum for many years. Erwin had certainly taken advantage of everything that was on offer in Victoria, and the very fact that he was running no less than four film arts organisations (the MFF, the Melbourne Film Society, the Victorian Federation of Film

Societies and the Australian Film Institute) from his Cardigan Street headquarters was seen by some as a blatant grab for power.

I saw these criticisms as indicative of the 'tall poppy syndrome' that I was already discovering was widespread in Australia. I thought it was entirely logical that Erwin, with his enthusiasm and resources, should run those four organisations. When I visited him in Melbourne, I was enormously impressed with the MFF office, which occupied the ground floor of a terrace house in the inner-city suburb of Carlton. Erwin and his second wife, Ann, lived above the office in a very comfortable flat with two grand pianos – music was Erwin's passion as much as film, if not more. The ground-floor offices included not only generous space for Erwin and his secretary but also a screening room equipped with both 35-mm and 16-mm projection, and plenty of space for film storage. This was the nerve centre of film culture in Victoria, referred to so warmly by the British Federation's Margaret Hancock, and it made our facilities in Sydney look shabby and paltry by comparison. I immediately resolved to rectify that as soon as possible. My meeting with the Melbourne committee, including Ed Shefferle, Pat Gordon and Ray Fisher, was extremely friendly; in basic principle, we saw eye to eye. But how, and when, would we succeed in achieving our new aims?

Back in Sydney the bureaucrats of the Censorship Board began to make their presence felt. Not only films had to be submitted to the censors but also still photographs, posters and press books. It was immediately obvious that any photograph which featured a scantily dressed woman or – horrors! – a naked woman, was seized by the censors and simply not returned. Were these offending images really destroyed, as we were told they were, or were they being added to someone's personal collection? Whatever the answer, I decided simply not to submit such photos in the future and simply filed them away, uncensored, in the Festival office.

There was another vital area where fences had to be mended, and that was with the commercial film distributors, most of whom, I soon discovered, were extremely suspicious of the Festival. One of the 'majors', Columbia Pictures, had always been on friendly terms with us and had in the past offered the Festival films they really didn't know what to do with, such as *O Cangaciero* in 1956, which had been the first Brazilian film ever screened in Australia. Columbia, whose Australian CEO was Colin Jones, seemed to appreciate that the Festival's reasonably efficient publicity machine could help create an audience for more 'difficult' product, and had in recent years entered two films, Stanley Kubrick's *Dr. Strangelove, or How I Learned to Stop Worrying and Love the Bomb* in 1964 and William Wyler's *The Collector* in 1965. It's probable that this friendly relationship was partly based on the fact that Jones was the brother of Phil Jones, the manager of the Gala Cinema arthouse in Pitt Street. Phil Jones was a great supporter of the Festival, which he saw as both a way to 'test' potential film releases with a discriminating audiences and to broaden the city's film education.

But if Columbia was 'on side', the other distributors – 20th Century-Fox, Paramount, Universal, MGM, United Artists – were not and nor were the independent distributors, which was a matter of graver concern. The major distributor of foreign-language and independent films in Australia in the mid-1960s was Blake Films, which was run by a man called Sid Blake. That was not his real name; I believe he was originally from Poland, as was his partner, whose English name was Fletcher. They were both amiable men, astute businessmen and, I suppose, film-lovers, because they imported a great many fine films, including the work of Ingmar Bergman, Michelangelo Antonioni, Federico Fellini, François Truffaut and others. However, Blake never publicly complained when the censors cut his films, which they did on a regular basis. Occasionally, the cuts were so severe that the released film was a travesty of the original: the Swedish actress Mai Zetterling's first feature as director, *Alskande Par* (*Loving Couples*), a harrowing story set in the early days of the twentieth century and based on a literary classic about three women betrayed by the men in their lives, originally ran for 118 minutes; the Australian version released by Blake ran 98 minutes after censorship. Whole scenes had been removed, but the long-suffering public who paid to see the film was not informed that they were seeing damaged goods which hardly reflected the intention of the original.

I discovered that Blake had actively lobbied overseas *against* participation in the Festival; he believed that the festival screening of a film would rob him of potential paying customers, and he refused to purchase any film screened at the Festival or to enter any of his films in the Festival. We were in a situation where the leading independent distributor took the opposite view to that held by Phil Jones, the leading specialist exhibitor in Sydney, whose cinema screened many of his films. There were also a couple of smaller independents, Kapferer Films (Robert Kapferer) and Scheinwald Films (Natan Scheinwald) whose attitude towards the Festival was similar to that of Blake, although neither man was as personally hostile.

Clearly, I had to attempt to change the attitudes of these distributors or, at the very least, try to prevent them from bad-mouthing us to our suppliers. I set about establishing cordial relationships with the CEOs of all of the major companies, and mending fences where necessary. I met with Blake, Kapferer and Scheinwald, but the atmosphere in every case was frigid. Blake was particularly antagonistic towards Erwin, and I wrote to my Melbourne colleague reporting this; Blake had complained about the very large number of subscribers in Melbourne, about Rado's 'huge' salary, and had even suggested that he took some kind of commission 'from entering into the commercial side of the business'. Erwin responded that he was 'amazed Blake dares to make libellous statements about me to you – I could take him to court, not that I would want to. No one can teach him a lesson in manners.'

There was clearly a lot of work to do mending fences. I decided to give these distributors an open invitation, not only to the Festival's opening night but also to any film they wanted to see in the programme, a gesture not extended to them before.

Meanwhile, the first films had started to arrive for the 1966 Festival. Because we had no screening facilities ourselves, Ian Klava had usually exercised the right of an importer to view the films at the office of the Censorship Board while they were being assessed; I decided there was nothing for it but to continue this policy, because we couldn't afford to rent a screening room for the purpose. One of the first films I saw in this way was an Italian film by Luchino Visconti, whose previous work had included masterpieces like *La Terra Trema*, *Senso* and *Il Gattopardo* (*The Leopard*). The new film was *Vaghe Stelle dell'Orsa*, known in English simply as *Sandra*. Given my attitude towards censorship, this first experience of being present while censors decided the fate of a film was an intensely unsettling one.

I should explain that spools of 35-mm film can run for a maximum of twenty minutes, so that the average feature consists of at least five spools. Every cinema in those days was equipped with at least two projectors, and cue dots on the top right-hand corner of the image indicated when it was time to start the other projector, to enable the projectionist to achieve a smooth transition from one spool to the next. These days, in multiplex cinemas, the 'platter' system is used, which means that the spools of film are spliced onto one continuous reel which is placed horizontally to the projector; with this system, as the film passes through the projector gate it automatically rewinds. As a result, many of today's younger projectionists probably don't know how to make reel changes, and if the film goes out of focus it's likely to stay that way unless the projectionist – who is usually servicing several different screens at the same time – happens to glance at the screen.

The projectionist at the censors' office was situated in a soundproof booth, just as he would be in any small screening room, but there seemed to be only one 35-mm projector instead of the usual two. The screening room itself was small and capable of seating only a handful of people. I was given a seat closest to the screen and three members of the Board were seated behind me at desks equipped with small lights, which stayed on most of the time. Prowse seated himself alongside his colleagues. Two of the censors were women, both introduced as 'Miss' and both in late middle age. They looked like, and probably were, retired schoolteachers. When the film started, the reason they hadn't bothered with a second projector became clear: at the end of each reel the projectionist would stop and the censors would talk about what they'd seen so far. It seemed hardly the best way to enjoy a film, but of course they weren't there for enjoyment.

Although I hadn't yet seen *Sandra* I knew its content and I was rather nervous because I hadn't included in the synopsis, which I was obliged to send to the censors' office prior to the screening, the fact that incest was involved. At the climax of the film, a brother and sister (played by Claudia Cardinale and Jean Sorel) engaged in discreet sex (just off-screen) on a woollen rug in front of a blazing fire in a sequence well in keeping with Visconti's operatic modern take on Greek mythology. How would Prowse and his colleagues react to the incest scene, even though it was very tactfully presented? I soon found out. After the screening, Prowse took me to one side. 'You film festival people are a strange lot,' he said. 'You like films no-one else can understand. Didn't you find that confusing? I thought, at the beginning, they were brother and sister.' The film was passed, without cuts.

A week or so later the news was less benign. Again I sat in with the censors, this time to see the wonderful Milos Forman comedy about young people *Laske Jedne Plavovlasky* (*Loves of a Blonde*). This is as true and honest a depiction of the turmoil of a naive girl's first love affair and her seduction by a youthful womaniser as has ever been made, and the sensitive way Forman juggles sequences of comedy and anguish has rarely been equalled.

I adored the film but the censors made no comment when it ended. A few days later I received a letter detailing the cuts they required before the film could be shown. Several subtitles had to be removed because the word 'Christ' was used in them, and this was deemed blasphemous. For example, there was a scene in a dance hall in which, according to the English subtitle, a soldier says 'Christ, let's get out of here'; that line had to go, and so did several similar ones. Far more crucial, though, was the censors' reaction to one of the key scenes in the film, which takes place after the couple have made love – in the girl's case for the first time. Although the couple were both naked, her breasts and his and her genitalia were discreetly covered; the dialogue in the scene was important, and sweetly funny. But according to the censors' directive, the entire scene, lasting about two minutes, had to go.

I was incensed. How could anyone with an ounce of sensitivity find something dirty in such an innocent and beautiful film? Without giving it a second thought, I sat down at the typewriter and wrote a furious letter to Prowse, pouring out my anger and frustration at his Board's actions. The next day, I had a phone call from Kirkwood, who told me that I had been very foolish and that Prowse would not respond to such a letter. He also advised me that unless I agreed to the cuts immediately, the film would be returned to its sender as a prohibited import.

It should be remembered that our policy at this time was to publicise and protest censorship cuts; it would be another couple of years before we would extend our anti-censorship campaign to the point that we would refuse to screen any film the censors had cut. With great reluctance, and frustrated anger, I agreed, after consulting with Erwin, to these cuts, which in my view bordered on the criminal. *Loves of a Blonde* wasn't the only film to suffer in this way at the 1966 Festival. Also cut was an East German anti-war film, *Die Abenteuer des Werner Holt* (*The Adventures of Werner Holt*), because a couple of the subtitles used the forbidden word 'shit' (this was a film about the military). Cuts were made, too, in

Kon Ichikawa's powerful film about the defeat of the Japanese army in the Philippines, *Nobi* (*Fires on the Plain*) – a scene in which a starving soldier resorts to cannibalism, which was the point of the entire film – and to Korean director Shin Sang-okk's period piece, *Sam-yong* (*The Mute*) – scenes of violence in which the protagonist is beaten up, again, essential to the film.

When a film is cut, two additional frames of the image are lost, one on each side of the deleted image(s). Additionally, when, after the Festival, the deleted scenes were replaced (prints had to be returned to the censors' office for this procedure), two more frames would disappear. In other words, valuable prints of films which did not belong to us were being damaged and returned to their owners in a less than pristine condition. On that level alone it was a deeply unsatisfactory state of affairs.

All these cuts were duly publicised in a Festival press release, and a very productive public forum on censorship was held during the Festival, organised by Beverley Burke. The greatest difficulty was to find pro-censorship speakers but the issues were well and truly aired. Several newspapers picked up on these events, which at least meant that, perhaps for the first time, the censorship of films in Australia was being discussed. But the situation left me with a heavy heart. I'd hoped for a quick decision in our favour from the Government, but the Customs Minister had rejected our position out of hand and Prime Minister Holt did not reply to our letter seeking his intervention. And then my worst fear materialised. I had invited Bernardo Bertolucci's magnificent second feature, *Prima della Rivoluzione* (*Before the Revolution*), to participate in the Festival but there had been no reply from his producer in Rome. About a week before the commencement of the Festival I received a letter from Italy telling me that the print was on its way. I managed to fit it into the schedule, but the print arrived at the airport on the Friday of the second week of the Festival, and the Censorship Board was unable, or unwilling, to review it that day. As a result we could not screen it. We were able to arrange a special presentation for subscribers a week later, but this was hardly a satisfactory outcome.

Thanks to Eric Dare, a new distributor on the local scene, we were able to obtain in its place a print of Sidney Lumet's *The Pawnbroker*, in which Rod Steiger gives a mesmerising performance as a New York Jew haunted by memories of the Holocaust. Dare had submitted *The Pawnbroker* for censorship himself, and I was unaware, until later, that the censors had cut from the film glimpses of Steiger's wife, half-naked, threatened by a Nazi guard; they had allowed, however, images of a black prostitute, also topless. Nudity was acceptable for blacks but not for whites in this kind of perverted decision-making. Talk about White Australia!

Despite these problems with the censors I was quite pleased with my first SFF programme. We decided to open with a pleasantly innocuous French film, Rene Allio's *La vieille Dame indigne* (*The Undignified Old Lady*), which was well received by the VIP audience, including the NSW Governor, Sir Roden Cutler. The programme also included such fine films as George Franju's *Thomas l'Imposteur*; István Szabó's first feature, *Almodozasok kora* (*The Age of Daydreaming*); Dušan Makavejev's first feature, *Covek nije Tica* (*Man Is Not a Bird*); Marco Bellocchio's debut, *I Pugni in Tasca* (*Fists in the Pocket*); Jerzy Skolimowski's second feature, *Walkover*; Satyajit Ray's *Charulata*; Chris Marker's *Le mystere Koumiko*; Cuban Tomas Gutierrez Alea's debut, *Cumbite*; Larissa Shepitko's *Znoy* (*Heat*) from the USSR; and Carl Theodor Dreyer's 1955 Danish masterwork *Ordet* (*The Word*) was given its first Australian screening. The domination of films from Eastern Europe reflected both the quality of films from that part of the world and also the willingness of the nationalised film companies to send their films all the way to Australia. I had no doubt that they had a propaganda agenda, but the films we selected were good enough to overcome that; however, I was unaware at the time just how interested the Australian Security Information

Office (ASIO) was in the Festival's activities. In addition, there were a great many high quality short films from all over the world. In the Appendix to this book I have listed all the major feature films programmed between 1966 and 1983, my years as SFF Director.

When the Festival ended the films had to be returned to their owners overseas, unless they had been sold to a local distributor. We also wrote letters of thanks to every entrant, and we prepared a press book in which every mention of every film was included from all the media; they were few and far between. In fact, press coverage of the Festival was pretty poor in those days, and though we sent a copy of the press book to every entrant, most would have discovered that their film wasn't mentioned at all. The Australian media simply wasn't very interested in the SFF in the 1960s; it was only after Paul Byrnes became Director in the late 1980s that press coverage improved, which was undoubtedly because Paul had been a journalist and knew exactly how the system worked. It's also true to say that there was far less general interest in film in the 1960s; later on, the media became much more interested in cinema (perhaps in part thanks to the accessibility of films on video) but in 1966, and for most of my time as SFF Director, the press could hardly care less.

I had learnt a lot in the five months since I commenced working as SFF Director, but if the Festival was to survive and prosper there was a great deal more to do. And, in any case, I needed to see my family. Some months earlier I had proposed that, if the Festival would pay for an economy class round-the-world ticket, I would combine an official trip to the key film-producing countries with a period of some time spent in England. On 20 July I boarded a Qantas flight for the first leg of that trip, first stop Honolulu.

Chapter Eight

Before I left on the first of the many overseas trips I would make on behalf of the Festival I met with Charles Higham, the film critic for *The Bulletin*, Australia's venerable weekly news magazine, who gave me some useful tips about visiting Hollywood, a place he knew well, and who to contact there. Charles also suggested that I write a few freelance articles on my overseas experiences for the magazine. This was my first opportunity for serious writing on film, and although I can't say that my articles – about six in all – were very good, I was encouraged that *The Bulletin* ran them.

Apart from a couple of flights to and from Majorca with my parents, the only air travel I had experienced prior to that time were trips to Melbourne and Brisbane. I'd never been on a long flight before and, truth to tell, I was rather nervous at the prospect. Airliners crashed with frightening regularity in the early 1960s; in the first three months of 1966 alone there had been three disasters, two in Japan (which had killed a total of

263 people) and one in the Alps (an Air India airliner crashed into Mont Blanc in January, killing 117). Although I have flown many hundreds of thousands of miles over the years I still can't say that I enjoy flying, and when I flew out of Sydney on that July day I was extremely tense.

I stopped over in Honolulu for a couple of days en route to San Francisco. My first visit to America got off to a bad start; a hostile immigration official objected to the fact that I'd completed my arrival card with a red pen ('Are you *joking*?' he demanded, not in the least bit amused at this inadvertent error of judgment on my part). I had to fill in a new form, in blue ink this time, and was allowed to enter the United States. I found a cheap hotel a couple of blocks from Waikiki Beach and within a short time of my arrival I was swimming in the surf. Later that day I went to see *Who's Afraid of Virginia Woolf?*, Mike Nichols's fine adaptation of the Edward Albee play and a film which, according to *Variety*, was likely to challenge international censors because of its strong language, though it didn't contain the four-letter words that would soon become acceptable.

After this brief vacation I flew on to San Francisco where Jo Webb, my father's cousin, was living with her mother, my great-aunt Marjorie. Jo, who had always been sympathetic to my passion for movies, was eager to hear about my new job, but Marjorie (correctly) guessed that my father would be extremely disappointed at the direction my life had taken. Although they lived in a small apartment in the centre of the city, they found room for me on their lounge and I spent a couple of days exploring the spectacular Bay Area which, as I got to know it better over the years, became my favourite American city. As always, I made sure that I saw some films. One of them was *Käre John* (*Dear John*), a Swedish film which was then running very successfully in a handful of American cinemas and which contained some scenes of sex and nudity that, although mild when compared to what would come later, would never have been allowed in Australia in 1966.

My next stop was Los Angeles. I wanted to explore the possibility of bringing a veteran Hollywood director to Sydney as guest at the 1967 Festival, and Charles Higham had helpfully suggested that I make contact with David Bradley, an eccentric film collector who personally knew many of these ageing icons. I found a cheap hotel, near Hollywood and Vine, and immediately after I checked in I called Bradley, who generously offered to take me to his house in the Hollywood Hills. He obviously came from a wealthy background, was clearly gay, slightly intense, but welcoming. He lived with his mother in a huge house filled with movie memorabilia and a very large collection of feature films on 16-mm. While at the University of Chicago Bradley had made a couple of independent feature films, *Peer Gynt* and *Julius Caesar*, both starring a young acting student named Charlton Heston. Although neither film enjoyed much in the way of distribution, even after Heston became a star, Bradley was given a chance to direct a Hollywood feature at MGM. *Talk about a Stranger* (1952) was a slight but well-made drama about a little boy convinced that his rather odd neighbour, played by Kurt Kaszner, has killed his dog. Those two well known Republicans George Murphy and Nancy Davis (Reagan) played the boy's parents, but despite remarkable photography by one of the masters of lighting, John Alton, Bradley's only studio film had no commercial impact and he never made another. He now seemed to spend his time viewing his enormous collection of 16-mm prints and meeting with some of the now retired directors who made them.

Bradley offered to screen me anything from his collection and I chose three films I'd been keen to see for years: Paul Leni's silent version of *The Cat and the Canary*, Buster Keaton's *Steamboat Bill Jr.* and Rouben Mamoulian's brilliant 1931 version of *Dr. Jekyll and Mr Hyde*. Mamoulian, who hadn't made a film since he was forced to quit the direction of the ill-fated *Cleopatra* earlier in the decade, was an obvious candidate for a festival guest, but Bradley suggested that Josef von Sternberg might be even better. Sternberg, who was born in Vienna and had made some remarkable silent films, including *Underworld* and *The Last Command*, was chiefly famous for 'discovering' Marlene Dietrich in Berlin when he went there in 1929 to make *The Blue Angel* for Paramount and UFA. His liaison with Dietrich, and her instant success, led to a triumphant return to Hollywood for both the actress and her director/Svengali, and to the production of a series of formally bold and visually exciting melodramas – *Morocco*, *Dishonored*, *Shanghai Express*, *The Scarlet Empress* and *The Devil is a Woman*. Sternberg was much admired by the *auteur* critics of *Cahiers du Cinema* and *Movie*, even though his Hollywood career slid to an ignominious end in the 1940s and 50s, after the relationship with Dietrich ended. He had made one last extraordinary film in Japan in 1953, but *The Saga of Anatahan* was more talked about than actually seen. Bradley phoned Sternberg, who was unable to meet me during the short time I was in Hollywood but who expressed interest in coming to the Sydney and Melbourne Film Festivals the following June.

The rest of my time in Hollywood was spent sightseeing, and watching movies. Thanks to Colin Jones, the CEO of Columbia Pictures in Australia, I had been given an invitation to visit the Columbia studios on Gower Street, and I was excited about my first trip to a place where the magic happened. Behind these nondescript walls, in these hanger-like studios, Frank Capra had directed *Mr Deeds Goes to Town* and Howard Hawks had made *His Girl Friday*. Gary Cooper, Jean Arthur, Cary Grant, Rita Hayworth and countless others had worked here when movies were not only glamorous but of a consistently high quality.

The studio's PR man, a good-natured veteran called Eli Levy, greeted me warmly and immediately took me to a sound stage where Phil Karlson was directing a western called *The Long Ride Home*. The star of the film was Glenn Ford, and the scene being shot was set in a bar. I watched, fascinated, impressed by the speed with which Karlson achieved the effects he wanted. At the lunch break I met briefly with Ford, who was relaxed and charming, and had a long talk to Karlson, who seemed surprised that I knew and admired the low-budget *films noir* he'd directed during the previous decade, films like *The Brothers Rico*, *Kansas City Confidential*, *The Phenix City Story* and *Scandal Sheet*. I joined him for lunch, and found him excellent company. In the afternoon I was taken to another soundstage where I met Dick Van Dyke, who was making a comedy called *Divorce American Style*, and then to yet another to meet Dean Martin on the set of *Murderers' Row*, a spy spoof.

My next stop was New York. On the daytime flight across America I watched my first in-flight movie (*A Big Hand for the Little Lady*) when I wasn't glued to the window and the spectacular landscapes we were crossing. I had been invited to stay with friends of my parents who lived just outside the city. Peter Roberts, a Canadian by birth, was a broadcaster who had the breakfast slot on a New York radio station, WOR; his distinctive voice could also be heard every week narrating the Metro Newsreels. Peter and his wife, Jo, had visited Wiltshire a couple of years earlier and had seen my mother walking her pug dog through the village of Lacock; pug owners themselves, they immediately made contact and a friendship was formed.

The Roberts lived across the Hudson River in a pleasant New Jersey town called Paterson. Every weekday, a chauffeur-driven car would call at four am to drive Peter into the city. On the first morning, I took a train into Manhattan at a more civilised hour. I didn't really have any serious appointments to keep; this was just a chance to explore New York and, as always, to see a few films – among them Antonioni's *Il deserto rosso* (*The Red Desert*) and Godard's *Une femme est une femme* (*A Woman Is a Woman*). On the second day I drove into the city with Peter, who had arranged for me to join WOR's traffic reporter in his helicopter. I don't recall his real name, but this combination of chopper pilot and broadcaster was known as Fearless Freddie, and I was taken to La

Guardia airfield to meet him. I had to be weighed before I was allowed to board the craft, and then we took off. This was a truly unforgettable experience – seeing New York from a chopper in the early morning light on a brilliant summer's day. When the time came for Fearless Freddie to broadcast his live traffic reports, he added the information that he had an 'Aussie' with him that morning; I didn't really feel like an Aussie yet, but I appreciated the sentiment. At the end of the exhilarating flight, Freddie flew *under* one of the bridges that span the East River and hovered on the level of the sixth floor of the United Nations building where his girlfriend worked. He was a lot of fun, and a few years later I was saddened to learn that, on a similar flight to the one I'd enjoyed, his chopper had crashed, killing him.

From New York I flew to London's Heathrow Airport, where my wife and daughter, as well as my parents, were waiting to meet me. It was, of course, wonderful to see them all again; Mary had grown appreciably in the six months since I'd seen her. She was now two years old, and a beautiful little girl, full of fun. I hadn't been looking forward to sitting down with my father and explaining, in person, why I had decided to stay in Australia rather than return home and fill the role in Strattons that he'd assigned to me. On the surface he seemed quite understanding, but I knew that he was disappointed and felt that I had let him down. Nor can it have been easy for my parents to know that, for the foreseeable future, I would be living, with my wife and their granddaughter, on the other side of the world. We all stayed at my parents' home for the remainder of that northern summer, but I made several trips away on behalf of the Festival.

In August I flew to Edinburgh to attend a film festival which I knew would be somewhat similar to the Australian festivals. The Edinburgh Director was a young man, about my age, named David Bruce; we became lifelong friends. Edinburgh was in many ways a model for the kind of event I thought we should have in Australia, and I learnt a lot from my few days there. I was a bit surprised that Bruce had chosen to open the Festival with David Lean's *Doctor Zhivago*, partly because of its length (almost four hours), but also because it had already been screening for several months in the major British cities, though this was the Scottish premiere.

From Edinburgh I flew to Venice via London. I was surprised and pleased to discover that, because I was the Director of a FIAPF recognised festival, I was given what amounted to VIP treatment: I was met at Venice airport and taken by launch to the Lido.

The Venice programme in those days was small compared to that of today. Two competitive films screened every day, plus a retrospective, which in 1966 celebrated Women Stars of Hollywood Films of the 1920s. But little consideration was given to visitors who spoke no Italian. The Italian films in competition screened with French subtitles and everything else had only Italian subtitles. Under these circumstances, my appreciation of many of the films was understandably limited.

I spent a lot of my time meeting people – networking, to use today's terminology. One of my most important contacts, and the beginning of another close friendship, was *Variety*'s legendary Paris representative Gene Moskowitz, known to all as 'Mosk'. Mosk had been born into a Hungarian-Jewish family in New York and like me he had become crazy about films at an early age. After serving in World War II, he took advantage of the GI Bill of Rights and settled in Paris, where he worked as a freelance journalist and, eventually, was given the job of covering France for the celebrated New York-based trade paper. Mosk reviewed every major French film released from the mid-1950s until his early death in 1982, and he also wrote about movements in French cinema, especially the New Wave, in *Sight & Sound* and other magazines. I was very familiar with his work long before I met him. Mosk was a large man, with a round face and sparse, crinkly hair. He was heavily suntanned, smoked cigars and looked for all the world like a caricature of a Mexican bandit. As soon as he discovered that I was knowledgeable about films and that I shared many of his enthusiasms he took me under his wing and introduced me to his many friends. 'My boy' he used to call me affectionately, and we used to hang out together for much of the time.

Mosk always travelled with a small portable typewriter, on which he composed the reviews he sent to the New York headquarters of *Variety*. I learnt later on that, although he was prolific, his colleagues back in America often dreaded the arrival of his copy because he wrote in a peculiar, haphazard style which was borderline incomprehensible and always had to be extensively rewritten.

Through Mosk I met the British director Lindsay Anderson, who was visiting Venice. In the autumn of 1956, Anderson had written a famous article for *Sight & Sound* entitled 'Stand Up! Stand Up!' on the subject of film criticism, and he was part of the Free Cinema documentary movement in the early 1950s. He had directed one of the best of the British New Wave films of the late 1950s and early 1960s, *This Sporting Life*, in which Richard Harris gave an electrifying performance as a damaged football player. Lindsay had also made a short film called *The White Bus*, which was designed as the middle section of a proposed three-part film to be called *Red, White and Blue*; the other parts were to have been directed by other New Wave Brits, Tony Richardson and Karel Reisz, but I don't think they were ever made. *The White Bus* itself had hardly ever been seen (it is still virtually unknown), so I was privileged to be allowed to sit in on a private screening Lindsay arranged for Mosk in one of the small cinemas in the bowels of the Palazzo del Cinema during the Festival.

I made another lasting friendship when I met the British film writer John Gillett, an endearingly eccentric man who loved cinema with a passion. John was as much the epitome of an Englishman as Mosk was of a certain type of American. They both loved all aspects of cinema – John was particularly knowledgeable about Japanese cinema – and they were men after my own heart. John, Mosk and I hung out every afternoon at the retrospective screenings of such films as Josef von Sternberg's *Underworld*, Frank Capra's *The Power of the Press* and Clarence Brown's *A Woman of Affairs*, which starred Greta Garbo.

The opening night screening of Roger Corman's *The Wild Angels* was scandalous enough (the film was subsequently banned in both Britain and Australia), but it wasn't the only scandal of the 1966 Venice Film Festival. The Swedish entry *Nattlek* (*Night Games*), the second feature directed by Mai Zetterling, dealt with a child who is traumatised by the erotic behaviour of his dissolute parents and the other adults around him. The Catholic Church protested at the inclusion of the film and Luigi Chiarini, the Festival Director, apparently caved in to the pressure. The press screening was cancelled and the film was given just one screening instead of the usual two or three. Needless to say, it was packed and many people were turned away. I managed to find a seat and, despite the fact that the film was in Swedish with Italian subtitles, managed to follow most of it. It was a bleak but impressive work. Afterwards, I introduced myself to Zetterling and her English husband, David Hughes (who had collaborated with her on the screenplay), and we spent a couple of pleasant evenings together. She was understandably appalled at the way her film had been treated by the Festival and the whole incident gave me an insight into yet another aspect of the censorship question – this was a case of a festival censoring itself, or at least restricting access to one of its official entries.

François Truffaut, another director whom I greatly admired, was in Venice for the screening in competition of his only English-language film, *Fahrenheit 451*, which was based on the science-fiction novel by Ray Bradbury and starred Julie Christie and Oskar Werner. I was able to meet Truffaut and his actors at a French reception. It was easy to meet the filmmakers at Venice then and even today it's the most accessible of all the major festivals. Roger Vadim, who was married to Jane Fonda at the time, was presenting his film *La Curee*, and I was amused to hear Fonda tell anyone who would listen that she was perfectly happy to do whatever Vadim told her to do. They were at the airport when I was checking in at the end of the Festival, and I asked her where they were heading for. 'I don't know, ask Vadim,' was her reply.

The winner of the Golden Lion at Venice that year was Italian Gillo Pontecorvo's remarkable film about the conflict in Algeria, *La Battaglia di Algeri* (*The Battle of Algiers*). The film, which screened in Venice despite the official protests of the French Government, dealt sympathetically with the contentious revolution in Algeria against French rule which had occurred only a few years earlier. It would be banned in France for several years, and it also gained notoriety because it became a kind of text book for radical insurgent groups. Handled in vivid documentary style, the film was enormously impressive and disturbing. I didn't meet Pontecorvo at the time but many years later, when he was Director of the Venice Film Festival, he invited me to be a member of the international jury.

After two exhausting but productive weeks in Venice, I flew back to London to spend a few days with my family before attending yet another festival, this time in Cork, Ireland. A much smaller affair which lasted just a week, Cork was, oddly enough, directed by Ireland's Chief Film Censor, a disarmingly charming man named Dermot Breen. I could never reconcile the fact that the censor also programmed Ireland's leading film festival; there was something very fey about the entire notion. A few years later, I was in Cork when Breen screened Milos Forman's great comedy-drama *Taking Off*, which is about teenage runaways and their foolish but concerned parents. One of the many songs in the film features a butter-wouldn't-melt-in-her-mouth blonde who sings direct to camera a song called *Ode to a Screw*. The word 'fuck' appears in just about every line of the song ('You can fuck the moon, and the stars and the sea; but before you fuck them, first you must fuck me'). But at Cork the f-word word was bleeped out. I tackled Breen about this afterwards and he said, with a perfectly straight face, 'Oh, but it's *funnier* that way!'

I was interested to see that the many guests attending Cork weren't necessarily representing films being screened; they were invited, it seemed, simply to bring some celebrities to town. Among them was Jack Palance, the American actor who had been so effective as a villain in films like *Panic in the Streets* and *Shane* and as a flawed hero in *Attack!*. There was also the formidable British character actress Peggy Mount – who could forget her as a nightmare mother-in-law in *Sailor Beware*? – and an up-and-coming Polish actor named Janusz Guttner. I spent a day shark-fishing with Peggy and Janusz, which was quite an experience; we also took a trip to nearby Blarney Castle to kiss the Blarney Stone. Films, it seemed, were quite low on the agenda in Cork – but the Festival was well managed and great fun.

Next I spent a week in Paris, my first visit to the French capital. I had arranged this through the French Embassy in Canberra and had received an official invitation. I was given excellent treatment, being met at the airport and taken to a smart little hotel on the Rue de Rivoli. An interpreter was placed at my disposal, which was very useful because my schoolboy French was pretty primitive. My main tasks in Paris were to meet Alphonse Brisson of FIAPF and Jacques Nicaud, the Deputy Director of Unifrance Film, the organisation which entered French films in festivals. Nicaud was extremely helpful and arranged for me to see several films.

My meeting with Brisson was more difficult. He made it clear that he still wasn't happy with the endorsement of both Melbourne and Sydney as long as the festivals overlapped and shared films. I went over all the arguments in favour of the status quo, and left with the feeling – correct as it turned out – that no changes were about to be made.

While in Paris I caught up with Gene Moskowitz and did a fair bit of sightseeing. My guide from the ministry also arranged for me to meet Jean-Luc Godard, who was one of my cinematic heroes. He was shooting *L'anticipation*, an episode for a multi-part feature, *Le plus vieux metier du monde* (*The World's Oldest Profession*), on location at Orly Airport, and I was taken there for the meeting, which turned out to be a pretty brief one. But watching him work was of great interest, and meeting his leading actress and muse, the Danish-born Anna Karina, who was appearing in the film with Jacques Charrier, was also a thrill. Oddly enough, this is one Godard film I've never seen.

I left Britain during the last week of October to start the journey back to Australia, but I had planned a number of important stops along the way. First, I flew to Stockholm. Sweden was a very important source of quality films in the mid-1960s, but Sid Blake, of Blake Films, who distributed quite a number of Swedish films, had made it plain that he disapproved of the Festival, so I had some serious lobbying to do. Swedish films were becoming more and more sexually explicit, so Australia's censorship problems were also very much in the forefront of my mind. During the course of less than a week in the chilly but very beautiful Swedish capital, I visited all the major production companies for meetings and discussions. There were three of them: Svensk Filmindustri, Sandrews and Europa Film, all located on Kungsgatan, the main street of the city. I also went to see the new Ingmar Bergman film *Persona*, which was in its first-run release at the Spegeln cinema. Thanks to the foreign sales agent of the film's producers, Svensk Filmindustri, I was armed with an English dialogue list, which I tried to read, surreptitiously, by the light of a torch as the film proceeded.

I was also shown a number of films, and introduced to some of the younger directors. Vilgot Sjoman met me after a private screening of his new film *Syskonbadd* (literally, *Bed for Brother and Sister*), a steamy drama of incest, and drove me from the screening room back to my hotel in his rickety car. During the journey he told me about the film he was currently shooting, *Jag ar nyfiken* (*I Am Curious*), a film which would prove of lasting importance in the censorship battle in the United States (he later divided the lengthy dramatised documentary into two parts which were named after the colours of the Swedish flag, *Yellow* and *Blue*). I was also invited to the apartment in the Old City that Finnish-born director Jörn Donner shared with Harriet Andersson, the star of his new film *Har borjar aventyret* (*Adventure Starts Here*). Donner and I hit it off, and he agreed to defy Blake's ban and enter his film in Sydney and Melbourne – furthermore, he agreed to travel to Australia himself to present it. Altogether, I had a very positive reception from the Swedes, thanks to the help of the Swedish Film Institute, and I was convinced that, from now on, we would be assured of regular Swedish participation in the Festival.

From Stockholm I flew by SAS to Prague. I had never been to a Communist country before, and I'd been led to believe, from what I'd been told and from all those Cold War spy films, that Czechoslovakia and the other members of the socialist bloc in Eastern Europe would be strange and unwelcoming places. On the other hand, I'd seen enough films from these countries to know that this couldn't really be the case. The Czech films of the early 1960s, especially those directed by Milos Forman, were peopled with recognisably human characters and dealt with an everyday reality common to many countries, Communist and non-Communist alike.

As it happened, my arrival in Prague coincided with celebrations being held to commemorate the anniversary of the Russian Revolution and red flags were fluttering everywhere in the cold air. I was met at the airport by Eduard Hais, the very charming and urbane deputy to the Head of Ceskoslovensky Film, Ladislav Pospisil. My hotel was located in the main street of the city, Vaclavske nam (Wenceslas Square), and Hais took me on a grand tour of the sights, including the magnificent Karlovy Bridge over the Vlatava River and the Old City, with its medieval Town Hall and Cathedral. It was all amazingly beautiful.

The following day I met Pospisil at the office of Ceskoslovensky Film, across the avenue from my hotel. Clearly the Festival faced no problems here, and I was shown a number of interesting films over the next couple of days. I had wanted to meet Milos Forman, but he was out of town. After a couple of days in Prague, Hais drove me to Brno, the main city of the province of Moravia, where some kind of local film event was taking place. He wanted me to see a brand-new film by a first time director called Jiri Menzel; the film was *Ostre sledovane vlaky* (*Closely Watched Trains*), the slightly whimsical story of a naive youth who gets a job at a country railway station during the German occupation. It was quite magnificent. Two years later it won the Oscar for Best Foreign Film.

On one of the nights I spent in Prague I went to a cinema to see Jacques Demy's sublime musical *Les Parapluies de Cherbourg* (*The Umbrellas of Cherbourg*), which, although two years old, had not yet been released in Australia. I always associate Prague with one of my favourite films which, despite being in French with Czech subtitles, was easy to follow.

From Prague I flew on to another spectacularly beautiful Central European city, Budapest. The elegant, if somewhat crumbling, buildings that flank the wide boulevards in the centre of Pest, on the west bank of the Danube, contrast with the narrower streets of hilly Buda, on the east bank, where the oldest parts of the city are to be found adjacent to the imposing Bastion, which towers over the river. I stayed in Pest, in the incongruously named Royal Hotel on Lenin Boulevard, and, as had been the case in Prague, the officials of the nationalised film company Hungarofilm were extremely kind and cooperative. They were mostly women: Leila Somogyi and Martha Ozorai were running the foreign cultural department and Edit Solti was assigned to be my interpreter and guide. Among the many films I saw in the few days I was there were Miklós Jancsó's visually stunning political allegory, *Szegenylegenyek* (*The Round-Up*).

My next stop was Warsaw, which, unlike Prague and Budapest, had been severely damaged during the war and rebuilt in a less than attractive Stalinist-era style. The tallest building in the city was the Palace of Culture, a hideous gift from the Soviet Union to the people of Poland: the locals joked that it offered the best views of the city because it was the only place in the city where you didn't have to look at the Palace of Culture. Waclaw Grabowski, of Film Polski, organised my itinerary, and I stayed at the famous Europejski Hotel (immortalised by Ernst Lubitsch in his great comedy *To Be or Not To Be*). It was now late November and very cold, with a significant coating of snow blanketing the city. Just as had been the pattern in Prague and Budapest, I was shown a number of films, the most impressive of which was Jerzy Skolimowski's *Bariera* (*Barrier*), the young director's third feature (we'd screened his second, *Walkover*, at the Festival earlier in the year). I was very much impressed with this former boxer's strangely romantic yet disenchanted vision of Polish youth, and asked if I could meet him. He spoke no English but, through an interpreter, we had a lively conversation.

One evening in the lobby of my hotel I bumped into Lindsay Anderson, who was in Warsaw directing a play. He remembered our meeting in Venice, and was interested to hear about the Polish films I'd been seeing, especially *Barrier*, which I warmly recommended.

I also caught up with Janusz Guttner, the young Polish actor I'd met at the Cork Film Festival. On the day of my arrival, a Saturday, he invited me to the name-day party of a girl who lived in an apartment on a courtyard right in the middle of the city, behind the office of British European Airways. The party was like any party in the West, a rowdy, noisy affair, and the Beatles' recently-released album *Revolver*, which I'd brought from England as a present for Janusz, was the music of choice. Vodka and borscht were consumed in great quantities, and there was a great deal of merriment. Some time after midnight it was decided that someone should go out to an all-night sausage stand nearby to get more food, and I was elected for this task. This was apparently because the hostess was afraid that the concierge would lock the gate and deny access back into the courtyard because of the noise but that I, as a non-Polish speaking foreigner, would be treated more tolerantly than a local. That, at least, was the theory. I purchased the food and was indeed denied access back into the building. When I rang the bell, the concierge called the police. I flashed my British passport and my friends came down from their apartment to protest at my exclusion from the building. The matter was only sorted out when some money exchanged hands. It was apparently a normal situation in Warsaw on a Saturday night.

Moscow, my final destination in Eastern Europe, was potentially the most challenging, and indeed it proved to be so. After a week in Warsaw I was scheduled to fly out on the Friday morning but, when the weather took a turn for the worse, all flights were delayed. My LOT Airlines flight finally departed about twelve hours late. I had arranged all my Eastern bloc visits through the film offices concerned and, in the case of Moscow, with the body responsible for sending films to international cultural events, the Committee for Cinematography. They had issued me with an official invitation and told me I would be met at the airport and taken to a hotel they had reserved for me, but by the time I finally arrived, quite late in the evening in the capital of the Soviet Union, there was no welcoming party. I had not been told in which hotel I had been placed, so I realised I had a fairly major problem. The uninvited tourist to the USSR was expected to pay in advance, in US dollars, for accommodation, and because I had not anticipated this situation I didn't know how to proceed. I went to the airport office of Intourist and sought help from a barely sympathetic official who, after much grumbling, found me a room in a hotel in the middle of the city. Naturally, he insisted that I had to pay cash in advance using American dollars. This was before the wide use and acceptance of credit cards, so I'd been using cash and traveller's cheques for the entire trip. Some of my few remaining US-dollar traveller's cheques proved acceptable and I was taken to a small but comfortable hotel. By the time I got to my room it was past midnight.

The next day being Saturday, the phones at the Committee for Cinematography (CFC) went unanswered, so I realised that I had to resign myself to a weekend without guidance or support. It was now the first weekend in December and the weather was bitterly cold, but I wasn't really dressed appropriately for the freezing conditions. I found that half an hour exploring the city was about all I could bear. I had even run out of books to read, so I searched for a bookshop which might offer anything in English, finally finding a copy of *Dodsworth* by Sinclair Lewis. That night I ate a solitary meal at a café.

The following day I thought I'd try to see a film, but the baffling Cyrillic alphabet made it not merely difficult but impossible for me to decipher street names. The hotel concierge advised me that no films were screening in the city in English but there was a French film playing in one cinema; the title he gave me meant nothing to me, but I thought I'd give it a go. I followed the directions he gave me, ending up in a large square. Finally, I saw what looked like the entrance to a cinema: people were flocking in and purchasing tickets at what seemed to be a box office. I joined the queue, indicated that I wanted one ticket, and followed the crowd – not into the auditorium of a cinema, as I'd imagined, but onto a platform of the Moscow subway! I never did find that cinema.

On the Monday morning, I finally made contact with Alexander Slavnov at the CFC. He didn't seem particularly perturbed at my difficulties over the weekend, but arranged for me to see a few films, including the first two parts of Sergei Bondarchuk's massive epic *Wojna I Mir* (*War and Peace*), which was then playing in a huge mid-city cinema.

My visit to Moscow proved to be the least successful of the entire trip. I had wanted to persuade the Russian film authorities to allow me the privilege of inviting the films I wanted for the SFF, because in the past they had invariably sent films of *their* choice and had supplied very little advance information about them. However, Slavnov made it clear that this was the way they did things in the USSR. They alone made the choice, he said, and they always picked films they thought would be the most suitable. In fact, I had to admit that their selections hadn't been bad so far, but still I insisted, on the grounds that festivals like Cannes and Venice were surely given some choice in the films they screened from the Soviet Union. I found the officials in Moscow far more bureaucratic and much less friendly than those in Prague, Budapest or Warsaw had been; and although it was exciting to be in the city, my time there was frustrating.

I flew from Moscow on a nonstop Aeroflot flight to New Delhi, where I stayed for a couple of days, mainly to have meetings with representatives from the Ministry of Information and Broadcasting of India's Film Division. The man in charge had an office in the Parliament building, and I was intrigued to see mice running around among the files and documents piled on the floor while we sipped tea and discussed Indian participation in the Festival. Then it was on to Calcutta, the final stop of my journey back to Australia, where I was to meet with Satyajit Ray, the director of the famous *Apu Trilogy* and one of the world's greatest filmmakers. I wanted to invite him to come to a future Festival as our guest. I stayed at the Great Eastern Hotel and was somewhat taken aback by the abundance of cockroaches and, I suspect, bedbugs which shared my room.

The crowded streets of the city were unlike anything I'd experienced before, but I made my way to the studio where Ray was working on his latest film, *Chiriakhana*. He was extremely cordial and we hit it off instantly. He introduced me to one of his famous actors, Soumitra Chatterjee, and over the inevitable cup of tea he promised to come to Sydney at the first possible opportunity. The contrast between the rather ramshackle studio where Ray made his sublime films and the studios at Columbia where big Hollywood stars made westerns and comedies couldn't have been more striking. Ray had just composed the music for the Merchant-Ivory film *Shakespeare Wallah*, and he very kindly gave me a signed LP of the soundtrack.

It was now mid-December and I was anxious to get back to Sydney, but fate intervened. Qantas staff were on strike and my Calcutta to Sydney flight was cancelled. At the airport I was advised to go to Sydney via Bangkok, so I flew to the Thai capital and checked in to a hotel until I was able to find a seat on an Alitalia flight bound for Sydney. I was exhausted, but stimulated, after my long journey home, and now I had to face the challenge of assembling my second Festival.

Chapter Nine

During the six months I'd been away from Sydney a significant event had occurred on the film scene. In August, a rival film festival had emerged, based at the University of NSW and boasting as its patron the Vice-Chancellor of that University. This was the brainchild of three UNSW graduates and seems to have been established because of what its organisers perceived to be a state of flux at the Sydney Film Festival. The NSW Film Festival, as it was called, had presented a mildly interesting programme that climaxed with the Australian premiere of Joseph Losey's latest (and some would say least) film, *Modesty Blaise*, one of the large number of spy spoofs being made at the time. The Festival had also invited a distinguished guest, British film writer Peter Cowie, who was the owner of Tantivy Press, publisher of the recently established *International Film Guide*.

It seemed clear to me that the presence of rival festivals in Sydney could spell disaster for us – not only from the point of view of FIAPF, who would surely take this as a sign of complete irresponsibility, but also from the perspective of the Customs Department. We had been arguing in favour of freedom from censorship for established film festivals, but how would the authorities react if they thought that new festivals could spring up at any time and make the same demands? Of course, logically speaking there was no reason why they shouldn't, but at the time the presence of a 'renegade' festival in Sydney seriously threatened to disrupt our campaign. As it turned out, there would be no more NSW Film Festivals; the 1966 event proved to be a one-off, either because it was a financial failure or because the organisers lacked the energy and the will to continue. One of them, Michael Robertson, approached me to offer his help to the SFF, which I accepted (he designed the catalogue in 1968), and later on he became a film director.

During my absence, another local film enthusiast had arrived on the Sydney scene. John Baxter loved both science fiction and film, and wrote about both in his spare time. He worked for the NSW Department of Railways, and he hadn't been part of the film scene before I left on my overseas trip; it seems that Cowie's visit had been the spark that encouraged him to try his hand at serious writing about film. Baxter had proposed to Cowie that he write some film books for Tantivy Press, covering such subjects as 'Science Fiction in the Cinema' and 'Hollywood in the 1930s' (Charles Higham and Joel Greenberg had also contacted Cowie, and had undertaken to write a book on Hollywood in the 1940s). Baxter was to be an influential figure on the local film scene until he based himself overseas a few years later.

As far as I can recall, Baxter started writing on cinema in *Film Digest*, one of a small number of privately produced film magazines to emanate from Sydney and Melbourne during the 1960s. These magazines were relatively primitive affairs: they were written on ordinary typewriters and then duplicated, but they produced the best local film writing at the time. Every so often I contributed an article myself, and these, really, constituted my first attempts at film criticism. I wrote mostly about films which were then banned in Australia – *The Night of the Hunter* and Godard's *Une femme mariee* among them.

At the Festival's Annual General Meeting at the end of 1966, Frank Bellingham resigned as President – probably he was never too happy at having to deal with an upstart like me, although on the surface we had enjoyed perfectly cordial relations. He was replaced by Dugmore Merry, the inventor and manufacturer of the Merry Tiller, a mechanical gardening machine which had been so successful it had been exported around the world; coincidentally, my father owned one. Merry was, in my view, a rough diamond with little interest in the kind of cinema that excited me; like Bellingham, he had come from the 8-mm home movie, cine-club side of the membership.

In terms of cinema, the big event to unfold in the second half of 1966 was the enormous success of Michael Powell's Australian-made comedy *They're a Weird Mob*, which opened at the State Theatre in Sydney in early December and ran there throughout the summer; it achieved similar success in other venues throughout the country. This was the first successful and widely screened locally made film in many years, but Australia had been a pioneer in the production of feature films. In 1906, J. and N. Tait had produced and Charles Tait had directed arguably the first feature-length (that is, more than an hour) film, *The True Story of the Kelly Gang*, but sadly this milestone doesn't survive in its entirety (it was partially restored in 2006). Between 1910 and 1929, during the period of silent film production, there was a relatively vibrant industry in Australia though, like the British film industry, it had always faced severe problems, especially in the face of the fierce competition which emerged from Hollywood after World War I. Raymond Longford, director of *The Sentimental Bloke* (1918) and *On Our Selection* (1920), had been the key figure during the silent period, but this great pioneer had ended his days working as a nightwatchman on Sydney Harbour. To make matters worse, the ever-present Australian censors had made life difficult for our pioneer filmmakers. Bushranger movies, including the popular Ned Kelly stories, were completely banned in NSW.

With the coming of sound, Australian film production went into a further decline. Frank Thring Sr produced a handful of features at his Efftee Studio in Melbourne, and Charles Chauvel, a tenacious pioneer, directed a film every few years, most famously *40,000 Horsemen* (1940) and *The Rats of Tobruk* (1944). Throughout the 1930s, Cinesound, a company owned by Greater Union, had backed Ken G. Hall in his production of a couple of feature films every year, including the much loved *Dad and Dave* series. But local production had been few and far between since the 1940s; the advent of World War II had brought to an end GU's involvement in feature films. Charles Chauvel had continued to make the occasional feature, including the ambitious *Jedda* (1955), Australia's first colour feature, which dealt with the stolen generation of Aboriginal children who were taken from their families by well-intended but patronising whites. A shortened version of *Jedda* had played on the lower half of a double-bill in Britain and I had seen it there without fully comprehending it; certainly it hadn't made much of an impression on me then. There were other mavericks too, such as Cecil Holmes and Rupert Kathner (whose story was told in the excellent 2006 feature *Hunt Angels*), but they faced an uphill battle to get their films made and an even greater battle to get them widely screened.

To make matters worse, the vast majority of cinemas were controlled by overseas companies with no interest in supporting local product: in the 1960s, Hoyts was controlled by 20th Century-Fox (USA) and Greater Union by the Rank Organisation (UK). The small number of independent cinemas tended to concentrate on foreign-language and other arthouse fare. The few Australian films that were produced found it difficult to secure cinema bookings. But all this was about to change.

John O'Grady, writing under the pseudonym Nino Culotta, had written the enormously popular bestseller *They're a Weird Mob*, published in 1957, which was required reading for every newcomer to Australia, including me. This funny story of an Italian migrant and his experiences with 'dinki-di' Aussies was colourful and, at the time, had an authentic ring about it. The Ocker slang used by O'Grady was, by today's standards, extremely mild but at the time of its publication some people found it vulgar ('bloody' was the commonly used expletive).

Director Michael Powell's considerable reputation as one of Britain's greatest filmmakers had been mainly based on the post-war films he had made with his partner, Emeric Pressburger (*A Matter of Life and Death*, *The Red Shoes*, *Black Narcissus*, *I Know Where I'm Going* and others). *They're a Weird Mob* was very far from being his best work, but it allowed Australians to laugh at themselves and it also featured a backdrop of familiar Sydney landmarks, such as Kings Cross and Bondi Beach.

Soon after my return home, Richard Prowse requested a meeting with me; he was seeking confirmation that, in the light of the events surrounding the 1966 Festival, our policy on censorship remained the same and I assured him that it did. During this discussion Prowse told me that, in his opinion, the Censorship Board was moving with the times. 'We made a big step forward with classifying *They're a Weird Mob*,' he told me, with a perfectly straight face. 'They use the word "bloody" eighty times in that film and we didn't cut it once!' I was so astonished I didn't know what to say; it had never occurred to me that the innocuous use of the word 'bloody' in the context of that film would ever have been considered offensive, and it was dispiriting that Prowse saw this as a mark of liberality.

Margaret was pregnant with our second child, and my mother decided to accompany her and Mary back to Sydney by sea; they left England early in 1967. In anticipation of their arrival, I rented a house at Ashfield in a pleasant suburban street; we already knew the area, and we were close to a park, to the shops and to the railway station. My mother stayed on with us for a few weeks and then flew to Los Angeles to meet my father there.

I was not, I'm sorry to admit, a successful husband or father. I was working long hours and I didn't spend nearly enough time with Margaret and Mary. But I do have happy memories of our time in Ashfield. We acquired a beautiful golden labrador, given the name of Goldie, and the house had a large backyard and plenty of space. I recall one interesting event from that period: television transmission was still in black and white in 1967 and one morning we got up early to see a special programme which featured segments broadcast live from a large number of countries around the world. This was trailblazing stuff, but it was a pity that, due to some escalation in Cold War tensions, Moscow and the Communist bloc pulled out of the transmission at the last moment. Nevertheless, it was still exciting to see – live to air – images from so many different places. Australia contributed a segment in which the first trams of the day left their depot in Melbourne, and the broadcast ended on a rousing note in London with the Beatles performing their hit single 'All You Need Is Love'; the Rolling Stones could be glimpsed among the back-up singers.

I was eager to move the Festival away from the environs of Sydney University. The arrival of the UNSW Festival had served as a warning that we could be in the midst of a war between the two universities, whereas I saw the Festival as belonging to the City of Sydney, not to the University. The NSW Government had sacked Jørn Utzon, and the interior design of the Opera House was being radically redesigned as a result; it now seemed clear that the projection facilities in the major hall which we had been promised by the Opera House Trust would not be available after all. We now urgently required an auditorium that would seat 2000, similar to the Palais in St Kilda which was used by the Melbourne Film Festival. In that way, we could fulfil our obligation to FIAPF and screen each film only once. The obvious venue was the State Theatre, but Sir Norman Rydge, the Chairman of Greater Union, which owned the theatre, and Keith Moremon, the company's CEO, refused even to discuss the rental of the magnificent old cinema.

The only solution seemed to be to move the Festival to the suburbs. So, with some trepidation, I agreed to a Committee decision of a one-off experiment which entailed splitting the main programmes between a cinema in the eastern suburbs, the Wintergarden at Rose Bay, which seated about 2000, and one in the north, the Orpheum at Cremorne, which in those days was single auditorium seating around 1800. Weekday screenings would take place at these two venues, with weekend screenings at the University and the Elizabethan Theatre at nearby Newtown. This effectively got rid of the unsatisfactory Teachers College venue. FIAPF had agreed to four screenings per film at the Union Theatre because its seating capacity was only 620 but I knew that Brisson would never allow films to be shown more than once in cinemas as large as the Wintergarden and the Orpheum. As a result, the Festival was carved into two, with different films screened in Rose Bay from those screened in Cremorne. For example, the opening night film in Rose Bay was John Frankenheimer's chilling sci-fi thriller, *Seconds*, while in Cremorne we opened with Jean-Luc Godard's equally chilling, even more radical, *Alphaville*.

Before we reached this stage, however, there was a lot of work to do. I invited one of America's leading independent animators, Chuck Swenson of Murakami-Wolf Films, to design the striking programme cover (a pair of pink hands with six fingers and a thumb on each hand for the fourteenth Festival) and Witold Giersz, one of Poland's leading animators, to design the poster. I had also decided that my antipathy towards Prowse and the Censorship Board was now so great that it was no longer advisable for me to attend censorship screenings as I had done in 1966 as a way of checking the prints of the films as they arrived in the country. Unlike the MFF, we had no access to a screening room, but it was at this moment that Phil Jones proved himself to be a great friend. He offered us the use of the Gala Cinema for screenings on Sunday mornings, free of charge. This meant that, as the prints arrived, I could view them in the Gala with members of my Film Panel. Phil was also kind enough to pass on his copy of the invaluable American trade paper *Variety* to me every week; we couldn't possibly afford to subscribe to *Variety* ourselves, and Phil's kindness meant that I was now able to check on the hundreds of film reviews printed in the paper, which was of inestimable help in keeping up with what was happening around the world. Many of the European reviews were, of course, written by my friend Gene Moskowitz.

I entered into further correspondence with Josef von Sternberg, who agreed to come to the festival as guest of honour and to supply us with a copy of *The Saga of Anatahan*, which had never been screened before in Australia. The BBC had recently produced a programme called *The Epic that Never Was*, which was about the unfinished Alexander Korda production *I Claudius*, which Von Sternberg had started making in Britain in 1936 with Charles Laughton in the leading role, and this was added to the programme. With assistance from the local office of Paramount, I also managed to acquire several of Von Sternberg's classic films for a retrospective.

The Sydney Festival had rarely attracted guests until now and so I was pleased that another filmmaker, Jörn Donner, was able to fulfil the promise he made to me in Stockholm the previous November and come to Sydney personally to present his film *Adventure Starts Here*. The rest of the programme also came together very satisfactorily.

One of the films invited to participate was a very fine independent British production, *The Private Right*. Directed by Michael Papas, the film dealt with the torture by British interrogators of EOKA rebels on the island of Cyprus, a theme as timely today as it was then. Another entry that would prove controversial was Japanese director Shohei Imamura's *Jinruigaku Nyumon*, a provocative film variously known in English as *The Amourist*, *The Pornographer* and *An Introduction to Anthropology*; the central character of the film is an eccentric purveyor of sex aids whose mission is to bring happiness to his customers.

As the overseas films began to arrive, censorship problems again arose. The censors banned both *The Amourist* and *The Private Right*, the former because of its sexual content, the latter, officially, because of its violence, though I formed the opinion that what really upset Prowse and his Board was the depiction of *British* soldiers committing atrocities. The censors also demanded cuts in Bo Widerberg's *Karlek 65* (*Love 65*) involving partial female nudity, and ordered the removal of a sub-title from the Danish film *To* (*Two People*); the offending line, spoken by one factory worker to another at the end of the shift, was: 'What's on tonight? Going to dip the wick?' This expression the censors found unacceptable. Once again, we issued a press release to publicise these outrageous decisions, and the media started to pay more attention to what was happening.

It would be two more years, however, before the public at large became aware of the activities of the censors, even though 1967 was the year of the release in cinemas of cut versions of Arthur Penn's *Bonnie and Clyde* and Michelangelo Antonioni's *Blow-Up*. The mainstream distributors were, I sensed, starting to feel that censorship in Australia was a problem that would have to be dealt with, although cinema owners were still very much against the adults-only classification proposed by the Festival. Dale Turnbull, the CEO of Hoyts, went so far as to say in an interview that he would rather have a film cut by ten minutes or even more than ask his box-office staff to decide the age of a patron.

My son, Giles, was born on 7 May, just a few days before the 1967 SFF commenced. His arrival coincided with the latest censorship confrontation and with a crisis which had arisen over a new ticketing system designed by John Griffin-Foley, a prominent journalist and Vice-President of the Festival. The previous year, several members of the Committee had become concerned that a few people had managed to obtain access to screenings without tickets. Griff had been given the task of devising a foolproof system but he had kept his ideas very much to himself, refusing to tell me what he had in mind. When he finally revealed his plan, about ten days before the start of the Festival, it seemed to me to be so cumbersome that it would cause more trouble than it was worth. At every session, each subscriber would have to go to the box office to show their pass, and only then would they receive an admission ticket for the session about to start. There was no way this was going to work and I had to go over Griff's head to inform the President, Dug Merry, that Griff would have to be told to scrap his ideas. Sadly, Griff took it badly and resigned. The old ticket system was reinstated and we vowed to be much cleverer about ticketing in the future.

Josef von Sternberg flew into Sydney from LA the day before the Festival began, having celebrated his seventy-third birthday on the plane. Dug Merry and I met him at the airport, where he was forced to undergo the obligatory press conference and some listless questioning by uninformed hacks. This was one of the most annoying aspects of journalism at the time; 'celebrities' arriving from overseas were, in their jet-lagged state, subjected to questions at the airport from journalists who seemed only to have the vaguest notion of who they were. It was embarrassing to witness. After this ordeal we drove into the city in Merry's car but had to stop because Sternberg felt ill and wanted to get out and get some air. I naturally became concerned about the state of his health, although he seemed to make a speedy recovery.

We had booked him into the Australia Hotel in Castlereagh Street and when he had unpacked and freshened up he wanted to see the city. He seemed surprised that there were so many people around; I think he had expected a much smaller city.

Before he left LA I had written to tell him I had located prints of all his major films with the exception of one of his best silents, *The Docks of New York*; to my surprise, he had brought a 16-mm print of it in his baggage and had not, of course, declared it to the customs people at the airport. He explained that, on his way to LA International, he had stopped at the home of film collector David Bradley and had 'borrowed' Bradley's copy of the film without telling him he was taking it to Australia. I had the feeling that Bradley would be extremely annoyed and I was later proved correct.

Sternberg had a reputation for being difficult. His career as an innovative director was long over and his recent autobiography, *Fun in a Chinese Laundry*, reflected his bitterness over the years in which he had been unable to practise his craft. Beverley Burke had volunteered to look after him and she carried out her assignment with dedication and, in the end, with great affection. Without her, Sternberg's visit might indeed have been a troublesome one. He didn't like to be subjected to newspaper interviews, though he agreed to be interviewed for *Spectrum*, an arts programme on ABC television, which was hosted by Mungo MacCallum Sr and produced by Brian Adams. At the ABC studios at Gore Hill, television veterans gazed in awe as the director of some of the most beautifully photographed Hollywood films ever made instructed the technicians where they should place their lights to obtain the best visual effect.

Apart from this single interview, Sternberg refused, at first, to meet with journalists. Barrie Pattison was very keen to talk to him and I arranged for him to do so, but Sternberg wouldn't allow Barrie to make a tape-recording of their encounter. John Baxter was also eager to meet this distinguished guest, another meeting to which Sternberg reluctantly agreed. But the old director was continually grumpy and matters came to a head on the night that I had arranged for him to have dinner with two prominent journalists, Anne Deveson and her husband, Ellis Blain. When I arrived at the restaurant I could see something was wrong. 'They were late,' Sternberg said. 'They kept me waiting.' There was a moment of total embarrassment and then I took the bull by the horns. 'Well, Jo,' I said, 'I'm sure it's not the first time you've been kept waiting in your life.' To my relief he smiled, and after that we became firm friends. It seemed that he responded to anyone who would stand up to him, and I never personally had another problem with him after that incident.

However, I was mortally embarrassed when he took the stage at the Elizabethan in Newtown a few days later to introduce *The Saga of Anatahan* and the microphone stubbornly refused to work; undeterred, the diminutive Sternberg projected his voice to the upper reaches of the cavernous venue without the assistance of any amplification.

Sternberg stayed on in Sydney for a few days after the Festival had ended. He was a keen collector of Indigenous art and I located a shop where Sepik River paintings and artefacts from New Guinea were on sale. He bought a great many items, including a throne, and then had everything delivered to Qantas, insisting that it all be freighted back to LA on the same flight on which he was booked. It was unacceptable, he said, for these valuable items to be sent on a separate flight. He had bought two of almost everything and told me that he intended to sell the duplicates at several times the price he'd paid for them, thus making a handy profit.

One item he refused to take with him, however, was David Bradley's copy of *The Docks of New York*. I had already received one angry letter from Bradley, who had by now realised that Sternberg had taken his precious copy of the rare film with him to Australia. Convinced, quite erroneously, that I had encouraged Sternberg in this subterfuge, Bradley made all kinds of threats directed at me. I sent the print back to him by air freight at the first opportunity but this didn't mollify him in the least. He detected a tiny scratch on the film's leader (not on the film itself) and insisted that the worry and stress of the whole affair had hospitalised him. He demanded that the SFF pay his hospital bills and when I naturally refused, he threatened to horsewhip me if ever I set foot in Los Angeles again!

Jörn Donner was an easier guest. He was very keen to inspect the unfinished Opera House and to meet with the new architect, Peter Hall. He gave an excellent introduction to his film, and as many interviews as we required. He fell in love with Sydney on this trip and returned, at his own expense, on two or three more occasions in the succeeding years.

One of the highlights of the 1967 SFF was *Forgotten Cinema*, a feature documentary made by Tony Buckley which explored the rich history of Australian film production. My eyes were opened by the excerpts included in Buckley's film and I became determined to see as many as possible of these vintage Australian films in their entirety.

Despite the serious censorship situation and the dubious decision to split the Festival in two, the fourteenth SFF was generally considered a success. In the end, it was the quality of the films that defined it and I felt very happy about that. We kept within our budget and we made a small profit. After it was over I was desperately in need of a rest – I'd been working and travelling nonstop, seven days a week, for over a year. It had been decided between Sydney and Melbourne that neither Erwin nor I would travel overseas that year; Erwin would travel in 1968 and after that we would take it in turns. So now I had time to step back and reflect on what, if anything, I had achieved.

Obviously, the censorship problem, which had reached crisis proportions with the outright banning of two festival entries in 1967, needed to be solved, but how? Together with Erwin I continued to lobby the Customs Department, but to little avail. However, a new and important ally was about to enter the scene. Ross Jannes, as he called himself when I first met him, before he reverted to his given surname of Tzannes, had been a prominent member of SUFG a few years earlier but I had never met him because he had been travelling in Europe with his wife, Suzanne, for the last couple of years. Now he had returned and within a very short time he was elected to the SFF Committee. Before long, Ross, a lawyer by profession, would become another lifelong friend. His contribution towards the battle against censorship was to prove vital.

In the second half of 1967, and for much of 1968, I became involved in efforts to start a National Film Theatre of Australia (NFTA). Most countries boast some kind of Cinematheque, where specially curated seasons of recent or not-so-recent films are programmed. Now there was a move to start something similar in Australia and I attended several meetings in Canberra and also in Melbourne, where I met and befriended film enthusiasts including Peter Hourigan, Geoff Gardner, Michael Campi, and Peter Carmody and his wife, Anna. Some of us thought that the festivals were the logical organisations to run Cinematheque screenings throughout the year. The model was London, where the National Film Theatre and the London Film Festival operated out of the same venue and with the same staff. But, as is so often the case in Australia, the tyranny of distance proved a stumbling block. Not only was it immensely expensive to air-freight prints of films to Australia from overseas, but it was also very costly to ship them around Australia, which would have to be done if the proposed NFTA was to be truly national.

An imported season of films by the Japanese director Kon Ichikawa, supplied by the Japan Film Library Council, was arranged to take place in the spring of 1968 to test how an NFTA might work, but, once again, the Customs Department made things difficult. *Shokei no heya* (*Punishment Room*), one of the films in the programme, was banned outright. Eventually, the Sydney Film Festival Committee decided it didn't want to be involved with the NFTA, and that was the end of my involvement with the embryonic organisation.

At around this time the Festival office moved from King Street to 52 Erskine Street in the city. This building was leased by Norman Little, a photographer, who had a studio on the first floor. Little had no use for the ground floor, which was an area large enough for offices and a screening room. Some of the handier members of the Committee constructed a projection booth, and the two ageing 35-mm projectors we owned were installed there and I was taught how to use them. The screening room itself was musty and prone to invasion by cockroaches, but, at last, we had somewhere to screen and store the films. The office itself was established at the front of the building in what was basically a shopfront.

It was also essential to solve the question of the Festival venue. The management of Greater Union still wouldn't discuss the possibility of renting us the State and we all felt that splitting the event should not be repeated so we decided, rather reluctantly, to pin our hopes on the Wintergarden at Rose Bay. Many older subscribers still harboured considerable nostalgia for weekends in the University of Sydney grounds, where they had been able to enjoy picnics and to discuss the films with friends in a relaxed atmosphere, so there was some opposition to my plan to leave the University altogether and to make the 2000-seat Wintergarden our headquarters. The new venue was located by Sydney Harbour and had excellent parking and bus (but not train) connections from the city. But it proved, from a technical point of view, far from ideal.

On 16 October 1967 I was invited to Canberra to attend the world premiere of another new Australian feature film. *Journey out of Darkness*, which had been partly funded by Darrel Killen, the owner of Canberra's Electric Shadows cinema where it was being premiered, was a story set in the Northern Territory in which an Aboriginal tracker is assigned to help a white policeman arrest a fugitive Aborigine wanted for murder. (Many years later, Rolf de Heer's *The Tracker* would tackle a similar story.) *Journey out of*

Darkness was the first feature from American director James Trainor and the white policeman was played by a little-known American actor, Konrad Matthai. The Aboriginal fugitive was played by the Malayan-born Tamil Hindu singer Kamahl, and the Aboriginal tracker was played by a white actor, Ed Devereux, in unconvincing black make-up; he looked like Al Jolson in *The Jazz Singer*.

The film wasn't just bad; it was shockingly, cringingly bad. The guest of honour that night was the Prime Minister, Harold Holt. I'd met Holt before at the 1965 SFF Opening, and at the conclusion of the screening he and his wife, Zara, stopped to chat with me. 'I'm sure you'd like to show a film like that at your Festival,' he said, and, once again, I was at a loss for words. I realised yet again the gulf between my ambitions for the SFF and the lack of knowledge, or even interest, in cinema on the part of Australia's politicians. About six weeks later, on a Sunday afternoon while I was watching a screening of Raoul Walsh's western *Distant Drums* on television, the film was interrupted by a solemn announcer who informed viewers that the Prime Minister had disappeared while swimming off a beach at Portsea near Melbourne. His body was never found.

Earlier in 1967 a referendum had given Australia's Indigenous people the vote for the first time; one of the activists fighting for the Aboriginal cause had been Faith Bandler, whose husband, Hans, had been on the Committee of the SFF. Looking back, I'm ashamed that I didn't get to know Faith better on the few social occasions when we met. It was a missed opportunity for me, but the truth was that I still knew very little about Australia and its politics. In that respect I had a lot of catching up to do.

Dug Merry resigned from the presidency of the SFF at the 1967 AGM, after only one year, and was replaced by Ian McPherson. Because of the decision not to send either Erwin or myself overseas that year we were forced to programme the 1968 Festivals without the benefit of overseas scouting. Instead I used the contacts I had made in the summer and autumn of 1966, and especially the advice of people like Gene Moskowitz and John Gillett, to assemble what I considered to be an excellent programme.

However, the programming was not without its difficulties. The Festival Committee, which met once a month, had established eleven sub-committees, under different chairs, to concentrate on specific aspects of the event; there were sub-committees for Delegates, Finance, Fund-Raising, Public Relations, Publicity, Technical, Transport, Theatres and Freedom from Censorship. The latter was chaired by Ian McPherson and included Ross Tzannes in its membership. As Director I was invited to attend any or all of these meetings and, as far as possible, I did.

Arguably the most important sub-committee of all was the Film Sub-committee, which, for the 1968 Festival, was chaired by John Baxter and included among its members Dorothy Shoemark and Barrie Pattison. I had great difficulties with this sub-committee. John and Barrie were steeped in knowledge about the cinema and they were forceful in their views. But those views weren't identical, and they weren't necessarily my views or those of my overseas advisors. The difficulty was that we were, in a sense, working blind. I was relying very much on the advice and opinions of overseas colleagues who had seen the films which were under consideration, and I found it exasperating that, at the monthly Film Sub-committee meetings, my proposals were being overturned. There was a big row over the Jerzy Skolimowski film *Le Depart*, which the Polish director had made in Belgium and which had won both the Golden Bear and the FIPRESCI (International Federation of Film Critics) award at the Berlin Film Festival; for some reason, both John and Barrie were against the film, and wanted it rejected, a decision I was simply not willing to accept. In the end, I was reluctantly forced to go over their heads and appeal directly to Ian McPherson as President of the SFF. Eventually, the Film Sub-committee was dissolved and a 'Film Advisory Panel' established, which was chaired by myself as the

Festival Director, who was from then on solely responsible, for good or ill, for the films selected and programmed.

Australian feature films were practically non-existent in 1968, but short films were often submitted by local directors. One such film, produced for the ATN (Channel 7) Social Club Christmas Party, was a comedy called *Count Vim's Last Exercise*. The film's young director, Peter Weir, a junior employee at ATN, showed plenty of promise but I didn't think the film was up to the standard of other Festival entries and I rejected it. I've since regretted this decision.

My problems were nothing compared to the dramas which unfolded at Cannes that May. That month virtually the whole of France was paralysed by strikes and the Film Festival was badly affected. Many of the young *nouvelle vague* directors – Truffaut, Godard, Louis Malle – demanded the Festival be shut down, which, eventually, it was, with no awards given for that year. I read all this in the pages of *Variety*, for which Mosk supplied vivid reports on the chaotic occurrances.

In the wake of the tremendous commercial success of *They're a Weird Mob*, Michael Powell was making another film in Australia. *Age of Consent*, based on an autobiographical book by artist Norman Lindsay about his relationship with a young model, was being produced by the actor Michael Pate, who had returned to Australia after more than a decade of playing minor but compelling roles, usually villains and Indians, in Hollywood films (one of his last films in America had been Sam Peckinpah's *Major Dundee*). Location shooting for *Age of Consent* had taken place on Dunk Island on the Barrier Reef, with James Mason playing the artist and Helen Mirren – in her first film – the young model who spends much of the film naked. The film unit had now returned to Sydney to shoot some additional scenes. Thanks to Tony Buckley, who was editing the film, I was invited to visit the set one day. In a Paddington art gallery Powell was directing Mason in a key sequence. I was able to have lunch with Powell,

Mason and Pate, and also to talk to Helen Mirren, who seemed slightly overawed about acting in her first film so far from home.

By the time the 1968 SFF was launched in June, Mason, Mirren and most of the other actors had returned to Britain, but Powell was still in Sydney working on the post-production of *Age of Consent* so I invited him and Michael Pate to the opening night at the Wintergarden. The opening film that year was Bo Widerberg's romantic tragedy *Elvira Madigan*. The occasion was a near-disaster and symptomatic of the problems we were to have at the Wintergarden. Keith Mortley, who was both manager of the cinema and the projectionist, seemed unable to keep the image in focus; he blamed the print, but I had seen the same print in another venue and it had looked sharp and clear. There turned out to be a problem with the projector lenses, which were very old, but Mortley was unwilling to concede this and wasn't exactly cooperative about updating his equipment.

The Festival was small by today's standards. Just twenty-eight feature films were screened in 1968, ten fewer than the previous year when we had been forced to programme separately for Cremorne and Rose Bay. The event was designed so that subscribers were able to see every film, and most of them did. The festivals of that time were far more manageable than they are today but critics could argue, with some justification, that there was less choice.

To my delight, Satyajit Ray fulfilled his two-year-old promise to attend the Festival. For some reason that I never quite understood, he didn't want to screen his latest film, *Chiriakhana*, but instead presented a six-year-old film, *Kanchenjungha*, which had been his first production in colour. I met Ray at Sydney airport and as I drove him to his hotel, he asked a favour. He explained that he was in negotiation with Columbia Pictures to direct a film for them using money earned by the company's films released in India which had been frozen by the government. He had submitted to the studio a screenplay called *The Alien*, which was about the arrival at a small village in Bengal of a friendly creature from another planet. Columbia had expressed interest in the idea and had suggested that Peter Sellers, who had a reputation for playing Indian characters, would be ideal casting as the villager who befriends the alien. The Blake Edwards film *The Party*, in which Sellers played an accident-prone Indian, had just opened in the US, and Ray wondered if there might already be a print in Australia which he might be allowed to see. I called the recently appointed CEO of United Artists, Ken Beaton, who, fortunately, knew Ray's work and who was a supporter of the Festival, and he told me the print of *The Party* had just arrived; nobody had seen it yet, Beaton said, but he was happy to let Ray watch it that afternoon if it would be of help him. He gave me permission to sit in on the screening.

Ray was not at all amused by the film; in fact, he was insulted by Sellers's broad caricature of an Indian, and he immediately cabled his agent to reject the project. Even today I can't watch *The Party* without recalling Ray's furious reaction to Sellers's performance. Years later, Ray told me he suspected Steven Spielberg might have stumbled across his screenplay of *The Alien*, because it bore a striking resemblance to Spielberg's *E.T.: The Extra-Terrestrial*, which was made in 1982.

Ray proved a popular guest of the festival, but I will never forget sitting with him in a taxi driving through the western suburbs of Sydney on our way to a dinner when we heard, over the radio, the news that Robert Kennedy had been fatally shot in Los Angeles. Earlier in that turbulent year, Martin Luther King had been assassinated. Apart from the paralysis of France, the Vietnam War was hotting up, and there were major riots during the Democratic Convention in Chicago. Anti-war protesters demonstrated on the streets of all western capitals, including Sydney. The world seemed to have gone crazy.

In August, I was horrified to hear the news of the Warsaw Pact invasion of Czechoslovakia. I thought of my friends in Prague:

Ladislav Pospisil, Edouard Hais and all the filmmakers – Forman, Menzel and the rest. I took part in my first-ever street demonstration, outside the Polish Consulate in Sydney, protesting the invasion. My visit to Prague eighteen months earlier had revealed to me that most Czechs were not Communists and that they resented the Soviet domination of their country. Their films had reflected this. Similar sentiments had been expressed to me in Hungary and Poland. The people of these Central European countries seemed to me to be culturally and philosophically more attuned to Western Europe than to Moscow, and the Russians were to them what the Americans were to many in the West – bullies who wanted to impose their way of life on reluctant allies. I was disgusted when Australia's Foreign Minister, Paul Hasluck, made a statement to the effect that what had happened in Czechoslovakia was some kind of internecine quarrel between two Communist countries and therefore not of any great concern to Australians.

My contacts with film distributors had paid off. With the exception of Blake Films, a company which still treated the Festival with barely disguised hostility, I was now on good terms with the managements of all the film companies and as a result I was regularly invited to preview screenings of Hollywood films. On 1 May 1968, I attended the Australian premiere of Stanley Kubrick's trailblazing *2001: A Space Odyssey*, at the Plaza cinema in George Street. The film had opened in the US exactly a month earlier (one wag suggested that the 1 April trade screening in New York was some kind of April Fool's joke), and one of its actors, Keir Dullea, had flown to Australia to introduce the film. Rather disarmingly, he admitted that he really had no idea what it was about. Lines of communication weren't as efficient in those days as they are today and I knew little about Kubrick's film other than that it was a science-fiction epic. The prologue, involving some actors in ape skins, had me totally perplexed, though I was transfixed by the magical moment when Kubrick cuts from the distant past to the future in one split second as a bone, hurled into the air, is transformed into a spaceship. At the intermission, which took place before the main spaceflight had even commenced, I chatted with Charles Higham, who, after the death of *The Sydney Morning Herald* film critic Josephine O'Neill, had moved to the *Herald* from *The Bulletin*; he was as baffled as I was. Only later on, when I saw *2001* a second time, did this amazing film begin to weave its magic spell. I've seen it many times since.

In 2006, a magnificent 70-mm print of *2001* was imported for a few screenings and I was asked by Paul Dravet, the manager of the Orpheum at Cremorne, to host a pre-screening discussion with the film's two principal actors, Keir Dullea and Gary Lockwood. It was great fun and an occasion to remember that, though most of the world's critics at the time were unimpressed by the film, the late Beverly Tivey, who in 1968 had become critic for *The Bulletin*, had named it one of the best of the year.

The 1968 SFF had been completely free from censorship problems. Not one cut had been demanded. Were the censors quietly backing off, or were the films we had selected really so unthreatening? The following year's experiences would, unfortunately, answer that particular question.

Chapter Ten

Nineteen sixty-nine proved to be a milestone year. Now that Ian McPherson was President of the Committee and was enthusiastically supporting the drive for censorship reform, we decided to up the ante. We informed Chief Censor Prowse, and the office of the new Minister for Customs, Senator Malcolm Scott (Liberal Party, Western Australia), that we would no longer accept cuts in film imported by the Festival, and that even the smallest cut would amount to a ban of the entire film.

Meanwhile, there had been a great deal of debate at Committee meetings over what some members perceived as a policy, instituted by me, to commercialise the Festival. I had made it clear that, in my view, our international sources of film – producers and distributors – saw the film festivals in Australia mainly as a means towards obtaining distribution in this country. This was especially true of countries like France, Italy, Japan and Sweden – all high-profile suppliers of commercial foreign-language films to local distributors – but it was increasingly true of countries like

Czechoslovakia, Hungary and Poland, whose films were now being distributed in countries like Britain and the US but not to any large extent in Australia. It made sense to me. Why would a French producer agree to go to the expense of sending a valuable subtitled print of a new film to Australia? It was true that in the past, with the encouragement of local embassies and consulates, films had been sent to the Festival in the name of culture, but several producers in Europe and Japan had made it clear to me that the 'honour' of having a film screen in Sydney or Melbourne was becoming less important than selling the film to an Australian distributor for cold hard cash. The writing was on the wall: it seemed to me that it was imperative that the Festival must do everything in its power to assist in the acquisition and distribution of the films it selected.

This imperative was simply not understood by some members of the Festival Committee. They argued that if we were successful in this aim, the result would be that most Festival films would later play in the country's art-house cinemas. If that were to be the case, they argued, what was the point of seeing them at the Festival? According to this reasoning, we should concentrate on programming films which had virtually no chance of distribution. I was completely opposed to any policy which would impact on the overall quality of the programme. The debate was often passionate and I was accused by some of selling out to commercial interests.

Despite all this, the 1969 programme came together very well. On a trip to Mexico the previous year, Erwin Rado had discovered a remarkable avant-garde film titled *Fando y Lys*, which was the first feature by theatre director Alejandro Jodorowsky (who would later make the notorious *El Topo*). Despite the dramatic events that had occurred in Czechoslovakia, we had also obtained the two best Czech films of the year, Jiri Menzel's tender *Rozmarne leto* (*Capricious Summer*), which had won the Grand Prix at Karlovy Vary a few days before the invasion, and Jan Nemec's subversive, satirical *O Slavnosti a Hostech* (*Report on the Party and the Guests*). The second feature from the brilliant Yugoslav director, Dušan Makavejev, *Ljubavni slucaj* (*Switchboard Operator*) was also in the programme and I was nervous about that one, from a censorship point of view, because of its free-wheeling nude scenes and its excerpts from old porno films Makavejev had discovered in the Serbian archives. To my surprise, the censors weren't concerned with the Yugoslav film. The trouble, when it came, was completely unexpected.

I was very excited about the film chosen to open the Festival, Lindsay Anderson's provocative *If . . .*, which, a few weeks earlier, had competed in Cannes where it had won the Palme d'Or; Paramount had agreed to allow this film to open the Festival, which confirmed, in my mind, that we now had much better cooperation with just about all the major distributors.

I had hoped that Anderson might be persuaded to come to Australia, but he was busy with other commitments. Since I had a budget for one guest, I was determined to use it. It was essential that whoever came was able to speak English, which ruled out some of the contenders. Erwin had invited three Swedish features and knowing that the Swedish directors would all speak English, I invited first Kjell Grede, whose film *Hugo och Josefin* (*Hugo and Josefin*) was a delight. When Grede was unable to come I tried Jonas Cornell, director of a sexy comedy called *Puss och Kram* (*Hugs and Kisses*), but he couldn't make the trip either. Finally I invited Stig Björkman, a young film critic whose first feature, *Jag alskar, du alskar* (*I Love, You Love*) was our third Swedish entry and who immediately accepted.

The first major problem occurred about three weeks before the start of the Festival, when Eric Dare, who had distributed *Elvira Madigan*, acquired Cornell's film and imported a print. He was quite happy for it to screen at the SFF, but when he submitted it to the Censorship Board they demanded two cuts, one of which was a shot in which the female star of the film, Agneta Ekmanner, the director's wife, undresses and gazes at her naked body in her bedroom mirror. Technically speaking, our policy of not screening cut films applied only to films that *we* imported, not to films owned by local distributors, over which we had no control. Despite that, I should have dropped the movie from the programme then and there, but the catalogue was already at the printer's and the film had been announced. I asked Dare if he would mind if we inserted, in the two cut sequences, the word CENSORED and, to my surprise, he had no objection. On this basis we went ahead with the screening, but we'd wrongly calculated the amount of footage cut from the film and so CENSORED appeared, rather fuzzily, on the screen for far, far longer than it should. The audience, understandably believing that the cuts had been more extensive than they actually were, erupted in fury.

There was worse to come. A couple of days before the start of the Festival I had a call from Lyn Kirkwood of the Censorship Board to inform me that the Board demanded a scene must be cut from *I Love, You Love*. The scene in question involved the leading actors, Evabritt Strandberg and Sven Wollter, embracing on a bed. Both were naked and Strandberg was (in real life) heavily pregnant. Her breasts and their genitals were covered, but the censors had decided that the couple was actually having sex, albeit in a sitting position. This had never occurred to me when I saw the film and at first I didn't take it seriously. But, Kirkwood assured me, this was deadly serious. 'Since you don't want cuts made, we're going to ban the film,' he told me. I tried to reach Björkman in Stockholm to tell him the news but he had already left for Australia. I tracked him down in Singapore and told him what had happened; he was shocked, but agreed to come on to Australia to help us fight the decision of the censors.

We issued a press release and, when Stig arrived in Sydney, a mob of reporters was present to greet him. This was news, front-page news. It was of great assistance to us that Stig was young, handsome, charming and articulate. He denied that he had filmed a scene involving actual sex, and implied that the Censorship Board had dirty minds, while I wondered, privately, if they had confused his film with Vilgot Sjoman's *I Am Curious Yellow*, which had recently caused a stir in America because it contained actual sex scenes. Stig announced that he would phone his actors to confirm their side of the story, and the phone call was made from the offices of *The Sydney Morning Herald*. Strandberg and Wollter denied they had been making love during the scene and were offended at the suggestion. But the denials of the director and his actors cut no ice with Prowse and his Board; the ban stayed.

It was in this tense atmosphere that the festival opened with *If*. . . I was rather disturbed to find that the NSW Chief Secretary, Eric Willis (the man responsible for censorship in the state), who had accepted an invitation on behalf of himself and his wife, had instead brought his daughter with him, a daughter who didn't look to be eighteen. I tried to tell him, when he arrived at the theatre, that there was a minimum age requirement of eighteen for festival attendance, but he brushed me aside. As the film unspooled, I was alarmed to discover that it had been cut since Alfred Jarrett, the CEO of Paramount in Australia, had screened it for me in his theatrette several weeks earlier; two or three scenes were gone. I would never have accepted the film had I known this was going to happen and it increased my sense of frustration and depression. I noticed, after the screening, that Willis seemed very unimpressed with the film, which wasn't surprising given that it ends with an explicit call for the overthrow of the establishment; his daughter, however, appeared to have enjoyed it.

When the news of the *I Love, You Love* ban became public, something quite unexpected occurred. Local filmmakers whose short films had been accepted by the Festival withdrew in protest. Among them was Peter Weir: though I had rejected *Count Vim's Last Exercise* the previous year I had very much liked his second short film, *The Life and Times of the Rev. Buck Shotte*, and had programmed it prominently. I wasn't convinced that withdrawing these films would have any effect on the censors, but Weir and the others obviously felt that it was a potent form of protest. I doubt that the Government was even aware of their actions; it was the Festival's programme that suffered from the decision of the film-makers to withdraw their work.

Although the frustration of the situation and the bad international publicity it engendered was the last thing I really wanted, it soon became clear that the *I Love, You Love* scandal was a blessing in disguise. Stig gave interviews to just about every television network, radio station and newspaper in the country. He was tireless in his advocacy for his film. Ross Tzannes came to the fore during the crisis and, in consultation with Ian McPherson, Erwin and myself, co-ordinated our response to the ban; Ross's legal background was of inestimable value.

We sought a meeting with the Customs Minister, Senator Scott, and his staff confirmed that he would meet us early one morning in Canberra at his office in Parliament House. Ross, Stig and I flew to Canberra on the first flight from Sydney on the day in question; unfortunately, fog in Melbourne closed Tullamarine airport and prevented Erwin from joining us. The Head of the Customs Department, together with Prowse, awaited us in the outer office. The Minister greeted Stig warmly but patronisingly: 'How are you enjoying Australia, laddie?' He mentioned in passing that the last film he'd seen was *The Sound of Music*. Stig assured him that Prowse and his Board were mistaken in thinking that there was actual sex in the film and that the disputed scene depicted only an affectionate embrace between a man and his pregnant wife. Prowse reiterated the fact that he and his Board members believed actual sex was taking place. Not surprisingly, Scott sided with Prowse. Despite our protestations he told us that the ban would not be lifted. Members of the press corps had gathered outside the Minister's office and Stig told them calmly but forcefully that the Minister was wrong.

The next day, the front pages of the newspapers were full of the story: 'Festival Film Banned' was the banner headline in *The Australian*. There were angry letters to the editor, some by well-known media names, all critical of the film's banning. We invited subscribers to the Festival to sign a petition and to pay ten cents each to enable it to be printed in *The Australian*; there was a tremendous response, and as a result we were able to take a full page in the national daily on which the hundreds of signatures were reproduced. The next day I was driving Stig to the Commonwealth Film Unit studios in Lindfield to meet with local filmmakers when we gave a lift to a schoolboy who was hitching a ride (yes, schoolboys hitched rides in Sydney in 1969!). The boy recognised Stig immediately and started a lively conversation with him, and I think it was at that moment that I first realised how deeply the story of the ban had penetrated the consciousness of ordinary Australians.

Shortly afterwards, Stig left for Melbourne to fulfil his obligations at the MFF. While he was there he was invited by the production company, Bilcock and Copping, to make a short film of protest and, in no time at all, he shot *To Australia with Love*, an ironic response to the events of the past few days. He brought a copy of the film back to Sydney with him and we added it to the closing night programme.

One other incident worth noting occurred during the 1969 SFF. I had included in the programme Tim Burstall's ambitious, if flawed, first feature film, *2,000 Weeks*, which was made rather in the style of the French New Wave and which dealt, quite tenderly, with the unhappy lives of a group of Melbournians. The film had already opened commercially in Melbourne and had received a hostile review from Colin Bennett in *The Age*; consequently it had done very little business. But I liked *2,000 Weeks* for its ambition and its style and I was certain the SFF audience would enjoy it too. I was wrong. Soon after the film began – with Burstall and his leading lady, Jeanie Drynan, in the audience – the snickering began and then turned into the occasional guffaw. 'Give it a go!' somebody yelled out but by that time Drynan had fled from the cinema in tears. The screening was a disaster and I was truly mortified.

Events on the censorship front moved fairly quickly after the Festival ended. It seemed that the media attention, and the public response, to the banning of *I Love, You Love* had touched a national chord. I have no doubt that Stig Björkman's affable, unthreatening presence had been a major contributor to the positive public reaction. Within two or three months the Prime Minister, John Gorton, had replaced Senator Scott in the Customs portfolio with the far more liberal and worldly Don Chipp, the future leader of the Democrats but at the time a Liberal Party frontbencher. I was unable to meet with Chipp before I left to go overseas on my next trip to seek films for the SFF, but he agreed to meet with me on my return. In his autobiography Chipp suggested that the Festival manufactured the censorship crisis in order to attract publicity; we had, he suggested, deliberately invited films which would arouse the ire of the censors. Nothing could have been further from the truth; on the contrary, the international publicity about the censorship of the Festival was proving extremely damaging, as I soon discovered.

At the beginning of July I embarked on my second lengthy overseas trip on behalf of the two Festivals. One of my most important stopovers was Tokyo, where I met with executives from the major companies, Toho, Shochiku, Nikkatsu and Toei, and was shown several new films. I also took the opportunity to discuss with Madam Kawakita, the Director of the Japan Film Library, the possibility of a future retrospective of Akira Kurosawa films and a visit from the great director himself. Madame K, as she was generally called, was a delightful woman who, against all current fashion, always wore a mauve-coloured kimono. She was married to the CEO of Toho, and they were both ardent film-lovers. Before my arrival in Australia she had already visited the

Sydney and Melbourne Festivals and she greeted me very warmly. She told me that Kurosawa was very busy at the moment with an ambitious new project backed by 20th Century-Fox; *Tora! Tora! Tora!* was an account of the attack on Pearl Harbor which showed both the American and Japanese versions of the event that brought America into World War II, and Kurosawa was directing the Japanese side of the story. After that he planned to start a new Japanese film *Dodeska-den* immediately, but Madame K thought that a visit to Australia in 1971 was not out of the question and we agreed to plan the retrospective with that date in mind.

One of the guests at the 1969 SFF had been the Russian director Stanislav Rostotsky, whose film *Dozhivyom do ponedelnika* (*Until Monday*), a last-minute entry, had proved very popular with the audience. Rostotsky and his actress wife, Nina Menshikova, who had accompanied him to Australia, had urged me to attend the 1969 Moscow Film Festival, and when I flew into Moscow from Tokyo Stan was at the airport to meet me. It seemed that his status in the Party – he was a war hero who had lost a leg in battle, and was now an acclaimed filmmaker – allowed him a considerable amount of latitude, because we bypassed customs and drove in his car straight to the gigantic, 5000-room Rossyia Hotel, near the Kremlin. Currency restrictions were severe in the Communist countries and it was only permitted to change Western money into Russian roubles at official outlets where the exchange rates were most unfavourable. Stan, however, quite openly volunteered to change US dollars into roubles at a much more favourable rate than the official one and when I queried the wisdom of this transaction, which was taking place in my room in a hotel where, I'd been led to believe, Westerners were kept under observation, he seemed highly amused.

The screenings at the Festival took place in a vast cinema inside the Kremlin and were attended by delegates from all over the world. For the most part, the films were fairly undistinguished, though I was pleased to be able to have a second look at *2001:*

A Space Odyssey under these unusual conditions. The film was the official American entry and was introduced by Vice-President Hubert Humphrey, no less; but I noticed that a brief scene between American and Russian astronauts was missing and I wondered how many other films in the festival had been 'modified'.

At mealtimes, seating in the vast dining room of the Rossiya was arranged according to nationality. The small Australian delegation included Eddie Allison, a former actor, proud member of the Communist Party and the CEO of Quality Films, a small distributor that specialised in releasing Soviet films in Australia; and director Tim Burstall, whose film, *2,000 Weeks*, was the Australian entry. My good friend Gene Moskowitz was also in Moscow reviewing for *Variety* and I spent quite a lot of time with him. At the American table, where there was a large delegation, I was thrilled to meet Lillian Gish, the legendary star of silent films, notably *The Birth of a Nation* (1915) and *Way Down East* (1920), the pioneering works of the great D. W. Griffith. Gish was utterly charming, and was happy to talk about 'Mr Griffith', as she always called him, and those long-ago days. She was also very informative about one of my favourite films, Charles Laughton's *The Night of the Hunter*, in which she had played a pivotal role.

While we were in Moscow we heard the momentous news that the Americans had landed on the moon, not that the Russian media exactly trumpeted the information; *Izvestia* mentioned it in a tiny paragraph on the back page. It struck me that it was an interesting coincidence that *2001* was the official American entry in the festival and I wondered if perhaps it hadn't been entirely accidental; perhaps the American Government was, in a sense, having a dig at the Russians by screening at the Moscow Festival a film which celebrated America's supremacy in space at exactly the same time as the moon landing. I asked Lillian Gish what Mr Griffith would have felt about all this. 'He would have been in ecstasy!' she replied, and she also thought he would eagerly have embraced the widescreen and stereophonic sound systems which had become standard in recent years.

John Gillett was also in Moscow and another member of the British delegation was director Richard Lester, famous for the Beatles' films *A Hard Day's Night* and *Help!*, and for the Cannes Golden Palm winner *The Knack . . . and How to Get It.* Lester's new film, *The Bed Sitting Room*, about a post-apocalyptic world, was one of the British entries. Another was *Oliver!*, Carol Reed's version of the Lionel Bart musical; Reed wasn't in Moscow but Ron Moody, who played Fagin, was, and he kept us in stitches with his anecdotes and backstage stories.

At the mid-point of the Festival, the organisers had arranged a trip for delegates to Leningrad, which today has resumed its original name of St Petersburg. We were taken to the Central Station late in the evening to catch the overnight train, and we arrived in Leningrad early the next morning. We were taken directly to the Hermitage Museum for a tour, where I was joined by Lillian Gish, who was visibly excited by the art treasures on display. After a morning at the Hermitage (which was, of course, far too short a time), and a brief lunch, we were taken to the old Summer Palace for a further tour, and then caught the night train back to Moscow. It was a very fleeting visit, but Leningrad made an indelible impression on me.

Two days after the Moscow Festival ended, the Pula Film Festival in Yugoslavia began. At the time Yugoslavia was making some very interesting, and often subversive, films and the iconoclastic Dušan Makavejev was one of the country's leading directors. Gene Moskowitz was also going to Pula so we sat together on the flight from Moscow to Zagreb, where we met up with Mosk's old friend Zelimir Matko, CEO of the famous animation studio Zagreb Film. Matko drove us to Pula, stopping en route at his favourite seafood restaurant just outside Rijeka for a meal. This drive from Zagreb to Pula with Mosk and Matko became a regular annual event over the following years and one I very much enjoyed.

The Pula Festival, which lasted a week, showed all the latest films from the various Republics of Yugoslavia but no international films. The screenings were held inside a magnificent, partly ruined Roman arena, rather like Rome's Colosseum, which was located by the sea, and the hot summer nights (it never seemed to rain) were made memorable by some very fine films. The guests, who included the celebrated British film critic Dilys Powell, were housed at a seaside hotel on the edge of town, and the days were spent relaxing by the pool, talking about films and preparing for another interesting evening of viewing. Mosk would write his reviews of the previous night's films on his battered portable typewriter and once in a while would place them in a large envelope and mail them to *Variety* in New York. He always became excited if an American guest was leaving to go home and would prevail on them to mail his reviews from somewhere in the US or, better still, to deliver them to the *Variety* office in person.

When Pula ended I flew, via Zagreb, to Budapest, and by the first week in August I was again ensconced in the Hotel Royal and spending my days at Hungarofilm, which was located at 10 Bathory Street, watching new films by, among other directors, Marta Meszaros and Miklós Jancsó. A few days later, in Warsaw, I was able to see Andrzej Wajda's remarkably personal story *Wszystko na Sprzedaz* (*Everything for Sale*), about a film director whose leading actor is killed when he falls under a train he is running to catch; Zbigniew Cybuksli, the charismatic actor who in 1958 achieved international fame in Wajda's *Popiol I Diament* (*Ashes and Diamonds*), had been tragically killed in just such an accident two years earlier. After some pleasant days in Warsaw I flew to Bucharest to see the latest Romanian films.

Although I hadn't really planned it, I arrived in Prague at the beginning of the week which saw the first anniversary of the Warsaw Pact invasion of Czechoslovakia. Pospisil and Hais were still in charge at Ceskoslovensky Film and Pospisil still had a photograph of the displaced Head of the Communist Party,

Alexander Dubcek, prominently displayed in his office. Hais screened several 'controversial' films for me, including one by Jan Nemec, who had managed to flee the country after making a documentary about the invasion a year earlier (for which Mosk had supplied the voice-over narration).

On the streets of the capital there was a genuine sense of unease. Soviet tanks and armoured cars were at every major intersection, but despite that, as the week wore on, more and more people gathered in Wenceslas Square, just across the road from the Ceskoslovensky Film office. On the evening of 20 August, the night before the anniversary, I went to see *Laterna Magica* (*Magic Lantern*), the celebrated mixture of theatre and film, but halfway through the performance was drowned out by the noise in the street outside and was then interrupted by the acrid smell of tear gas seeping into the auditorium. Outside there was chaos as the people of Prague blocked the way of Russian soldiers, who had obviously been ordered to clear the streets. I had my camera with me and took several photos until I saw some Russian soldiers watching me. Before I could leave the area I was grabbed by two Russians and dragged to the back of a truck. I shouted at them in English and showed them my passport. They let me go but they took the roll of film from my camera.

The next day the city was closed down. The manager of my hotel invited guests to help themselves to food and wine from the cellar ('Better you drink it than the Russians,' he said). I drank far too much, and became very ill. Next morning, with a terrible hangover, I returned to the Ceskoslovensky Film office to find that business was far from usual. A tear gas shell had penetrated one of the windows and the theatrette was unusable. As I was commiserating with Pospisil and Hais they received an unwelcome visitor; his name was Tugan Vesely, and he had been appointed by the Party to replace Pospisil. He was a large, bland fellow – a caricature of a Communist *apparatchik*, and very different from the sophisticated, urbane man he was replacing. I said my goodbyes to my friends and left sadly, feeling, correctly as it turned out, that I would not see them again.

Next morning I flew to Vienna. At Prague Airport I was approached by a man who said he was from *Time* magazine and that he had taken several rolls of film of the events of the past few days which he had to get urgently to the magazine's office in the Austrian capital. I agreed to take them and he slipped them into my bag; luckily nobody noticed. Later that afternoon, in Vienna, I delivered the films and the following week I was pleased to see vivid photographs of the tumultuous events in Prague prominently featured in *Time*.

My next stop was the Venice Film Festival, after which I spent a week in Paris. One of the films I saw there was *Easy Rider*, which had received its world premiere in Cannes three months earlier. Directed by Dennis Hopper, *Easy Rider* would launch a whole wave of youthful, anti-establishment, American movies. The story of a pair of bikies involved in dope dealing who ride across the American South, confronted at all times by prejudice – against their long hair and their alternative lifestyle – and violence, was naive but strangely affecting, and Jack Nicholson achieved star status with his riveting performance in the small role of a 'straight' guy who goes along for the ride. When I saw the film I wondered, as I often did at this time, what the censors in Australia would make of it.

It shouldn't be forgotten that the anti-censorship campaign being waged by the SFF was not only for freedom from censorship for the Sydney and Melbourne Film Festivals; we also wanted a better deal for all cinemagoers, and we argued that it was high time that an adults-only classification, similar to the British X-rating, be introduced to allow films to be shown in their integral versions. A large number of films of the past year or so had been released commercially in Australia with substantial censorship cuts, among them *Bonnie and Clyde*, *Lilith*, *A Fistful of Dollars*, *For a Few Dollars More*, *Blow-Up*, *The St. Valentine's Day*

Massacre, *The Green Berets*, *Barbarella*, *Rosemary's Baby* and *Secret Ceremony*; *The Wild Bunch*, which the Australian censors would shred, was due for release later in the year.

I celebrated my thirtieth birthday in Paris. I can't remember why I didn't spend the evening with Mosk but perhaps he was out of town or otherwise engaged. I had a rather lonely dinner before going to see Eric Rohmer's beautiful film, *My nuit chez Maud* (*My Night with Maud*).

A few days later I flew to London to be reunited with my parents. Over the previous year, my father had been very ill. A heavy smoker all his life, he had developed phlebitis, or hardening of the arteries, a disease undoubtedly exacerbated by the stress involved in running Stratton Sons & Mead. A brilliant surgeon saved his life with what was then a fairly new operation, which involved replacing his blocked arteries with plastic tubes, but not only was he now forbidden to smoke, he was forced to retire. At the early age of fifty-six my workaholic father had to relinquish the reins of the family business.

Roger, who was just twenty-two at the time, was, I suppose, considered by my father to be too young and certainly too inexperienced to assume such an onerous position; and Uncle John wasn't, in my father's opinion, up to the job, and anyway I think John was only too happy to seize this opportunity to reinvent himself. He retired too, and moved with his family to a small town in Cornwall where, for many years, he ran a souvenir shop. And so, after about 145 years in the grocery trade, Stratton Sons & Mead was absorbed into another company and the name was lost for ever. Perhaps if I'd returned from Australia things might have been different, although frankly I doubt it. The increasing willingness of the shopping public to patronise large supermarkets rather than small family grocers would inevitably result in the demise of family businesses like Strattons. However, I felt, once again, that I had let my father down. Fortunately, he recovered completely from his illness and lived for another twenty years.

I spent a few days in London, where I saw Sam Peckinpah's tragic epic *The Wild Bunch*. I also encountered Derek Hill, a former film reviewer – he had famously attacked, with rare venom, Michael Powell's *Peeping Tom* – who was now an anti-censorship campaigner. Derek ran a members-only film club in Soho where he was able to screen uncensored films, including Nagisa Oshima's *Shinjuku dorobo nikki* (*Diary of a Shinjuku Thief*), which had been banned by the British censors. Also in London I saw the Costa-Gavras political thriller *Z* (which I would select to open the 1970 SFF), John Schlesinger's remarkable *Midnight Cowboy* and a preview of Ken Russell's adaptation of D. H. Lawrence's *Women in Love*. The strong sexual content of many of these films convinced me that, at home in Australia, *something* had to give on the censorship front.

I sought advice from John Trevelyan, the Secretary of the British Board of Film Censors and thus Britain's Chief Film Censor. Unlike Dick Prowse, Trevelyan was a cultured and immensely intelligent man whose love of film was very evident. During the first of several meetings we would have at his office overlooking Soho Square, he interrupted our conversation to take a phone call from Gene Kelly, who, it seems, was a personal friend. Trevelyan listened sympathetically to my stories about the situation in Australia and seemed convinced that changes would be forced on the Censorship Board by the film industry itself. I was forming the same impression. He was also kind enough to invite me to join him at the occasional screening of films his Board had yet to see.

After London I made quick visits to Brussels, Amsterdam and Munich, which were followed by slightly longer stays in Stockholm, Copenhagen and Helsinki. From Finland I flew to New York and stayed at the Taft, a small hotel near Times Square. When I checked in, I received a message from the CEO of Columbia Pictures with an urgent invitation for me to meet with him at his office on Fifth Avenue. With him was Bosley Crowther, the celebrated former film critic of *The New York Times* who, since his retirement as a reviewer, had been engaged as a consultant to Columbia. I was intrigued to meet Crowther who, during his long stint at *The Times*, had been generally accepted as America's leading film critic, but I was wary. Two years earlier he had virulently attacked Arthur Penn's trailblazing *Bonnie and Clyde* after seeing its world premiere at the Montreal Film Festival. He returned time and again to attacking this remarkable film in his column, and there was some suggestion that *The Times* had let him go *because* he seemed so out of touch with a film everybody was talking about and just about everyone wanted to see.

The reason for this meeting was that *Easy Rider*, Columbia's greatest money-spinner of the year, was in trouble in Australia. I was told that the film had initially been banned outright but that, after strong appeals by Colin Jones, Columbia's Australian CEO, the censors had agreed to pass it but only after they had made a considerable number of cuts which eliminated, among other things, most of the pot-smoking sequence by the camp-fire.

I had always secretly hoped that one day the Censorship Board would take a decision which would impact on the bottom line of a major Hollywood company. As long as the cuts they made in mainstream films were relatively minor, none of the American distributors would be willing to rock the boat; but the case of *Easy Rider* was different. This was potentially a major money-spinner and the cuts required by the censors would effectively gut the film. After a lengthy discussion with Crowther and lunch at 21, the famous Manhattan restaurant, the Columbia executives made it clear to me that it was now in their interests to support the Sydney and Melbourne Film Festivals in their anti-censorship campaign. Colin Jones was, at the time, head of the Motion Pictures Distributors of Australia (MPDA) and I was led to believe during the course of this lunch that he would be instructed to use his senior position in the distribution industry in Australia to persuade the other major companies to back the

Festivals in calls for censorship reform. Now that Don Chipp was Minister for Customs there seemed, for the first time, a real possibility that something positive would develop.

After leaving New York I spent the next two weeks at the Chicago Film Festival, a world-class event which had been started the year before by Michael Kutza who, nearly forty years later, is still its director. I'd already seen many of the films in the programme but I was able to make some excellent contacts and to see such contentious films – at least from a censorship point of view – as Vilgot Sjoman's *491* and *I Am Curious Yellow*. I also agreed to take part in a discussion about the current state of world cinema on a Chicago television arts program; one of my co-panellists on the programme was the novelist Harold Robbins.

On the West Coast, I paid a quick visit to San Francisco mainly to spend some time with Jo Webb. While there I also made contact with Francis Ford Coppola, a young filmmaker whose work I admired; he was the same age as me, having turned thirty earlier that year. Despite having had a box-office flop with his last film, the sensitive *The Rain People*, Coppola seemed excited about his new project, *The Conversation*, a story about surveillance; he had just completed the first draft of the screenplay of this film which would actually not be made for another five years, after Coppola's success with *The Godfather*. When *The Conversation* was released in 1974, in the wake of the Watergate revelations, it was seen by many as a response to current political events, but, as I know from first-hand experience, a draft of the film had already been written in November 1969.

Coppola had established his company, American Zoetrope, in an old warehouse in the city and he was encouraging young filmmakers to join him there in a convivial work environment. On a tour of the building he introduced me to Jim McBride, who had recently made a fine independent film, *David Holzman's Diary*, and to George Lucas, a nerdy, pale-faced youth who was busy expanding his student film into a feature-length screenplay called

THX 1138. There was little indication this rather unprepossessing young man would eventually be the creator of a massive franchise like *Star Wars*.

I then flew on to LA, where I had a number of appointments and screenings and where I paid my second visit to Columbia Studios. This time the most important film being produced on the lot was *I Walk the Line*, which John Frankenheimer, a director I very much admired, was making with Gregory Peck. Peck played a small-town sheriff and the scene being filmed was on the porch of his house at night in which he was talking to his elderly father. Frankenheimer had cast his own father-in-law in this part, but the old man wasn't a professional actor and had trouble remembering his lines. When he finally *did* deliver the lines required by the script, it was an embarrassed Peck who dried up. Once the shot was finally in the can, Frankenheimer came over to meet me and started talking to me about my 'sensational' film; I realised he had mistaken me for the Swedish director, Vilgot Sjoman, who was also bearded and wore glasses. After we set the record straight, I had a most enjoyable discussion with him and with Peck.

I was eager to see Josef von Sternberg, with whom I'd kept up a correspondence for the past two years. He had sent several handwritten letters to me since his departure from Sydney, including one from the city of his birth, Vienna. Sadly, the file in which I kept this correspondence has been lost. On 4 December, Jo, as Sternberg liked to be called by his friends, arrived at my small hotel in his elderly Jaguar and drove me back to his house, stopping on the way to buy fruit at Farmers Market. We spent the afternoon in his study, where he was eager to show me photographs and other memorabilia from the days of his career as a director. One of the most interesting items was a telegram he had received from Sergei Eisenstein concerning *An American Tragedy*, the Theodore Dreiser novel. During a brief sojourn in Hollywood in the early 1930s, Eisenstein had attempted, without success, to adapt Dreiser's novel for the screen; Sternberg eventually directed a version at Paramount in 1931. I was also fascinated to see the rare photographs in his collection, which included one taken on the set of *Duel in the Sun* which confirmed Sternberg's contention that he had directed some scenes of the epic film, which is credited only to King Vidor. Jo gave me an autographed copy of his book, *Fun in a Chinese Laundry*, and also went through it with a red pen to correct two or three errors in the text.

His wife, Meri, a teacher, and their thirteen-year-old son, Nicholas, came home late in the afternoon; Nicholas was excited to hear that I'd seen *Easy Rider* and he wanted to talk about it, but Jo seemed upset at what he considered to be idle chatter and told his son, in no uncertain terms, that 'He came to see *me*!' In the evening, Jo took us out to a Japanese restaurant, where he insisted on showing me how to use chopsticks, an art I hadn't at the time mastered. He left the table at one point to go to the men's room and Meri told me, rather anxiously, that he hadn't been well; he was supposed to be resting and wasn't meant to drive. When it was time to leave the restaurant I wanted to call a taxi, but Jo insisted that he drive me back across town to my hotel. We took a fond farewell of one another.

I flew home via Mexico City, where I saw some recent productions. A few days later, finally back in Sydney, I read in the paper that Josef von Sternberg had died at his home on 22 December, just eighteen days after our meeting. I was deeply saddened by the news that this great director, who had become a good friend, was dead.

Chapter Eleven

My role as Director of the Sydney Film Festival was a demanding one. For the first half of every year I often worked seven days a week and was behind my desk, or attending screenings, far beyond the usual hours of nine to five. By the standards of today's arts organisations, we were very understaffed and seriously underpaid. In addition, from 1969 onwards I spent up to five months a year overseas. It was obvious that I was neglecting my wife and children, but I was caught up in a situation that was difficult to control and, to be perfectly honest, I enjoyed my job as Festival Director so much that wild horses wouldn't have made me give it up. And somehow I found the time for other activities.

In February 1970 I had a call from Di St John, a Sydney journalist whom I'd met a few years earlier when she was working for the *This Day Tonight* television programme. She wanted me to meet the man she was about to marry, Brian White, who, at the time, was hosting a top-rating afternoon radio current affairs programme on 2GB. Brian and I hit it off immediately and he invited me to contribute a regular film review segment on Friday afternoons, saying – to my surprise – that he liked the sound of my voice. I was a bit nervous about this and I arrived on the first afternoon with a script, which I had written out in great detail, for a review of the Tony Richardson version of *Hamlet*. I proceeded to read this over the air. Afterwards Brian advised me that this was not the way to go about things and suggested that in future I simply talk to him, in a relaxed fashion, about the films that opened every week. I came to enjoy those chats, and Brian and I became good friends. When, some time later, he became editor of a short-lived offshoot of *Vogue* called *Men in Vogue*, he asked me to contribute the film reviews, and when he wrote his excellent book on the media, *White on the Media* (1975), he autographed my copy with the generous words: 'To David Stratton, a good friend who, whether he realises it or not, has had a lot to do with this book.'

After a few years with 2GB, Brian moved to 2SM and I moved with him; but that was short-lived and soon he relocated to Melbourne, where he managed 3AW for several years. When he returned to Sydney to work for 2UE he asked me if I would resume my Friday afternoon reviews with him, which I happily did – until the sad day in May 1990 when Brian died suddenly, aged only fifty, soon after returning from Turkey, where he had covered the Anzac service. I missed Brian a lot and it was difficult to accept that someone so young and vital had died so suddenly. Since Brian's death I have been reviewing films on 2UE on Friday afternoons with John Stanley, who took his place, and have hardly missed a week.

When I joined the ABC some years later, some people there thought it was strange that I continued with my 2UE broadcasting slot, but I felt loyalty to the station and, especially, to the broadcaster who had supported me over the years. Even when I'm overseas I try to phone in with my weekly broadcast; there's something strangely comforting, when you're in a foreign country, in hearing an Australian voice report on traffic conditions in Sydney while you wait to go on air. John, who has a winning sense of humour, often makes good-natured reference to my complete lack of knowledge of, and interest in, any kind of sporting event; he also never lets me forget the occasion when my weekly live-to-air broadcast took place when I was in Los Angeles having dinner at the home of Phillip Noyce and his wife, Jan Sharp. Among the guests at dinner that evening were Nicole Kidman and Uma Thurman – I was seated between them – and when it was time to go on air they thought it would be amusing to try to make me laugh.

I'd been acquainted with Nicole for many years and always appreciated her down-to-earth approach. When *The Portrait of a Lady* premiered at the Venice Film Festival in 1996 she was so anxious to learn my opinion that she gave me not only the number of the hotel where she was staying but the pseudonyms she and her then-husband, Tom Cruise, were using. I wasn't surprised that Kidman and Cruise had been forced to use cover names to protect them from the less responsible members of the media; I have a profound hatred for the paparazzi who make the lives of people like Nicole a misery and for the trashy newspapers and magazines that pay them to invade the most private moments of actors and others who surely, despite their celebrity status, deserve a degree of personal space and privacy.

But back to the early 1970s. I was at this time also contributing occasional articles on film to *The Age*, the Melbourne daily broadsheet. The newspaper's critic, Colin Bennett, whom I had met through Erwin Rado, had suggested that I might write a few general articles on film during the summer holidays. The first piece I contributed was on the British director David Lean, based on a meeting I'd had with him the previous year, and it was well enough received that, for a while, I was invited to contribute more articles.

Now that I was effectively working as a regular film reviewer for radio I started attending all the previews of forthcoming films, which were arranged on a regular basis by the various film distributors. Usually these were straightforward affairs: the films would screen in small theatrettes located in the offices of the distributors and the reviewers would be handed production notes, which included a cast and credit list, before the screening began. I've been to thousands of such screenings over the past forty years, not only in Sydney but also in London, Paris, New York and Los Angeles. But one preview stands out.

It was early in 1970 and the film in question was a British production with an ungainly title: *Can Heironymous Merkin Ever Forget Mercy Humppe and Find True Happiness?* It was co-scripted and directed by the actor Anthony Newley, who had scored a success with the stage musical *Stop the World I Want to Get Off!*, which I'd seen in the West End before leaving Britain. The new film had received withering reviews and it seemed that its only *raison d'être* was the copious amounts of female nudity on display. Some indication of this could be gleaned from smuggled-in copies of a recent banned copy of *Playboy*, but the censors had, of course, removed all of the film's titillating scenes, leaving behind a pointless and singularly unamusing shell.

The distributor of this wreck was Universal, and the company's publicist at the time, Hans van Pinxteren (later manager of the cinema in Roseville), hit upon an original idea to rekindle interest in what was obviously a disaster. He invited a selection of male reviewers to a screening of the film which took place not at Universal's Pelican Street theatrette but on Goat Island in Sydney Harbour. On a chilly April evening the scribes were taken by boat to the island, where a makeshift screen and an ancient 35-mm projector were set up, and where there were generous amounts of beer and wine on hand to assuage the jaded palate. More than that: a stripper had been hired for the occasion, and before the screening began she decorously removed her clothes, presumably to show the startled film critics what we were about *not* to see in the film. In the event, the screening itself was even more of a fizzle than might have been expected; the projector functioned for a while and then sputtered out, so another, more traditional, screening of the film had to be arranged a few days later. Some of the reviewers were a bit worse for wear by this time, but we were taken back to Circular Quay, where the unfortunate stripper was abandoned. I was chivalrous enough to offer her a lift home.

On the censorship issue, I had the full support of the SFF Committee. I think Ross was concerned that Dorothy Holt, one of the Vice-Presidents of the Committee, might, because of her Liberal Party connections (her husband, Edgar, had been an office bearer of the party), baulk at our campaign but, on the contrary, she was totally supportive. On the question of four-letter words, which were still strictly forbidden in films, she once remarked: 'I cannot conceive that any combination of Her Majesty's alphabet could possibly be obscene.'

The reforms were taking a long time to be put in place and at the seventeenth SFF in 1970 two films were banned. *A Married Couple* was a fly-on-the-wall Canadian documentary by Allan King, in which the director observes a couple in their thirties during a period when their marriage is starting to disintegrate. There's no sex in the film – rather, the issue for the censors was language: there were four-letter words and plenty of them. The other banned film was from Sweden; Jonas Cornell's second feature, after the now notorious *Hugs and Kisses*, was *Som natt och Dag* (*Like Night and Day*), which deals with tortured relationships in contemporary Stockholm. Towards the end of the film there was a very brief scene of a coupling between three people: the central character, Agneta Ekmanner, her lover, Gosta Ekman, and her sister, Claire Wikholm. We had printed a warning advice in the Festival catalogue about this scene but, nevertheless, Prowse and his Board were not willing to let it pass. I suspect that Chipp was a bit frustrated about these bans because I don't think he welcomed the inevitable publicity.

After the Festival Chipp did something his predecessors would never have done. He arranged a screening in Sydney of both films, and invited members of the media and state and federal politicians to attend. He gave me the opportunity to introduce the screening, which I did, and the invited audience seemed impressed with *A Married Couple*, despite its bad language. They were clearly bored by *Like Night and Day*; but after Chipp had talked to a few people at the end of the screening, he whispered in my ear: 'I think you've made your point.'

Under the terms of our loose agreement, it was Erwin's turn to go overseas in 1970 to select films for the 1971 Festivals, but he had decided he didn't want to travel that year. Once again I found myself living out of a suitcase, attending the same events and visiting most of the same places I had the previous year. In Budapest that August I saw, at the Magyar Film Laboratories, a rough cut of István Szabó's third feature, *Szerelmesfilm* (*Love Film*), the deeply touching story of two young people whose love affair is interrupted by the Cold War – he lives in Budapest, she in a provincial city in France. The film had been invited for Venice.

After spending a few days in Budapest I made a side trip to Bucharest by train, and was welcomed by the people at Romania Film, but I was very disappointed with the new films on offer. On my last evening in the attractive but impoverished city, I was taken by the CEO of Romania Film and his deputy to what was supposed to be the best restaurant in town. They told me I didn't need a menu; they would order the specialty of the house for me. During the dinner I was supposed to tell them which films I'd chosen for Sydney, but in fact, apart from a short animated film, I hadn't found anything worth inviting. While I was breaking this news, the food that my hosts had ordered arrived: plates of rather large, greasy-looking liver, accompanied by a few chips. I loathe liver and find even the smell of it distasteful. My companions tucked into their food with considerable enthusiasm while I played with my meat, eventually managing to tip it into the cloth napkin on my lap and hope they hadn't noticed. From my lap the offending meat went into my pocket, and it seemed as though I'd got away with it – until we got up to leave and I displayed a large brown stain across the area of my crotch.

The next evening I took the train back to Budapest, across the Transylvanian Alps. I had a meal in the dining car, but the menu was written in Romanian and Hungarian and the waiter didn't speak English or French. There were no other diners from whom I might have sought advice and so I was forced to point at something on the list and hope for the best. Just as the waiter arrived with the food, all the lights on the train went out. With the previous night's experiences foremost in my mind I smelt the mystery food very suspiciously, but it turned out to be a kind of stew which proved to be very tasty. The lights went on again just as I finished it.

One of the films in competition at Venice in 1970 was Jerzy Skolimowski's *Deep End*, which was set in London but which had been made in a film studio in Munich. It was an intimate but intensely filmed drama involving two young people, played by Jane Asher and John Moulder-Brown, and I thought it was well up to the standard of the young Polish director's best work. Since I had met him in Warsaw four years earlier, Skolimowski had learnt to speak excellent English, and we hung out together in Venice; he promised to come to Sydney the following year with the film. I also met Bernardo Bertolucci, whose television feature *Strategia del Ragno* (*The Spider's Strategy*) was screening. At Berlin a few weeks earlier the young Italian had scored a major success with his magnificent film *Il Conformista* (*The Conformist*) and there seemed a good chance he might also be able to come to Australia the following June, bringing the two films with him. I had to remind myself that I had already extended an invitation to Akira Kurosawa, whose film *Dodeska-den* was nearing completion, and I wondered if we would ever be able to afford to invite three such important guests.

Szabó's *Love Film* screened in Venice with great success, but I was sad to see that he had removed a couple of scenes since the rough cut I'd seen in Budapest the month before. I've seen the film many times since and I still miss those deleted sequences. Skolimowski, Bertolucci and Szabó were all about the same age as I was and we spent a lot of time together in Venice that year. I also got to know and like Szabó's actors, Andras Balint and Judith Halasz.

I did a bit of zigzagging across Europe that summer; after Venice I spent time in Paris, where there was an unusually strong line-up of films, including Claude Chabrol's intense portrait of a jealous husband, *La femme infidele* (*The Unfaithful Wife*). It had occurred to me that Chabrol, an admirer of Hitchcock and the prolific director of wickedly clever thrillers about the world of the bourgeoisie, might make an excellent guest at some time in the future, and Mosk gave me his address so that I might be able to make contact with him when the opportunity arose; sadly, however, it never did.

In London that October I had an encounter with a young American student who would become another firm friend. I met Todd McCarthy through Linda Strawn, an American freelance writer, and a dead ringer for actress Ali McGraw, who I had encountered at the Karlovy Vary and Venice Film Festivals during the summer. She had met Todd earlier in Cannes, and when I got in touch with her in London (via American Express, whose mailing service I always used when I was travelling) she brought Todd with her to our meeting. Later on, Todd found work as an assistant – first to Elaine May and then to Roger Corman – before becoming, eventually, the senior film critic for *Variety*, a position he holds, with distinction, to this day.

While I was in London that autumn I was invited to a special screening at the Barbican of my favourite film of all time, *Singin' in the Rain*. I had seen this masterpiece several times since I first experienced it as a teenager and I have always loved its energy and style, its infectious sense of humour, the skill of the direction by Gene Kelly and Stanley Donen, and the fascinating era in which it's set – Hollywood during the transition from silents to talkies. Kelly had come over from LA to introduce the film and I observed that he looked not a day older than he did when it was made almost twenty years earlier – there wasn't a grey hair on his head. After the screening I was introduced to him and I told him how much I admired his work. I was thinking of recording a career interview with him on audio tape for possible use on 2GB and he readily agreed to be interviewed, but not in London because his visit there was a very brief one. However when I told him that I would be in LA the following month he gave me his home address and telephone number and told me to call him.

Once again, I flew home via America. Cinema was changing, and radical films like John Avildsen's *Joe* (about a redneck anti-hippy), Paul Morrissey's *Trash* (with Joe Delassandro as an impotent drug addict) and Bob Rafelson's *Five Easy Pieces* were screening in cinemas. So was Mike Sarne's devastatingly poor adaptation of Gore Vidal's funny novel *Myra Breckinridge*.

It was at the San Francisco Festival that October that I met Pierre Rissient for the first time. Pierre was a French film enthusiast who worked in Paris as a publicist in partnership with the future director Bertrand Tavernier. Earlier in his career he had championed the work of American directors such as John Ford, Howard Hawks, Jules Dassin and others, and had helped programme a small Paris arthouse cinema which rediscovered many of the works of these gifted filmmakers. Pierre had also been on the margins of the *nouvelle vague* and had worked as one of Godard's assistants on *A bout de souffle*. He not only loved films, he personally knew many of the Hollywood greats; Fritz Lang and Jean Renoir (who lived in Hollywood) were close friends. Pierre, who had a seemingly endless supply of colourful stories, was excellent company.

Skolimowski, Bertolucci and Szabó were also in San Francisco that year, and I quickly decided that this was my ideal film festival, the kind of event I would like Sydney to be. The Festival

Director was Claude Jarman Jr, a former child actor whose most famous appearance had been in *The Yearling*; every evening for two weeks he programmed two new films representing the best of international cinema, the same kind of films that we screened in Sydney and Melbourne. By day, the Festival venue – the imposing Palace of Fine Arts, located near the Golden Gate Bridge – was given over to Albert Johnson, an African-American blessed with a hypnotic charm, who programmed 'tributes' to Hollywood greats and always persuaded them to attend in person. These Johnson tributes were famous: the previous year they had included Bette Davis and Fred Astaire. In 1970 he paid tribute to Frank Capra, Vincente Minnelli and David Lean, all of whom I met because Jarman and Johnson gave me free access to the Green Room backstage. For a film-lover like me it was a once-in-a-lifetime opportunity to meet these giants of the cinema; I sat with Minnelli and his wife during a screening of his Van Gogh biopic *Lust for Life*, but was saddened to see how badly the rich colours had faded.

One day during the Festival I rented a car and drove north to Bodega Bay, where Alfred Hitchcock had filmed *The Birds* about seven years earlier. I bought a postcard there and seeing Claude Chabrol's name in my address book prompted me to send it to him, even though we'd never met. I knew him to be an admirer of Hitchcock, so I wrote: 'I'm in Bodega Bay, where Hitchcock filmed *The Birds*, thinking of you.' Strangely enough, I never got to meet Chabrol in person over the years until 2004, when I encountered him in Venice. I asked him if he ever received the postcard thirty-four years earlier and he became quite excited: 'So it was you!' he exclaimed.

From San Francisco I phoned Gene Kelly and he told me he could set aside a day to see me at his home. I was scheduled to fly back from LA to Sydney that evening, so I caught the first flight from San Francisco in the morning and, unable to afford a taxi, stored my bags in an airport locker and took the bus from LAX to the Beverly Hills Hotel. From there I walked to Kelly's home on Rodeo Drive and rang the bell. The door was opened by a little old man who was completely bald; at first I thought it was Kelly's father until he greeted me with that distinctively husky voice. This was Gene Kelly, sans toupee!

He was a marvellous host who entertained me in the living room of a house whose decor demonstrated his love of all things French. On the walls hung impressionist paintings and framed posters; there was even a Paris street sign. He talked about his career in great detail, contradicting a story Minnelli had told me the previous week about the climax to their film *The Pirate*, prepared us a light lunch, and seemed in no hurry to send me away. Finally I realised I must leave to return to the airport for my flight to Sydney. He wanted to call me a taxi but when I seemed hesitant, he understood that I was low on funds and drove me there himself. I found him to be an extremely kind and generous man, and my day with him remains one of my most pleasant memories.

As is often the case, my plans for the 1971 Festival didn't work out the way I hoped. Kurosawa had indicated, via Madam Kawakita, that he was willing to come and we had programmed a retrospective of his films. However, he was badly affected by the poor box-office response in Japan to his personal production, *Dodeska-den*, which had closely followed the humiliation of being fired by Darryl F. Zanuck from the production of *Tora! Tora! Tora!*. In a fit of depression, the giant of Japanese cinema had attempted suicide. Thankfully he survived, but coming to Australia was obviously now the last thing on his mind. Nor was Bernardo Bertolucci able to come. That left Jerzy Skolimowski who, true to his word, showed up, dressed for the summer rather than the winter – he borrowed a jacket of mine which he never returned.

Soon after Skolimowski's arrival in Sydney I made a mistake that I still regret. Jerzy was upset to find that his film *Deep End* was programmed in Sydney near the end of the Festival, after he'd been to Melbourne and back. He took the view that he wouldn't 'get laid' until his film had been seen and so he demanded that it be screened earlier. He suggested I swap it with *The Conformist.* 'My friend Bernardo wouldn't mind,' he said. Foolishly, I agreed to his request but I hadn't thought it through, and a large number Festival subscribers, who had planned their schedule already, were furious at the change.

An innovation at the 1970 Festival had been a competition for Australian short films. We had for some time experienced difficulty programming locally made shorts. Features weren't a problem, because there were hardly any of them, but the selection, or even worse the rejection, of local short films almost always caused a stir. From 1970 onwards, we instituted a competition for short films. Films running less than an hour were eligible to enter in one of three categories – Documentary, Fiction and Experimental (subsequently the latter was changed to General) – and were pre-judged by three viewing panels, who viewed them at the SFF office in the city. Twelve finalists were selected, four in each section, and these were screened at the Festival and seen by a different judging panel. The event was sponsored by the cigarette company Benson and Hedges, and became known as the Benson and Hedges Awards. Not surprisingly, we copped a fair bit of flak for aligning ourselves with a tobacco giant. One of the finalists that first year was *Could It Happen Here*, which had been made by a student at North Sydney Boys' High School. The boy, Chris Noonan, was too young to attend the screening of his film. Twenty-five years later, Noonan would direct the much-loved *Babe*.

There was always a special interest in the Fiction Section, and the four finalists in 1971 were Chris Lofven's *Part Two: The Beginning*, Michael Thornhill's *The Machine Gun*, Brian Davies's *Brake Fluid* and Peter Weir's *Homesdale*. The three judges of the finalists were Skolimowski, Jörn Donner, who was making a return visit to Sydney at his own expense, and Sydney film critic Beverley Tivey.

Weir's film had been by far the most popular with the local audience and so there was considerable surprise when Davies's film, a Melbourne-made production very influenced by the French *nouvelle vague*, was singled out by the judges. At a reception afterwards the actress Kate Fitzpatrick, who had appeared in Weir's film, berated the judges in general and Skolimowski in particular; but she wound up leaving with him and he disappeared for several days after that until I tracked the couple down in the home of director Jim Sharman to remind Skolimoski of his obligations to the Festival.

When the usual post-mortems were conducted by the Committee that year there was considerable criticism of me over my handling of Skolimowski's visit. I was accused of spending too much time swanning around with the visiting 'star' director and not enough time keeping control of the Festival. I was certainly guilty of making an unnecessary change of programme which I should never have done, but I actually spent very little time with Skolimowski, who was quite capable of looking after himself. Unfortunately, his amorous activities caused him to be unavailable for some of the interviews we had arranged for him. Some members of the Committee, in my absence, called for my dismissal, and I learnt later that there was a school of thought that Ian McPherson was too close to me to take the necessary action called for by his role as President.

As it happened, Ian had chosen this moment to spend several months overseas with his wife, Trish. Ross Tzannes was voted to take over the Presidency and I discovered later that his brief was, in effect, to sort me out. I don't remember in detail the discussions Ross and I had about the situation, but I felt sobered by the experience. The change of President ushered in a highly productive era for the SFF; Ross stayed in the Presidency until after I had resigned my position twelve years later. We understood each other very well and we worked hard in our different ways to make the SFF as successful as it could possibly be.

Ever since I had started work as Director of the SFF I had, thanks to the generosity of Phil Jones, used the American newspaper *Variety* as a major source of information. *Variety* had been the brainchild of a colourful New Yorker named Sime Silverman, who had published the first issue on 16 December 1905. The aim of the paper was to cover all forms of show business – theatre, vaudeville, circus, burlesque, minstrels, fairs and circuses. Within a year *Variety* was reviewing films and as the years went by the paper incorporated coverage of all forms of entertainment – radio, television, the recording industry, video, DVDs. *Variety* was originally very much a family affair; Sime and his colleagues were friends without, at first, much money but with boundless enthusiasm. Legend has it that, not long after publication began, William Randolph Hearst offered Sime $1.2 million for the paper and he turned it down. Sime appointed Abel Green editor in 1931 and it was largely thanks to Green that, after Sime's death, the paper stayed very much the same as it had always been. The language of *Variety* – terse, hard-boiled, amusing, very New York – was famous, as were its headlines ('Wall Street Lays an Egg' was the first headline after the 1929 Crash). In 1956 Sime's grandson, Syd Silverman, had taken over the publishing of the paper.

In the 1960s and 70s, *Variety* was printed with a form of ink which tended to get all over your fingers as you read the paper. I was always amused by a story Mosk used to relate. He was awoken very late one night in his Paris apartment by a phone call from the director Henri Verneuil. 'Mr Moskowitz,' complained the filmmaker. 'I have been reading your newspaper in bed. Now I have to change the sheets!'

In addition to my great friendship with *Variety*'s Paris bureau chief, I found, as I travelled the world, that in every major city there was usually a *Variety* 'mugg', as they were called, who would be of invaluable assistance with advice, contacts and moral support. Bob Hawkins, one of Syd's most trusted lieutenants, seemed to cover whatever territory was required, and turned up at many of the major film festivals. The Rome bureau chief was Hank Werba; in London, there was the exuberant Roger Watkins; from Copenhagen, Keith Keller covered all of Scandinavia; in Madrid, there was Peter Besas, who became the paper's archivist and historian; in Chicago, there was Frank Segers, a specialist in Asian cinema; and so on.

The editorial office in New York was located at 154 West 46th Street. The editor sat on the first floor at the front of the building, where a large window enabled him to look down on the passing parade in the street below; the printing presses were out in the back. You expected to see James Cagney or Joan Blondell pass by at any moment. In addition to the box-office reports, the news, the gossip and the obits, *Variety* published reviews of just about every film which screened publicly in most countries of the world. The reviewers signed their pieces with traditional four-letter nick-names – Mosk, Werb, Besa, Kell, Hawk.

In the late 1960s there had been a *Variety* stringer in Melbourne called Raymond Stanley who contributed the occasional review, but I had noticed that these contributions had recently ceased. Not that there were many Australian films to review in those days, and *Variety* didn't cover short films. But in February 1971 I saw *Three to Go*, a three-part film produced by Gil Brealey for the Commonwealth Film Unit which featured the work of three young, up-and-coming directors: Oliver Howes, Brian Hannant and Peter Weir. The film was impressive and I thought it was a shame that it would probably not be covered in *Variety*, so I decided to submit a review myself.

I copied the paper's house style as closely as I could and wrote a very positive review ('. . . a large step towards valid, wholly-indigenous local film production'); I signed it 'Strat' and mailed it to the editor in New York. It hadn't occurred to me that 'Strat' consists of five letters, not four, and it obviously didn't occur to the editor either because my review duly appeared in the paper on 7 April 1971. There had been no correspondence from New York about this but I waited eagerly to see how much my fee would be. No money arrived and nobody contacted me. I learnt later that stringers were expected to invoice the paper for their work. Disappointed at the complete silence from the other end, I decided not to write any more unsolicited reviews. To this day I've never been paid for the review of *Three to Go*.

It was not originally intended that I should travel overseas in 1971 because I had now been two years in a row and it was Erwin Rado's turn. Erwin was preparing to leave to select films on behalf of both Festivals when a crisis blew up with FIAPF. Alphonse Brisson made one of his occasional demands that we sever the links between Sydney and Melbourne or lose accreditation. In this emergency the Committee authorised me to go to Paris and to join Erwin to make a joint approach to Brisson. This approach proved successful and we were given yet another reprieve.

My visit to Paris that September was marked by a curious occurrence. Over the past five years my marriage had been greatly affected by the onerous job I had undertaken and by the long months I spent overseas or in my Sydney office. I had proved to be a neglectful husband and ineffectual father. I had also indulged in the occasional affair while away from home, most notably one with a Finnish actress I had met at the 1969 Moscow Film Festival.

When I had been in Budapest the previous year I had noticed a very attractive receptionist who worked behind the desk at the Royal Hotel. She always smiled very sweetly at me and she seemed to be very friendly. My last night in Budapest that year was a Saturday and, left to my own devices, I asked this young woman if she could recommend a place where I could spend the evening. She suggested a bar on a boat moored on the Danube and she told me that was where she was going to be that evening. It was obviously an invitation, and, sure enough, when I arrived at the boat, she was there. Her name was Elizabeth and we had a pleasant, though inconclusive, evening together.

Now, over a year later, as Erwin and I left the offices of FIAPF on the Champs Elysées in Paris, there was Elizabeth, standing on the pavement. I knew how difficult it was for Hungarians to obtain permission to travel abroad in those days, which made her presence there unusual enough, let alone the coincidence that she should be there, at that spot, at that very moment. She greeted me with affectionate enthusiasm and we went for a drink at a bar, where she told me she was staying in a flat that had been loaned to her by friends who were visiting South America. To cut a long story short, I moved out of my hotel and into her flat for the rest of my stay in Paris. Erwin very much disapproved, and maybe he was a little suspicious too. I must say that I had my suspicions as well. Elizabeth seemed thrilled to see me and amazed at the coincidence that had led to our paths crossing; she also seemed eager to embark on a brief affair. But there were moments, especially in bed, when it seemed to me that it was all an act; that she didn't really feel as enthusiastic as she was pretending to be. It was a nagging feeling that stayed with me for the few days we spent together.

One evening Gene Moskowitz came to dinner at the flat and Elizabeth cooked him a Hungarian meal. He, too, seemed to think there was something odd about the entire situation; after all, this was at a time when the newspapers and cinemas were filled with stories about espionage. But why would the Hungarians want to spy on me, or perhaps, through me, on Hungarian-born friends, like Mosk and Erwin? I never knew the answer. Elizabeth and I spent a few pleasant days in Paris, during which time I took her to see the James Bond movie *Thunderball*, which she enjoyed although it was dubbed into French, and then she caught a train back to Budapest. I wrote to her, but never received an answer. The following year, there was a different receptionist at the Royal Hotel.

By the end of the year I was back once again in Australia. I had stayed in touch with Tim Burstall after the disappointing screening of *2,000 Weeks* at the SFF and our subsequent stay in Moscow and I was pleased to be invited by him to the premiere of his new film, *Stork*, which took place in Melbourne at the Palais Theatre, St Kilda, home of the MFF, in December 1971. This funny screen adaptation of David Williamson's play was, in contrast to *2,000 Weeks*, a triumph, with wonderful performances from tall and gangly Bruce Spence, as the eponymous Stork, and Jacki Weaver as his diminutive love interest. So successful was the film commercially that it must really be considered the beginning of the Australian film revival. Unlike the Michael Powell films, or such other recent trailblazers as Nicolas Roeg's *Walkabout* and Ted Kotcheff's *Wake in Fright*, which were both, in their different ways, quite remarkable, *Stork* was made by an Australian for a specifically Australian audience. I was delighted for Burstall.

It was thanks to Burstall that I was given my first television assignment; Brian Adams was the producer of the ABC TV arts programme *Spectrum*; I had met him when Josef von Sternberg was interviewed for the programme, and now he asked me to interview Burstall about *Stork*. The interview, filmed in black and white, still exists in the ABC's archives.

On another visit to Melbourne about six months later I was invited to Burstall's home in Fitzroy for lunch. Tim's wife, Betty, had prepared a number of salad dishes, and the guests had been asked to bring a bottle of wine and to help themselves. I arrived at about the same time as Bob Ellis, the Sydney writer, and playwright David Williamson and his wife, Kristin. Ellis was wearing a duffle coat and clutching a bottle of Mateus Rosé. We moved to the table talking about various things while Ellis struggled to extract the cork from his bottle. Eventually, he reached into the pocket of his duffle coat and produced a handkerchief which he wrapped round the bottle opener. As the cork finally emerged so, too, did a used condom which fell out of the handkerchief and into a bowl of Greek salad. David Williamson and I both observed this unsavoury spectacle and Bob, seeing the expressions

My maternal grandparents, Jessie and Frank Wells. It was Jessie who introduced me to the cinema.

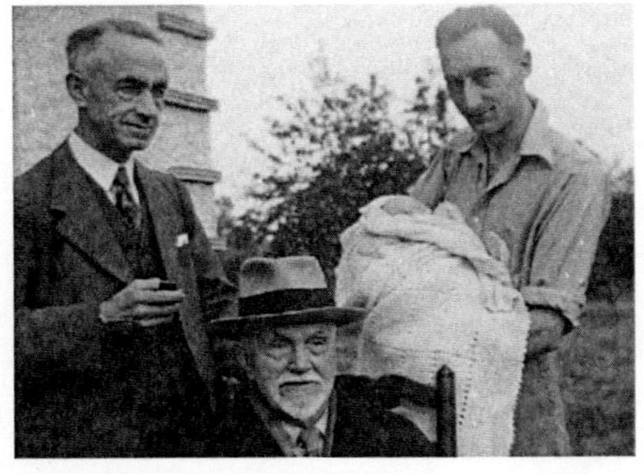

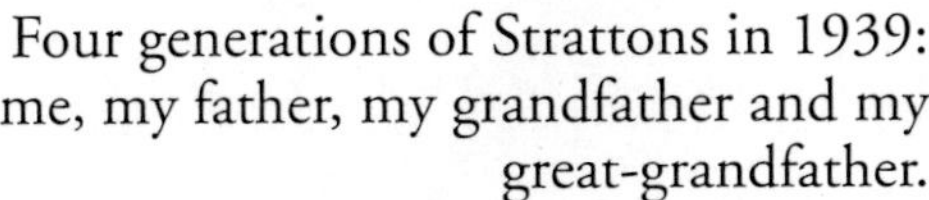

Four generations of Strattons in 1939: me, my father, my grandfather and my great-grandfather.

At Chafyn Grove School, Salisbury, with my best friends, John Martin (*left*) and John Newman (*right*), and the headmaster's dog. *Photo courtesy of John Martin*

With my father, before he left for the Far East.

A photograph I took of Gerry Bartlett, who brought me to Australia, with his wife-to-be, Gwenda (1963). *Photo courtesy of Dr Gerry Bartlett*

With Glenn Ford on the set of *The Long Ride Home* at Columbia Studios (1966).

Facing the media with Josef von Sternberg (1967).

With director John Frankenheimer (1969).

Stig Björkman, director of *Jag Alskar, Du Alskar (I Love, You Love)*, the film that brought our fight against censorship to public attention at the 1969 Sydney Film Festival. *Photo courtesy of Stig Björkman*

Gene Moskowitz – Mosk – my mentor, in the early 1970s.

With Kate Fitzpatrick at the Sydney Film Festival opening night, 1974. I'm wearing the clothes Robert Redford wore in *The Sting*, courtesy of Universal Pictures!

On stage at the State Theatre with Warren Beatty (1975).

With director Miloš Forman (1975).

With Peter Weir at the Sydney Film Festival (1975).

In middle Europe (1976).

With Michelangelo Antonioni at the Sydney Film Festival (1976).

Agra, India, with Akira Kurosawa, Michelangelo Antonioni and Satyajit Ray (1977).

With actor Elizabeth Alexander on the set of *The Killing of Angel Street* (1981).

At the 1982 Berlin Film Festival. *From left to right:* Joe Hembus, James Stewart, Brigitte Fossey, me

The International Jury of the 1982 Berlin Film Festival. *From left to right:* me, Helma Sanders-Brahms, Sergei Baskakov, Joe Hembus, Joan Fontaine, Mrinal Sen, Brigitte Fossey, Gian-Luigi Rondi, László Lugossy

Devizes, 1985. *From left to right:* my brother, Roger, my parents, Mary and Jim, and me

With Clint Eastwood (1985).

With Barry Humphries (1986).

With Paul Hogan (1987).

In Hong Kong with author Linda Jaivin, and Zhang Yimou and Chen Kaige, two of the most famous Chinese directors (1987).

The *Variety* team at Cannes in 1988. *Back row:* Bob Hawkins, Maril Thomas, Jack Kindred, two colleagues, Hal Scott, Mike Evans, Mark Silverman, Keith Keller, Bruce Alderman, Hy Hollinger, Frank Segers, Don Groves, Frank Meyer, me, Blake Murdoch. *Front row:* Larry Cohn, Hank Werba, Peter Besas, Edna Fainaru, Roger Watkins, Marty Feldman, Art Anderman

With Roman Polanski (1988).

With director George Miller and actress Gosia Dobrowolska (1990).

With Wim Wenders in the outback (1990).

Assisting cameraman Robby Muller filming Max von Sydow and Jeanne Moreau in *Until the End of the World* (1990).

With Margaret Pomeranz on the set of *The Movie Show* in 1993.

The 1994 Venice International Jury. *From left to right:* me, Carlo Verdone, Festival Director Gillo Pontecorvo, David Lynch, Mario Vargas Llosa, Gaston Kaboré, Nagisa Oshima, Olivier Assayas, Margherita Buy, Uma Thurman

Relaxing, post-Cannes, in the early 1990s. *From left to right:* Dan Fainaru, Derek Elley, me, Edna Fainaru

The Movie Show team at SBS (2000). *From left to right:* Brendan Walls, Margaret Pomeranz, me, Terry Toaldo, Deb Spinocchia, Electra Manikakis

Variety farewell lunch at Cannes in 2003. *Back row:* Lisa Nesselson, Deborah Young, Scott Foundas, Derek Elley. *Front row:* Todd McCarthy, me, Pierre Rissient

on our faces, and realising what had happened, reached into the salad and retrieved the offending rubber. 'I suppose you think I'm very old-fashioned,' was all he said. We all avoided that particular salad.

Brian Adams also asked me to interview the visiting American director Peter Bogdanovich for *Spectrum;* his film *The Last Picture Show* was the movie of the moment in 1972. During the course of the interview I asked Bogdanovich if he was influenced by John Ford and he denied it; many years later, filmmaker George Hickenlooper, who was making a documentary about Bogdanovich, called me to ask permission to use my question and Bogdanovich's answer in his film, because in later years Bogdanovich always acknowledged the influence of Ford. The back of my head can be glimpsed in Hickenlooper's film as I ask the question. In 2006 I met Bogdanovich again and reminded him of the incident. 'You're the one who got me in trouble,' was his reply.

Events on the censorship front, meanwhile, were coming to a head. Despite the fact that I sensed that the commercial distributors were, behind the scenes, pushing for reform, Australian cinemas continued to screen films which showed obvious signs of censorship interference. Robert Altman's *That Cold Day in the Park* and his Cannes prizewinner *M*A*S*H* were two of the casualties, but there were many others. We were given the strong impression that Don Chipp was also seeking a solution to the problem but, in the meantime, I was determined not to play it safe with programming in order not to rock the boat, as some people advised. At no time did I ever fail to invite a film I wanted for the Festival because I feared it might cause censorship difficulties but, at the same time, I never invited a mediocre film just in order to create a censorship sensation.

At last, in the second half of 1971, the Sydney and Melbourne Film Festivals were formally advised that films imported for these events would no longer have to be actually viewed by the Film Censorship Board. Instead, we would be required to furnish details (title, country of origin, synopsis, running time, etc) to the Board after which we would automatically receive a censorship classification valid for Festival screening only. At the same time, an R-classification was introduced for commercial films. The battle had been won – at least for the time being. I was elated that the principles I had stood for had been vindicated. Ross Tzannes, Ian McPherson and Erwin Rado, who had contributed so much to the success of our campaign, shared my delight at the outcome of our five-year campaign.

The R-rating was introduced just in time to allow a new wave of bolder films to be screened commercially in Australia without censorship interference. I believe that the first R-classified film publicly screened was Robert Altman's revisionist 'western' *McCabe and Mrs. Miller.* I firmly believe that the Festival's campaign had the effect of allowing the screening in this country of films like *A Clockwork Orange*, *Straw Dogs* and *Last Tango in Paris*, all of which played, uncut, over the next few years. The R-rating was also a boon to the fledgling local film industry, whose early successes were raunchy comedies like the *Barry McKenzie* and *Alvin Purple* films, which were made by Bruce Beresford and Tim Burstall respectively.

Of course, not everyone was happy with the changes Chipp had made. About eighteen years later, there was a fuss over the release of Martin Scorsese's *The Last Temptation of Christ*, which the Festival of Light and other conservative Christian groups wanted banned. On the evening the film opened in Sydney I was walking past the cinema where the premiere was taking place when I noticed a large crowd of demonstrators outside. I paused for a moment to watch and an elderly lady approached me. She seemed very pleasant and asked if I was David Stratton. When I replied that I was she told me I had changed her life. 'Many years ago,' she said, 'I saw you on television speaking against censorship. I listened to what you said, and the next day I joined the Festival of Light.'

In 1972, the SFF, which had made a small but significant profit every year since its inception, moved its office again. Suzie Tzannes had noticed that a two-storey house was for sale in Glebe Point Road, and we managed to acquire it. It was a beautiful building with ornately carved ceilings and plenty of space for offices and a screening room. There was one problem, though. The area wasn't zoned for business and the only solution, according to Leichhardt Council, was that it be both a residence *and* an office. Accordingly, Modesta Gentile made the top floor of the building her home and the ground floor was converted into offices, screening room and film storage area. A few years later, after Modesta left the Festival, the restriction eased, and the entire building was taken over for offices. To help offset the large costs involved – the building was sold to us for what was then the hefty sum of $44,000 – it was suggested that the Sydney office of the Australian Film Institute also be located there, and that the AFI pay us a small rent and share secretarial costs. Erwin Rado, who was trying to lessen his workload, had recently stepped down as the Director of the AFI and his replacement, Richard Brennan, was a good friend of mine. However, after a year, Richard left the AFI to concentrate on producing films, and his replacement, David Roe, saw no need for a Sydney base and terminated the arrangement.

Meanwhile, I basked in the obvious relief of not having to face any more censorship problems. The new censor-free era, and the resulting greater ease in the importation of the films themselves, plus our increased international status, meant that the SFF was entering a golden age. I can give two practical examples of how the lifting of censorship affected us. In 1973, we decided to present a special programme of previously censored films. At the time the SFF was still taking place at the Wintergarden, but, with the appointment of a new CEO at Greater Union, David Williams, we were finally in negotiation to move to the State Theatre from 1974. As a kind of test run we presented, immediately after the 1973 Festival proper had concluded, a special season of eight banned films at the State, for which a separate subscription ticket was required. The programme included the already legendary *Performance*, the Nicolas Roeg/Donald Cammell film starring Mick Jagger about 'swinging' London, as well as *I Am Curious Yellow* and, finally, *I Love, You Love*. We sold out all of the 2000-plus seats of the State, and with the proceeds we were able to complete payment for the house in Glebe Point Road. We now owed no money to anyone, plus we owned our own office. No wonder we were confident.

Four years later I invited Nagisa Oshima's very controversial *Ai no corrida* (*In the Realm of the Senses*) to the 1977 SFF. When we announced that this Japanese film, which was notorious for its actual sex scenes, was to be part of the programme, I received a call from Richard Prowse telling me he wanted to see it prior to the Festival screening. I pointed out to him that his request was not in accordance with the agreement we had with what was now the Attorney-General's department (responsibility for censorship had shifted from Customs to the AG under the Whitlam Government). In my view, I did not have to let Prowse see the film in advance of the Festival screening and I had no intention of doing so. Instead I invited him and every member of his Board to attend the screening at the Festival, which he agreed to do. Before the film commenced I warned the audience about its content and announced that latecomers who had missed my warning would not be admitted. The reason for this was so that subsequently nobody would be able to claim they had been subjected to material they hadn't been warned about in advance. The film screened without any incident and afterwards Prowse told me he thought it would have been even more explicit. When it was submitted for commercial distribution it was cut to shreds and then given an R-rating.

Censorship reared its ugly head again in 1980 after Prowse had retired and Janet Strickland had been appointed Chief Censor.

At issue was Volker Schlondorff's epic *Die Blechtrommel* (*The Tin Drum*), which Strickland claimed featured a scene which could be deemed child pornography and thus fell outside the boundaries of the agreement between the Festivals and the AG's Department. We vigorously contested this and appealed to the Board of Review, which gave the clearance for the film to be shown. The following year, a similar problem occurred with the Brazilian film *Pixote*, the tragic story of a slum kid; again, Strickland refused to allow the Festival to screen the film on the grounds of child pornography and again we appealed and won. Both films were later screened in commercial cinemas without cuts and, later still, on SBS.

After I had left the SFF, it became common practice for other organisations, apart from the Sydney and Melbourne Film Festivals, to take advantage of the freedom from censorship privileges originally granted to us by Don Chipp. National film weeks proliferated, as did other film events – such as the Gay and Lesbian Film Festival, held in conjunction with the Mardi Gras – and all of them applied to import films without having them subjected to commercial censorship or classification. The organisers of these events, however, sometimes seemed not to be aware of the privileges that we had been given. In the late 1980s, the Gay and Lesbian festival imported a print of the 1986 Spanish film *Tras el cristal* (*In a Glass Cage*), by director Agustin Villaronga, which I had seen at the Berlin Film Festival that year. It was, as I noted at the time, a well-made and serious film but the subject matter (it dealt with a man who derived sexual pleasure from molesting and murdering young boys) was repellent. The Censorship Board demanded that the festival submit the film for censorship, and subsequently banned it.

After this incident, even the Sydney Film Festival found itself again under threat. In 2003, Festival Director Gail Lake programmed the controversial Larry Clark/Ed Lachmann film *Ken Park*, which had premiered the previous year at Venice and which showed, explicitly, sexual acts among bored teenagers living in an ugly suburb. It was a film of merit, but Lake erred in allowing its commercial distributor to submit it to the Office of Film and Literature Classification instead of handling the application herself. The film was refused classification. It was like history repeating itself when the Festival that year opened with the news of a banning.

My television co-star, Margaret Pomeranz, who is a passionate and very active member of the Watch on Censorship committee, attempted to defy the ban and to screen the film, on DVD, at Balmain Town Hall, but she was prevented from doing so by the police. Once again, it seems, censors are able to interfere with the programming of arts organisations, though it must be said that some recent decisions of the OFLC have been encouragingly liberal. At the time of writing it's too early to say if Donald McDonald, the previous Chairman of the ABC Board, who was appointed to head the OFLC in the autumn of 2007, will continue with this welcome trend.

Chapter Twelve

For the remainder of the 1970s and into the 1980s my annual routine changed relatively little. I was now travelling overseas *every* year to select the next year's programme, to keep all our contacts alive and, very often, to deal with the demands of FIAPF. I usually left Australia in July, about three weeks after the SFF ended, and stayed away until late November or early December. When I returned home I had time for only a short period of relaxation before the pressure of the next event began early in the New Year, and so the cycle continued.

At about this time one of my colleagues suggested to me that I seemed to have more friends overseas than I did in Australia, and that was probably true. I had become a kind of drifter, spending five months of each year travelling and seven months putting together the festival. My job had taken an irreparable toll on my marriage, and Margaret and I separated in 1973 and divorced in 1975. I tried to see my children, Mary and Giles, as often as possible, but after Margaret relocated to Wollongong, where she had a teaching job, this became rather more difficult. I was depressed that my marriage had been such a failure, a failure I blamed entirely on myself. My parents were less than pleased. For the next few years my relationships tended to be transient ones; it was especially difficult in the case of relationships in Australia, none of which survived those five month absences.

I was never able to attend the Cannes Film Festival, which was the pre-eminent event on the international film calendar, because it took place in May when I was in the final stages of preparing the Sydney Film Festival for June. But I would avidly read in the pages of the invaluable *Variety* reports and reviews from the event, many of them written by Gene Moskowitz. I could imagine him and other friends hanging out at the Petit Carlton or the Blue Bar, legendary waterholes on or off the Croisette, after screenings. Later I would read more considered reports in *Sight & Sound* and other film journals. In those days, Australian newspapers weren't at all interested in covering Cannes; they still barely covered the Sydney Film Festival.

My first stop on my annual trip was usually the Berlin Film Festival, which, in those days, took place in mid-July. I would then go to either Moscow or Karlovy Vary; at the time, these took place on alternate years. Karlovy Vary was held in the old Czech spa which is also known as Carlsbad, and which is close to Marienbad, the town featured so famously in the Alain Resnais film. One year, when I was about to attend the Karlovy Vary Festival, I had a call from Jerzy Skolimowski; somewhere or other he had met an Australian girl of Czech origin and was desperate to see her again. He wanted to meet up with her in Karlovy Vary, but she had nothing to do with the film business so she couldn't obtain accreditation to the Festival. He asked me if I would pretend that she was my secretary which would give her a legitimate reason for coming to KV, and I agreed. Her name was Sonia and she was happy to be part of the charade. She did, indeed, attend the Festival as my 'secretary' and she managed to spend as much time with Skolimowski as possible.

At the 1973 Moscow Film Festival an Australian film titled *The Office Picnic* was in competition. The director was Tom Cowan and he came to the Festival along with his leading lady, Kate Fitzpatrick, who (according to her memoirs) had a great time and enjoyed flirting with luminaries like the Japanese actor Toshiro Mifune. One evening, we were all invited to the home of Maxim Shostakovich, the son of the famous composer, who lived in an apartment which was unusually lavish by Moscow standards and was located at the top of a building with a panoramic view of the city. One of the other guests was a man who, it was claimed, knew the secret of levitation. Through an interpreter he explained that he wasn't in the mood to carry out levitations on humans that evening, but he did achieve a trick with my glasses. He told me to hold them in my hand, look him in the eyes (he had intense, piercing blue eyes) and then let go; the glasses hovered in the space between us. While this was going on, the record player was going at full volume and other people were talking, laughing and drinking; it was an uncanny experience. Was this strange man a latter-day Rasputin?

After the official screening of each film in Moscow, there would be additional screenings at cinemas in the outer suburbs of the city. Tom and Kate had left to go on a trip to the Soviet Republic of Georgia when one such screening of *The Office Picnic* took place, so as an 'Australian film worker' I was delegated to represent them. I made a speech to the effect that bureaucracy was a worldwide phenomenon, which got a bit of a laugh, and I was presented with a red carnation for my trouble.

My friend John Gillett, the British critic and film historian, was notorious for being accident-prone. That year in Moscow, at the opening night party in the Kremlin, he was gesticulating enthusiastically about the disappointing Russian film we'd just seen when his cufflink attached itself to the hair of a diminutive

American journalist called Betty Denby. As John continued to wave his hands about, her entire head of hair – revealed to be a wig – was waved about too, and there was some confusion as Betty attempted to reclaim it. A few days later John was supposed to join a group of 'British film workers' at a screening of one of the official British entries in the Festival out in the suburbs. He missed the official car which was taking the British delegation to the cinema, but was confident that he knew where he was going and took a taxi, which promptly delivered him to a cinema. There he joined the line of dignitaries on stage without, at first, realising that they were all strangers to him. It was only when he was introduced as a member of the East German delegation that he realised he'd come to the wrong place. That was typical of John – he was notoriously muddle-headed.

After Karlovy Vary or Moscow I would usually wend my way through Eastern Europe – Warsaw, Budapest, Prague – before attending the Pula Festival and then the Locarno Festival, which was located in a beautiful spot by Lake Maggiore. In the 1970s Locarno was run by Moritz de Hadeln, who put together a very fine programme. Alexander Walker, the long-time film critic of the London *Evening Standard*, often went to Locarno and constantly complained about the left-wing bias of the films Moritz presented. One year he took to dropping notes off for Mosk at his hotel: '*Another* piece of Communist propaganda tonight!' Alex was in many ways a curious man. When he saw Tobe Hooper's very confronting *The Texas Chainsaw Massacre* at Locarno in 1975, he was so impressed that he campaigned to have the British censor's ban on the film lifted, yet twenty-four years later, at Venice, he came out of a screening of David Fincher's *Fight Club* and immediately phoned the British censor to demand that it be banned. His contradictory nature embraced his appreciation of films but he became a champion of the new Australian cinema in the 1970s and he wrote some exceptional books.

At all these Festivals, and usually at Venice, too, which came later, I would hang out with friends like Mosk, Ken Wlaschin, the director of the London Film Festival, Peter Refn, a cheerful Dane who ran an arthouse cinema in Copenhagen, and Derek Hill, among others. Later I befriended the much-travelled Israeli critics Dan and Edna Fainaru and spent a good deal of time with them.

Sometimes I made it to the Edinburgh Film Festival, which at the time was run by Lynda Myles, who I believe was, in the early 1970s, the world's only female festival director. I was in Edinburgh in 1975 when Martin Scorsese presented his film *Alice Doesn't Live Here Any More*; he told me at a reception afterwards that he was exhausted because he'd just finished filming *Taxi Driver*, and he was full of praise for Robert De Niro's performance in his new film. Edinburgh often had excellent retrospectives in those days which highlighted the careers of Hollywood genre directors like Samuel Fuller, Roger Corman and Raoul Walsh. One evening in the Festival Club I struck up a conversation with Peter Wollen and Laura Mulvey, who were representatives of a new school of criticism which was influenced by semiology; Wollen's book *Signs and Meanings in the Cinema* had recently been published. They were working on a monograph on Raoul Walsh, and I offered to lend them the taped interview I'd made with the famous Hollywood director in San Francisco the previous year. 'Does he discuss his castration complex?' Mulvey asked, and I had to admit that he didn't. 'Then it wouldn't be much use to us,' she said, and that was the end of that.

The Venice Festival commences at the end of August and ends usually ten days or so into September. At around the same time, in Canada, festivals in Montreal and Toronto take place, so there was no shortage of events to attend in the late summer. I always tried to cover as much ground as possible, but Venice remains my favourite festival, mainly because of its location. However, in its brief heyday under Jarman and Johnson, San Francisco was the closest to my ideal of what a non-competitive festival should be.

More often than not, when attending the Venice Festival, I've been lucky enough to stay at the Hotel des Bains. This elegant edifice looks as though it's seen better days. The parquet floors creak, the rooms – each one completely different from the next – vary between the large and the pokey. There's a magnificent swimming pool in the garden. Breakfast is served in the Thomas Mann Room, named after the author of *Death in Venice*, and there's also a banqueting hall called the Visconti Room after the director of the film version of Mann's novel, which used the hotel as a backdrop. I've always found it disconcerting that dining room is invaded, every morning, by voracious sparrows, which peck at the food which has been laid out for the guests – the bread, the breakfast cereals, even the spoon used to ladle scrambled eggs out of the bain-marie. I go out of my way to avoid the food, which seems most vulnerable to this bird plague, but the waiters seem completely unfazed by the unhygienic goings-on in this upmarket and immensely expensive hotel. I was always expecting to read about a bird flu epidemic which started at the Hotel des Bains in Venice, but in 2007 the hotel staff seemed to have realised the problem and had taken elaborate means to solve it.

The first few years I attended Venice were exciting not only for the contemporary films that screened, but for the impressive guests and the easy accessibility to them. You could, for example, sit down and talk with King Vidor and the silent-era actress Colleen Moore, who came to Venice in 1972 for a Vidor retrospective, or with Dennis Hopper, whose follow-up to *Easy Rider*, *The Last Movie*, received one of its very rare screenings at the Festival in 1971. There were still only two screening of films in competition per day, one in the late afternoon and the other later in the evening. Apart from that, there was a retrospective (usually an excellent one) and nothing else. So the mornings were free to sit on the beach or swim in the pool at the Des Bains. Sitting on the beach wasn't so easy, since the beaches on the Lido, and, indeed, throughout the Mediterranean, are controlled by the adjacent hotels and you have to rent a 'cabana', or changing hut, to access them. Such luxuries were outside my budget but Mosk always knew which cabana-renters were most amenable to having freeloaders share their facilities. His usual benefactors were Mr and Mrs Kawakita, who gave me access to the facilities as well (in truth, they rarely used the cabana themselves). As a result, a Festival like Venice, in those days, was pretty much like a holiday. It's very different today, when vast numbers of films screen in different cinemas from 8.30 am until well after midnight.

After the 1972 Festival, Venice fell victim to political events, and there was no festival in 1973, or, indeed, for five years after that. It was re-established in 1979, and has been running ever since. The 2007 Festival was called Venice 64, but the suggestion that the Festival has run continuously for sixty-four years since its inception in 1933 is, obviously, a misleading one.

At the beginning, the restored Venice Festival was still quite a modest affair. Press-screenings took place in the tiny 300-seat Sala Volpi, which easily accommodated the journalists in attendance, with one notable exception. In 1980 the Festival had programmed the world premiere of a new film by John Huston titled *Phobia*. This creaky thriller, which Huston made in Canada, is, today, the great director's least-seen work and rightly so; but at the time there was much anticipation about a new Huston film. A crowd of press people assembled outside the Sala Volpi – heavens knows where they came from, but there had never been so many of them at a press-screening before. When the doors were opened, they filled every seat, squatted in the aisles, and even sat on one another's laps. The ushers were dismayed; clearly this was unacceptable and the start of the screening was delayed. Finally, a legendary announcement was made, in Italian and English: 'Until the theatre is completely emptied, the film will not commence.' Nobody took any notice whatsoever. After another delay, the lights dimmed and the film began. Within half an hour of enduring the inanities of the preposterous production, the cinema was practically empty.

Often, after leaving Venice, I flew to London. On several occasions in the mid-1980s I observed a wealthy looking couple flying business class on the same flight. They were elderly and obviously very distinguished, with elegant, embossed luggage, and they looked vaguely familiar. I finally realised that he was John Profumo, the former Tory government minister who in 1963 had been at the centre of a sex scandal because of his relationship with Christine Keeler, a high-class callgirl. His wife was Valerie Hobson, once the leading light of Rank productions, star of *Kind Hearts and Coronets* and other major films. I was very tempted to talk to her but I never did.

In mid-September I usually spent a week in Paris, where there were always arguments with Brisson over FIAPF membership, discussions with Unifrance over the value to French cinema of the Australian festivals and pleasant evenings with Mosk and a parade of visiting filmmakers.

I also had to set aside time to visit the Low Countries and Scandinavia. Jörn Donner used to let me stay in his apartment on Helsinki Harbour when I was in the Finnish capital, because he was almost never there in summer. One August, when the brief Scandinavian summer was already giving way to autumn, I rented a car and drove to the west coast of Finland, near the old capital, Turku, where Donner had a small island, Kustavi, on which there was a summer house. He had asked me to bring some provisions – ham, bread, cheese, wine and so on – and to phone from a call box when I arrived at the point opposite the island. There I parked the car and Jörn rowed across the stretch of water separating the island from the mainland to pick me up. 'We're all having a sauna,' he told me. 'Come and join us.' This was my first experience of a communal sauna and my British reserve kicked in with a vengeance, especially when, stark naked, I entered the tiny, boiling hot steam room, where half a dozen naked strangers of both sexes were sitting on benches. I found myself sitting next to the beautiful Harriet Andersson, the actress who had appeared in so many Swedish films made by Ingmar Bergman and others. Making small talk in circumstances like that isn't easy and after a while it was suggested that we all go for a swim in the sea. Off we raced across the rocks. Still feeling awkward about this very Scandinavian situation, I tripped on a rock and grazed my knee. It was Harriet who held back from the others to make sure I was all right and, in close proximity to this beautiful naked woman, I had great difficulty to keep from demonstrating the extent of my lust in what would have been a wholly inappropriate way.

I was often in Stockholm for the annual crayfish festival, an occasion on which the Swedes drink a lot of aquavit and eat crayfish which, already in the 1970s, were being imported from Turkey because there were no more to be found in the Swedish lakes and rivers. It all sounds like a lot of fun and, indeed, it was, but there was also a lot of work to do – films to see, face-to-face discussions about film entries, problems to iron out. It was from this sort of activity that the SFF programmes of the 1970s emerged, and I'm still very proud of them.

During the autumn I sometimes stayed in Europe to attend the San Sebastian Film Festival in Spain and then move on to London, but often I went to North America, to see films in Canada and New York and to attend the San Francisco Film Festival. One memorable day in San Francisco in 1972 Pierre Rissient introduced me to both Howard Hawks and Raoul Walsh in the Green Room. These were titans of old Hollywood: both had careers dating back to the silent days. Hawks had directed such iconic classics as *Bringing Up Baby*, *His Girl Friday*, *The Big Sleep*, *Red River* and *Rio Bravo*, while Walsh had been responsible for directing Errol Flynn in *They Died with Their Boots On* and James Cagney in *White Heat.* Pierre invited me to join him and Walsh for dinner afterwards; the veteran director, who, as an actor, had played John Wilkes Booth in Griffith's *The Birth of a*

Nation, and who had lost an eye in the early 1930s while on location in the desert, was quite a character. Dressed like a cowboy, complete with ten-gallon hat, he entertained us hugely with anecdotes involving the people he'd known in the golden days of Hollywood – Flynn, Mae West, Charles Chaplin, John Barrymore and many more.

That year I rented a car after the Festival ended and drove north-east into the Yosemite National Park, a most beautiful area where wildlife, including some not very friendly bears, ran free. Yosemite is situated in the High Sierras, and it's a pristine area of mountains, rivers and waterfalls. From there I drove steeply down into Death Valley and stayed a night at Zabriskie Point, which is the lowest spot in the United States, and the location of Michelangelo Antonioni's recent film of the same name. My next stop was Las Vegas, which wasn't really my scene, and on 1 November, with light snow starting to fall I drove into the mountainous desert country near Flagstaff, Arizona, where I saw the Woody Allen comedy *Play It Again, Sam* at the Flag East Cinema. Next day I drove on to the Grand Canyon, which was just as spectacular as all those movies located around it had indicated. In Phoenix a few days later I saw Bogdanovich's *What's Up, Doc?* at the first multiplex cinema, situated in a new suburban shopping mall, that I'd ever experienced. Little did I realise at the time that this would be the future of cinema-going for the next twenty-five years at least. I then undertook the long drive from Phoenix to Los Angeles.

I have always thoroughly enjoyed the experience of driving through unfamiliar countryside, visiting small towns, seeing a variety of landscapes, staying in small hotels, finding interesting places to eat. Over the years I've been lucky enough to drive through quite a lot of North America, not only in the south-west, but also in the north-west (Oregon, Washington, Montana) and north-east (Massachusets, New England, southern Canada).

My unfailingly happy American experiences have, however, been slightly tainted by my inability to understand the country's devotion to firearms. Every time we hear news of a fresh massacre, and a spokesman for the National Rifle Association (sometimes Charlton Heston himself) comes out with the old bromide about 'guns not killing people, people killing people', I become more sickened. But I've learnt not to talk to my many American friends about it. I made this mistake in 1972, during a dinner party at the Los Angeles home of writer-director Theodore (Ted) Flicker, whose most famous film remains the 1967 satirical comedy *The President's Analyst*. Ted and his wife were intelligent, cosmopolitan people and during the course of a conversation on violence, I said, 'Well, I'm sure there's no gun in *this* house.' There was an embarrassing silence and then Ted admitted that he did, indeed, keep a gun. 'But you see,' he said, 'Sharon Tate lived just around the corner from here.' This reference to the 1969 killings by the Manson family quickly ended the talk about guns.

Then in its second year, the Los Angeles Film Festival, known as Filmex, was run by a gay couple, Gary Essert and Gary Abrahams. The programme was an excellent one and screenings took place at the famous Chinese Theatre on Hollywood Boulevard. Guests stayed at the venerable Hollywood Roosevelt Hotel across the road from the Chinese and the atmosphere of the Festival was an attractive combination of nostalgia and modernity.

One of the guests was Jacques Tati, the great comedian whose handful of films – *Jour de Fete, Monsieur Hulot's Holiday, Mon Oncle, Playtime* – had resurrected the purely visual comedy style of the great silent comedians. Like many funny men Tati was, in real life, quite melancholy; his latest film, *Traffic*, was being released by a major studio, Columbia, but he worried over the fact that he wasn't getting sufficient royalties for his past work. He told me that a few weeks earlier, in New York, he had been a passenger in a taxi which collided with another car; he emerged from the cab shaken and bruised, to be greeted by a traffic policeman who had witnessed the incident. The cop, obviously a film buff, recognised Tati as the accident-prone Monsieur Hulot, and instantly burst out laughing, to the unamused comedian's mortification.

A few months later, Tati visited Sydney and I was able to introduce him to Ross Tzannes, who agreed to act as his lawyer and attempt to recover the Australian royalties that were due to him. Tati kept a notebook and whenever he saw anything amusing he'd make a note of it for possible future use in a film. I was having breakfast with him in his room on the top floor of the Chevron Hotel one morning when we saw, through the window, a man and a dog emerge onto a rooftop across the street. The man was in shorts and singlet, and he stretched as he breathed in the morning air; the dog made precisely the same stretching gesture as his master. It was a very Tati moment and Jacques duly made a note of it.

I made it a point to make contact with as many major film-makers as possible. While in Los Angeles that year I called the office of Robert Altman, whose recent films *M*A*S*H* (1970) and *McCabe and Mrs. Miller* (1971) had been remarkable. We spent an hour talking about his work and he invited me to a rough-cut screening that evening of the film he was now working on, an adaptation of Raymond Chandler's novel *The Long Goodbye*. The screening, which took place at the Samuel Goldwyn studios, was a very incomplete one, without music or sound effects, but it was exciting to be present in the company of Altman and his other guests, who included the film's star, Elliott Gould, and the elderly Groucho Marx. Sadly, Altman was never able to come to Sydney as our guest but over the years he allowed us to screen many of his best films, including *California Split* (1974), *3 Women* (1977) and *A Wedding* (1978). We also screened a movie he produced, *Welcome to LA* (1976), which was the first film directed by Alan Rudolph.

I've never been terribly comfortable at parties making small talk to people I don't know, but in those days, when film festival parties were even more common than they are today, I usually put in an appearance. I still have a copy of an invitation to 'Brunch with Jane Russell' which I attended, but I found myself a bit overwhelmed by the (still beautiful) woman whose mammaries had created so much fuss in her very first film, *The Outlaw* – one of the 'forbidden' films my grandmother had taken me to see. I had made the serious mistake of bowling up to Sylvia Sims to tell her that I had fallen in love with her when I was a teenager; she didn't seem amused by that awkward attempt at small talk (I was pleased to see, though, that she's still going strong, though her role as the Queen Mother in *The Queen* is light years away from the pony-tailed heroine of *My Teenage Daughter*, the film which first brought her to my adolescent attention).

On the rare occasions that my father would talk about his taste in films and film stars he confided that his favourite actor had been Gary Cooper and his favourite actress Myrna Loy. When I met Ms Loy at an LA party in 1972 I could hardly tell her that, but, in the meantime, I had also become a great admirer of this consummately sophisticated and witty actor, though I'd been forced to see her greatest successes, such as *The Thin Man* and *Manhattan Melodrama*, on television in the days before video. Perhaps, too, I was tongue-tied because the very elegant Ms Loy was smoking a joint: this was, after all, Los Angeles in the early 1970s, but I don't think my father would have approved. I never again met anyone who looked so effortlessly stylish while enjoying pot.

The closing night film at Filmex in 1972 was Luis Buñuel's *Le charme discret de la bourgeoisie* (*The Discreet Charm of the Bourgeoisie*). I had already seen it in Paris a couple of months earlier, but this was the North American premiere and Buñuel himself was in attendance. It was a great occasion because Buñuel rarely came to such screenings. The Garys were, of course, thrilled to have him and arranged for cocktails at the Hollywood Roosevelt before the screening. George Cukor, a patron of Filmex, was there as were several other celebrated Hollywood figures. I was introduced to Buñuel, a remarkable director who had tweaked the noses of the Franco regime in Spain when he made the Cannes Palme d'Or winning *Viridiana* in 1960, a film which, as we have seen, was subsequently banned in Australia on the grounds of blasphemy. We talked about the new phase of his career, which had taken him from making films in Mexico, exiled from his native Spain, to directing prestige productions, like *Belle de Jour*, in France. Gene Moskowitz was a friend of Buñuel and the mutual affection we had for the *Variety* reviewer ensured our meeting was a very relaxed one.

As we were talking a messenger delivered a note to Gary Essert which revealed that the projectionist had discovered that the last reel of *The Discreet Charm of the Bourgeoisie* was missing. This was potentially a disaster but help was at hand. The film was being distributed around the world by 20th Century-Fox and a Fox executive was at the cocktail party. He had a print of the film at his home on the other side of LA, and he offered to send his driver to pick it up. This would take some time but we all crossed the street and took our seats in the theatre where an announcement was made to the audience that the start of the screening would be delayed by up to an hour. Buñuel seemed completely unfazed by this turn of events which, on reflection, was a rather Buñuel moment – his 1962 film, *The Exterminating Angel*, is structured around a smart event – in this case a dinner party – which the guests are mysteriously unable to leave; in this case, the well-dressed guests were sitting in a cinema facing a blank screen waiting endlessly for the film to start. The missing reel eventually showed up and the film screened to a very enthusiastic audience. A few months later it won the Oscar for Best Foreign Film.

The day after the Filmex screening Cukor hosted a lunch at his home in honour of Buñuel. Among those present were Billy Wilder, Alfred Hitchcock, William Wyler, Rouben Mamoulian, Robert Wise and John Ford. A group photograph appeared in

The LA Times the following day and I keep a framed blow-up copy of it on my office wall.

After two weeks at Filmex I flew to Mexico for a couple of days where a Mexican film director friend, Juan Lopez Moctezuma, who specialised in making horror films, drove me out of the city to see the famous pyramids, an unforgettable experience.

I returned to Australia that year (1972) to discover that significant changes were taking place. The Labor Party had just won the federal election and Gough Whitlam was the new Prime Minister. There was a fresh spirit in the air, especially in the world of the arts. In the past year or so a movement had been launched to revive the Australian film industry and to increase Australian content on television. The 'Make it Australian' campaign was a powerful one and was taken up by several prominent people from different sides of the political spectrum. They included: Peter Coleman, a NSW Liberal MP; Barry Jones, who was famous as the most successful winner of the television quiz show *Pick-a-Box* and who would be a future President of the Labor Party; Phillip Adams, who was partner in an advertising company and who had directed a low-budget feature film; and Tony Buckley, a film editor and also a member of the SFF Committee. These men, among others, lobbied the government tirelessly, and Coleman, Jones and Adams embarked on an overseas study tour to examine film production and film teaching centres abroad. On their return their published report contained positive proposals for the re-establishment of a film industry in this country.

As a result, the Gorton (Liberal–Country Party) Government had announced a three-tiered scheme of support for the film industry. First was the establishment of a Film School, to be based in Sydney. The inaugural Director of the School was Jerzy Toeplitz, the head of the famous Polish Film School at Lodz, which had been the training ground for, among others, Andrzej Wajda, Roman Polanski and Jerzy Skolimowski. The first intake of students at the new school would undertake what was called the Interim Year during 1973, which was a pilot for the full programme to be introduced the following year. The students for this interim year included Phillip Noyce, Gillian Armstrong, Chris Noonan and James Ricketson, all of whom became directors. Another of the 1973 intake was Graham Shirley, who became one of Australia's leading film historians.

Secondly, the government had announced the establishment of an Experimental Film Fund to assist young people with the cost of their first attempts at working in the medium. And thirdly, a film bank was established, a lending organisation that would provide the seed money for feature films but which would also assist cultural organisations. This was initially called the Australian Film Development Corporation (AFDC) but it wasn't long before it was re-named the Australian Film Commission (AFC). Later still, its funding activities were taken over by the Film Finance Corporation (FFC). Spurred on by this example of federal munificence, the states got into the act, starting with South Australia where Don Dunstan's Labor Government established the South Australian Film Corporation (SAFC) under Gil Brealey. The aim was to produce documentary and feature films in the state. The long-standing voluntary treasurer of the SFF, John Burke, was given the job of Administrator of the new SAFC so, to my great regret, he and his wife, Beverley, who had both been so supportive of me, left Sydney and moved to Adelaide. Soon after this, to my surprise, I was offered the position of Head of Marketing at the SAFC, a position I declined; there was still too much work to be done at the Festival in Sydney.

The first feature production of the SAFC was Ken Hannam's richly textured film of John Dingwall's screenplay about outback shearers, *Sunday Too Far Away* which, though it had a troubled production history, turned out very well indeed and was selected for a non-competing slot at the Cannes Film Festival in 1975. In the succeeding months the other states joined South Australia in establishing film production entities; the most prominent were the NSW Film Corporation and Film Victoria.

In 1973 the last SFF was held at the Wintergarden in Rose Bay and I'll never forget the closing night which strangely paralleled what had happened at the closing night of Filmex a few months earlier. As the closing film I had originally programmed Lina Wertmuller's cheeky comedy *Mimi the Metalworker*, but the print had failed to arrive from Italy, and I had to find a last-minute replacement. I usually tried to close the festival with something fairly light, so I persuaded 20th Century-Fox to let us screen the Australian premiere of Ralph Bakshi's R-rated animated film *Fritz the Cat*. In those days, the SFF ended on the Bank Holiday Monday and Fox duly delivered the print of *Fritz* to the Wintergarden on the Friday afternoon. On the Sunday, as the projectionist, Keith Mortley, was checking the prints for the next day, he discovered that the last reel of *Fritz* was missing.

I still don't remember how I managed it but somehow I located the home phone number of Eric Davis, the CEO of Fox in Australia, and called him about the disaster. He was very helpful and rang me back to say that there was a print of the film in Melbourne. It was now Sunday evening but he promised to have the last reel sent up by air the next day and I agreed that we'd pick it up at the airport. From midday onwards Peter Witton, the SFF Committee member in charge of transportation, waited at the airport but the anticipated package stubbornly refused to show up. I called Eric again and he assured me it was on its way. It was time to start the session so I took a deep breath and authorised Mortley to start the film without warning the audience that, as of that moment, the last reel had still not arrived. Thankfully, after the film had been unspooling for about twenty minutes Peter turned up with the missing reel and all was well.

Sometimes I would end the European summer at the San Sebastian Film Festival, which was located in Spain's Basque country. This was another Festival that always assembled a great retrospective and in 1973 there had been a retrospective of the films of Rouben Mamoulian. The veteran film and stage director was appointed President of the International Jury of the Festival. Gala events begin late in Spain and the opening-night film, a mediocre Hollywood thriller titled *Night Watch*, was scheduled to commence at ten pm in the beautiful old theatre, the Victoria Eugenia, which was the Festival's headquarters. The film's stars were Laurence Harvey and Elizabeth Taylor – and Taylor, at the time a superstar, had agreed to attend. I don't think anyone was very surprised when the start of the ceremony was delayed because the guest of honour wasn't ready to appear.

Certainly Mamoulian would have been well used to this behaviour from Taylor, who had played the leading role in the last film on which he had worked: it was mainly due to lengthy delays caused by Taylor, and her eventual illness, that production of *Cleopatra*, the film Mamoulian was directing, was shut down for several months. When it resumed, a new director, Joseph L. Mankiewicz, had taken over and Mamoulian never worked in Hollywood again. I was talking to Mamoulian and his wife about all this while we waited for Taylor's arrival and he made it plain that he was no fan of the celebrated actress. After an hour had passed he looked at his watch and noted resignedly: 'This film was aptly titled!' Finally Taylor arrived, looking marvellous, and the film was screened, to a very muted response. At the reception afterwards I was introduced to the woman many considered to be the most beautiful screen actress of all. She was, indeed, a beauty and her eyes were particularly striking. They were of a distinctive shade of violet and I don't think any of the films she made quite captured their extraordinary colour.

Another important guest at San Sebastian that year was the legendary Orson Welles, who was presenting his film *F for Fake*. We were both staying in the same hotel, the Londres, which over-looked the near-perfect seashell-shaped beach for which San Sebastian is famous. Welles wasn't very communicative, though he gave a press conference which proved to be quite entertaining. He was accompanied by a very large mastiff, and when Welles and the dog occupied the hotel's small, cage-like lift, there was no room for anyone else.

That year in San Sebastian I witnessed a fascinating spectacle which suggested that, although Spain was changing, the old Fascist outlooks were still not far below the surface. The best film in competition was a local production, *El Espiritu de la Colmena* (*The Spirit of the Beehive*), the first feature made by a young man called Victor Erice. The film was set just after the end of the Civil War and although on the surface it dealt with a pair of young sisters who have been freaked out by a screening of James Whale's *Frankenstein*, there was obviously a lot going on beneath the surface. At the conclusion of the screening, while a few of us warmly applauded the film, the vast majority of the audience booed, hissed and stamped their feet. A few days later I was delighted when Mamoulian announced that his jury had chosen Erice's film to win the Festival's main prize, the Golden Shell, but again the decision was greeted with loud boos and when poor Erice came on stage to collect his prize I thought the old theatre would collapse with the din and the palpable feeling of hate on the part of those members of the audience who objected to his subtle anti-Franco message.

Nine months later both Mamoulian and *The Spirit of the Beehive* were featured at the Sydney Film Festival. Mamoulian's innovative use of sound in early talkies like *Applause* and *City Streets* ensures his place in film history but he had also worked with both Garbo (*Queen Christina*) and Dietrich (*Song of Songs*), and had reportedly slept with both of them. In addition, he had directed the first three-strip Technicolor feature, *Becky Sharp*, and the original Broadway productions of *Porgy and Bess* and *Oklahoma!*. Since 1974 was the first year the Festival was taking place entirely at the State Theatre, we decided to arrange a very special opening night. With the help of a number of friends, led by Andrew Jakubowicz, we planned to stage an evening which would be typical of the early days of this magnificent cinema, which that year was celebrating its forty-fifth birthday. I managed to persuade the BBC to loan us their pristine 35-mm copy of *Love Me Tonight* (1932), Mamoulian's masterpiece, a musical-comedy starring Maurice Chevalier and Jeanette MacDonald, which has a great score by Rodgers and Hart, including standards like 'Isn't it Romantic?'. Also from 1932 we obtained, with the help of the National Film and Sound Archive, a newsreel, a Betty Boop cartoon and a short travelogue, in colour, about the gardens of Melbourne.

With the help of theatre director Rex Cramphorn and actors Kate Fitzpatrick and Jacki Weaver, we presented a stage show before the feature, just the kind of entertainment which was often staged at the biggest cinemas in the early 1930s. The Bankstown Symphony Orchestra provided the music and our wonderful cast sang and danced to the show-stopping numbers from the film. An unusual form of entertainment was provided by a classy stripper, who was discovered by Cramphorn; as she divested herself of her clothes, she used balloons to cover herself! Much time and effort was spent on this spectacular opening, which was co-ordinated by John Rochester, who ran the Opening Night Sub-committee for many years.

A year earlier, Benson and Hedges, the sponsor of our short film awards since 1970, had withdrawn their support in protest after the judges selected a strong anti-smoking film as one of the finalists in the competition. I can't say that I was sorry to see them go. Whenever B&H reps came to my office they ostentatiously lit up their cigarettes and offered me a smoke, which I always refused (I've never smoked cigarettes, though for a while I did enjoy puffing on thin cigars – the kind Clint Eastwood smoked in the *Dollars* trilogy). During our negotiations with David Williams over the State Theatre we asked if Greater Union would be interested in sponsoring the awards in the future. He said that they would and so the Greater Union Awards for Australian Short Films were inaugurated in 1974.

That was also the year we instituted the Rouben Mamoulian Award, a special prize given to the best finalist in the opinion of a visitor (or visitors) to the Festival. Mamoulian himself viewed the twelve finalists and selected *Castor and Pollux*, directed by Phillip Noyce, who had just completed his first year at the Film School. The Festival was officially opened by the Prime Minister, Gough Whitlam, and without telling him or his staff, I had arranged for Barry Humphries, who was in Australia at the time, to present the PM with a bunch of his trademark gladioli. It was a good-natured moment and altogether truly a night to remember.

There was another reason why the 1974 SFF was important. That was the year Peter Weir presented his first feature, *The Cars That Ate Paris*, which was, perhaps, the first 'serious' film of the New Australian Cinema. Although the film, a very black comedy, was a great success with the Festival audience, it failed to make any kind of impact at the box office when it opened a few weeks later.

The Australian film revival had got off to a good start with the success of raunchy comedies like Tim Burstall's *Stork* and *Alvin Purple* and Bruce Beresford's *The Adventures of Barry McKenzie* and *Barry McKenzie Holds His Own* (working title: *Barry McKenzie Pulls It Off*). I had invited Pierre Rissient to the festival that year, because I wanted him to assess this new Australian movement; this was the first of many visits he made to Australia. During the Festival Pierre was invited by a former film critic of *The Australian*, Michael Thornhill, to see a rough cut of the first feature film he'd directed, *Between Wars*, a very ambitious movie which explored Australian politics in the 1920s and 30s while at the same time presenting a personal story. Pierre didn't like the film at all and I was embarrassed for Thornhill at the forceful way he expressed his dislike.

Another visitor to the SFF in 1974 was the Polish director Krzysztof Zanussi, whose films were cool, intellectual and cerebral. Ross invited him to dinner one evening at his home along with the author Frank Hardy, the Federal Attorney-General Lionel Murphy and me. It was a very convivial evening, at the end of which addresses and phone numbers were exchanged. Several months later Hardy was visiting Warsaw for a writers' conference. While he was checking out of his hotel, a maid examined his room and found that it was in a terrible mess; the carpet had been ruined by some noxious substance. She phoned this information through to the desk, and the hotel management refused to allow Hardy to leave until he paid for the damage in US dollars. He didn't have enough money and, after some argument, he remembered that he had Zanussi's phone number. He called the director and sought his help. Zanussi agreed to pay for the damage, in Polish zlotys, not dollars, but told Hardy that he would need speedy repayment because the sum involved was considerable. Weeks went by and the money wasn't forthcoming; letters to Hardy went unanswered. Finally Zanussi wrote to Lionel Murphy asking him to intervene with Hardy, and the money duly arrived a few days later.

Complicating the running of the first SFF at the State were events of which the public was barely aware. While in Rome the previous year I had seen an excellent documentary made by Michelangelo Antonioni for RAI-TV – *Chung-kuo: La Cina* (*Chung kuo: China*). This was a period during which we saw hardly any films from or about China so Antonioni's documentary, which was made at the invitation of the Beijing Government, was, I thought, essential viewing. But not long after I first saw the film the Chinese authorities mysteriously decided that Antonioni had made an anti-China film; I can't remember now just what it was that upset them, but it was some relatively minor image of which they disapproved. At any rate, the Chinese Government began to put pressure on any organisation in the world that planned to screen the film. My position was that RAI had entered it in the SFF and I saw no reason not to show it.

As soon as we announced our programme for the year I had a call from the Chinese Embassy in Canberra demanding that I withdraw the film. I refused. Then I had another call asking me to meet two representatives from the Embassy in Sydney. I invited them to my office but they wanted to meet on neutral territory, so I agreed to a meeting in a small, obscure hotel in the city somewhere near Central Station. They were very young men and they seemed nervous. Their hotel room was small and a bit smelly. They produced beer, which I declined, and then told me, quite politely, that to show the film would be an insult to the people of China. I asked them if they'd seen it and they admitted that they hadn't. But, they assured me, they *knew* it insulted the Chinese people. I offered to show them the film, but that didn't interest them. I told them I thought that opposition to the film was misplaced and that furthermore I'd been fighting Australian government censorship for years, and now that battle was won I wasn't going to accept censorship from the Chinese Government. I don't think they understood my argument, but there was no more to be said and so I left.

Then the telephone threats began. A personal friend of Ross Tzannes called him at home to ask him to forbid the screening of the film. The Theatrical Employees Union informed us that if we screened the film they would boycott the Festival. I told the State's projectionist, Bill Dirou, about this and he scoffed at the idea. 'They won't stop me,' he said; but it was this threat that persuaded Erwin Rado not to screen the film in Melbourne. 'What if,' he asked, 'the union really does black-ban us? There'd be no festival.' Erwin was not happy that I was determined to go ahead with the screening in Sydney, but I was adamant and Ross gave me his full backing. Soon, people with strong Australian accents phoned to warn me that my life would be in danger and so would the life of the projectionist if the film was shown. Again, I talked to Dirou about the threats, but he wasn't in the least bit fazed. After some consideration,

I added the following note to the description of the film in the Festival catalogue:

> Since the Festival selected and programmed Antonioni's film we have been made very much aware of the great concern within the People's Republic of China which this film generates . . . We cannot see this film as an attack on the People's Republic of China and nor can we see that by presenting the film at the Festival it can be said that the Australian people are in any way unfriendly towards the Chinese people. We have always believed, and always will believe, in freedom of expression, and freedom for the film maker and also freedom for the Festival to select and programme the films of its choice. We have no wish to offend the People's Republic of China but, after careful consideration, we have decided to proceed with our presentation of the film as planned.

The screening of *Chung-kuo: China* went ahead as scheduled. There were absolutely no incidents or repercussions; the threats had been empty ones.

The drama over Antonioni's film wasn't the only example of controversial programming at the 1974 SFF. Argentina was, at the time, in the grip of a brutal military dictatorship and opponents of the regime were beginning to 'disappear' – in other words, to be kidnapped and then quietly murdered. *Los Traidores* (*The Traitors*) was produced anonymously by a group calling themselves 'Cine de la Base' and concerned itself with the gradual ideological and moral decline of the Peronist union movement. The actual director of the film was a radical young Marxist, Raymundo Gleyzer, who, to my surprise, decided to come to Australia to present the film at the Festival. I asked a friend of mine, Alexandra Lamas, to work as a Festival volunteer and to look after Raymundo during his stay.

Alex, a beautiful young woman, was, I thought, ideally suited for this role. Her father was the Argentinian actor, Fernando

Lamas, who had played leading roles in a series of MGM films of the early fifties, among them *The Merry Widow* (1952), opposite Lana Turner, *Rose Marie* (1954), with Ann Blyth, and *Dangerous When Wet* (1953), with Esther Williams. Alex's mother, Lydia, was Italian-born, but a naturalised Australian; the couple divorced when Alex was five years old, after which Fernando married Arlene Dahl, his co-star in *Sangaree* (1953). In 1969, he had married Esther Williams. Raymundo and Alex fell in love almost immediately. The screening of *The Traitors* was a success and attracted quite a bit of publicity; but I remember being concerned that diplomats from the Argentinian Embassy might be watching Raymundo and following his activities in Australia.

Raymundo stayed on for some time after the Festival ended, living with Alex in her Paddington flat. I had lunch with them the day before he finally decided to return home. Not long afterwards Alex followed him. They lived together in Buenos Aires for a year before the deteriorating political situation prompted them to separate for safety reasons. Alex lived with her aunt for a while, and then purchased a small apartment from members of Raymundo's family, where the couple could meet at every opportunity. On 27 May 1976, Raymundo was leaving the office of SICA (the Union of Filmmakers) when he was kidnapped. He was never seen again; tragically, he joined the legion of the 'disappeared', a victim of the dictatorship. Alex still lives in Buenos Aires.

Rouben Mamoulian's visit to Australia did not end well. Although we had gone to great trouble to locate and screen copies of most of his films, he seemed to think we hadn't done enough for him. I think his wife, who accompanied him and who was very protective of him, persuaded him that we weren't honouring him sufficiently, although he had been the focal point of that memorable opening night and I had promised him that the award of the visiting filmmaker(s) would, in perpetuity, be named after him. I had even taken the risk of screening a nitrate 35-mm print of his bullfight epic, *Blood and Sand*, at the State, with the full support of Bill Dirou – nitrate prints, which were highly flammable, had been the norm prior to the late 1940s, when safety film was introduced, but many older films were only available in the format – this particular copy had come from a private collector.

After his return to Sydney from the Melbourne Film Festival, Mamoulian developed a very bad cold. He and his wife were staying in a suite at the Sebel Town House, and it became obvious that they would not be willing to leave when the Festival came to an end. This was liable to cost us a lot of money but, of course, the health of our guest was a major consideration. Perhaps I handled the matter badly, but matters reached the stage where Mamoulian would no longer talk to me; his main contact with the SFF was through Ross and Modesta Gentile, my assistant. I had promised to drive Pierre Rissient to Melbourne and Canberra immediately after the festival and, since the Mamoulians were in good hands, I saw no reason to cancel the trip.

After a year without a car (following the separation from my wife) I had purchased a second-hand Ford from my friend Andrew Jakubowicz, who was leaving on a trip to Europe. I don't know a thing about how cars work and I didn't know, until too late, that the engine of this particular vehicle tended to die if there was a hint of moisture in the atmosphere. On one occasion I was driving across the Harbour Bridge when it started to rain and the engine immediately cut out, to my great embarrassment. In addition, a family of small cockroaches had made a nest inside the upholstery of the passenger's seat and would occasionally make an unwelcome appearance. Under the circumstances, it was foolish of me to embark on the trip with Pierre; the car gave up the ghost somewhere near Yass, and the rest of the journey was a disaster. When I finally returned to Sydney some time later, the Mamoulians were still in the suite at the Sebel and the manager of the hotel, Henry Rose, was furious because their rooms were needed for Nana Mouskouri, who was about to arrive in Sydney for a concert.

Things became really nasty. Mamoulian's cold had developed into flu and although he was on the mend his wife insisted he couldn't leave. She threatened to jump from the window if they were forcibly moved, and Rose, in turn, threatened to cut off the water and power to their room. Finally, they agreed to leave and I breathed a sigh of relief.

Chapter Thirteen

In 1974 the Committee of the Sydney Film Festival decided to start a Travelling Film Festival (TFF). There were several reasons for this initiative. The most obvious was to promote the kind of quality films that the SFF screened in regional cities throughout Australia, especially in New South Wales. Another, of equal importance, was to help gain distribution for films shown at the SFF. It was always a matter of concern, by FIAPF and some national producers associations, that not enough films which had been screened at the Festival were picked up for local distribution and this was, after all, the main reason most of them were entered in the first place. So it was made clear from the outset that the TFF would *only* screen films which had been presented at the SFF. The TFF would pay a reasonably generous rental for the films selected for its annual tour and so acted as a real inducement for their commercial distribution. After I left the SFF, the TFF started showing films which had *not* played at the SFF and I always felt that this was a mistake.

The third reason for establishing the TFF was to help pay for our full-time staff. In addition to Modesta Gentile, we had recently hired Carol Hughes, an Australian who had briefly worked for Ken Wlaschin, the Director of the London Film Festival and of Britain's National Film Theatre. We employed Carol as an executive assistant and for a short period of time we shared her with the Australian Film Institute. When that arrangement fell through, the TFF, which had been given a modest financial grant by the Australian Film Commission, was able to pay a percentage of Carol's salary, and we also had enough money to pay the wages of a part-time TFF Director.

I spent some time during 1974 setting up the TFF and visiting the regional centres where we planned to screen films. It was a wonderful opportunity for me to explore parts of NSW I'd never visited before. Through the Arts Council I made contact with local arts groups in some of the larger centres. Some were more interested than others in our proposal of a mini-film festival which would be held over a weekend. The people in Lismore were particularly keen, but I discovered that some large centres, like Grafton and Tamworth, no longer had cinemas, which ruled them out. The cinema owner in Dubbo flatly refused to discuss renting out his cinema. In the end, the first season of the TFF visited Lismore – where the local federal member, Doug Anthony, Leader of the Country Party, opened the event – Bowral, Wagga Wagga, Albury, Newcastle and Wollongong. The films we screened that first year included Peter Weir's *The Cars That Ate Paris* and Francis Ford Coppola's *The Conversation*. The event was successful enough to make it worth continuing, and in future years we expanded interstate, eventually visiting such centres as Mount Gambier (SA), Pomona (Qld), Broken Hill and Darwin.

At around this time a new Film Festival was launched in Perth. The Director was Sylvie Le Clezio whose partner, David Roe, had succeeded Richard Brennan as the Director of the Australian Film Institute. For a couple of years in the mid-1970s the Perth

Film Festival presented a problem for the SFF. Films which I had secured for Sydney, including the early work of Werner Herzog, were suddenly withdrawn and soon afterwards were announced for the Perth programme. Meanwhile the AFI – using AFC money – started distributing foreign arthouse films, some of which had previously screened at Perth, among them some Herzog films. The suspicious observer might have deduced that the Perth Festival was accessing films thanks to a distribution deal with the AFI, which was very different from the SFF's arrangements since the SFF had no relationship with the distributors of the films which were selected for the TFF.

During the latter half of 1974 I also spent some time in Canberra viewing classic Australian films at the National Film and Sound Archive. The time had come, I felt, for the SFF to present a comprehensive retrospective of Australian cinema. It was clear that something exciting was happening with the emergence of new filmmakers like Peter Weir, Phillip Noyce, Fred Schepisi and Gillian Armstrong, and I thought the time was right to celebrate this by reminding our audience of the past achievements of our filmmakers.

You'll notice the 'our'. After eleven years in Australia I was beginning to feel like an Australian. I decided that 1975 was the year to celebrate Australian cinema and I concentrated a great deal of time over the next few months on the preparation of the Australian retrospective. Tony Buckley's *Forgotten Cinema* had confirmed that there was a great deal I didn't know about the very rich heritage of Australian cinema and with the help of the Archive's Ray Edmundson I spent several days in Canberra filling in the gaps.

Eventually, I decided to screen a representative number of Australian-made features as well as films made in Australia by foreign production companies, screenings which would take place during the afternoons on each weekday of the Festival. I also invited as many surviving participants as possible from these films to introduce them. These are the feature films I screened in full: *The Sentimental Bloke* (Raymond Longford, 1918); *The Overlanders* (Harry Watt, 1946), introduced by one of the actors in the film, Peter Pagan; *The Man from Kangaroo* (Wilfred Lucas and Bess Meredith, 1919); *Smithy* (Ken G. Hall, 1946, introduced by Hall); *On Our Selection* (Longford, 1920); *The Sundowners* (Fred Zinnemann, 1960); *A Girl of the Bush* (Franklyn Barrett, 1921), introduced by actress Vera James; *Wherever She Goes* (Michael S. Gordon, 1950); *The Adventures of Algy* (Beaumont Smith, 1925); *Robbery Under Arms* (Jack Lee, 1957), introduced by Lee; *Romance of Runnibede* (Scott R. Dunlap, 1928), introduced by Dick Collingridge, son of lead actor Gordon Collingridge; *Mike and Stefani* (R. Maslyn Williams, 1951), introduced by Williams; *The Back of Beyond* (John Heyer, 1953), introduced by Heyer; *The Cheaters* (Paulette McDonagh, 1929); *For the Term of His Natural Life* (Norman Dawn, 1927); *Wake in Fright* (Ted Kotcheff, 1971); *Mr Chedworth Steps Out* (Ken G. Hall, 1939), introduced by Hall; *The Kid Stakes* (Tal Ordell, 1927); *Captain Thunderbolt* (Cecil Holmes, 1955), introduced by Holmes; *A Son Is Born* (Eric Porter, 1946), introduced by Porter; *His Royal Highness* (F. W. Thring, 1931); *The Power and the Glory* (Noel Monkman, 1941); *Forty Thousand Horsemen* (Charles Chauvel, 1940); *Jedda* (Chauvel, 1955); and *Sons of Matthew* (Chauvel, 1949), introduced by lead actor Michael Pate. I also prepared a number of excerpts from the films we didn't have time to screen in full, and we printed a separate booklet about the event.

We opened the 1975 Festival, for the first time, with an Australian film: *Sunday Too Far Away*, despite its chequered production history, had screened the month before in Cannes to great acclaim. We were conscious of the fact that the 1974 opening had been a very special one and we wanted to make this one equally exciting; John Rochester's Opening Night Committee came up with the great idea of seeking permission to close Market Street between Pitt and George Streets and to invite Jack

Thompson, the film's leading actor, to shear sheep out in the open. Thompson was agreeable to this kind of publicity and we managed to acquire the help of Australia's gun shearer to work with him. The problem was finding the sheep; in the end, we had to buy them, and then, after they were shorn, to sell them to the abattoir. The purchase and then sale of a large number of sheep made for an unusual entry in our books for the year. The event made the front pages of the newspapers the next day, which of course was exactly what we wanted. Unfortunately, the film's director, Ken Hannam, was in Europe, but I arranged for Thompson and most of the actors who played shearers in the film to appear on stage the moment the film ended. As I hoped, they received a rousing reception.

One of the highlights of the 1975 SFF was the visit of superstar Warren Beatty. After the success of *Bonnie and Clyde* (1967), which the actor had also produced, Beatty was 'hot' and had appeared to advantage in a number of excellent films, including Robert Altman's *McCabe and Mrs. Miller*. He had also produced his latest film, *Shampoo*, which was directed by Hal Ashby, and in it he played a randy Beverly Hills hairdresser servicing clients played by Julie Christie and Goldie Hawn. *Shampoo* wasn't just a sexy comedy, however; it contained a sharply progressive political undercurrent if you cared to look for it. I invited the film and was surprised, but pleased, when Beatty expressed an interest in attending the Festival.

This, of course, made it a very big deal. Columbia, the distributors, were extremely cooperative and we worked together on publicity and presentation. Beatty's arrival at the airport, accompanied by his brother, who acted as his personal assistant, and by his latest girlfriend, was instructive for me; he was able to bypass Customs completely and leave by a side exit to avoid the waiting press. It was decided to hold a press conference at the Hilton Hotel because Beatty wasn't willing to submit to a lot of one-on-one interviews with the media. I was to host the press conference, and when Warren and I walked into the room to face a large media scrum my eye was immediately caught by Gary MacDonald, an actor I'd met a few months earlier in South Australia when I visited the location of Peter Weir's second feature, *Picnic at Hanging Rock*. MacDonald had played a policeman in the film and I couldn't imagine what he was doing at the Beatty press conference. He seemed to have cut himself shaving and was accompanied by a television crew. *The Norman Gunston Show*, a comedy series in which MacDonald played a gormless interviewer, hadn't yet started its run on television so I had no idea what was going on. MacDonald asked the first question: 'How many women have you had sex with since you arrived, Mr Beatty?' Warren whispered to me: 'What *is* this? Is it a joke?' and I replied that it must be, so he replied to the deliberately insulting question with good humour and the press conference went ahead. I have often thought that Sacha Baron Cohen must have seen episodes of *Norman Gunston*, because his style of comedy is so very similar.

We screened *Shampoo* on a Saturday night and the State was packed to the rafters. Warren made an excellent speech on stage and as we left he expressed interest in the very long throw from the projection room to the screen so I asked him if he'd like to go upstairs to see the bio box. He said he would, so we walked up many stairs and, to the surprise of Bill Dirou and his assistant, Hollywood's number-one superstar at the time did a tour of the State's projection facilities. By the time we'd walked back down the stairs into the cinema lobby the film must have been running for about ten minutes, but as we reached the ground floor a couple emerged from the auditorium, obviously having just walked out.

Warren greeted them in some surprise. 'You don't like it?' he asked. 'Pile of crap, mate!' came the reply from the man and the couple walked on and out into the night. Warren was both amused and annoyed. 'Pile of crap! That I understand,' he said. 'But why did he call me "mate"?'

An important addition to the SFF staff in 1975 was Antonia Barnard, who had arrived earlier that year from the UK. I hired her as my secretary and in a very short time she demonstrated her creativity and enthusiasm so that we became close friends. After she left the SFF she became a producer and she has worked on a number of important films, including Stephan Elliott's *Welcome to Woop Woop*, Phillip Noyce's *The Quiet American* and John Curran's *The Painted Veil.* Carol Hughes also entered the production side of the film industry when she left the Festival.

Greater Union had for many years concentrated mainly on exhibiting films in the cinemas the company controlled but now David Williams and his senior staff had decided to start distributing a small number of films themselves. This policy didn't last very long, but one of the first films GU acquired was Miloš Forman's adaptation of *One Flew Over the Cuckoo's Nest*, the film which finally brought the exiled Czech director a measure of success in America; Miloš won the 1975 Oscar for Best Direction, Jack Nicholson won Best Actor, Louise Fletcher was Best Actress and the production itself was voted Best Film. To launch *Cuckoo's Nest* in Australia, GU invited Forman, Nicholson and producers Saul Zaentz and Michael Douglas to Australia for a publicity tour. David Williams invited me to a small lunch at the San Francisco Grill in the Hilton to welcome them. Warren Beatty, who was a friend of Nicholson – they had just filmed Mike Nichols's *The Fortune* together – had been full of praise for Sydney the city and also for the Sydney Film Festival, and so I had the impression that Nicholson knew something about me; in any event, the lunch was a convivial one. A couple of days later I joined Forman, Nicholson and Douglas on a Harbour cruise, which was also arranged by GU.

I had screened Yugoslav director Dušan Makavejev's remarkable first film, *Man Is Not a Bird*, at my first Festival and since then I'd presented all his work – *Switchboard Operator*, *Nevinost bez zastite* (*Innocence Unprotected*), and the very controversial

W.R.: Misteriste organizma (*W.R.: Mysteries of the Organism*). Makavejev finally found time to come to Sydney himself in 1975 to present *Sweet Movie*, which he'd made as a co-production with Canada. Not everyone understood or liked the film, but one who did was the former Attorney-General Lionel Murphy, who was now a Judge of the High Court; he was very enthusiastic about it and invited Dušan and myself to lunch to discuss some of its more intricate aspects. Makavejev and Murphy got on very well, and Dušan told me later that few people had understood his work as well as Murphy.

I always used to present guests of the Festival with a gift when they left the country and in Dušan's case I gave him a copy of *The Americans, Baby*, by Frank Moorhouse, which I thought he would appreciate. He did. He phoned me from Hawaii to tell me he'd loved the book and especially one of the stories in it, *The Coca-Cola Kid*, and that he'd be very keen to make a film of it. He eventually did just that, though it took him almost ten years, but it was a pity that, when the film was finally made, Makavejev's celebrated improvisational style of working and his fondness for introducing tangential material were suppressed and replaced by a far more linear structure. The producer was David Roe, and although *The Coca-Cola Kid*, which was released in 1985, wasn't a bad film, it certainly isn't one of Makavejev's best.

Visits from film people weren't confined to the periods in which the SFF actually took place. By now I'd acquired something of an international reputation, it seemed, and from time to time I would receive a call from someone seeking advice or contacts. There was a period in the late 1960s when the British director, Michael Winner, enjoyed something of a reputation for free-wheeling anti-establishment movies like *The Jokers* and *I'll Never Forget What's 'Is Name*; this reputation tarnished over the years, but when he came to Sydney in 1969 to film the Australian segment of *The Games*, a movie that followed the fortunes of four marathon runners from different parts of the world, I received a call inviting me to drop in on the location, which was situated at one of Sydney's Northern Beaches. Whatever his qualities as a film director, Winner was an avuncular character and watching him at work was fun.

Barbet Schroeder was a French producer and director whose reputation in the latter area rested on *More*, a sexy movie about hippies on Ibitha. He passed through Sydney in 1971 with his talented cameraman, Cuban-born Nestor Almendros; they were on their way to Papua New Guinea to shoot a film called *La Vallee*, and Barbet was interested in contacting Australians who might be willing to work – for minimal wages, I gathered – on the film.

An altogether larger project which was nearly made in Australia was Francis Ford Coppola's *Apocalypse Now*. Sometime in 1974, the year I screened the world premiere of Coppola's magnificent film, *The Conversation*, at the SFF, I received a visit from Dean Tavoularis, who was the director's production designer, and Fred Roos, one of his producers. They told me that Coppola was planning to make a screen version of Joseph Conrad's *Heart of Darkness*, updated to the conflict in Vietnam. They wanted to shoot the film in far north Queensland, and they were passing through Sydney touching base with local production companies that might be of assistance. It sounded like an enormously exciting project, but it hinged on the willingness of the Federal Government to make available to the production men and material, including helicopters, from the armed forces. This the Government was, as it turned out, unwilling to do, and so in the end *Apocalpyse Now* was shot, with great difficulty, in the Philippines, where access to military hardware was easier but where the weather proved to be extremely treacherous. The film wasn't completed until 1979. Over twenty years later, American director Terrence Malick was able to shoot *The Thin Red Line*, based on the James Jones book about the World War II battle for Guadalcanal, in North Queensland.

Another exciting film project that nearly got made in this country in the mid-1970s was a screen adaptation of Patrick White's novel *Voss*. The entrepreneur Harry M. Miller, famous at the time for bringing *Hair* to the stage in Australia despite the strict censorship of the period, had acquired the film rights, but White, who regularly attended the Sydney Film Festival, was something of a film buff and was certain that the only contemporary director who would be able to make a film of *Voss* was the exiled American Joseph Losey. Losey, who had made some fine *films noir* in his home country, had become a victim of McCarthyism and had been blacklisted; he had relocated to London and had, during the 1960s, made a remarkable number of films there, many starring Dirk Bogarde, including *The Servant*, *King and Country* and *Accident*. He had almost made a film in Australia before this: he had been the first to show an interest in *Wake in Fright*, which, had he filmed it, would have starred Dirk Bogarde as the intimidated schoolteacher.

Losey was very keen to make *Voss*, and he had in mind Maximilian Schell for the leading role, but it was not to be. Miller needed funding for the project from the Australian Film Commission, and though the AFC was, apparently, happy to accept a foreign director and leading actor, they demanded more than just locations and the source novel as Australian content if they were to invest. Australia had already had demonstrated that local cameramen, such as Russell Boyd, Don McAlpine and Peter James, were world-class, and there were excellent post-production facilities here too. But Losey insisted on using his own camera crew and handling the post-production in London. I had a couple of discussions with him, but it was clear there would be no meeting of minds. *Voss* has not, as yet, been filmed.

In 1974 I had closed the Festival with a 70-mm print of Richard Lester's *The Three Musketeers*. For the 1975 closing night, Cinema International Corporation (CIC), the distributor of Paramount and Universal films at the time, offered me a choice between Steven Spielberg's *Jaws* or John Schlesinger's *Day of the Locust*. They didn't have a print of either film at the time my decision had to be made, so I had to make the choice sight unseen. Nor did I have overseas reviews to rely on because neither film had opened. After some deliberation I chose Schlesinger's film, which, of course, was a mistake; I'd always liked Schlesinger's work, and the prospect of a drama set in 1930s Hollywood was appealing. On the other hand, I'd liked both *Duel* and *The Sugarland Express*, Spielberg's first two features, but I thought a film about a giant shark might turn out to be a bit silly. *Day of the Locust* was a major disappointment; *Jaws* turned out to be something of a triumph.

A few months later, in September, I was attending the San Sebastian Film Festival where *Jaws* was receiving its European launch. *Variety*'s Robert Hawkins asked me to join him at a lunch he was having with Gerry Lewis, the head of international publicity for CIC, and Steven Spielberg. 'Gerry says Spielberg's a bit of a film buff,' Bob told me, 'and I know you are, so I thought you might hit it off.' We did indeed; I found that Spielberg and I shared an affection for many of the same films, and after a long lunch we returned to his hotel room to talk more about our favourite directors and movies. He gave me his phone number and told me to call him whenever I was in LA. I never did, though, partly because my visits there were so fleeting and so rushed. Looking back now, I wish I had.

Another European director whose work I'd loved and championed during this period was Wim Wenders. I showed all his films – *Die Angst des tormanns beim Elfmeter* (*The Goalkeeper's Fear of the Penalty*), *Alice in den Stadten* (*Alice in the Cities*) and *Falsche Bewegung* (*Wrong Movement*). I programmed his masterpiece, *Im Lauf der Zeit* (*Kings of the Road*), sight unseen – because Wim sent me a copy direct from its Cannes premiere. He had always hoped to attend the Festival, because he was a great traveller, but he never managed it. Then, in the December of 1977, I had a call from

Wim who was in Darwin. He had been attending a German Film Week in Jakarta and had hopped on a boat. Now he wanted to come to Sydney but he had run out of money. Could I help? I transferred some funds to a bank in Darwin and he phoned again a couple of days later to say he'd hitchhiked down to Alice Springs and that he was overwhelmed by the beauty of the landscape of the outback. He finally arrived in Sydney just before Christmas with seemingly hundreds of rolls of colour film he wanted developed urgently. I sought the help of a photographer friend who very kindly dropped everything to develop the films, and I persuaded Antonia Barnard to let Wim stay in the spare room of her house. It was a very fleeting visit; after a couple of days in Sydney he set off to hitchhike north again; but out of that Australian experience came his 1991 film, *Bis ans Ende der Welt* (*Until the End of the World*). To this day, he hasn't repaid me the money I loaned him, or the cost of developing the photographs, but he did buy me a hamburger the next time we met in Berlin.

While Wim was in Sydney a mutual friend, Tom Luddy, phoned my office from San Francisco looking for him. I'd met Tom when he was programming the Pacific Film Archive with Albert Johnson and he had also been a programmer at the San Francisco Film Festival. He was now working for Francis Ford Coppola and he wanted to tell Wim that Coppola had given the green light for Wim to direct *Hammett*, a film noir inspired by an incident in the life of the writer, Dashiell Hammett. The following year I went on holiday with Carol Hughes and her boyfriend, Steve Elliott, a cheerful Welshman who had moved into the apartment I had been sharing with Carol. We flew to Los Angeles, rented a car, and drove up the Californian coast meeting Wim in San Francisco where he was working on *Hammett*.

The success of the Australian retrospective at the 1975 Festival had an interesting sequel. Brian Adams, the former producer of the ABC arts programme *Spectrum*, was no longer working for the national broadcaster and had decided to make a feature-length documentary about the history of Australian film; he asked me to write the script. We enlisted the help of Graham Shirley and I worked on the project for a couple of weeks. When Brian managed to interest Jack Thompson in reading the narration, my script underwent a major change; I had envisioned the narration as being confined to a voiceover while clips from the films themselves were on screen. But Brian thought audiences would want to *see* Thompson, who was the most popular Australian actor at the time, and so we rewrote it to have Jack speak the narration directly to the camera in various locations which were important landmarks in film history such as Collins Street in Melbourne, site of the first Australian cinema, and Port Arthur in Tasmania, where much of *For the Term of His Natural Life* was filmed in 1926. This decision considerably slowed down *Sunshine and Shadows*, as the documentary was called, and, in the end, greatly diminished it. I don't think Brian was happy with the result and nor was I. Some time later the writer/producer Joan Long made a series of three films about the Australian film industry which were not only far superior to our effort but were models of their kind.

The focus of the 1976 SFF was Italian cinema and Gideon Bachmann, a Rome-based film writer and documentary director, agreed to programme the event for me. We opened the festival with Lina Wertmuller's *Pasqualino Settebellezze* (*Seven Beauties*) and the star of the film, Giancarlo Giannini, flew in to attend the ceremonies. The evening was somewhat marred by the fact that the Lord Mayor of Sydney brought as his guest the Mayor of Jerusalem, Teddy Kollek, who took exception to Wertmuller's approach towards some events that took place during World War II and walked out, rather noisily, during the screening. This wasn't the first time a VIP had taken offence at an aspect of the opening night film; six years earlier the Festival's patron, NSW Governor Sir Roden Cutler, expressed displeasure at the opening film, *Z*, Costa-Gavras's examination of a political assassination in his native Greece. Apparently the Governor was annoyed by the film's final scene, in which the director focuses his camera on the military medals worn by the film's villains, the colonels who had seized power in Greece. In any event, that was the last opening the Governor attended.

The 1976 Festival, which included the premiere of Fred Schepisi's *The Devil's Playground*, closed with Luchino Visconti's *L'Innocente*, which had screened a couple of weeks earlier in Cannes. Visconti, director of such fine films as *Senso* and *Il Gattopardo* (*The Leopard*) had died in Rome the previous March, before his last film had been publicly screened.

One morning in 1975 I received an unexpected call from the *Variety* office in London. Harold Myers (Myro), a British-based troubleshooter for the paper, was on the phone. Since it was obvious that big things were happening in film production in Australia, he said, Syd Silverman, the paper's publisher, had decided to establish a *Variety* bureau in Sydney; was I interested in running it? I was amazed by this proposition, because, apart from my occasional contributions to *The Bulletin*, *The Age* and *Men in Vogue*, I had no experience – and certainly no training – in journalism. I wondered if someone at *Variety* had been impressed with my unsolicited review of *Three to Go*, or perhaps I'd been recommended by some of my friends who worked for the paper? Although I was very flattered to be offered the job I didn't think I was suited for it; but I knew who'd be perfect in the position.

Mike Harris was, at the time, reviewing films for *The Australian*, having taken over from Michael Thornhill when the latter left to direct films. Mike was American-born, British-raised and was married to an Australian, Carolyn. He was a born journalist, erudite, amusing, witty – a lover of food and drink and good company. He and Carolyn lived at Palm Beach and at weekends they regularly invited friends, who were entertained with 16-mm films projected onto a sheet and were treated to Carolyn's superb cooking. The Harrises' home was an oasis for me at a time when I was personally a bit rootless. When Harold Myers arrived in

Sydney to discuss the *Variety* position with me I told him that I thought Mike would be a far better candidate for the job and I drove him and his wife, Maxie, up to Palm Beach to meet the Harrises. As I expected, they hit it off immediately and before long Mike was establishing *Variety*'s first Australian bureau in a small office in Albion Place, just behind the George Street cinemas. Mike arrived on the scene in time to cover the Australian film revival for *Variety*, which he did with wit and perception.

In addition to my drives through rural America, I also took time, whenever I could, to travel by car during the weeks I spent in Europe. The most extensive drive I undertook was in the Northern summer of 1976, when I hired a car in Warsaw, after seeing the latest Polish films, and drove to the ancient city of Cracow. I had intended to take a train from Cracow to Budapest, but I discovered that the last moment that a Czech visa would be required because the train made a stop in Czechoslovakia. There was no Czech consulate in Cracow; the nearest was in the coalmining city of Katowice, several kilometres away. It was Friday afternoon, and the Consulate would close in an hour's time. I drove furiously on bad roads through heavy rain but – too late. The Consulate had closed. I spent the weekend in Katowice and was waiting outside the Consulate when it opened on the Monday morning.

After seeing the latest Hungarian films in Budapest, I went to the Pula Film Festival and from there to Trieste, where I rented a car in which I drove first to Venice, for a short break, and then to Locarno for the Film Festival. I then drove through Germany and into Denmark, then by ferry from Helsingor (the site of Hamlet's castle) to Helsingborg, in southern Sweden. From there it took two days to drive to Stockholm, after which I went on to Oslo and then to Bergen, where I caught a ferry to Newcastle, in England, and drove on up to Edinburgh for the Film Festival.

My companion on this lengthy drive was Karen Jaehne, an attractive, fun-loving American who, at the time, was living in

Berlin. Karen was twenty-nine and though she didn't talk much about her past I gathered she had been married and divorced. She was a great film enthusiast and very good company, but the distances between us ensured that our relationship ended in Edinburgh. I saw her occasionally in succeeding years after she returned to America and married for a second time. For a while she also reviewed films for *Variety*, but her life ended tragically young when she died of cancer in 2000 at the age of fifty-one.

In Paris in December 1976, I saw Bernardo Bertolucci's *1900*, which was screened in two separate parts. I was so impressed that I saw it again, a few days later, in Munich, where it was dubbed into German. I was very keen to screen *1900* in Sydney in 1977, especially when I heard that the English release version of the film was expected to be a cut-down combination of parts one and two with about two hours of footage removed.

For the first half of 1977 I kept in touch with Bertolucci, who tried hard to arrange for the only English-subtitled copy of the integral version to be sent to Sydney; right up until the last moment, I hoped he would succeed, and I left the final two sessions open for a 'surprise' event. But in the end Bertolucci wrote to say he couldn't deliver as hoped, so once again I was faced with the problem of finding a last-minute closing-night film. An interesting candidate was *Star Wars*, which had opened in America during the last week of May to generally positive reviews. Pierre Rissient, who was again visiting the Festival, knew some people at 20th Century-Fox in LA and phoned them for me; they agreed to let us have *Star Wars* for closing night and promised to send us a print, but before I could even announce this good news they rang again to say that the film had become such an unexpected success at the box office that they needed every print available for North American cinemas. They suggested another Fox release, Joseph Losey's *M. Klein,* which wasn't exactly a cheerful closing-night film – it dealt with the Holocaust – but at least was a respectable one.

Pierre and I had become good friends. On one of my trips to Hollywood, he had taken me to see Clint Eastwood shooting his film *Breezy*, with William Holden, and this was the start of several meetings with Eastwood over the years. I loved Pierre's enthusiasm for films ('It's not enough to like a film, you have to like it for the right reasons!' he would maintain) and I also appreciated his admiration for some of the more obscure figures of Hollywood history, like Harry D'Abbadie D'Arrast, who had directed a handful of remarkable films in the late silent and early sound period. Whenever I met him in Paris Pierre always knew the best restaurants and the most interesting up-and-coming filmmakers. He had been in partnership with Bertrand Tavernier in a company promoting films, but now Tavernier had branched out to become a director himself. Pierre directed a couple of films too – *One Night Stand* and *Cinq et la Peau* (*Five and the Skin*) – which were most interesting but which never captured much public attention.

In January 1977 I attended the New Delhi Film Festival. It was a very impressive affair, not so much for the films that screened but for the people who came to India for the event. Satyajit Ray had been an advisor to the festival and he had arranged for many of his colleagues to attend. Mosk was there, of course, and John Gillett, and other critics and film professionals. One of the highlights of the Festival was a trip to Agra to see the Taj Mahal. When we arrived at the car park adjacent to the world-famous tomb, Satyajit called me over to pose for a photo with him in company with Akira Kurosawa and Michelangelo Antonioni; afterwards he insisted that the celebrated Japanese and Italian directors ride on an elephant, and eagerly took photographs of them looking rather uncomfortable atop the swaying animal. Later I strolled around the Taj in the company of Spain's Carlos Saura, Sweden's Bo Widerberg and Switzerland's Alain Tanner. A few days later, the Prime Minister, Indira Ghandi, invited some of the Festival guests to a breakfast in her rooms at

Parliament House. Once again, Satyajit was influential in assembling the guest list; I was there, so was Mosk and so were Antonioni and Kurosawa, as well as Elia Kazan. It was, indeed, a memorable occasion, one of the most memorable during my eighteen years as SFF Director.

Chapter Fourteen

Greater Union and Hoyts were very well-established cinema owners, or exhibitors in Australia but the Village-Roadshow company was relatively new on the local scene. V-R had commenced operations in Victoria with an exhibition chain and, by the mid-1970s, had become a major force with cinemas across the country and an active distribution arm, which included the entire output of Warner Bros. V-R was run by Graham Burke in Melbourne and Greg Coote in Sydney. I got to know Greg quite well, and in 1978 he approached me with the suggestion that I programme the smaller of the two cinemas the company operated in Double Bay on the site of what had previously been the Greater Union Vogue. The idea was to specialise in foreign-language and independent films and Greg made it clear that in his opinion my profile as SFF Director would carry some marketing weight. Ross Tzannes and the SFF Committee had no objection to this proposal and so the 'David Stratton Showcase' came into being. In the beginning, Greg had been generous enough to offer me a small percentage of gross ticket sales, and since my salary from the Festival had been on the spartan side for all these years this was the first opportunity for me to earn real money. For the first time I was able to buy a new car.

In later years I came across many people who assumed I owned the Showcase, which was, of course, still operated by Village-Roadshow. It was also confused with Dave's Encore Cinema, a tiny repertory cinema near Central Railway which usually screened films on 16-mm and with which I had no connection. The Showcase ran quite successfully for some time and was promoted skilfully by V-R so that the box office actually increased. Inevitably, though, tensions arose when Village wanted to programme a so-called 'arthouse' film which I didn't like; the first of these was Menahem Golan's *The Magician of Lublin*, which was programmed at the Showcase in my absence and against my wishes. The problem was eventually sorted out and the Showcase continued until Greg left the company, after which the arrangement lapsed.

Dorothy Holt, a long serving member of the SFF Committee, was also active in the Art Gallery Society of NSW, and she came up with the idea of a joint initiative by the Gallery and the SFF to present the work of Andy Warhol. Warhol was the most famous pop artist in the world; his silk screenings of Marilyn Monroe and reproductions of Campbell's Soup cans had made him a celebrity in his own right. He'd been making experimental films since 1963, some of which were notoriously long (*Sleep*, which depicted a man asleep, ran for eight hours) and some of which, like *Blow Job*, were reported to be sexually explicit (a false report, in the case of that particular film). Since 1968 Warhol had handed over the direction of his films to Paul Morrissey, starting with *Flesh*, and the films had improved, become more structured and more audience-friendly, though they were still on the far side of way-out. I'd programmed the Warhol-produced, Morrissey-directed *Trash* in the 1973 Festival and though, as I told Dorothy,

I had some misgivings about the prospect of a Warhol film retrospective I agreed to visit The Factory, Warhol's legendary headquarters, when next I was in New York.

This was indeed an experience! The place was laid out as an open space, and Warhol's 'superstars' (Ultra Violet, Viva, Candy Darling, Joe Dallesandro) drifted around aimlessly. Warhol didn't seem to grasp what I was talking about; perhaps he was stoned (though it was midafternoon) but I clearly wasn't getting anywhere with him.

Morrissey was much more approachable but told me candidly that he didn't think that such an ambitious plan – combining the films and the artworks in retrospective exhibitions in the same city – would work, especially in Australia. I came away empty-handed.

In 1978 the SFF celebrated its twenty-fifth anniversary, and I wanted to make an opening-night splash just as we had in 1974 and 1975. The first production of the NSW Film Corporation was *Newsfront*, which is still, today, my favourite Australian film. David Elfick was the producer, Bob Ellis the principle writer and Phillip Noyce the director. All of them had a close association with the SFF. Noyce had not only won the first Rouben Mamoulian Award four years earlier but, in 1977, I had encouraged him to allow me to screen his 60-minute film, *Backroads*, a low-budget road movie of considerable interest, in a prominent feature slot at the Festival; Noyce has often said that this encouraged him to continue with a feature film career. Both Noyce and Elfick, who had screened a rough cut of the film for me and Ross Tzannes in January that year, were keen for the SFF to open with his film. I was very excited about opening with *Newsfront* and we were already planning a big event along the lines of the *Sunday Too Far Away* opening; to add to the interest, the film was about a Cinesound newsreel camera team, and Cinesound had been owned by Greater Union. The synergy was all there. But it was not to be.

The CEO of the NSWFC, Paul Riomfalvy, vetoed the participation of *Newsfront* in the Festival. The official reason he gave us was that he and his Board had concerns that the Festival screening might detract from the film's subsequent commercial career. It was true that, after its 1974 SFF premiere, Peter Weir's *The Cars That Ate Paris* had not succeeded in cinemas, but *Sunday Too Far Away* had been a commercial success and in my view the Festival screening would only add to the lustre of *Newsfront*, a film I was certain would be a commercial and critical success. I wondered whether the decision was in any way due to David Roe, who had moved from the AFI to become the Corporation's Marketing Director, or to Michael Thornhill, who was a member of the Corporation's Board; neither of them had been very good friends of the SFF.

We used all our considerable clout to appeal to the NSW Premier, Neville Wran, who agreed, in principle, that it would be a good idea to have a NSWFC film open the Festival. There was, however, another film from the same source: the Corporation's *second* production was Tony Buckley's film *The Night the Prowler*, based on an original screenplay by Patrick White and directed by Jim Sharman (who had scored a huge cult success with *The Rocky Horror Picture Show* three years earlier). Riomfalvy offered us *The Night the Prowler* instead of *Newsfront* and we were hardly in a position to refuse. *The Night the Prowler* was an interesting film, even a bold one, but it was hardly opening-night material. Nevertheless, we made the best of it and I was always pleased that Patrick White agreed to appear on stage before the screening. But to this day I regret that we were unable to open with *Newsfront* as planned; it could have been the greatest opening of all.

Newsfront wasn't the only Australian film refused to us in 1978. In April John Duigan screened me his film *Mouth to Mouth*, a fine piece of work about a pair of runaway Melbourne teenage girls. I invited the film but, to my surprise and disappointment, the distributor, Roadshow, a company with whom I thought I had good relations, refused to allow participation. The decision was made by Roadshow's Director of Marketing, Alan Finney, who was implacable in his opposition to a festival screening. It was very frustrating not only for me but, I think, also for Duigan. When it was eventually released some months later, *Mouth to Mouth* didn't perform spectacularly at the box office.

That year we screened Alan Rudolph's first feature, *Welcome to L.A.*, a poignant film about the music scene, produced by Robert Altman; the film had not been picked up for distribution in Australia. Rudolph was unable to come to Sydney but the film's lead actor, Keith Carradine, agreed at the last moment to attend. Before I knew that Carradine was coming, I'd scheduled a late-night screening of the uncut print of Orson Welles's *Touch of Evil* to follow *Welcome to L.A.* on the first Saturday night of the Festival so there was no opportunity for the actor to take part in the usual Q&A after the screening of the film. Accordingly, I slotted in a time for Carradine to talk about the film to the audience the following afternoon. The discussion went well but the audience was starting to arrive for the next screening, Shyam Benegal's *Manthan*; Carradine was in the middle of answering a question when someone yelled out: 'Get off, you wanker!' Carradine left the stage immediately and was extremely angry and upset. I was furious at the boorish behaviour of the unknown heckler.

However, there also were moments to cherish. The alternative newspaper, *Nation Review*, which provided some of the best reading in the mid-1970s (Bob Ellis wrote the film reviews and Sam Orr's restaurant reviews were hilarious), printed a small announcement in the personal column one week announcing an engagement: 'We met at the Film Festival. Thank you David Stratton!'

I had become fascinated with the evolving Australian film industry and I decided to write a book about it. At every opportunity during 1979 I interviewed the new Australian film directors who had emerged during the 1970s – Peter Weir, Bruce Beresford,

Tim Burstall, Michael Thornhill, Phillip Noyce, Gillian Armstrong, John Duigan and others. These interviews formed the basis for *The Last New Wave*, which was published in 1980 by Angus and Robertson. I dedicated the book to Gene Moskowitz and sent him the first copy. He was very touched, I think, that I'd acknowledged our friendship in this way. I was thrilled when the former Prime Minister Gough Whitlam agreed to launch the book at the Film and Television School.

Reactions to the book were mainly positive but I was very disappointed by the review in the magazine *Cinema Papers*, which criticised the book not for what it *was* but for what the reviewer thought it should have been. This taught me a lesson; that it's all too easy for a critic to review not the film, or book or whatever, which the artist has made but, instead, to review what the critic thought he *ought* to have made.

Mike Harris had been reviewing all the films of the Australian New Wave for *Variety* but, in May 1979, the paper had asked him to join the team at the Cannes Film Festival. Aware that two new features were about to be released, he asked me if I would review them in his absence. One of them was John Duigan's *Dimboola*, which, I thought, was a major disappointment, but the other was George Miller's *Mad Max*.

Seven years earlier, Miller, then still a medical student, had submitted a short film titled *Violence in the Cinema Part 1* in what was then still called the Benson & Hedges Awards for Australian Short Films. Sitting in the projection box while the judges viewed the entries that year, Ross Tzannes and I were both struck by the originality of this provocative meditation on cinema violence. Although the judges failed to select the film as a finalist in the competition, we decided it had to be screened. I phoned Miller the next morning and sought his permission to screen the film out of competition; he agreed.

The film was programmed on the afternoon of the holiday Monday that year in support of a feature from Yugoslavia, and the audience response was immediate. After the screening, John Fraser, of Greater Union, told me he'd like to distribute it. Miller was nowhere around (we had never actually met) but I phoned him the next day to tell him that Greater Union wanted to distribute his film. He seemed surprised, and not really aware as to what the distribution of his film involved.

Now he had made his first feature. I thought *Mad Max* was an extraordinary achievement for this young doctor (Miller was a GP) with no formal training in cinema. Obviously inspired by great traditions of genre cinema, both American and Japanese, Miller had made a cult movie for the ages and, in the process, had made a star out of a young actor named Mel Gibson. *Variety* published my reviews of both *Mad Max* and *Dimboola* on 16 May that year, my second and third reviews for the paper.

Meanwhile, after a quarter of a century at the helm of the Melbourne Film Festival, Erwin Rado retired at the end of 1979. I was genuinely sorry to see him go. We'd worked very harmoniously over the years and I'd become very fond of him. But I was pleased that his replacement was to be Geoff Gardner, whom I knew and liked a great deal. I think that, to begin with, Geoff found Erwin's presence behind the scenes intimidating and even restrictive, and since many of the films had already been selected for the 1980 festival he had little room to manoeuvre. That European summer Geoff and I spent some time together at the Venice and San Sebastian Festivals and I came to respect his taste and enthusiasm even more.

Geoff only directed three Melbourne Festivals. After the 1982 event he left to work for Gareth Evans, the prominent federal Labor Party politician. In the wake of the 1983 election, which swept Bob Hawke to power, Evans became Attorney-General, and Geoff saw to it that the censorship regulations pertaining to the festivals were formalised in a way that had not been carried out by Chipp or even by Lionel Murphy. The Melbourne Festival scene became rather chaotic after Geoff's departure; his replacement,

Franco Cavarro, seems to have made rather heavy weather of the preparations for the 1983 Festival and Erwin came out of retirement to take over. He wound up directing the 1983 and 1984 Festivals before retiring for a second time. Erwin had become interested in film production and had written a screenplay he wanted István Szabó to direct; in the meantime he also became involved with some projects by Paul Cox and he makes 'guest' appearances in a couple of Cox's films made at this time. In 1985 Erwin suffered a stroke at home; help didn't reach him soon enough to save his right arm from contracting gangrene, and it had to be amputated. This was a terrible blow for Erwin but he bore it bravely. Sadly in 1988, a second stroke brought to an end, at the age of seventy-four, a rich and fulfilling life, and robbed me of a close friend.

Ten years earlier, in 1978, Ian McPherson had given up his job at CSR and joined the staff of the SFF as Administrator. It was good to have someone with his enthusiasm and knowledge in the office but, sadly, his time with us proved to be all too short. Early in 1980 he was diagnosed with cancer. 'I'm going to beat it,' he assured me when I returned from the Berlin Festival that year. 'I'm too young to die.' Nevertheless, his illness progressed and he was forced to resign in June after the Festival ended. He died in August while I was away attending the Edinburgh Film Festival. The following year, we inaugurated an annual lecture, the Ian McPherson Memorial Lecture, with the intention of inviting overseas guests to deliver it. I missed Ian's cheery optimism; he was one of my first, and closest, friends in Australia.

At about the same time that Ian became ill Gene Moskowitz was also diagnosed with a form of cancer. Mosk had recently married a young American mime artist, Vernice Kleber, who had come to visit him in his tiny Paris apartment and had simply stayed on. To Mosk's delight, Vernice had given birth to a son, Justin. But my old friend's happiness was short-lived; when I saw him in Paris in September 1981, I was shocked at his appearance;

the cheerful, rotund man I knew so well was now painfully thin and barely recognisable. Nevertheless, he soldiered on. The following February he came to Berlin and I returned with him on the flight to Paris after the Festival, dropping him off at his home. He went to Cannes that year too, for the last time. The final film he reviewed for *Variety* was his friend Lindsay Anderson's *Britannia Hospital.* Pierre Rissient, who was one of several friends who cared for Mosk in Cannes that last year, remembers that Anderson kept badgering him over the review of the film, constantly calling to ask when it would be completed and when it would be published.

Throughout the summer of 1982 Mosk lingered on, with Vernice caring for him. I visited them in the Paris apartment in September. Gene had been re-watching old films on video and he told me that he wept through *The Grapes of Wrath* and *Limelight.* I was in my office in Sydney on 29 December when the new Festival Administrator, Lyn McCarthy, told me the sad news. Mosk was dead. But there was worse to come. His cancer had apparently been transferred to his little son. Justin, the handsome boy of whom Gene was so proud, died not very long after his father.

Many years later I discovered that, throughout the 1970s and into the early 1980s, the period I had been directing the Sydney Film Festival, I had been the subject of interest from the Australian Security and Intelligence Office (ASIO). ASIO operatives had observed me whenever I visited the Consulate or Embassy of a Communist country, which was usually to collect a visa so that I could visit the country concerned. More than that, though, an ASIO file I've seen reported that I attended a function at the Polish Consulate in Sydney on Poland's National Day and that I was wearing a red tie! Horrors! If keeping tabs on me was typical of ASIO activity, then you really have to question the competence of the organisation.

Throughout this period the Sydney Film Festival had been evolving gradually but significantly. By the early 1980s, we were screening an annual retrospective on weekday afternoons and I was inviting a guest programmer ('curator', as they're called these days) to make selections for the weekday 5.30 pm sessions with the aim of opening up the event to radical, cutting-edge material. But I was beginning to feel that political correctness was affecting the responses to some of the festival films. In 1982, for example, I invited Paul Bartel's scabrous black comedy *Eating Raoul*, which had been well-received at other festivals. Bartel, a former protégé of Roger Corman, was well-liked in the industry but during his Q&A session at the State Theatre he was pilloried by feminists in the audience who evidently had failed to see the funny side of his film. At the same Festival I had invited Lindsay Anderson to present *Britannia Hospital* and to deliver the first Ian McPherson Memorial Lecture. Lindsay, a lifelong fighter for quality cinema, had some pertinent things to say about the kind of film being financed by the British Film Institute, which he saw as too narrowly based, too political and often badly made. Again, some militants in the audience reacted in anger to Anderson's comments.

The poor treatment afforded to such talented directors as Bartel and Anderson by segments of the audience depressed me. Also depressing were the deaths of my friends Ian McPherson and Gene Moskowitz and the resurgence of censorship controversy over the films *The Tin Drum* and *Pixote*. I was beginning to feel that I should follow Erwin's example and retire from the Festival. Two other important considerations then came into play; one was my growing closeness to Susie Craig, the woman who became my second wife; we married in 1985. I was keenly aware that my first marriage had failed mainly because I was away so much and had worked such long hours on behalf of the SFF and I was determined that I would make more of a success of my second marriage. Susie had a son, Ben, by her first marriage and over the years he and I became very close.

The other consideration was Prime Minister Malcolm Fraser's decision to start a multicultural television service, to be called the

Special Broadcasting Service, or SBS. I was only dimly aware of the existence of SBS Radio, which had been established in the late 1970s to provide programming in different languages for many ethnic communities within Australia. The first I knew that a television equivalent of the radio station was to be opened was when I had a call from Bruce Gyngell, the man who had made an indelible mark when television began in Australia in 1956; his was the first face viewers saw. Speaking on TCN9, Gyngell's famous 'Good evening, ladies and gentlemen, welcome to television' had made him a household name. Now he had been assigned the task of bringing an ambitious, and very different, new television network to air.

The charter of SBS called for multicultural programming, and that meant programmes, including films, from around the world. Gyngell explained to me that he needed my input since few people in Australia at the time knew as much about world cinema as I did. He was offering me the role of Feature Film Consultant to the network, which was an extremely exciting challenge.

Because I was becoming involved at the very outset I was in a position to make a few suggestions. It was the policy of the new network to screen every programme in the original language with English subtitles, so that was never in question. I also asked that the films be screened, as far as possible, in the correct ratio (that is, to be 'letterboxed' if they had been shot in a widescreen format) – this often proved difficult to achieve, but I felt it necessary because most television networks 'panned and scanned' widescreen films, a device that filled the square-shaped television screen but which removed about half the original image. My final suggestion was that the films not be censored; I said that I would rather not screen a film at all than screen it with cuts. We came to an agreement that films could be discussed on an individual basis if an issue of censorship cropped up. Gyngell told me that, like the ABC, the new network was to be permitted to appoint its own censorship classification officer who would be responsible for classifying the programmes using the guidelines of the Censorship Board, which now had the grand name of the Office of Film and Literature Classification.

I cleared my involvement with SBS with Ross Tzannes, and entered into an agreement to work part-time as Feature Film Consultant in January 1980; SBS was scheduled to go to air for the first time the following October. From then on I spent much of my spare time compiling lists of titles of films and, where possible, international film contacts. To begin with we concentrated on films which already had Australian distribution, because it was quicker and easier to obtain the rights to them. Unfortunately, many of the prints held by local distributors were badly scratched and damaged after some months or even years in release, and it was impossible to clean them up. This problem was solved once we started dealing directly with producers to obtain pristine copies of the films we acquired for broadcasting.

I was in Europe when SBS television launched in October. The first feature to be screened was Bo Widerberg's *Elvira Madigan* followed by an eclectic selection of international cinema. But when I checked in with Gyngell on my return he wasn't entirely happy. He liked the films I'd selected but he felt that he, and the wider audience, would appreciate them better if they were contextualised. With this in mind he invited me to host a weekly 'movie of the week' which, to begin with was called *A Whole World of Movies*. Gyngell suggested that I wear a tuxedo for the presentation but fortunately I was able to talk him out of that idea. I hosted my first movie, Claude Gorretta's *La Dentelliere* (*The Lacemaker*), with Isabelle Huppert, on 1 February 1981.

I was awful. I had no idea how to use an autocue, and the producer of my segment didn't really show me how. I was too vain to wear glasses so I peered shortsightedly at the camera. I was awkward and hesitant and downright embarrassing. Unfortunately, at about this time video recorders started to become widely available and I still have a few copies of my early movie introductions. They're a grim reminder of just how terrible it's possible to be on television. At least the films that I was introducing were worth seeing. A week later I presented Shyam Benegal's *Junoon*, followed on 15 February by Bertolucci's *The Conformist* and on 22 February by Wenders's *The American Friend*.

Somehow Gyngell persevered with me. Indeed, we became quite friendly and, early in 1982 he made me an interesting proposition. This was the time of 10BA, the period when tax breaks to assist Australian film production were unusually generous. Some major players had entered the film industry as a result; Kerry Packer had formed an unlikely partnership with Phillip Adams to form Adams-Packer Films, a company that produced some significant movies, including Paul Cox's *Lonely Hearts*, Igor Auzins's *We of the Never Never* and Donald Crombie's *Kitty and the Bagman*. Australian ex-pats Rupert Murdoch and Robert Stigwood had also joined forces and formed a company, Associated R&R Films, with the aim of producing local movies; in the event, they only made one, Peter Weir's *Gallipoli*, but it was a magnificent one.

Inspired by this, Gyngell proposed starting a film company himself and invited me to be, in effect, executive producer, choosing key personnel and inviting top directors, like Weir, Armstrong, Noyce, Schepisi and others, to bring their projects to the company. We had several secret meetings about this project, one at Gyngell's home, one in Melbourne, and one at Beppi's Restaurant in Sydney, where Gyngell introduced me to some of the financial people who would back the new company. I was stimulated by these ideas, and went so far as telling Ross Tzannes that, if Gyngell's plans worked out, I would resign from the Festival after the 1982 event. Luckily, Ross kept this to himself because, in the end, nothing ever eventuated. I don't know what happened. Maybe Gyngell lost interest, or got a better offer, or it all became too hard. But suddenly it was all off, and I was left with a feeling of considerable frustration, and contemplating what might have been.

The beginning of the 1980s saw the start of a revolution in the way we were able to see films; video had arrived. Until that time the only way to see older films had been on television or in repertory. Once a film had completed its commercial run it might disappear forever, which made programmes like Bill Collins's *Golden Years of Hollywood* on network television so important. Bill loved Hollywood films and although it was a fairly indiscriminate love, he was able to popularise movies of the 1930s, 40s and 50s because of his enthusiastic introductions. True, the films were interrupted every ten minutes or so by inane commercials, and the widescreen films of the 1950s and later decades were panned and scanned, but it was better than nothing. In Britain the BBC and Channel 4 had attempted to educate viewers by screening widescreen films in at least a partial 'letterbox' format, which kept reasonably closely to the correct ratio of the original, but despite this progressive form of presentation, audiences would complain about the blank spaces at the top and bottom of the screen. In the US and, sadly, Australia, no attempt was ever made to educate audiences in the value of showing widescreen films in the correct ratio until I started programming films on SBS. It was painful to see how such films, especially the early CinemaScope films, were destroyed visually on the box. The 3 x 4 format of films made prior to the advent of Scope in 1953 made them more suited to television transmission.

In the early days of video there were two rival formats: Betamax and VHS. The smart thinking was that Betamax, which used a slightly smaller tape, was the superior system and that was the system I first acquired as soon as VCRs became available in Australia. Later on I, along with everyone else, was forced to switch to VHS, when, in a triumph of marketing, that system became so dominant that Betamax tapes disappeared from the market. I managed to save some of my Betamax recordings by copying them onto VHS.

Since my childhood I'd collected everything to do with film – newspaper advertisements, film magazines and other printed memorabilia and also movie soundtracks. I'd recorded the latter from radio and television ever since, in 1957, I bought my first tape recorder, and by 1980 I had a huge collection of film soundtracks on tape. From an early age I'd also bought recordings of film songs and music.

So the advent of video was something I'd been waiting for all my life. To begin with it wasn't possible to buy films on video; you could only rent them. It was a long time before the film distributors tapped into the market for people, like me, who had a compulsion to *own* movies; in fact, in Australia, it wasn't really until the advent of DVDs that collectors could own their own movies. In America there was much more of a market for sell-through VHS movies, but the American television system, NTSC, was incompatible with the Australian and British PAL systems. On a trip to the US I bought an NTSC player and started collecting American tapes. Later, VCR machines sold in Australia were capable of playing both systems. Within a very short while a new and better system of buying movies was introduced: the Laser Disc. This was a disc the size of a vinyl LP, and though the system never caught on in Australia it was popular for several years in America and Asia. Films on Laser Disc were presented in the proper format for the first time and though the discs were expensive, the joy of owning widescreen copies of favourite films more than made up for the cost.

By the time DVDs were introduced, in the early 1990s, I already had a considerable collection of films on Laser Disc and VHS, both in PAL and NTSC formats. The quality of DVDs was so superior (though, initially, Australian pressings were rather poor) that I became determined to collect everything exclusively in this format. Out went the old tapes and Laser Discs to be replaced by superior DVDs. Of course, there are also hundreds, maybe thousands of films which have never been released on video in any format, though new titles are being issued every week.

When I was a child and was discovering films I never could have predicted that one day I would be able to own copies of these films compressed onto tiny discs. Many of my friends and colleagues are collectors too, and we exchange information about what new film is available in which country. I still find it thrilling to be able to relax in my home theatre and to see excellent copies, presented in the correct aspect ratio, of films I first saw when I was a teenager. Usually I find the original thrill I had on first seeing these films all those years ago returns to me when I see them again.

Chapter Fifteen

The films that participate in competitive film festivals are judged by panels of juries. The principal jury is the one selected by the Festival itself and usually consists of up to eleven people from different countries and from different backgrounds in film. A President is appointed to keep order and the jury is given instructions about the number and type of awards it is permitted to hand out. Most juries at the major festivals give awards for best film, runner-up, best director, best actor, best actress and sometimes also a special, or consolation, prize.

The official jury is often just one of the juries at work during a festival. FIPRESCI, the International Federation of Film Critics, has a jury at most festivals, and there's usually an Ecumenical jury too, representing a variety of religious faiths. On two occasions during the mid-1970s I was invited to be a member of the jury at the Chicago Film Festival, and on both occasions the film critic of the *Sun-Times*, Roger Ebert, was also a juror. Ebert was a Chicago resident who co-hosted a very popular national television film review programme with another critic, Gene Siskel. The fact that Siskel and Ebert rarely saw eye to eye with one another – in fact, they seemed to have little in common – had helped popularise their programme.

In 1982 Moritz de Hadeln had moved from directing the Locarno Film Festival to Berlin and he invited me to be a member of his international jury. The jury President was Joan Fontaine, the British-born actress who had won an Oscar for her role in Hitchcock's *Suspicion* and who had given a luminous performance in Hitchcock's first Hollywood film, *Rebecca*. Fontaine, the sister of Olivia de Havilland, had also starred in one of my favourite American films, Max Ophuls's *Letter from an Unknown Woman* (1948). Joan arrived in Berlin bringing with her a book on 'How To Run Meetings' and a steely determination to have things done her way. She was an outspoken supporter of President Ronald Reagan and she made it clear that she had no time for Communists.

The other jury members included the German director, Helma Sanders-Brahms, the French actress, Brigitte Fossey who, as a child, had given a heartbreaking performance in Rene Clement's *Les jeux interdits* (*Forbidden Games*), Italian critic and future Venice Film Festival Director Gian-Luigi Rondi, Indian director Mrinal Sen and a Soviet bureaucrat called Sergei Baskakov. Joan took an instant dislike to Baskakov, who was the only member of the jury who spoke no English – he didn't speak German, either, and for some reason the Festival couldn't find an interpreter who could translate from Russian into English. As a result, whatever the poor man said had to be filtered through two translators.

Undeterred by this, Joan had decided that jury meetings would be conducted under a strict regimen. Anyone who had something to contribute would have to receive approval from the President (herself) before speaking and then would be given the floor for two minutes only. She had brought with her a stopwatch to ensure strict adherence to this rule. At our inaugural meeting Baskakov started by making a speech in which he attempted to say how pleased he was to be in Berlin with comrades from all over the world and how the art of the film would be well served by such an illustrious jury – the usual meaningless blather doled out on formal occasions in the Eastern Bloc – but by the time those sentiments had been translated twice his time had well and truly expired, and Joan refused to allow him to continue. This method of running jury meetings obviously wasn't going to work so Helma and I had a word with Moritz who, I assume, spoke with Joan. The stopwatch didn't reappear.

I had dinner almost every evening with Joan and some of the other members of the jury, but I took one evening off to have a meal with Donald Crombie, the director of the Australian competition entry, *The Killing of Angel Street*, and his leading actress, Elizabeth Alexander, though I felt a bit guilty about doing so because jury members weren't supposed to fraternise with filmmakers whose work was in competition.

Joan was always willing to sign autographs for members of the public, but whenever anyone had the temerity to ask her about her sister, with whom she was not on good terms, she would simply pull a photograph of a sadly overweight De Havilland from her handbag and show it to the disappointed fan.

Towards the end of the Festival, I received a formal invitation, on Joan's private letterhead, inviting me to a dinner at the most expensive restaurant in Berlin. I arrived to find the other male members of the jury present but we soon discovered that neither the women members of the jury nor Baskakov were present. When Mrinal Sen wondered aloud why these jurors weren't at Joan's dinner, she explained, without embarrassment, that, as hostess, she saw no reason to invite them and that was the end of it.

As a member of the jury in Berlin I discovered something about the pressures involved. István Dósai, the head of Hungarofilm, was an intelligent and charming man and had been very helpful to me in recent years. But I was dismayed when he phoned me in my hotel room early one morning to urge me to give the Best Director award to Zoltán Fábri, the veteran director of the Hungarian entry. I told him that he was out of line to make such a request and he apologised; but when the final jury meeting was held I was surprised to find that there was a successful push, led by Gian Luigi Rondi, to give Fabri the director prize.

The previous November I had visited Warsaw when the city was in turmoil over the activities of Solidarity, the union movement, led by Lech Walesa, that stood against the Communist regime. One of the films I saw there was *Dreszcze* (*Shivers*), a powerful drama by director Wojciech Marczewski about the indoctrination of pre-teen children into Stalinism at a so-called 'Pathfinders Camp' in 1955. Two of the actors appearing in the film, Bogdan Koca and Gosia Dobrowolska, later migrated to Australia. *Shivers* was the Polish entry in the Berlin competition and I persuaded Joan that, although it was made in a Communist country, the Communists in the Soviet Union would strongly oppose it. We ended by giving it the second prize, or Silver Bear. But no sooner had we ended the jury meeting than I had a call from a friend who worked for Film Polski telling me that the new military regime in Poland had, in the past twenty-four hours, banned the film, and that if it won an award in Berlin there might be trouble. By then it was too late.

I became quite friendly with Helma and Brigitte during the Festival and we decided to lend our support to the German competition film, which was Rainer Werner Fassbinder's *Veronika Voss*. Joan was all in favour of the American entry, Sydney Pollack's *Absence of Malice*, and offered to vote for *The Killing of Angel Street* to receive the runners-up award if I'd support her. I think she thought I was very unpatriotic when I declined. *Veronika Voss* won the Golden Bear, and this was the only occasion that Fassbinder, perhaps Germany's most controversial and certainly prolific director at the time, ever won a major award at a festival.

James Stewart had been brought to Berlin to hand out the awards and Moritz hosted a dinner for the jury to meet him before the ceremony. Helma declined to attend on the grounds that Stewart had piloted one of the planes that had carpet-bombed the city of Dresden in World War II.

I don't think Joan had any information about Fassbinder's background, or what sort of person he was, so when, dressed in leather and chains, he shambled on to the stage to accept the award, she turned to me and whispered: 'Just look at him! We made a terrible mistake.' I cherish the image of James Stewart, looking urbane and relaxed in his tuxedo, shaking Fassbinder's hand. Fassbinder died of a drug overdose four months later.

The week after the Berlin Festival the César Awards – France's version of the Oscars – were held in Paris and Brigitte Fossey had agreed to be one of the presenters. When she learned that I was spending a few days in Paris that week she asked me if I would be her date for the evening and I was happy to agree. Evening dress was mandatory and I was forced to go to the expense of buying a tuxedo in Paris. I picked Brigitte up at her apartment on the night in question and we were mobbed by fans when we arrived at the theatre where the awards were to take place. I hadn't realised what a popular actor she was. The cream of the French film industry was present and afterwards there was a dinner at Fouquets on the Champs Elysées, where Brigitte and I found ourselves sitting at the same table as the director Bertrand Tavernier, Isabelle Huppert, the star of *The Lacemaker*, Jean Rochefort, Philippe Noiret, Anouk Aimee, who had given such a lovely performance in Jacques Demy's *Lola*, and the Polish actor Daniel Olbrychski.

In August the same year I was invited by Serge Losique to be a member of the international jury at the Montreal Film Festival, which he'd been running successfully for several years. This time my fellow jurors included Madam Kawakita, James Quinn of the British Film Institute and Australian-born, LA-based writer/director Colin Higgins, who had written the screenplay of the cult movie *Harold and Maude*, and who was the writer-director of *Foul Play* and *Nine to Five*. Earlier in 1982 the conflict that the British called the Falklands War and the Argentinians the Malvinas War had taken place in the South Atlantic. Argentina had occupied the British-owned islands and Prime Minister Margaret Thatcher had sent forces to drive them off. As it happened, the two most interesting films in the Montreal competition that year were Argentinian and British: *Tiempo de Ravancha* (*Time for Revenge*), by Adolfo Aristarain, was a subversive drama about loss of personal privacy, while Richard Loncraine's *Brimstone and Treacle*, written by Dennis Potter, was an equally subversive drama about the machinations of a contemporary Devil, who was played by Sting. After some lively debate, and over the strenuous objections of James Quinn, a very proper and very patriotic Englishman, a majority of the jury decided to give the main prize jointly to these two films. Neither of the filmmakers was present at the closing ceremony and there was some unseemly jostling for position when the Argentinian Ambassador and the British High Commissioner took the stage to accept the awards.

As 1982 wore on I became aware of the fact that I would have to make a decision about my future as Director of the SFF. The Festival had been my life's work and my passion for almost eighteen years, but I knew that it was time that I moved on. I was very pleased with the way the Festival had developed and evolved during the period I had been its Director. Not only did we present a strong line-up of international cinema every year but we had never lost money. That was undoubtedly as much a credit to my tiny, underpaid, intensely loyal staff and to the work of many volunteers, not least the Festival Committee and Treasurers John Burke and, after him, Kevin Troy, as it was to me. But I also felt that changes would have to be made in the near future. I felt, for instance, that the days of selling only subscription tickets were numbered. Most of all I thought it was time for someone else to bring a fresh outlook on the event.

Fortunately, I was earning enough money from SBS to provide for me in a post-SFF environment. I had also been approached by Jim Murphy, a senior writer for *The Age*, who had been given the task of establishing a magazine – *The Video Age* – to cover the new area of feature films released on video. Jim, whom I had never met before, invited me to contribute reviews of movies released on video and this would provide another source of income. I decided to start a consultancy company and to offer my services to anyone interested.

On 1 November 1982 I wrote to Ross Tzannes to advise him that I would step down as Director of the SFF after completing work on the next year's event, which would be the thirtieth Festival. I told Ross that I wouldn't be going to a specific job but that I would freelance for a couple of years. I also told him I was concerned that my departure would create some worry for him; I knew that he was thinking of resigning as President after ten years in the position, and I wanted, perhaps selfishly, to get my resignation in before he did.

I mailed that letter from London, where I was attending the Film Festival, and the first person I told about my decision, apart from Ross, was Roger Watkins, the London Bureau Chief of *Variety*. Roger was one of those immensely likable people who always seemed to be cheerful and easygoing but who was obviously a formidable entertainment journalist. I admired him a great deal and tried to catch up with him whenever I was in London. We were having lunch together when I told him about the changes I was planning. To my surprise, he immediately suggested that I review films for *Variety* on a regular basis. This was just a few weeks before Mosk's tragic death, but it was already obvious that a replacement would be needed for the man who, for a quarter of a century, had been the paper's main reviewer in Europe. I'd always written programme notes for the SFF catalogue and had contributed the odd review and article here and there; I'd also been writing on Australian cinema for Peter Cowie's

International Film Guide since 1973, but I still didn't see myself as a reviewer. Roger had the confidence in me I didn't have in myself and I'll always be grateful to him for that.

I wanted to make my final Festival a great one. We opened with Peter Greenaway's stylish first feature, *The Draughtsman's Contract*; Greenaway was already familiar to Festival audiences because I'd shown most of his early short films. He agreed to come for the screening and so did Michael Nyman, the composer of the striking music scores for his films. On stage before the screening, Nyman played music from the film on a harpsichord. I was also pleased that other good friends, London Film Festival Director Ken Wlaschin, and Carole Myer, who worked for the British Film Institute, came to Sydney for the occasion.

One of the finalists in Fiction section of the Great Union Awards during my final Festival was Jane Campion's *Peel*, which the New Zealand-born filmmaker had made at the Film School. Jane has told me since that when she first arrived to live in Sydney, and knew no-one, she started attending the SFF and, through this experience, fell in love with cinema. She was determined then to make a film which would one day screen at the Festival and she fulfilled that ambition. She says that her love of cinema and her determination to be a film director was born sitting in the State Theatre at the SFF.

I spent the period of my last Festival in something of a daze but I never doubted that I'd made the right decision. Everything was running very smoothly thanks to my loyal and hardworking staff and the volunteers who had always made the event possible, and by the time closing night arrived (Martin Scorsese's *King of Comedy*), I felt exhausted but content. The SFF Committee, through Ross Tzannes, asked me what I would like as a parting gift; someone had suggested a 16-mm projector, but I could see that 16-mm didn't have much of a future, that video was the way films would be viewed in homes in the future. Instead I suggested a complete set of *Variety* film reviews, which covered the years

1906–1980, and which were available in handsomely bound volumes. I still refer to these volumes on an almost daily basis. I was also made an honorary Life Member of the SFF.

The leading candidate to replace me was an Englishman, Derek Malcolm, the well-known film critic of *The Guardian*. Derek was frustrated with his role at the venerable newspaper because he was never allowed to cover the Cannes Film Festival, an assignment which was given, instead, to former New York Film Festival Director Richard Roud. At my suggestion, Ross and Derek entered into long-distance negotiations and for a while it seemed as though the deal would be done. But as soon as Derek informed his arts editor at *The Guardian* that he was leaving he was suddenly given everything he'd wanted – coverage of Cannes as well as a rise in salary. He immediately informed Ross and gave up any idea of directing the SFF, though not long afterwards, when Ken Wlaschin resigned as Director of the London Film Festival and programmer of the National Film Theatre, Derek took over the former role for a few years.

My replacement at the SFF was Rod Webb, a former Director of the short-lived National Film Theatre of Australia. I liked Rod, who was very knowledgable and energetic, though he could be a touch abrasive at times, but after two or three years he had a falling out with the Committee over the amount of control to which he was entitled and he was replaced by *Sydney Morning Herald* film critic Paul Byrnes. Under Paul and his successors, Gail Lake and Lynden Barber, the size of the SFF increased enormously. There was a tendency all over the world to swell film festival programmes, a tendency which probably started in Toronto and Montreal. No longer was the SFF subscriber with the stamina and time at their disposal able to see *every* film in the programme. Now screenings were taking place simultaneously in several different venues, and the number of feature films screened grew from 30 to 40 to up to 300. At the same time it could be argued that the *quality* of international cinema was in decline, so that more films were on offer but they tended to be of lower quality. All this was in the name of giving the filmgoer more choice, of making the role of the festival programmer less monolithic; but I wonder, sometimes, if it has been in the best interest of the festival. It has surely increased the costs of running the event, but has it really added to the quality? And is this why the SFF has been steadily losing money in recent years? On the other hand, the Melbourne Film Festival annually assembles an equally gargantuan programme and it seems to fare well on the financial front.

In recent years the Sydney Film Festival has been overshadowed by Melbourne and also by Brisbane, where Anne Demy-Geroe has run an excellent, challenging film programme, and Adelaide, which is now held every other year and is able to contribute to the financing of Australian films which then form part of the programme. But the Sydney Film Festival, neglected for far too long by a seemingly indifferent state government in NSW, has fallen on hard times. High hopes are held for Clare Stewart, who took over the event in 2007.

Stewart's first Festival was, artistically at least, a success, and later in 2007 the NSW Arts Minister, Frank Sartor, announced a funding boost to enable the Festival to hold a competition with an international jury. It was optimistically suggested that this would, eventually, put it on a par with Cannes and Venice. This seems most unlikely, given that the world is already full of competitive festivals (among them Montreal, Locarno, Moscow, Karlovy Vary and San Sebastian) with far bigger budgets and – let's face it – more convenient locations, which are still unable to compete with Cannes, Venice or even Berlin. Still, the much overdue government support might at least help Sydney to keep level with its rivals in other Australian states.

Meanwhile at SBS, the new programmer, Peter Barrett, had cleared the way for me to start a second programme, *Cinema Classics*, which began on 1 February 1983 with a Jean Renoir season that included *La Grande Illusion* and *La Regle du Jeu*. In addition to being paid as the SBS feature film consultant I was now being paid for two presentations a week, and these payments – plus the income from *The Video Age* and increasing assignments to write occasional reviews for *The Sydney Morning Herald*, and my contributions to *Variety* – gave me an encouraging, regular income.

In addition, I had been engaged as a consultant by three overseas clients. Michael Tarant, who had replaced Colin Jones as CEO of Columbia Pictures in Australia in the 1970s, had now moved to New York to run Columbia TriStar Home Video and he hired me as a consultant to advise on acquisitions. Similarly, the German producer Klaus Hellwig sought information about up-and-coming Australian filmmakers whose work he might be interested in supporting. And Derek Hill, who was now programming films for Channel 4 in London, used my services to keep him informed about forthcoming Australian films.

One night, not long after leaving the SFF, I was awoken from a deep sleep by a phone call from London. Leslie Hardcastle, the ebullient Director of the National Film Theatre, and his assistant Helen Loveridge were on the line. They told me that Ken Wlaschin had resigned as NFT programmer and London Film Festival Director and asked me if I would be interested in taking on the job? This was an overwhelming proposition, something I had dreamed about in the past. But the timing was all wrong: I couldn't suddenly uproot and leave for London and I really didn't feel like embarking on another stint as a film festival director. Very reluctantly, I declined the offer.

A couple of weeks after my final Festival ended I was invited to lunch by the CEO of the Australian Film Commission, Joseph Skrzynski, who wanted to sound me out on becoming an AFC Commissioner. This three-year term on the board of the AFC was my first, and so far only, experience of serving on a government board. The Chairman was Phillip Adams, and board members included Jonathan Chissick, the CEO of Hoyts, and Gil Appleton, a writer and media expert and the wife of the former Whitlam Government minister and later Maralinga Royal Commissioner Jim McClelland. Gil and I formed a friendship which has grown over the years, especially since we've become neighbours in the Blue Mountains.

At almost exactly the same time I left the SFF, Mike Harris left *Variety* to take up the position of running the AFC office in Los Angeles. It was the perfect job for him and I think he thoroughly enjoyed it. His place at *Variety* was taken by Don Groves (Dogo), who had been writing a showbiz section for a daily paper. Reviewing films wasn't Don's strong point (as he readily admitted after suggesting that *Crocodile Dundee* wouldn't be a great box-office winner), and after a while I took over all the reviewing of local films for *Variety*. I was now also covering the Budapest, Berlin, Cannes, Venice and Montreal Film Festivals for the paper, so I was travelling almost as much as ever.

I went to Cannes for the first time in 1984. In contrast to my expectations, it rained almost every day. Mike Harris met me at Nice airport – as an AFC Commissioner I was there in a semi-official capacity, though I was paying for my own hotel. Mosk had told me so much about the place over the years that I was saddened to be there without his formidable presence. I explored with interest all the bars and hotels he'd talked about – the Blue Bar, the Petit Carlton, the Majestic.

I reviewed a large number of films for *Variety* and halfway through the Festival the latest edition of the weekly paper arrived containing reviews of films screened in the first few days (in those days *Variety* did not publish a daily paper, as it does today). Soon after the paper hit the streets I visited the AFC office on the eighth floor of a building on the main street, the Croisette. Access was via a tiny lift and also crushed into this confined space was the Australian producer Joan Long, whose latest film, *Silver City*, was premiering in the Festival market. A third passenger was a large man smoking a cigar. I asked him, politely, to put it out. He glared at me. 'You're David Stratton, aren't you?' he growled. I confessed that I was. It turned out he was the director of an Icelandic film which I'd panned in the paper and that he'd just read my review. 'You're a fucking idiot!' he hissed at me, puffing the cigar more fiercely than ever. It was the first occasion in which I have been confronted by the hostile recipient of one of my reviews, but it would not be the last.

On the other hand, one distinguished filmmaker was apparently very happy with my review of his film. I was delighted to be assigned to review John Huston's *Under the Volcano*, which was based on the book by Malcolm Lowery and which boasted a magnificent performance from Albert Finney as an alcoholic diplomat in Mexico in the 1930s. Several days after the film screened, and my review appeared in *Daily Variety* in Los Angeles, I received a call from a representative of 20th Century-Fox to tell me that the celebrated director would like to meet me. He was staying in a suite at the Carlton Hotel, and was attached to a respirator to help his very laboured breathing. I'd assumed he would want to talk to me about what I'd written, but he didn't even mention my review, instead asking me about Australia in his deep, wheezy, voice. It was an odd, and rather unsatisfactory, encounter.

There's always some confusion in the public mind about a Festival like Cannes, which has so many different sections. Berlin and Venice also have a great many sections, but Cannes beats them all. The Official Section includes a competition of about twenty-five new films which may not have been screened before outside their country of origin, although this rule is broken from time to time. 'Un Certain Regard', which is also programmed by the official selectors, consists of films with 'a certain look' which were liked but not liked enough to make the competition. The Directors' Fortnight is programmed by a separate committee and sprang from the 'Events' of 1968, when the Festival was closed down as part of the strikes that rocked France in May of that year. The Critics' Week consists of films selected by the French critics and there's also a sidebar of new French films and a retrospective. On top of all that there's the Market. Any film can play in the Market; the producer, or his agent, only has to hire one of the screening rooms made available by the Festival. Each year, several new Australian films which have not been selected by the Festival are screened at the Market for potential buyers, and we often hear later that the film 'screened at Cannes', which is true in the strictest sense but which is basically misleading.

The town of Cannes is virtually shut off to traffic during the festival; half of the Croisette is transformed into a pedestrian walkway and in the small back streets the traffic is severely congested. Although most screenings take place in the Festival Palais, a significant number of screenings, including the Directors' Fortnight and the Critics' Week, take place some distance away and interviews are conducted in hotels all over the town. There's a great deal of running around to be done, an activity complicated by the enormous influx of sightseers and movie fans who clog the pavements. Many of them have small dogs on leads or babies in strollers so that getting quickly from one place to another is at times frustratingly impossible; in addition there is a serious problem with dog poo, though the city seems to have waged a reasonably successful campaign in recent years to cut down on this form of pollution.

My typical day at Cannes starts at six am (it started at five am when I was writing for *Variety* and had to file regular reviews), when I compose my notes on the films I saw the previous day; these notes will form the basis for later reviews. I also check emails and then head out to pick up the daily trade papers, of which the *Variety* daily, with its wealth of reviews, is by far the best. I glance through the trades over a quick breakfast and then head for the Palais to get a good seat for the 8.30 am press screening of the first competition film of the day. That's followed through the day with interviews, other screenings in various sections, and eventually dinner, which probably doesn't take place before ten pm. Most nights I'm lucky to be in bed by midnight. This is an exhausting regimen, and by the end of twelve days I'm wiped out but, depending on the quality of the films that year, mentally stimulated. I go to very few parties and official dinners mainly because I just don't have the energy for them.

After my first experience of Cannes I planned to visit Athens for a few days. I mentioned this to Roger Watkins and he asked me to represent him and *Variety* in a delicate matter. For the past few years Greek films had been reviewed by a woman whose *Variety* name was Rena. This arrangement hadn't been working out; her English was poor, her reviews had to be substantially rewritten, and the London office was becoming exasperated with her. I was asked to meet with her and to tell her that her services would no longer be required. Since I wasn't an employee of the paper but only a casual reviewer, I thought this was a rather unusual assignment but Roger insisted and so I met with Rena in my hotel and told her the bad news.

While I was in Athens I also took the opportunity to write a long article for *Variety* on the history of Greek cinema and to review all the upcoming films, which were screened for me at the Greek Film Centre. For some time after that I became *Variety*'s expert on all things Greek.

For the next few years Roger would frequently asked me to coordinate the reviews at the festivals I attended and to assign them to the other reviewers. In the late 1980s, I would also write the 'wrap' stories from the Berlin, Cannes and Venice festivals, and for several years I covered the Montreal Festival for *Variety* with the help of just one other reviewer sent up from New York. I worked closely with colleagues like Deborah Young, who reviewed films out of Rome, and Edna Fainaru, who was based in Tel Aviv. One of the great benefits to flow from my love of film is to meet people with similar interests, and these contacts often transform into lifelong friendships: so it was with Deborah and Edna. Indeed, I soon started spending a few days after Cannes each year on a much-needed break in the company of Edna and her husband, Dan, whose wisdom, humanity and sense of humour I came to appreciate keenly. After a couple of years we were joined by Derek Elley, an Englishman with a gift for languages (he speaks Mandarin and German), and a love for the same kind of widescreen movie epics of which I'm also very fond.

Early in 1986 Roger Watkins approached me about a special assignment within *Variety*. He was now the paper's Editor-in-Chief and had relocated from London to New York. He wanted to rationalise the way films were reviewed and the festivals that the paper covered in Europe. Todd McCarthy, whom I'd known for sixteen years, was now the senior reviewer for the paper in North America and was effectively coordinating the review coverage there. Roger wanted me to come to Europe, to be based either in Paris or London, and to take over the film review coverage of the paper for the rest of the world outside America. It was an exciting prospect. Roger was very keen but the final decision had to be made by the owner of the paper, Syd Silverman. I met with Syd in Cannes in 1986 and we had a very positive discussion about the proposal. He agreed in principle, but the stumbling block was the cost of my relocation from Australia to Europe. I told him I'd work out a figure and phone it through to him after my return to Sydney. When I phoned him I could tell he'd gone cold on the idea, and I think now it was probably because he was in the process of negotiating the sale of the paper. In any event, the idea came to nothing and after the paper had been sold Derek Elley assumed approximately the role that Roger had been talking about with me. Of course, if the *Variety* job in Europe had come about, there would have been no *Movie Show*.

When Syd Silverman finally sold the paper, he sent me a note thanking me for my contributions and enclosing a cheque for US$500. Since I had only been writing for the paper on a regular basis for three or four years I thought this was remarkably generous. Syd was a gentleman of the old school and this gesture was typical of him. *Variety* was sold to Cahners, a division of Reeds, and it wasn't long before Roger Watkins departed as Editor-in-Chief. The new editor, Peter Bart, had spent seventeen years as a Hollywood executive; he was Vice-President of Paramount for much of the 1970s and Executive Vice-President of MGM in the early 1980s. He wasted little time in moving the paper's headquarters from New York to Los Angeles and firing many of the old-timers, the 'muggs' who had worked as reporters or reviewers in different parts of the world. He seemed determined to populate the paper with new writers but Todd McCarthy survived as Senior Film Critic, and so did I as a roving reviewer.

The paper changed immensely under Bart's editorship; for one thing, the old device of the four-letter nicknames was dropped and the full names of the reviewers were printed. It also became far more Hollywood oriented, and much less interested in international coverage. And Bart's own op-ed pieces, often in the form of letters to famous filmmakers ('Dear Steven . . .') were sometimes quite embarrassing. But the review section, thanks to Todd's firm hand, remained incredibly strong, and I still think that *Variety* film reviews are among the best in the world. I wrote for the paper for twenty years and I'm very proud of my association with it.

On average I wrote 100 reviews a year for *Variety* during this period and I covered just about all the Australian releases as well as films from all over the world that I was able to see at the various film festivals I attended. As a reviewer I have always liked to see the positive side; it gives me no pleasure to denigrate the efforts of filmmakers, though, of course, sometimes this becomes a necessity. Some reviewers delight in tearing a film to pieces but I don't. It gives me pleasure to think that a positive review from me can help an up-and-coming filmmaker; I've been pleased to see interviews in which Gus Van Sant has acknowledged that he got a big boost at the beginning of his career from the positive review I wrote in *Variety* for his first film, *Mala Noche* (1986).

At the 1991 Venice Film Festival, I was faced with a tricky moral dilemma. The Polish entry was the work of my old friend Jerzy Skolimowski; in recent years his career as a director had faded away almost to nothing, though he had made the occasional striking acting appearance (for example as a Russian KGB agent in Taylor Hackford's *White Nights*). The new film, titled *Ferdydurke*, and co-written by one of his sons, under the pseudonym Joseph Kay, was made in English, and I thought it was incredibly poor. How could I possibly trash the film of someone I'd once been so friendly with? I don't know what I *should* have done, but in the end I simply didn't write a review of the film at all. I've often wondered why I made that decision; after all, I'd written negative *Variety* reviews for other directors I'd been friendly with in the past (Wim Wenders being just one example) but somehow, in the case of Skolimowski, I couldn't bring myself to demolish what has proved, so far, to be his last film. He has, however, reinvented himself as an artist and he still acts occasionally, giving a fine performance in David Cronenberg's *Eastern Promises* (2007).

My closest *Variety* colleagues were Todd McCarthy and Derek Elley. Todd and I have remarkably similar tastes in films; sometimes, after watching a film during which I have been making notes about various themes and connections, I read Todd's review and see that he made precisely the same connections. However, Todd is a far better writer than I am. Derek's range of film interests is extraordinary; he taught himself Mandarin so that he could appreciate the Chinese films he saw in cinemas in Asia when he visited his wife's family in Singapore, but he also became steeped in the cinema of Germany, Turkey, Hungary and even India – he's one of the few western critics with a true appreciation for Bollywood films. I don't think he's quite so keen on British films and there have been times I didn't agree with him at all (what *did* he see in Joel Schumacher's film of *Phantom of the Opera*?), but generally speaking he's a tremendously reliable reviewer.

Because he's the senior film critic, and based in LA, Todd naturally gets to review all the major Hollywood films, but in 1990 he took a leave of absence from the paper to make a documentary film. That year the new Clint Eastwood film, *White Hunter Black Heart*, was due to have its world premiere in Cannes; Todd would normally have reviewed the film, but in his absence Joe Hyams, a Warner Bros executive who usually looked after Clint's films, called me and asked me if I would handle the review. Since Bart had just taken over as editor I wasn't sure what the protocol was, but Hyams went ahead and sent a print of the film to Roadshow with the request that they arrange a private viewing attended only by myself. I was enthusiastic about the film, in which Eastwood had cast himself as a John Huston-like filmmaker shooting a movie a lot like *The African Queen*, and I wrote a positive review. When I arrived in Cannes with this review under my arm Bart was obviously a bit suspicious as to how I came to see the film before anyone else, but he allowed my review to run after making a few amendments.

A similar thing happened with the *Variety* review of Jane Campion's film *The Piano*, which Pierre Rissient, who had worked for the French company that financed the film, screened for me privately in Paris in February 1993, just after the Berlin Film Festival that year. No-one else was shown the film prior to its Cannes screening the following May so my enthusiastic *Variety* review was the first one published. It was typical of Pierre that he told me, after my private screening, not only that the film would be in competition in Cannes and on which date it would screen (which surely couldn't have been formally confirmed that early in the year) but also that it would open in cinemas across France the following day *and* that it would win the Palme d'Or (which it did, *ex aequo* with Chen Kaige's *Farewell My Concubine*; Jane Campion became the first woman to win the coveted prize.)

I've always been able to make quick decisions, and as a result I gained a reputation, at *Variety*, of being a swift reviewer; I wasn't the best reviewer on the paper, but I was the fastest. Consequently, I was often assigned a film if the deadline was a tight one. In 1997, the Venice Film Festival was opening with the new Woody Allen film, *Deconstructing Harry*. Up until the last moment, Todd thought he'd be able to see the film in LA, and when I flew out of Sydney bound for Venice, via London, I assumed that he would have already covered it. But when, after the usual very long journey – exacerbated in Venice by the need to catch a boat from the airport to the Lido and then a car from the dock to the hotel – I finally arrived, David Rooney, an Australian who was then running the Rome bureau for the paper, advised me that Todd had emailed to report that he'd been unable to see the film and that he wanted me to write the review; furthermore, the press-screening was starting in half an hour and the review had to be filed *immediately* after the screening ended. I had the fastest shower ever, raced to the accreditation office for my festival pass, and arrived in the cinema as the lights were going down. I thought the film was one of Allen's best, and the review I wrote, in my jet-lagged and exhausted state, is still, I think, one of my most authoritative.

I heard the following day from Allen's producer that Woody had read my review in New York and had liked it. You don't very often get positive feedback for your reviews, but after I reviewed British director John Boorman's *The Tailor of Panama*, based on a book by John Le Carre, in Berlin, I received a handwritten note from Boorman thanking me and telling me that my review had persuaded his distributor, Columbia, to give the film, which apparently they hadn't much liked, more of a push.

By the beginning of 2003 I'd decided to try to do less work, and, with great reluctance, I decided to end my association with *Variety*; I had been reviewing films for the American paper for twenty years. One of the results of this decision was that I would no longer be able to make annual visits to the Hungarian Film Week in Budapest and to the Berlin Film Festival. The organisers of both events, when they heard this news, were kind enough to make presentations to me; some vintage wine from the Hungarians and a magnificent book on art from the Berlin Film Festival Director, Dieter Kosslick.

Todd McCarthy made several attempts to persuade me to stay on as a reviewer, which was generous of him, but my mind was made up. At Cannes that year he hosted a farewell lunch for me, attended by all my *Variety* colleagues, plus Pierre Rissient. In September, in Venice, the paper's Elizabeth Guider also hosted a dinner for me. I wrote my final review for *Variety* from the 2003 Venice Film Festival.

In April 2005, without any warning, the Sydney bureau of *Variety* was closed down and Don Groves, who had faithfully served the paper for many years, including a stint in the London bureau (when his place in Sydney was very capably filled by Blake Murdoch) was out of a job. Peter Bart didn't even phone Don personally to tell him the news, but left that chore to one of his underlings. Don had been a first-class reporter for the paper for more than twenty years and he was very popular among members of the film industry both in Australia and overseas. It was deeply disappointing to see him – and his deputy, Jane – treated so shabbily by the paper they had served so loyally.

I hadn't heard from *Variety*'s previous owner, Syd Silverman, for almost twenty years and then, in 2005, I received an invitation from him to attend a dinner at Sardi's in New York to celebrate the centenary of the founding of the paper. This function had, I discovered, been organised by Syd personally, and was nothing to do with Peter Bart or the current owners of the paper. It was another generous gesture on the part of the founder's grandson, but my first instinct was to decline, albeit reluctantly. The dinner was on a Saturday night (24 September), and I had a weekly television programme to record as well as a weekly lecture to deliver;

at most, I could be in New York for two days and it seemed foolish to make such a long trip for such a short stay. But then I had a phone call from Todd, who urged me to come, and so I decided that, crazy as it might be, I would regret it if I missed out.

I flew out of Sydney on the Friday morning, arriving in New York at about 5.30 that evening. After checking into my hotel I called Todd, who told me Syd was hosting drinks at the Waldorf-Astoria; there I met old friends and colleagues I hadn't seen in a long time – with the exception of Todd and one or two others, most of the pre-Bart contributors to *Variety* had been let go since the paper was sold. Syd and his wife, Joan, generously invited those of us who had travelled long distances to join them for dinner that evening, after which Todd and I dashed across to Central Park where the Opening Night party of the New York Film Festival was in full swing. Next day I fitted in a brunch in Greenwich Village with Todd and David Rooney and a trip to the theatre before attending the dinner at Sardi's, which was a very nostalgic occasion. Everyone present was given a coffee mug with his or her name on it, as well as a bound book on the history of the paper, which including a couple of photographs of me looking rather idiotic. The only sad thing about the evening was that Roger Watkins had recently been taken ill and was unable to fly from London to be there. His presence would have made a great night complete and his death a few months later greatly saddened me. The next day, after catching a couple of films and checking out the DVD stores in Times Square, I caught the evening flight back to Sydney. I had spent just forty-eight hours on the ground in New York, and it had taken about forty-eight hours' flying to get there!

Chapter Sixteen

My association with SBS, which began in 1980, was to last for more then twenty years. In the beginning my main role was as Feature Film Consultant; I made regular reports and recommendations based on my own viewings at the various film festivals I attended and on the recommendations of trusted colleagues. I also checked lists of films which were regularly submitted to SBS by sales agents all over the world to select the most interesting of them for screening.

I was in Europe when SBS first went to air in 1980 and a year later I was in Europe again when the network celebrated its first anniversary. I was attending a documentary film festival at Nyon, in Switzerland, when I received a call from the Head of Programming, who wanted me to tape a brief celebratory piece about movies on the network; he told me that a film crew would make contact with me when I was in Paris the following week. Sure enough, one morning an English television crew arrived at my hotel, having just flown in from London. They seemed to have been given only the vaguest brief, and because I was still new to television I had only a vague idea as to what was required of me. But I tried to look confident and I led the way to the Champs Elysées, where we set up the camera in front of a cinema advertising a wide variety of films. I was in the middle of attempting, not very successfully, an ad-lib about the exciting movies scheduled to screen on SBS in the coming months when, out of the corner of my eye, I saw my friend, Pierre Rissient, laughing at me; he had been walking down the street when he observed the odd spectacle.

Before I left to spend five months overseas in 1982, the last year I selected films for the SFF, I had spent several hours in the SBS studio at Milsons Point in Sydney recording introductions to some twenty feature films in a marathon session. Unfortunately, somebody accidentally wiped out the tapes and I was obliged to go through the entire process again a couple of days later.

The weekly 'pick of the week', which I introduced myself and which was originally called *A Whole World of Movies*, had, by 1984, been given the title *Movie of the Week*. On 1 February 1983 a second programme, *Cinema Classics*, was introduced, which I also programmed and hosted, and, for a while, there was a third programme, *Movie Legends*; altogether, I selected, programmed and introduced two, sometimes three, movies every week.

These movies, screened without commercial breaks and, as far as possible, in the correct language and often (but not often enough) in the correct aspect ratio, became a kind of de facto Cinematheque. On *Movie of the Week* the connoisseur of international cinema could see films by Bernardo Bertolucci (*The Conformist, The Spider's Strategy*), Carlos Saura (*Raise Ravens, Elisa My Love, Cousin Angelica*), Claude Chabrol (*La femme infidele, Les Biches, Le Boucher*), Wim Wenders (*Kings of the Road, Alice in the Cities*), Michelangelo Antonioni (*The Red Desert, Identification of a Woman*), Rainer Werner Fassbinder (*The Marriage of Maria Braun, Effi Briest, Fear Eats the Soul*), Ingmar Bergman (*Cries and Whispers*), Victor Erice (*Spirit of the Beehive, The*

South), Andrzej Wajda (*Man of Marble*, *Man of Iron*, *Land of Promise*), Chris Marker (*Sans soleil*), Aki Kaurismaki (*Crime and Punishment*), François Truffaut (*The Last Metro*), Federico Fellini (*Orchestra Rehearsal*), Theo Angelopoulos (*The Travelling Players*, *The Hunters*, *Alexander the Great*), Jiri Menzel (*Capricious Summer*, *My Sweet Little Village*) and countless others.

The *Cinema Classics* programme was initially structured around mini-retrospectives. I featured the work of Jean Renoir, Akira Kurosawa, Sergei Eisenstein, Marcel Carne, Ingmar Bergman, Luis Buñuel, Dušan Makavejev, Yasujiro Ozu, Andrzej Wajda and Roberto Rossellini. I also tackled thematic programmes: Prague Spring (Miloš Forman's *Black Peter* and *Loves of a Blonde*, Menzel's *Closely Watched Trains*), for example, and Spotlight on Youth (István Szabó's *The Age of Daydreaming*, Bergman's *Summer with Monika*, Maura Bolognini's *La Notte Brava*, scripted by Pasolini). There were films directed by such iconic directors as Miklós Jancsó, Jean-Luc Godard, Pasolini, Satyajit Ray, Vittorio de Sica and Max Ophuls. There were also special seasons of the 1930s Cinesound features directed by Ken G. Hall and special screenings of the original versions of Sergei Bondarchuk's five-part *War and Peace*, of the original extended television versions of Luchino Visconti's *Ludwig* and of Fassbinder's *Berlin Alexanderplatz*, and Masaki Kobayashi's epic three-part anti-war film *The Human Condition*.

Some of the films I screened were still, technically, banned by the censors, including Buñuel's *Viridiana* and Godard's *A bout de souffle* (*Breathless*). As time went by I was able to introduce to Australian viewers the new Chinese cinema – important films from Taiwan and Hong Kong as well as the mainland – and the new Iranian cinema. I have been immensely gratified to be told on several occasions that the many hundreds of fine quality films I screened on SBS in the 1980s and 90s exerted a powerful influence on young film enthusiasts, who were able in this way to access otherwise unavailable material. On the downside, I've heard that copies of some of these films have been sold or offered for rental in the US and elsewhere, still preceded by my introductions!

The films we programmed were translated by a formidable group of subtitlers, whose work in making films in a great variety of languages accessible to Australian television audiences has scarcely received the recognition it deserves. Most of the subtitlers seemed to enjoy working on the films I'd programmed, and sometimes they consulted me about details. One of them had the brilliant idea of subtitling the voice of the ominous computer in Godard's *Alphaville* in blue letters rather than the usual white ones. This was a great idea and I think it added to the film's enjoyment.

However, I had constant problems with a Hungarian subtitler who was an avowed anti-Communist. He reacted very badly to my programming of some of the classic Hungarian films of the 1950s and 60s, claiming that they were Communist propaganda. The fact was, of course, that most of these films were made by directors *opposed* to the Communist regime: most of them were directors who attempted, with some success, to create subversive works of art despite the constraints of a heavy-handed bureaucratic system. The Hungarian subtitler employed by SBS remained unconvinced by this argument, and even succeeded in suppressing two of the films I'd programmed: Miklós Jancsó's first feature, *A harangok Romaba mentek* (*The Bells Have Gone to Rome*, 1958) and Andras Kovacs's tense film about a wartime atrocity, *Hideg Napok* (*Cold Days*, 1966). These were the only instances of political interference in my programming of films on SBS.

During my overseas travels and visits to film festivals I often met directors whose films I had programmed, and whenever possible I took the opportunity to tape their introductions. Among the directors who introduced their films on SBS were Miklós Jancsó, Wim Wenders, Dušan Makavejev, István Szabó and Roman Polanski. I filmed Polanski's introduction to *Knife in the Water* at the small hotel where I used to stay in Paris. The staff of the hotel, which was located near the Champs Elysées, were thrilled that the famous man was coming to their establishment and they allowed me to use the breakfast room as a location for the interview. Unfortunately, the ancient electrical wiring in the hotel wasn't able to cope with the lights my camera crew was using and after about a minute we were plunged into darkness. Quick as a flash, Polanski ad-libbed: 'Day for night,' he said, a reference not only to Truffaut's film of that title but also to the custom of shooting night scenes in daylight using dark filters.

I had a wonderful time at SBS in the early days of the network. I was given a free hand to choose movies and the response was generally favourable. However, from time to time minor incidents occurred that are worth recording.

In September 1984, the Head of Programming, Peter Barrett, was preparing a week of films about Indigenous Australians, and he wanted a *Movie of the Week* to tie in with this theme. I suggested *Wrong Side of the Road*, Ned Lander's 1981 film about two Aboriginal rock bands travelling across the outback. The problem was that the film was laced with four-letter language which, at the time, hadn't yet been allowed on television. Fortunately, it turned out that a 'softer' version of the film was available – not censored, but redubbed with slightly less confronting language. I recorded my introduction to what I assumed would be this version of the film, but on the night it went to air the wrong version – the four-letter word version – was screened. Strangely enough, there were no complaints; the only phone calls were complimentary ones and we realised we could be less cautious about language in the future.

I think it was some time in 1987 that I programmed the Brazilian film *Pixote*, which had initially been banned by the Film Censorship Board but which had eventually been passed, on appeal, without cuts. I was expecting to hear from the in-house classification officer about the film, but no memos were forthcoming. On the day I was set to record the introduction to *Pixote*, I thought I had better talk to him first, but I was told he was away. Peter Barrett, too, was away, and the chief executive was in a meeting and couldn't be disturbed. It was my call, said the producer, so we screened *Pixote* uncut.

In the early 1980s, John Baxter, who had been living in America for several years, returned to live in Sydney with his American wife, Joyce Agee, niece of the famous writer, James. John suggested that we work together on a series of six profiles of film directors to air on Radio National. He would conduct the Australian interviews, which included Gillian Armstrong and Peter Weir, while I was assigned the task of finding three major international directors to interview on my overseas travels. I was able to record a lengthy career interview with Sydney Pollack at that year's Berlin Film Festival. After Berlin I went to London, where I was able to talk to David Lean, whose last film, *A Passage to India*, was being previewed for the press. Unusually, I was granted enough time to record an extended interview with Lean for the programme. I thought he was one of the great figures of cinema. The third extended interview I conducted for the series was with Bernardo Bertolucci, which was taped a few months later in Tokyo. I was very pleased with the interviews, but John gave me no input into the way they were edited for the programmes; when I finally heard them I was disappointed to discover that my questions had been entirely deleted.

That same year, 1985, I became a grandfather. I was in the *Variety* office in Cannes on 11 May when one of my colleagues from the newspaper gave me the good news that Mary had given birth to a son, Nathan. This momentous event made me feel suddenly very old and now, more than twenty years later, when Nathan occasionally borrows my car, I feel positively ancient. His brother, Riley, followed six years later. They are wonderful young men and I'm very proud to be their grandfather.

After Cannes that year I was invited to the Tokyo Film Festival, where Akira Kurosawa's *Ran* was receiving its world premiere; I had been assigned to review this important film for *Variety*. Before the Festival started there was a little time to spare and I went with Susie, who had flown in from Sydney, to visit the ancient city of Kyoto, travelling on the bullet train from Tokyo. We stayed at a Japanese inn located inside one of the shrines, which was a magnificent, serene experience.

A large number of film people, mostly actors, were in attendance for the opening ceremony of the Festival, among them Glenda Jackson, Donald Sutherland, Harrison Ford and Rod Steiger. All the guests were taken by bus from our hotel to the cinema well in advance of the screening; the film was magnificent but, annoyingly, was projected slightly out of focus for most of its running time. Despite that it was a splendid occasion marred only by the fact that Kurosawa himself had been taken ill and wasn't able to attend – or perhaps it was a question of nerves, because a few days later some of us were taken to meet the Grand Old Man of Japanese cinema and he seemed healthy enough.

As I have previously mentioned, for the first three years of this post-SFF period I was also serving as an AFC Commissioner. When Jo Skrzynski decided to leave the post of CEO I was a member of the interviewing panel that selected Kim Williams, the son of my friend David Williams of Greater Union, to replace him. Kim had been the Director of Musica Viva, and music was his first love; I knew that his father, himself a former AFC Commissioner, harboured some misgivings at the thought of his son becoming involved in the film industry, but Kim, who has since held many important executive positions related to film and television, proved an excellent CEO of the Commission. Though the 10BA period is not normally remembered as a vintage time for Australian films, some very good projects came up for assessment by the AFC. I remember being especially excited about Paul Cox's *My First Wife*, although it seemed so autobiographical that there were fears that Cox's first wife might lodge some objections.

One of my suggestions to the AFC board was that we play a more proactive role in the selection of Australian films for the major international film festivals, especially Cannes. I suggested that we hire Pierre Rissient as a consultant; Pierre, I knew, was already fulfilling a similar role for other countries. So began Pierre's annual visits to Australia, which continued until 2000. Every year in the autumn he would come to view the new output of features and shorts. Through him a great many films were proposed to Cannes and other festivals. He had his favourites; he liked the work of Bill Bennett, Jane Campion (whose *Peel* won the Palme d'Or for Best Short), Frank Shields (director of the genre thrillers *Hostage* and *The Surfer*), Rolf de Heer and others. He had his dislikes too, and they were strong ones. He wasn't at all impressed with work of Jocelyn Moorhouse and he thought Hugo Weaving was an uninteresting actor. *Muriel's Wedding*, a popular success at Cannes in the Directors' Fortnight, was never one of Pierre's favourites. But despite this, Pierre's work on behalf of Australian cinema over a fifteen-year period resulted in much-needed international attention for the industry.

About twenty years after Pierre started advising the AFC on Australian participation in Cannes and other festivals, Todd McCarthy decided to make a documentary about this colourful character, whose role in international film many still found mysterious. It took more than a year for Todd to film *Man of Cinema: Pierre Rissient*, which eventually screened in Cannes in 2007 as an unacknowledged 'work in progress' (after the Cannes screening, Todd added a couple more interviews, including one with Claude Chabrol). From the film Pierre emerged, as his friends expected, as a complex, passionate character, very set in his ways and determined to assist the films he felt needed assistance. 'Talking heads' filmed by Todd included some big names: Clint Eastwood, Quentin Tarantino, Oliver Stone, Sydney Pollack, Jane

Campion, Jerry Schatzberg (Cannes Palme d'Or winner in 1973 for *Scarecrow*), the Iranian director Abbas Kiarostami, and many others, all of whom had been advised or helped or nurtured by Pierre over the years. Derek Elley made some important contributions, and I was featured as well, though my indiscreet comment about a famous film star with whom Pierre claims to have had a one-night stand was bleeped out, which was probably just as well. The screening took place in the Salle Buñuel (named after Luis), which I thought strangely appropriate. Here I was in a screening room named after one of the great directors, the director of *Viridiana*, whose banning had begun my crusade against censorship, which had led to my involvement in the Sydney Film Festival; I was looking at myself on the giant screen as I talked about one of my close friends in a film directed by another close friend; there seemed to be a certain symmetry there.

In the mid-1980s I met a woman who would have a powerful influence on my life both as colleague and as friend. Margaret Pomeranz had been employed at SBS as a producer/writer. Born and raised in Sydney, she had worked as a schoolteacher before travelling to Europe, where she settled for a while in Austria before returning to Australia and marrying Hans Pomeranz, the Dutch-born founder of Spectrum Films, a leading post-production house, and the director of the little-seen feature film, *Stockade* (1971). Margaret and I had passed one another in the corridors of SBS but had never had a conversation – she thought I was stand-offish – until she was assigned to produce my movie introductions (or 'hostings', as they were called). She immediately came up with some radical ideas as to how these should be done: she suggested, for example, that I wear a ponytail and open-necked shirts, and that I stroll onto the set to start my introduction. I, just as immediately, reacted against those ideas. I just wanted to sit in a comfortable chair and talk about the movie the viewers were about to see. After a while, we reached a compromise and I discovered that Margaret knew what she was talking about – she *knew* how television worked, far better than I did – which wasn't surprising, really. I've never been a television addict; apart from watching movies and news and current affairs programmes, there's not a lot on television, especially in recent years, that interests me.

As Margaret and I got to know one another better we occasionally had lunch and talked about the movies we loved and why. It was at of these lunches that the idea for what became *The Movie Show* was hatched. I'd always thought that there should be a film review programme on Australian television, like the one Barry Norman hosted in Britain, or the one on which Siskel and Ebert frequently disagreed in America. We weren't aware, at the time, that for a short while Channel 7 in Melbourne had produced a programme called *Two on the Aisle*, in which Jim Murphy and the film critic Ivan Hutchinson had discussed new movie releases. That programme had only screened in Victoria and had now come to an end, which is why we were ignorant of it.

We first pitched the idea of a film review programme some time in 1985 to Lachie Shaw, who was then Managing Director of SBS, and David Leonard, who was Head of Television. Gyngell had gone by this time and Shaw and Leonard were showing less interest in classic movies, especially those in black and white. There was a time – mercifully a brief period – when it looked as though my *Cinema Classics* might be cancelled, though in the end it was, for a period, expanded. The idea of a movie review programme didn't appeal to Shaw and Leonard, who seemed far more interested in news and current affairs.

Not surprisingly, given the fact that we've argued over films for twenty years now, Margaret and I disagree about what happened next. She believes it was *her* idea that the show, if it ever got off the ground, should feature two people. She says that she wanted to bring out 'the other side' in me – the funny side, the raconteur – and that two people would bring a fresh visual dimension to the programme rather than one talking head. As far as I can remember, I *always* thought such a show should have two people – on the Siskel and Ebert model rather than the Barry Norman model – and I always felt that the second person should be a woman.

The first problem to solve was: who should the other person be? I wasn't certain that I could work harmoniously with any of the women critics who were working in Sydney at the time, and we knew that, financially, it would be out of the question to bring in someone from interstate. I began to think outside the frame of established film critics; I talked to a female writer and to an actress, but nothing could proceed because SBS was unwilling to make the commitment.

By the middle of 1986, though, things were looking more positive. Ron Brown was now Managing Director, Paddy Conroy was Head of Television and Peter Barrett was Head of Programming. Margaret had been producing a ten-minute filler programme called *Sneak Preview*, which was hosted by Silvio Rivier and which looked at upcoming programmes on SBS. When Barrett asked her to expand *Sneak Preview* to half an hour, in order to fill a gap on Thursday evenings at 8.30 for twelve weeks, she saw a window of opportunity. She persuaded Barrett that half an hour of self-promotion would be tedious and that this would be just the spot for the movie review programme we'd been talking about for so long. At first, Barrett suggested that such a programme should include reviews of forthcoming films on SBS, but I was very unwilling to do this. I wanted to confine the programme to reviews of the new feature films that opened in cinemas every week. Finally, Barrett gave Margaret the green light to produce what we called *The Movie Show* and a budget of $12,000. At $1000 per show, that was hardly a budget to get excited about but at least it didn't include studio facilities. Clearly, though, it didn't include a fee for a woman reviewer.

It was, I believe, me who suggested that Margaret appear in front of the camera. In her own words, she pooh-poohed the idea but Peter Barrett liked it and proposed that she do a screen test. We did two pilots; in one, we reviewed Woody Allen's *Hannah and her Sisters* and, in the other, Donna Deitch's lesbian drama *Desert Hearts*. Again, our recollections are somewhat at variance. I recall thinking that this experiment wasn't going to work, but Margaret felt that it seemed to be reasonably successful. Certainly, she took to television like a duck to water once her initial nervousness had been overcome. And so the die was cast and the roller-coaster ride began.

Those first twelve programmes (I can only remember six, but Margaret is certain there were twelve) were hosted by Silvio Rivier. He acted as a kind of compere and handled the introductions and news segments, while 'the team', as he called Margaret and me, confined ourselves to reviewing the films. The first programme, which went to air on 30 October 1986, featured an interview with Bruce Beresford and a review of his film *The Fringe Dwellers*, which had competed at Cannes earlier that year. Ron Brown, Peter Barrett and some other guests, including film director Phillip Noyce, came to a party at Margaret's Mosman house that evening to watch the programme go to air; none of the SBS hierarchy had seen it until that moment. It seemed to go off fairly well – though, looking back, those early shows are extremely embarrassing.

The next show featured an interview with Peter Weir about his film *The Mosquito Coast*, and by the time the twelve (or maybe six) weeks were up we'd already been given the green light to continue into the New Year. When Silvio was assigned to a documentary project in what was then Yugoslavia, he dropped out. Margaret thought that the show would be slower without him, but it worked well and actually sped up. She was also concerned that some weeks there might not be enough material to fill a half-hour programme, but that has never been the case. The ratings started building gradually right from the start, though we both think we're lucky that there weren't very many viewers to watch our first, faltering steps. And so *The Movie Show* was born.

Who would have imagined on that October evening in 1986 how long the show would last? The public acceptance of our format has been gratifying. I'm quite certain that there's a fascination in seeing two people who come from totally different backgrounds but who share a love for cinema discuss, and sometimes argue and fight, about movies. The arguments were never faked or created for the sake of the programme, and I think that shows. Usually, when I arrive at the studio to record the show on a Wednesday morning I'm unaware of Margaret's views on the films we're about to discuss. Thus there's a spontaneity about our arguments, though I often find myself remembering, too late, something I *should* have said. I'm often approached by people who tell me they invariably agree with my views rather than Margaret's, and I know that people tell Margaret exactly the reverse. But whether we like a film or we don't, I think both of us convey an enthusiasm for the medium and a knowledge of what makes it work or not work.

One of the best scripts to come our way during my time as an AFC Commissioner was one written by Frank Moorhouse about a paedophile ring based in Sydney. *The Everlasting Secret Family* was a provocative and confronting screenplay, which obviously needed very careful handling if it were to be passed by the censors. Michael Thornhill, whose last film, *The Journalist*, had been an unmitigated critical and commercial disaster despite a cast that included Jack Thompson, Sam Neill and Elizabeth Alexander, was set to produce, but not direct, the film, and the idea, we were told, was to make it in black and white. Some really offbeat casting – Jack Thompson, say, as the head of the paedophile ring – would have made the project even more interesting.

Sadly, the film that was finally made wasn't very interesting at all. Thornhill, despite his earlier thoughts on the subject, decided in the end to direct it himself, and it was made in colour. Arthur Dignam was a too-obvious choice for the leading role, and everything about the film was predictable and bland rather than cutting-edge and provocative.

The film was scheduled to release in February 1988 and, unknown to Thornhill, I'd already seen it at a private screening. I knew I'd be covering the film on *The Movie Show* but I was more concerned about my role as a *Variety* reviewer; a review in *Variety* can make or break a small film's reputation and severely impact on its international sales, and I was always very conscious of this. I was concerned about worsening my already tenuous relationship with Thornhill and so I decided to make every effort to avoid having to write a review for the American trade paper. I ran into him at a Christmas Party late in 1987 and suggested that he send a print of the film to London where one of my British colleagues could see it and review it. This he did, and I heaved a sigh of relief. Adam Dawtrey, who wrote the *Variety* review, found the film not very convincing, but gave it a more positive review than I would have.

But then Paul Byrnes, the *Sydney Morning Herald* film critic, asked me to fill in for him while he took a vacation at the end of February. I was leaving for Berlin and I agreed – as long as I didn't have to review Thornhill's film, which Byrnes assured me he'd cover. But I returned from Berlin to discover there had been no advance press previews – very unusual for an Australian film and suggesting that a negative reaction was anticipated – and that Paul counted on me to review the film for the *Herald*. I went to see *The Everlasting Secret Family* for a second time, at the Academy Twin in Paddington, and was uncomfortably aware of the negative audience reaction. I wrote my review, which was published a week after the film opened, and which infuriated Thornhill so much that he took an ad in the *Herald* the following week to claim that 'Stratton gets it wrong'.

That summer was a sad one for me because of the death of my mother. The year before, my parents had driven down to Cannes the day after the Festival ended. We'd decided to spend a few days together in the hills of Provence. I thought they both looked very well and very relaxed. On the first evening we had dinner at a charming little restaurant in a small village. I noticed out of the corner of my eye that a woman at another table was looking at me, and as she and her partner got up to leave she came past our table to tell me that she was from Melbourne and that she loved *The Movie Show*. I think this was the first time that my parents were really aware of what I was now doing. I had always felt that they were disappointed with my career, and I certainly knew that they wished I'd stayed in Britain. At any rate, this stranger's comment made my mother visibly excited. 'He's my son!' she told the woman. A couple of days later they dropped me off at Nice airport.

A few weeks later, suffering from bad back pains, my mother sought medical advice and was diagnosed with cancer. Despite treatment, the pain grew worse. By the end of the year she was having difficulty functioning and she spent a miserable Christmas. I had spoken to her regularly on the phone and was now so concerned about her illness that I decided to leave earlier than usual for Berlin, but I wanted to stay in Sydney long enough to celebrate the bicentennial celebrations on 26 January with Susie and her family. On 27 January I flew to London, arriving early the next day. My father wasn't there to meet me; instead, one of his friends had come to Heathrow to pick me up. We arrived in Devizes mid-morning. My mother was in hospital in Bath; my father had spent the morning with her and she was eagerly looking forward to seeing me. Visiting hours didn't start again until after lunch so I ate a meal with my father in the café my sister-in-law, Laura, was now running in Devizes Market Place.

When we arrived at the hospital my father pointed out my mother's bed and went to talk to the nurse in charge. My mother appeared to be asleep; I tried to wake her, but there was no response. I put my hand on top of hers, and she covered it with her other hand. That was the only acknowledgement she made of my presence. I sat and talked to her while we waited for the doctor. She never regained consciousness and died that night.

The funeral was held a few days later, and I was able, under such sad circumstances, to meet many old friends I hadn't seen in very many years, including my uncle, John. Nor had I seen much of my brother, Roger, or his children, Richard and Helen, for quite some time. It's ironic that such reunions occur at times of such great sorrow. A few months later, in August, I had just arrived in Venice when I received a phone call from Susie to tell me that her father, Harry, had died very suddenly and unexpectedly. Harry, an RAAF pilot in World War II and owner of a successful Queensland property until his retirement, was a wonderful man with a great fund of stories which always made for riveting listening. I was saddened that I was unable to attend his funeral.

In January 1989 my father flew to Auckland where Susie, Ben and I met him, together with Susie's mother, Fran. Sadly, that summer was one of the wettest ever, both in Australia and New Zealand. It rained every day as we travelled over much of the North Island, to the Bay of Islands and the Coromandel Peninsula, unable to escape the bad weather.

When we returned to Sydney with my father, who was planning to stay for a few weeks, the rain followed us. I felt desperately sorry for him because, unlike me, he loved the sun and the beach and had been planning on a lot of swimming. Instead, while Susie and I went to work, he spent almost every day in our house in Seaforth while the rain poured down outside. Although he didn't much like films, he came with me to the occasional screening, including a preview of Phillip Noyce's *Dead Calm*, which I was reviewing for *Variety*.

While my father was in Australia, Roger was building an annexe to the house where my parents had lived in Devizes; the plan was for Roger and his family to live in the main house, and Father in what was, in effect, a 'granny flat'. This was completed by the time he returned home from Australia at Easter but he only lived in it for a year. He was increasingly troubled with angina, which developed into serious heart problems. When I arrived in England a few days before the 1990 Cannes Festival he was in hospital, having suffered a heart attack a few days earlier. He was in the same hospital and, as it happened, the same ward in which my mother had died two years earlier. His cheeks were sunken and he looked terribly ill. While I talked to him, he suffered another attack. He was stabilised and when, a couple of days later, I left for Cannes, it was in anticipation of seeing him after the Festival; but he died, at the age of seventy-six, the day the Festival opened.

One of the films in competition that year was Bertrand Tavernier's *Daddy Nostalgie*, a touching story in which a sickly man, played by Dirk Bogarde in his final screen role, comes to terms with his estranged daughter, Jane Birkin, before his death. Under the circumstances, the film had an unusually strong impact on me; I saw my own father in Bogarde's truthful, heartbreaking performance. As it happened, the morning I flew from Nice to London to attend my father's funeral, Bogarde was on the same flight. I'd never met him before, but we were seated in the same row. I don't usually approach famous people, but I couldn't resist telling him how much the film had meant to me, and why, and he was tremendously warm and sympathetic.

I rented a car at Heathrow and drove to Devizes for the funeral. Once again, it was a truly sad occasion, and it was also the last time I saw my uncle, John, who would die of cancer a couple of years later. I went back to the house to meet with family and friends, before driving back to Heathrow and catching an evening flight back to Nice and from there a taxi to Cannes. I had to see a film late that evening. It was a very strange day.

Losing one's parents is a very traumatic thing even if, as in my case, you have only seen one another fleetingly over the years. However, I am still able to hear their voices because I had the foresight to spend some hours in the late 1980s recording them as they talked about their lives. I asked them questions about their earliest memories and they talked, frankly and freely, for long periods of time. I cherish these recordings and only wish that I'd had the foresight, and the equipment, to capture them on video.

Back in Australia there was always plenty of work to do. I had written film reviews for *The Sydney Morning Herald* on and off until August 1989. I knew that the paper was looking for a full-time writer, which was not something I wanted to be, and when Paul Byrnes finally returned permanently the paper had no more use for me. About a year later I received a call from Maria Prerauer, the Arts Editor at *The Australian*. She told me she was experiencing difficulties with one of her film reviewers, who seemed to have trouble filing on time, and asked me if I would take on the position. I was reluctant at first, because I had no wish to put another reviewer out of work, but Maria insisted that, whatever my decision, she would not keep working with this particular person, so I agreed. My first review appeared in *The Australian* in October 1990, and I don't think I've missed a week since. My fellow reviewer, Evan Williams, and I divide up the films to be covered each week in what is a very amicable arrangement. I also cover the Cannes and Venice film festivals for *The Australian*.

Shortly before these events, I'd decided to write a sequel to *The Last New Wave*. I had in mind a book about the Australian cinema of the 1980s, a decade which, while not as exciting and rewarding, perhaps, as the 1970s had been for Australian film, still produced some remarkable works. I called the book *The Avocado Plantation* to emphasise the fact that the crazy world of tax concessions embraced not only films but almost any kind of produce, including avocadoes. I set about interviewing as many people as I could during the last four or five months of 1988 and first weeks of 1989.

Pan Books had commissioned the book but during the period I was writing it they were taken over by Macmillan, forming Pan Macmillan, and the new owners seemed not so interested in what I was doing. There was no money for a proper launch, but we combined the launch with the *Movie Show* Christmas Party in November 1989. Once again, reactions to the book were mixed: *Cinema Papers* attacked it, but Gary Maddox wrote a great review in *Encore*, a trade paper, and seemed to appreciate exactly what I was attempting.

However, the experience of having my second book published was a bad one; a minor player in the industry objected to something I'd written about him. He had directed one of a small series of low-budget horror films for producer David Hannay and, according to Hannay, had made such a botch of it that it had to be completed by somebody else. The aggrieved director, who has never, to my knowledge, directed another feature film since, took legal action against me; Pan Macmillan wasn't very supportive and most of the money I earned from the book went into settling the matter.

In addition, there was almost a legal dispute over what I wrote about the film version of David Williamson's play *Emerald City*. Two of the film's actors, Robyn Nevin and the late John Hargreaves, objected to the fact that I wrote that they had insisted that Williamson's pared-down screenplay adaptation of his stage play be expanded to incorporate speeches and dialogue from the original theatre production. In interviews for the book, both Williamson and the producer, the late Joan Long, had confirmed this information, but the two actors, both of whom I very much admired, seemed convinced that my observations were damaging, and I promised them, reluctantly, that if the book were ever to be republished I would amend the text according to their wishes. This never happened; the book wasn't nearly successful enough to warrant a paperback edition. The result of all this was that I decided never to write a third book in what I had planned to be an ongoing series.

In 2006 the Perth Mint issued a coin to celebrate fifty years of Australian television. I was surprised and pleased to discover that one of only six programmes included on the coin (along with Graham Kennedy's *In Melbourne Tonight*, *Playschool* and *Hey Hey It's Saturday*) was *The Movie Show*; the 'spats' between myself and Margaret were, according to the brochure, one of the reasons for our inclusion. Of course, we often disagreed over the years and one of our most celebrated disagreements was over the Australian film *Romper Stomper*. Geoffrey Wright, the director, had previously made *Lover Boy*, a medium-length film which ran just under an hour although it had been marketed as a feature; in it, Noah Taylor had given a fine performance. I had read the script of *Romper Stomper* before it went into production and I thought, despite some reservations, that it had the potential to be an interesting film on an incendiary subject: the brutal clashes between neo-Nazi skinheads and members of the Vietnamese community in an Australian city.

When I saw the film at a Market screening in Cannes in 1992 I was quite depressed by it. It was formidably well made, with superlative performances by Russell Crowe (indeed, it made his reputation as an actor) and Jacqueline McKenzie. But the misgivings I had from reading the screenplay were exacerbated by the film itself. There was no voice for moderation; the 'hero' was a vicious, racist thug. I had no doubt that Wright was attacking racism and antisocial behaviour, but I feared that the film could be used as an incitement to violence.

When we came to discuss it on *The Movie Show*, I expressed these misgivings. Margaret very much admired the film; so did I, in a way, but the implications of it frightened me, and for that reason I felt I couldn't give it a score. It's not true to say I gave it a zero; I just didn't want to score it at all. Roadshow, the distributors, made my 'non-score' part of the marketing campaign of the film; it had already been misreported from Cannes that I had said something about burning the negative of the film, which was entirely untrue. For a while there was quite a fuss about my opposition to *Romper Stomper*, and many people whose taste I respected admired the film. On the other hand, I received several letters from members of the Vietnamese community thanking me for my stand against what they saw as a rabble-rousing exercise. For years afterwards Alan Finney, Roadshow's Head of Marketing, made veiled comments about my giving 'zero' to the film and how irresponsible my attitude had been towards an Australian production.

Two years later, Wright's follow-up film, *Metal Skin*, screened in Venice. I hadn't seen the film prior to the Festival. I presume that the producers had imagined, wrongly, that I harboured some kind of antagonism towards Wright and that a negative review in *Variety* would be expected from me. Instead, a decision had been made to screen the film for the trade press in Los Angeles and the – very negative – *Variety* review had been written by Todd McCarthy. Nevertheless, I planned to see it in its non-competing slot at the Festival. I was a member of the International Jury in Venice that year, and the Australian Film Commission had hosted a cocktail party – coincidentally, on the evening of my fifty-fifth birthday – at the Hotel Quattro Fontane to celebrate Australian participation. I had never met Wright, and when he came into the room I was talking to some other people and was unaware of his presence. I was completely taken aback when a shrill voice cried out 'Stay away from my film, you fucker!' and a glass of wine was thrown all over me. Before I could react Wright was gone, leaving behind some very startled festival-goers (I heard later that his action lost the film an English sale because the potential buyer was so appalled by his behaviour). Ironically, when I saw the film the next day I liked it much more than most people; there's no doubt that Wright is an accomplished director and his faltering career in Hollywood has been a disappointment. Sadly, his return to filmmaking in Melbourne with a modern version of Shakespeare's *Macbeth* has been less than distinguished.

In July 2006, a few weeks before the release of *Macbeth*, Wright gave an interview to Karl Quinn for *The Melbourne Magazine*, a glossy monthly insert in *The Age*. After boasting about attacking his American agent with a plate of spaghetti marinara, Wright launched into a wholly inaccurate account of that Venice encounter. He managed to get the location wrong (bizarrely, he claimed it took place in a New Zealand tent) and he claimed that he engaged me in conversation, asking me why I said he was a racist on television. According to him, I replied, 'Because you are,' which is when he threw the wine over me. He then suggests that a waiter offered him another glass of wine, and 'everyone cracked up'. Not only is this account far from the truth, but it also poses the question: why, twelve years after the event and with a new film about to open, would Wright want to remind *Age* readers that he reacts violently to criticism?

Film critics enjoy a sometimes uneasy relationship with film distributors. On the one hand, distributors seek good reviews for their films and court the critics who might supply them; but on the other, some distributors become very vexed when the expected positive reviews aren't forthcoming. While most distributors are very cooperative in arranging advance screenings for reviewers, some – exasperatingly – attempt to second-guess the critics, holding advance screenings of films they *think* certain critics will like and denying access to critics they think will not be impressed.

As already noted, previews are usually held in private theatrettes; sometimes a 'big' film will be screened in a large cinema, and when that occurs it often only screens once, which can present difficulties when, like me, a critic has a busy schedule. Some critics don't take these previews very seriously; one prominent Sydney critic for a major newspaper invariably arrives after the start of the screening and has been known to miss up to twenty minutes of the film. But for the most part the relationship between critics and film distributors is a relatively harmonious one.

There are exceptions, however. When Alan Finney was Marketing Director at Roadshow he often took an unpredictable approach to previews for reviewers. A case in point was James Foley's excellent *At Close Range*, a powerful drama with Christopher Walken and Sean Penn, which I'd seen at the 1986 Berlin Film Festival. The film had, apparently, performed badly in the US, and though I pleaded with Finney to allow Margaret to see it so that we could discuss it on *The Movie Show*, he refused.

An even more annoying example of this practice occurred in December 1994, when one of Roadshow's big Christmas releases was scheduled to be Neil Jordan's *Interview with the Vampire*, with Tom Cruise. All requests to screen the film in time for us to include a review of it in our final show of the year fell on deaf ears. Generally speaking, I liked Jordan's films, and I was looking forward to *Interview with the Vampire* but, for some reason, Finney refused to screen it for us, although he was quite happy to let us have film clips from it to screen on the programme. As it happened, *The Movie Show* had some money left in the year's budget, and so we decided on a radical act of defiance. On 9 December I flew to Honolulu, where, because of the time difference, I arrived late at night the previous day. As soon as the cinemas opened the next morning I went to the first session of *Interview with the Vampire* at the Waikiki Twin. I spent the rest of the day seeing three more films, all of them upcoming Roadshow releases, after which I had dinner and caught the midnight flight back to Sydney.

The following Wednesday, after taping the show earlier in the day with my (moderately favourable) review of *Vampire*, I attended a Christmas Party at the office of the Australian Film Commission, where I ran into Finney, who had flown up from Melbourne for the occasion. 'Have you attacked me on tonight's show for not letting you see *Interview with the Vampire*?' he asked me. I assured him that I hadn't and he never raised the subject again, but I have often wondered if he worked out how I got to see the film and if it had occurred to him that I flew to Hawaii just to see a movie.

We're often accused of being soft on Australian films (I was sometimes accused of this in my *Variety* reviews as well), but the truth is that, on the whole, I *like* Australian films. I get rather weary of all those films set in Los Angeles or New York, or even London, and I tend to embrace a film which tells an Australian story in an Australian setting with Australian accents. Some may call this parochial, and perhaps it is, but it's a prejudice to which I readily admit. On the other hand, my instinctive enthusiasm for local product took a bit of a battering with some of the woeful comedies produced and released in 2003 and 2004.

From the start of the show we included interviews wherever possible. These were usually with directors but sometimes also with actors. It's not very often that these interviews are a relaxed affair. Usually the film's publicist allows only ten minutes with the 'talent' and sometimes, especially at festivals like Cannes and Venice, it's as little as five. These 'junkets', as they're called – for reasons I can never understand – usually include not only the film's director but also several of the actors. Sometimes this proves to be a complete waste of time as we only have time on the programme for brief interviews and usually the director of the film is more interesting and authoritative than the actors.

One of the most interesting filmmakers I've interviewed is Clint Eastwood; my acquaintanceship with him from the early 1970s has been maintained, and I've been able to conduct the occasional formal interview with him in recent years, once in Cannes (for his film *Bird*) and once in Australia. When he came to Australia for the first time in 1990 to participate in the opening celebrations for the Warner Bros. Movie World on the Gold Coast, he agreed to participate in only two television programmes. One of them was *The Movie Show*. In recent years, Eastwood has invited me to private functions he's held in Cannes for friends and a select number of reviewers.

One of the best interviewees is Quentin Tarantino. The first time I talked to him was in Cannes in 1992, just after the first screening of *Reservoir Dogs*. For some reason, I hadn't been able to see the film but I'd heard a lot about it. The publicist was apparently working on a limited budget and hadn't been able to reserve a room for the interview, so it was to take place on the beach. Tarantino arrived and cheerfully squatted in the sand. I tentatively asked him the first question – something about the influence of Sam Peckinpah – and fifteen minutes later he was still talking. Two years later, when *Pulp Fiction* premiered in Cannes, we were required to travel out to the inconvenient Hotel du Cap in Antibes to interview a man who was now a Major Figure in the industry.

If Tarantino gives the best interviews (Dustin Hoffman is another who is very easy to talk to), American director James Ivory gives the worst. I had always found the director of *Howard's End* very stiff and unrelenting but at the 1993 Venice Film Festival he was on the Jury and Peter Weir was the Jury President. I often had lunch with Peter that year and Ivory frequently joined us. Having, as I thought, befriended this rather chilly man, I looked forward to interviewing him the following February in Berlin for his film *The Remains of the Day*, which I very much liked. My first question was about the complicity between some members of the British aristocracy and the Nazi Party in the years prior to World War II: I said that I hadn't been aware of this. It gave Ivory the chance to talk about the themes of the film, but instead he expressed amazement that I could be so ignorant, and then dried up completely. We couldn't use his interview at all.

I've always found Kate Winslet a charming and intelligent interviewee, and I've talked to her on several occasions. A few years ago, in Venice, I interviewed her for the film *Finding Neverland*, which was about the genesis of J. M. Barrie's play *Peter Pan*. When I arrived in the room to talk to her, Kate told me that she'd heard on the grapevine that I'd been moved to tears by the film, which was true. I was naturally surprised, though, that she knew about it. On the same occasion, I interviewed the talented Johnny Depp, who played Barrie in the film; my assistant at the time was Edwina Throsby, who was wearing a T-shirt with a complicated text written across it. Depp took some time to read this information, and Edwina was able to tell her friends that 'Johnny Depp looked at my breasts!' She was later presented with a T-shirt displaying this momentous information.

Perhaps the most surprising interview was one Margaret conducted at her Mosman home with the American actress Rosanna Arquette. When Margaret asked her what she thought her greatest asset was she replied, without guile, 'Well, I've got big tits!' and then collapsed into laughter. Margaret often found herself being chatted up while interviewing men of a certain age. Both Richard Attenborough and David Hemmings flirted with her as she tried to ask them questions about their latest films.

We were often invited to visit the set or the location of Australian films in production and we regularly filed reports for the show on these works in progress. But in 1991 I visited the set of one of the biggest productions ever made in Australia and I wasn't able to film a report for the show. *Until the End of the World* was conceived when its German director, Wim Wenders, visited Australia for the first time in December 1976 and it was eventually made, in the winter of 1990, as a co production between France, Germany and Australia, with Roadshow acting as the Australian production company. Wim and his partner, Solveig Dommartin, spent several months living in Sydney working on the pre-production of the film; they rented a house at Rushcutters Bay and I saw quite a lot of them. When production started on the film in the winter of 1991 near Alice Springs, Wim invited me to come up for a few days.

On the set, things were pretty fraught. William Hurt, who had been cast one of the leading roles, was apparently being difficult; he didn't want any strangers turning up at the location. Despite that edict, Julia Overton, the production manager, drove me to the location, where I met several friends and acquaintances – not only Wim and Solveig, but also Max von Sydow, Sam Neill, Jeanne Moreau and Rudiger Vogler, all of whom I knew from previous occasions. That night I was invited to watch rushes in the ballroom of the hotel and I was excited by the scope and vision of the film. But the post-production proved to be extremely difficult. Wim's cut ran for a whopping four hours and forty minutes, which was far too long for most of the distributors involved. The film bankrupted the French producer, Anatole Daumon, whose Argos Films had been responsible for some great films in the past (works by Alain Resnais and Chris Marker, as well as Nagisa Oshima's *In the Realm of the Senses*). Anatole's daughter, Florence, was a friend of mine; she'd been living for some years in the US but after the bankruptcy, and her father's subsequent death, she returned to Paris to run the company.

In most countries of the world, including Australia, *Until the End of the World* was released in a version running approximately two and a half hours, which dramatically reduced Wim's vision of the epic story. Perhaps because of this, it was a commercial failure just about everywhere, and the talented director's career has never quite recovered, though he did have great success with his affectionate documentary about Cuban musicians, *The Buena Vista Social Club*. At the time of writing, it is only possible to obtain the director's cut of *Until the End of the World* on DVD in Italy.

The year I visited the Alice Springs location of Wenders's film was also the year my apartment in Cannes was burgled. At the time, *The Movie Show* would pay my airfares to Cannes and Venice but *Variety* looked after my accommodation; it was an arrangement that suited everyone. In the early 1990s *Variety* booked apartments in the ancient Miramar, which was impressively located on the Croisette between the Carlton and Martinez hotels but which wasn't a hotel. The apartments in the Miramar were so musty and run-down that Margaret quickly dubbed it the

Barton Fink hotel, after the hotel in the Coen Brothers' film of that name. On the Saturday night while I was having dinner my apartment was broken into. My passport was stolen, along with my air ticket and all my money.

Early the next morning I had to find my way to the police station to report the theft, not that anything was ever recovered. As it happened, I had been assigned by *Variety* to review the competition film being screened for the press that Sunday morning, Maurice Pialat's *Van Gogh*, which I did as best as I could under the circumstances, though my mind was elsewhere. The next day I flew to Paris, where I spent several hours at the Australian Embassy, Air France and American Express organising replacement passport, ticket and traveller's cheques. It's not an experience I'd like to go through again.

Later that year, I was asked by Paul Cox to appear in a cameo role in a short film, *Touch Me*, which he was making for a series of films titled *Erotic Tales*. Cox often invited friends to make guest appearances in his films and I accepted the invitation, which involved a day of filming in Cox's own house in the Melbourne suburb of Albert Park. The film dealt with a lesbian romance between an art teacher, played by Gosia Dobrowolska, and a model, Claudia Karvan. Cox had turned the lounge room of his house into an art studio, and for most of the day Claudia, who had first come to public attention as a child when she played the daughter of Judy Davis in Gillian Armstrong's excellent film *High Tide* (1987), had to pose, naked, on a couch while a motley group of art 'students', played by Norman Kaye, Chris Haywood and myself, attempted to capture her likeness under the instruction of Gosia.

I had been instrumental in bringing Gosia and Cox together some three years earlier. I had met the Polish-born actress when her first Australian film, *Silver City*, screened at the Cannes Market in 1984; coincidentally, she and her husband, Bogdan Koca, had both acted in *Dreszcze* (*Shivers*, 1981), the film which had won second prize at Berlin when I was a member of the jury. Bogdan was an actor and theatre director of great talent, though he was somewhat surly; Gosia, on the other hand, was a charmer – a genuinely sweet woman. She was also an excellent actor who, probably because of her strong Polish accent, was often unemployed (an accent was no bar to the success of Dietrich, Garbo and others in the 1930s, but in Australia in the 1980s it seemed to pose a problem for audiences). Gosia did particularly good work in John Dingwall's low-budget drama *Phobia* (1988) as a wife suffering from agoraphobia, and Pierre Rissient had very much admired the film she made with Frank Shields, *The Surfer*.

At the 1988 Venice Film Festival Paul Cox was presenting his film *Island* in competition. He told me about the next film he was planning, an erotic drama titled *Golden Braid*, and asked me if I knew of an actress who might play the leading role. He was thinking of casting Deborah Unger, later known as Deborah Kara Unger, who had made an impression at the National Institute of Dramatic Art (NIDA) and had just acted in three Australian films one after another, none of which had yet been seen. I suggested he also consider Gosia, which he did, and she was immediately cast in the role and gave one of her best performances in *Golden Braid*.

That was the start of a significant professional and personal relationship between Gosia and Paul. She acted in his films *A Woman's Tale*, *The Nun and the Bandit* and *Lust and Revenge*. And this was the background to my cameo appearance in *Touch Me*, which, I have to say, was not a happy experience. The room in which we filmed was tiny, and most of the people involved smoked incessantly. Paul smoked a pipe while Gosia and other members of the crew smoked cigarettes. By the end of the shoot I was feeling quite ill and, in fact, developed pneumonia a few days later. If you see the film, you might blink and miss me. I have just one line to say, which I don't say very well. The experience made me glad I had never followed my childhood dream of becoming an actor.

In July 1999 Paul was making his most ambitious film on location on the Hawaiian island of Molokai, and he asked me to come and visit him. Susie and I flew to Honolulu and stayed for a few days at the Royal Hawaiian before boarding a small plane to fly to Molokai, which was famous for being the site of a leper colony founded in the nineteenth century. Paul's film was *Molokai: The Story of Father Damien*, a Belgian–Dutch co-production about the life of the famous Belgian saint. Father Damien had travelled to this remote spot to care for the lepers and had lived for years with them, finally dying of the disease.

Paul had suggested casting the young Australian actor David Wenham as Damien; he looked a lot like the priest and he had given impressive performances in Rowan Woods's powerful drama *The Boys* and in the television series *Sea Change*. The Belgian producers accepted the unknown actor provided a number of 'name' actors were cast in minor roles; this was, after all, one of the most expensive Belgian productions ever made. This explains why Peter O'Toole, Kris Kristofferson, Leo McKern, Tom Wilkinson, Derek Jacobi and Sam Neill appear in small roles in the film, although Paul made certain that many of his 'regulars', such as Chris Haywood and Aden Young, were also involved and that the crew was also composed of his frequent collaborators.

Paul was used to producing his own films; he didn't take kindly to being told what to do, and the Belgian producer wasn't happy with the rushes coming out of Hawaii. Filming was taking place in the leper colony itself, on the very spot where Damien had lived and worked and died. It was a barely accessible location, at the foot of sheer cliffs said to be some of the tallest in the world. To get there you had to take a perilous flight from the upper island on a small plane, buffeted by the high winds for which the area was notorious. While we were still in Honolulu, we heard that the producer had fired Paul from the film. Then we heard that the lepers themselves had gone on strike because of the dismissal and that Paul had been re-instated.

We arrived to find an uneasy situation, but fortunately the producer had left and filming had resumed. We watched the shooting of a church service and other scenes which took place on the plateau beneath the enormous cliffs, a plateau situated above more cliffs which rose from the rough sea below. It was a most spectacular place. The first night we stayed in the main part of the island, above the colony, but subsequently Paul persuaded us to move into the house where he was staying, in the leper colony itself. While we were there none of the 'big names' were around and it was fun spending time with Wenham, Haywood, Paul and the others.

Molokai had a chequered history. When shooting in Hawaii was completed Paul went to Belgium for the editing, but his version of the film was rejected by the producer, who ordered extensive re-cuts. When the film opened in Brussels it was a commercial disaster. Paul took legal action and was given the right to restore the film as closely as possible to his original concept, though it was never a great success. But Wenham is brilliant in the leading role, and although some of the scenes featuring the 'stars' (with the notable exception of Peter O'Toole) are somewhat awkward, the main scenes on the island are very impressive indeed, thanks in no small part to Wenham's presence.

Chapter Seventeen

In 1991 Susie and I moved from Sydney to live in the Blue Mountains. Though commuting is a bore at times, it's a move I've never regretted. The fresher air of the mountains, the differentiation of the seasons, the excellence of the cafés and restaurants and the new circle of friends we've been able to make have more than compensated for being away from the city. We've also enjoyed some memorable holidays over the last fifteen years, notably travelling through Central China and the now-flooded gorges on the Yangtse River in the company of Derek Elley and his wife, Bee See, and my very good friend from Canada, Gerald Pratley. Gerald also came with us when we explored the North of Scotland. I celebrated my sixtieth birthday in 1999 in Venice, and I was very pleased that so many of my family and friends, including my brother, Roger, his wife Laura, and their children, Richard and Helen, plus their partners, as well as Susie and her son, Ben, were able to attend. Also present on this memorable occasion was a gaggle of international film critics – Derek Malcolm, David

Robinson, Alexander Walker, Margaret Pomeranz, Sandra Hall (from Australia), and Dan and Edna Fainaru; Dan and Edna actually helped me organise the event, and booked the excellent restaurant. I was also pleased that my former Sydney Film Festival colleague Lyn McCarthy and her husband, Graeme Tubbenhauer, were able to attend, along with Gerald Pratley from Toronto and former Edinburgh Film Festival Director David Bruce, who travelled to Venice from Helensburgh in Scotland.

It often strikes me as strange that I, whose formal education ended when I was sixteen, who never sat for, let alone passed, the equivalent of HSC, and who never went to university, except to attend film screenings, should late in life discover that my most satisfying role would be as a teacher in film. This came about thanks to Jim Sait, who was planning courses for the Centre for Continuing Education at the University of Sydney and was eager to develop a film course. Jim had known my friends Gaby Hyslop and Geoffrey Borny when they were at the University of New England in Armidale and they recommended that he contact me. My initial reaction was to refuse; I had more than enough work to do and certainly I didn't have the qualifications to be a teacher. Jim calmly overrode my objections and urged me to try. 'The trick,' he explained, 'is never to let the class know that they know more than you do.' This seemed fair enough and so, in 1990, I began to teach classes with a brief to choose any subject that interested me.

At the beginning I decided simply to talk about some of my favourite films. Later, in an attempt to structure things more, I taught a term on film censorship in Australia. It was in July 1993, when I was on holiday in China, that I had the idea of teaching film history. Aboard a boat sailing up the Yangtse River, through the famous gorges, I discussed the matter with Gerald Pratley, who was then teaching a film history course at Ryerson University in Toronto. It seemed like a great idea, and as soon as I got back to Australia I pitched it to Derek Peat, who was now the head of Continuing Education, and to his deputy, Chris Downes. In February 1994, I started a five-year Film History course, which proved very successful – so much so that, when it was drawing to a close, I suggested to Chris, who had succeeded Derek as head of CCE, that I commence a ten-year course at the beginning of 1999.

Teaching this ten-year course, in which I've been examining the history of world cinema in chronological order, has been an exhilarating experience for me. Apart from anything else, it's given me the chance to go back over the films of the past, sort them out into some kind of order, and reassess them. Because I believe that it's important to contextualise the films, I prepare information about the important political and social events of the period in question, which is handed out before each class.

As an example, what follows is typical of the structure of one of my lectures; this one, the one-hundredth session of the ten-year course, took place on 16 October 2003. On that evening, arriving class members were greeted with documentation listing some of the key events that occurred between October and December 1949: Mao Tse-tung proclaimed China a Communist Republic, the German Democratic Republic (DDR) was established in the Soviet zone of occupied Germany; work began on the Snowy Mountains Hydro-Electric Scheme; rockets were tested at Woomera for the first time; and, on 10 December, Robert Menzies's Liberals defeated Ben Chifley's Labor Party in a federal election. Film-related events were included in the documentation: Sigourney Weaver was born on 8 October, Jeff Bridges on 4 December and the character actress, Maria Ouspenskaya died on 3 December at the age of seventy-two. In the lecture I concentrated on British films of 1949, screening excerpts from several of them, including the great Ealing comedies *Kind Hearts and Coronets*, *Passport to Pimlico* and *Whisky Galore*. There were also excerpts from Richard Burton's first film, *The Last Days of Dolwyn*, and from such classic dramas as *The Third Man*, *The*

Blue Lamp and *Morning Departure*. The film I screened in full that evening was rather a rare one: *Give Us This Day*, which was made in London by the blacklisted American director Edward Dmytryk, and which starred the blacklisted actor Sam Wanamaker in a drama set in New York in the 1920s. A discussion took place afterwards, as it does at the end of every evening.

The early weeks of this course traced the origins of cinema and the development of silent cinema until the arrival of 'talkies' with *The Jazz Singer* in 1927. Later on we looked at the arrival of musicals, screwball comedies, gangster movies and westerns. We saw how French cinema of the 1930s reflected the ominous events in Europe and how the exodus of Jewish filmmakers from Germany affected film production in the countries where they found work, including France and America. We saw how popular comedians attracted audiences during the Depression in Britain and also in Australia. Chinese and, especially, Japanese cinema of the 1930s and early 40s were not neglected. World War II brought about a new dynamism in British cinema, and the post-war period saw the blacklist begin to affect quality American cinema, as well as the arrival of wide screens and location-based spectaculars. The popularity of the samurai film in Japan, the spaghetti western in Italy, the gangster movie in France and the kitchen-sink drama in Britain – all these have been extensively covered, as has revolution in the 1960s brought about by the lessening of censorship and a more relaxed attitude towards sex and violence. New waves in France, Britain, Germany, Australia and Latin America have all been covered. The course is designed to end at about the time we reach the year 1980. Class numbers have been gratifyingly high, and many friendships have formed among class members.

Membership now hovers around the 100 mark and, when the current course is completed at the end of 2008, I have every intention of starting another ten-year course in 2009. Chris Downes, who was immensely supportive during the period that I was establishing this marathon course, resigned from the CCE in 2001, which was a blow for me because he had personally attended every one of my lectures. The obvious appreciation shown by members of the class, have given me some of my happiest professional moments in recent years.

Throughout the 1990s I was making a minimum of three overseas trips a year to attend the major festivals in Berlin (February), Cannes (May) and Venice (August–September). At these festivals I would review films for *Variety*, conduct interviews for *The Movie Show* and write wrap stories for *The Australian*. After serving on the international juries of the Berlin and Montreal Film Festivals in 1982, it was twelve years before I was invited onto the jury of one of the other key festivals.

I had been holidaying with Susie and Gerald Pratley in Alaska in the northern summer of 1994 and we arrived home to find an urgent letter from the Venice Film Festival. The VFF Director, Gillo Pontecorvo (winner of the Golden Lion for his film *The Battle of Algiers* in 1966), was inviting me to serve on the International Jury. We were only at home a short time before taking off again for Venice via Rome in first class seats on Alitalia provided by the Festival. We were treated like royalty and stayed in a magnificent suite in the Excelsior Hotel. The Jury Chairman was David Lynch, known for his mysteriously dark melodramas (*Blue Velvet*, *Twin Peaks*), and he proved to be an extremely pleasant man but a rather ineffectual Chairman. The dominant figure on the Jury, at least in his own mind, was the Peruvian author Mario Vargas Llosa, whose dogmatic, opinionated style alienated many of the other jury members. These included actor Uma Thurman, French director Olivier Assayas (who knew more about films than most of the rest of the jurors put together) and the Japanese director Nagasa Oshima.

For two weeks we watched films together, often ate together, regularly met and argued. The decisions were difficult; the jury was divided. Olivier and I favoured an exquisite, relationship-based

Taiwanese film, *Vive L'Amour* by Tsai Ming-liang, which Vargas Llosa detested; he very much liked a Macedonian film, *Before the Rain*, which Uma also liked but I wasn't very impressed with it. Peter Jackson's scary film about murderous schoolgirls, *Heavenly Creatures*, almost slipped in as the compromise choice, but David was keen to award Oliver Stone's *Natural Born Killers* the Golden Lion. This was the same year *Pulp Fiction* had won the Palme D'Or in Cannes and some of us thought it was sending too strong a message to give similar status to Stone's film. The jury meetings became quite heated. Susie told me that on one occasion she was sitting, with Vargas Llosa's wife, outside the room where we were meeting, she heard him shouting out loudly that David Stratton and Uma Thurman were making the choice impossible. In the end, a tired and frustrated jury shared the Golden Lion between *Vive L'Amour* and *Before the Rain*, and *Natural Born Killers* sneaked in as the runner-up; Peter Jackson missed out altogether. Nobody was very happy about the decisions that were made but, as Uma said to me on the last night, 'at least we survived'.

It often seemed to happen that tragic events occurred when I was away and it sometimes seemed as if festivals were harbingers of doom. On one occasion in the 1980s when I was in Venice, the Russians shot down a Korean airliner that strayed into Soviet airspace. I was also in Venice in 1997 when Princess Diana and Dodi Fayed were killed in Paris. Incidents like these are emblazoned in the memory, but nothing could compare to 11 September 2001.

That year we had decided to present *The Movie Show* from the Toronto Film Festival for the first and, as it proved, the last time. Margaret and I went to Venice first and then met our producer, Brendan Walls, and director, Terry Toaldo, in Toronto, where we hired a local crew. It proved more difficult for us to get interviews in Toronto because the event is geared towards the North American press, unlike Cannes and Venice, which are more cosmopolitan. On 10 September I celebrated my birthday by having dinner with friends, including Todd McCarthy, Derek Elley, Dan and Edna Fainaru, Eddie Cockrell and Shane Danielsen. I was still writing for *Variety* then and I was supposed to attend the press screening of Fred Schepisi's new film, *Last Orders*, that night, because I'd been assigned to review it. However, Todd had agreed that, under the circumstances, I could attend the public screening at nine am the next morning, provided that I filed the review through to LA as soon as possible after the screening ended.

On the morning of 11 September I breakfasted with Jan Rofekamp, a film buff who runs Film Transit, a Montreal distribution company, and then walked to the Bloor Cinema for the screening of *Last Orders*. As I was walking into the lobby I ran into Schepisi, who looked a little pale. I asked him if he was nervous about the screening but he explained that he'd just heard that a plane had crashed into the World Trade Center in New York. I assumed that he meant a small commuter plane but there was no time for elaboration as the film was about to commence. He introduced *Last Orders* to a packed cinema without mentioning this incident and for the next two hours I was entranced by his masterful depiction of the lives of four London friends, played by Michael Caine, Tom Courtenay, David Hemmings and Helen Mirren. As I left the cinema to hurry back to my hotel to write the review I became aware, from the attitudes of passers-by in the street, that something very dramatic had occurred, though I didn't know what. Toronto is in the same time zone as New York and back in my hotel room I turned on the television and watched with mounting horror as the twin towers collapsed. I knew from that moment that things would never be the same again.

I tried to call Susie, who was on the NSW Central Coast at the bedside of her mother, who, after some difficult hip surgery, had suffered a stroke; she died two days later, unaware of what had occurred in New York. Meanwhile in Toronto, the Festival came to an abrupt stop; screenings were cancelled but nobody could leave the city because all the planes were grounded. Some Americans rented cars to drive home but the rest of us just had to wait. Brendan and Terry, who had planned to leave on 12 September to edit the programme back in Sydney, instead were forced to rent an editing suite in Toronto to assemble the programme and, at great expense, satellite it back to SBS in Australia.

I had intended to fly home via San Francisco to see Jo but this was now out of the question. After several days in limbo we were told that, because flights across America were still cancelled, the best way to return home was via London. Toronto airport was crowded when we checked in. In the British Airways lounge I chatted to István Szabó who had been in Toronto with his film *Taking Sides* and, later, to Jan Chapman and Ray Lawrence, the producer and director respectively of one of the finest of all Australian films, *Lantana*, which had been selected to close the Festival in what was intended to be a major North American launch. The actors – Anthony LaPaglia, Barbara Hershey, Geoffrey Rush – had been unable to leave New York, however, so the launch had been a sadly muted one.

We flew into Heathrow early in the morning and, after a shower, I called my niece, Helen, who was free for lunch. The situation was really quite bizarre; I ran into an old friend, Derek Hill, as I walked towards from Victoria Station towards Helen's office in the Westminster Council building, and for some reason I remember being angered that the people sitting at the next table in the Italian restaurant where we had lunch were smoking. I'd become very fond of Helen as I got to know her better; we seemed to have a lot in common and to share similar viewpoints, and I also liked her partner, Jon, very much. Our lunch was an oasis of calm in a fraught period. Since the flight to Sydney wasn't departing until eleven pm, I went to see a film after Helen returned to work. By the time I got home to Australia I'd missed my mother-in-law's funeral. 2001 was a very bad year.

Now that I'm in my mid-sixties I should, I suppose, be working less – but I seem to be busier than ever before. Each week I'm required to see every film that opens in Australia; at one time this would have been a pleasure, but these days I have to say that, more often than not, it's a chore. It sometimes seems that Hollywood has almost entirely gone over to making films for teenagers. When I was young, American films were made with wide audience appeal, but today the appeal is much narrower. The plethora of sequels, remakes and 'franchises' is indicative of a lack of real imagination among American filmmakers. The endless teen romances and comedies are becoming increasingly tiresome and things have reached the stage that when, occasionally, a film made for adults emanates from a major studio, I tend to embrace it like a drowning man. Sometimes the embrace might be too eager and it's infuriating that more often than not these films are all released at the same time of the year – Oscar season.

Independent American cinema has gone some way towards filling the gap and in doing so has tended to displace the quality Australian (or New Zealand) film, which, fifteen years ago, stood much more chance of finding international distribution than it does today. Of course, Australian filmmakers haven't helped themselves with the depressing collection of lowbrow comedies that emerged at the beginning of the new century, though some much more ambitious films – *The Proposition, Little Fish, Oyster Farmer, Three Dollars, The Magician, Look Both Ways, Jindabyne, Ten Canoes, Suburban Mayhem* – improved the situation during 2005–6. The films of 2007 have been an uneven lot, with the independently financed *The Jammed* one of the stand-outs.

Since moving up to the Blue Mountains I have determined to stay at home on Fridays in order to write reviews and prepare lectures for the following week. Unless something unexpected happens I try not to visit Sydney at weekends. A typical week now involves previews on either Mondays or Tuesdays (hopefully not both, though occasionally this is necessary), taping *The Movie*

Show on Wednesdays, and then more previews on Thursdays until, during spring and autumn, I report to the University at 5.30 pm to prepare my three-hour lectures, which begin at 6.30. Even after quitting *Variety* I travel to Europe at least twice a year, to attend the Cannes and Venice Film Festivals. During these festivals, Margaret and I tape interviews with the talent available – directors and actors, usually – which are used when the films open later on in Australia. We also assemble a special programme on the festival. In addition, I always provide a general piece for *The Australian* and phone through a weekly audio report and review for John Stanley on 2UE.

After it gained power in 1996, the Howard Government made no secret of its antipathy towards the country's public broadcasters, the ABC and SBS. That wasn't new; Paul Keating and Bob Hawke had their run-ins with the ABC, and it's only right and proper that an independent broadcaster *should* be critical of the government, no matter which political party is in power. But Howard's feelings towards the ABC seemed to go deeper, and he had the power to do something about them. An attempt to neuter the broadcaster by the appointment of a totally unsuitable chief executive, Jonathan Shier, failed only because of public and media outcry and the courage of the chairman of the ABC Board, Donald McDonald. But with the appointment of right-wing commentators like Janet Albrechtsen, Keith Windschuttle and Christopher Pearson to the boards of the ABC and SBS, the Government was still clearly determined to bring about changes.

In October 2006 *The Movie Show* would have been on the air for twenty years, which seemed like a pretty good run. My movie selections and introductions would have been aired continuously for twenty-five years. I had in mind that 2006 might be the year to retire, and I even imagined the farewell celebrations that might take place at SBS. However, like most major events during my life, things didn't run that smoothly. Instead of being a happy occasion, my departure from SBS was a bitter one.

The SBS equivalent of Jonathan Shier was Shaun Brown, who had previously run TVNZ; if you've ever been to New Zealand you'll know that, whatever the merits of the place, quality television isn't one of them. Errol Simper, author of a weekly column for *The Australian* called 'A Certain Scribe', wrote on 8 June 2006: 'When Shaun Brown was appointed head of SBS television in January 2003 the industrious scribe made a number of telephone calls to New Zealand . . . The scribe was surprised and faintly alarmed at reactions when he told a number of NZ sources who'd worked with Brown that he'd been put in charge of SBS television. There's no kind, gentle way to put this, so we must be blunt. Brown running SBS television appeared to provoke a good deal of mirth and hilarity. There seemed to be a view that Brown might have a bit of difficulty running a bath.'

Brown has said that, when he was in Sydney for interviews about the job, he spent some time in his hotel room watching SBS. Nothing on the network interested him, apparently, apart from *The Movie Show* and the *IF Awards* (Independent Film), which happened to be screened that week and which had been produced by Margaret Pomeranz. He seems not to have been very attracted to the kinds of programmes which were, at the time, SBS staples: movies, documentaries and current affairs programmes.

In the weeks after Brown was appointed Head of Television at SBS, I was somewhat surprised that he made no attempt to contact me. After all, I was the network's Feature Film Consultant, and movies were an important part of the schedule; I was also co-host of one of the top-rating programmes SBS produced. But he didn't even call to say hello. All of his predecessors had been more courteous, but I put it down to the fact that he was busy and would get around to it eventually.

I heard later that, about six weeks after Brown joined SBS, Rod Webb, who had been acting Head of Television before Brown, was briefing him on a number of matters. Among other things, he mentioned that the marketing department had wanted *The Movie Show* to be sponsored by a brand of coffee, which they wanted Margaret and me to endorse on camera. We hadn't been consulted about this in advance, and when we heard about it we weren't enthusiastic. Rod had backed us, and he explained to Brown why. Brown listened to what he had to say and then asked: 'Who's David Stratton?'

When I was in Cannes that May, I heard that Rod Webb, who had done a splendid job as SBS Head of Programming, had been fired. This was the first of many firings of good people from SBS; it seemed as though Brown (or 'Beige', as he was being called around the station) was determined to get rid of the people who had made the network what it was. I should have seen the warning signs, but I didn't.

When I returned from a brief holiday with Susie in New Zealand that July, I received an urgent phone call from Margaret to tell me that my movie presentations were to be dropped. I couldn't believe that this would be done without any consultation with me but Margaret assured me it was true. I asked to meet with Brown and this meeting was the first time I'd talked to him face to face. He confirmed what Margaret had said; from September (which was less than two months away), the two sessions a week in which I programmed and hosted quality movies would be cancelled. No more 'hostings' would take place anywhere on SBS, he told me; the network was being given a new look. On reflection, he allowed the *Cinema Classics* to continue, but at the impossible time of midnight on Sunday night (and this was probably a way of using up the backlog of black-and-white movies). He assured me that he was a fan of *The Movie Show* and keen for it to continue, as well he might be: in the week that I met with him, the show had rated in the top five programmes on SBS.

To say that I was shattered would be an understatement. Brown was a totally underwhelming character; he gave the impression of knowing little and caring nothing about the kind of programming that had given SBS its reputation. If this was the kind of person the Board of SBS thought was the best to run the network then obviously things had changed more drastically that I had imagined.

I still could hardly believe that, after more than twenty years of working for the network, I hadn't been consulted in any way at all about these fundamental changes. And I was still in a state of shock when the CEO of SBS, Nigel Milan, invited me for lunch. I'd always liked Nigel and he was reassuring. *The Movie Show* was not in jeopardy, he assured me; I was, he said, an integral part of the network.

Margaret, too, was unhappy with the new regime. Ever since I'd known her, she'd been a producer at SBS. She was the executive producer of *The Movie Show* (which occasionally resulted in a minor conflict when she wielded her producer's stick) and of other programmes, such as *Front Up*. But she was appalled when the contract of Craig Collie, the well-liked Head of Production, was not renewed. Was he being dumped because his 'style' didn't fit with the 'new' SBS, or was it because there was a long-term policy to abandon in-house productions altogether? Collie's initiatives, like *Fat Pizza*, had scored top ratings; during his time at SBS he had given enormous impetus to local productions.

Before long, Glenys Rowe, a producer of quality feature films, who had been Head of SBS Independent (a quality-driven feature-film unit within the organisation) was appointed overall Head of Production. This appointment lent further fuel to speculation that the future of SBS would be towards outsourcing programmes and, as Margaret has often said, the heart of any television station is what it actually produces itself. The ABC has been greatly diminished since its internal drama production resources were disbanded because of budget cuts.

While many of the best and most loyal employees of SBS, some of whom had worked at the station since its inception, were being let go, the bureaucracy increased. Where it was once necessary for a producer to go through two levels of management to greenlight a new programme, there would now be five.

During this tense period, Margaret ran into the then Head of ABC Television, Sandra Levy, at a function. Levy had in the past expressed to Margaret an interest in working with her, and she asked how things were going under the new regime at SBS. 'Don't ask!' said Margaret. 'Let's talk,' said Levy. The two met in private to discuss the idea of *The Movie Show* moving from SBS to the ABC. After their first meeting, Margaret told me what was in the wind. I felt so betrayed by Brown, so hurt and so insulted by what he had done, that I jumped at the idea of a move. Margaret and I met Sandra at her home for further discussions.

There were several such secret talks with Sandra and, later, with the Executive Producer of Arts Programmes at the ABC, Courtney Gibson, as well as with lawyers on both sides, and over the summer months as an agreement was worked out. Somehow we managed to keep our plans a secret, though of course we had to tell the members of the production team who worked with us to put *The Movie Show* to air every week. Sandra had given us the option of producing the new programme ourselves with our own team, but our director, Terry Toaldo, our production assistant, Electra Manikakis and our assistant director, Deb Spinocchia, decided to stay with SBS. Our producer, Brendan Walls, was offered the job of producing the new programme at the ABC and accepted, a decision he has never regretted. The worst element in the move was leaving behind Terry, Electra and Deb because they had become as much family as colleagues over the years. We would also miss Ian Phipps, our resourceful publicist.

I wasn't able to go to SBS on that Monday before Easter in 2004 when Margaret broke the news to Shaun Brown in his office. In a carefully choreographed move, the ABC had prepared a press release to be sent out to the media the moment the meeting was over. Margaret phoned Kris Way, our ABC publicist, as soon as she left Brown's office, and the next day the news was in all the papers, making the front page of *The Sydney Morning Herald.*

In retaliation SBS issued a press release in which they implied that they were considering getting rid of us anyway. At the next Senate Estimates Committee in Canberra in May 2004, Nigel Milan was asked no fewer than fourteen questions by Senator Mackay about our departure from SBS and the comments Margaret had made in the press release expressing her disillusionment with the direction the network was taking.

SBS owned the title, *The Movie Show*, and so we had to find a new name for the programme without delay. Margaret's favourite was *Talking Pictures*, but this was already being used for a segment of the ABC's *Insiders* programme. Susie came up with *Two with a View*, which I thought was promising, but in the end we compromised with *At the Movies*, which Margaret jokingly calls ATM. Most people I meet usually refer to it as *The Movie Show on the ABC*.

Terry, Electra and Deb were put to work on a replacement programme for SBS; auditions were held and it was decided to employ three hosts, plus a DVD reviewer, instead of two. With a markedly different format, the show resumed but then, in June 2006, it was axed by SBS management. Several months later it was revived, after a fashion, with two more hosts in a ten-minute Saturday night timeslot. At about the same time Shaun Brown, who had been promoted to Managing Director of SBS by the Board, announced that commercial breaks would interrupt programmes every ten minutes in future, thus spelling the death knell for what was once a quality television network which was highly regarded the world over. The evening news now contains two commercial breaks and even movies are regularly interrupted. The departure, in angry circumstances, of the immensely talented and much admired newsreader Mary Kostakidis during August 2007 was the final nail in the coffin for SBS. It is now nothing more than a low-rating commercial station with little to recommend it (apart from the occasional documentary). If the original aim was to destroy the network, that aim has surely succeeded.

Our new team at the ABC consisted of Brendan, who repeated his SBS role as producer, Amber Ma, who was recruited from one of the smaller film distributors to be associate producer, Natalie Owen as the director's assistant and Pat Downie, producer's assistant. Amanda Duthie was our executive producer. Margaret and I soon found that the ABC provided a very different working environment from SBS. Our former home had been small enough that we knew just about everyone; it was – or had been, until the arrival of Brown – a family. We now record our programmes at the vast ABC headquarters at Ultimo in Sydney, and their preference is to record two at a time, so that we no longer have the opportunity to include up-to-the-minute elements, such as obituaries.

Our first show at the ABC went to air on Wednesday 1 July 2004, just a day after our SBS contracts had expired. We were both nervous and unsettled by our new environment, by the unfamiliar studio and production crew. I was surprised to find that I now had a 'wardrobe consultant' and was no longer encouraged to wear my own clothes. But we soon relaxed into the new regimen. Everybody was incredibly welcoming and pleasant towards us and the show, with its bright opening titles and music, looks slicker and more polished than it ever did before.

The ABC is more ratings-conscious than SBS had been, but the ratings weren't bad considering the fact that, after six months at 9.30 pm (at SBS we had gone to air at eight pm) we were put back to 10.05 pm, which is a late timeslot for many viewers. We were also given a six pm Sunday evening repeat slot, which has proved quite popular. By the middle of 2007 about a million viewers a week, including regional areas, were watching the programme.

All these changes took place a few weeks before my sixty-fifth birthday. My plans to slow down and think about retirement had to be put on hold. There was more work than ever. But since it's work that I enjoy so much, how can I complain?

I'm often asked if critics can really influence the success or failure of a film. I don't think we have any effect whatsoever on how the big Hollywood blockbusters perform, but when it comes to Australian films it's a different matter.

Take the case of *The Jammed*, a no-budget film written and directed by South African-born, Melbourne-based Dee McLachlan. This thriller, about a young woman who inadvertently becomes involved in the odious sex-slave trade, was bypassed for funding by the federal agencies but McLachlan, a determined woman, went ahead and made it anyway, shooting over a nineteen-day period on high-definition video with an excellent cast of actors led by Veronica Sywak, who plays the gutsy protagonist. The film had screened at the Sydney Film Festival in June, but I'd missed it there. A few weeks later I was in Brisbane, having just flown into the city for the Festival. I hadn't planned to see *The Jammed* until, by chance, I ran into Dee in the lobby of my hotel and she told me something about it. I decided to catch the screening that afternoon and was hugely impressed. When Dee told me that the film had not been taken up by any of the local film distributors, but was being self-distributed and was starting a brief run at the Nova in Melbourne the following Thursday, I was determined that we should include it on the following Wednesday's *At the Movies*, even though Brendan Walls, our producer, had already settled on the content of the show.

I borrowed a DVD from Dee and Brendan, who had also just arrived in Brisbane, saw it and was equally impressed. Margaret arrived the next day and shared our views. Brendan interviewed Dee and Veronica, and the following Wednesday we reviewed the film enthusiastically, both giving it four stars. The following morning there was an equally positive review by Jim Schembri in *The Age*. The response was immediate; suddenly distributors and cinemas were interested. Roadshow agreed to hold back the DVD release to allow for a theatrical window, which previously had seemed out of the question. The next day *The Sydney Morning Herald* ran a positive story about the 'discovery' of this little film. The film opened at the Nova in Melbourne to outstanding figures and was immediately booked into Palace cinemas in Sydney. In late 2007 *The Jammed* won the IF Award for Best Film. It all goes to show that sometimes you can make a difference, and it's wonderful when you can.

Several years ago the great director Billy Wilder was awarded with a Lifetime Achievement Award at the Berlin Film Festival. I was present at the ceremony and Wilder, American cinema's resident cynic, was on top form. The man who made the film many consider the greatest of all Hollywood comedies, *Some Like It Hot*, in 1959 and followed it with one of the most perceptive films about American ambition and ruthlessness, *The Apartment*, the following year, gave a wickedly funny speech in which he equated lifetime achievement awards with haemorrhoids. 'Every old arsehole gets them eventually,' he proclaimed.

I have been honoured to receive this kind of recognition in the years since I turned sixty. In 2001 I received a very special honour from the French Government at a ceremony in Sydney presided over by the French Ambassador to Australia. I was made a Commander in the Order of Arts and Letters, the highest cultural award France can bestow. The citation read that I was been honoured for services to cinema in general and French cinema in particular. I wear the discreet little green and white lapel pin with considerable pride.

Later the same year I received the Raymond Longford Award from the Australian Film Institute at the annual AFI awards, which that year took place in Melbourne. This award, presented to me by the actor John Wood, was in recognition of a lifetime given to celebrating film and filmmakers.

And then, after teaching film history at Sydney University for over fifteen years, I was immensely gratified to be honoured with an Honorary Degree of Doctor of Letters, which was bestowed on me by the Chancellor, Justice Kim Santow, on 9 June 2006. I was invited to deliver the Occasional Address to the Arts graduates assembled in the University's Great Hall, and I spoke about the need for passion and commitment in the arts. At the same time I was reflecting, yet again, on my great good fortune.

There was more to come. For nearly fifteen years I had hosted a question-and-answer session following the presentation of the Chauvel Award (in memory of film pioneers of the 1920s and 30s, Charles and Elsa Chauvel) to Australians in recognition of their contributions to Australian cinema. Among the recipients had been George Miller, Paul Cox, Rolf de Heer, Gillian Armstrong, Geoffrey Rush and Jack Thompson. In 2007, Festival Director Anne Demy-Geroe was generous enough to bestow the honour on me. Since I could hardly host a Q&A session with myself, Margaret Pomeranz was given the unenviable task of interviewing me on stage and there were also some unexpected, and very gratifying, on-screen tributes from such diverse friends and colleagues as Australian reviewers Paul Byrnes, Adrian Martin and Tom Ryan, directors Rolf de Heer, Paul Cox and Phillip Noyce, producer Jan Sharp, *Variety* colleagues Todd McCarthy and Scott Foundas, and actors Nicole Kidman and Hugh Jackman. Margaret also read out a very warm letter from Pierre Rissient.

To top it all, at a ceremony held during the sixtieth Cannes Film Festival in May 2007, I was one of a handful of international journalists awarded a commemorative medal for my work in covering the Festival. Todd McCarthy and Dan and Edna Fainaru were also recipients.

My love for cinema has undergone some turmoil in recent years. There's no doubt that American films aren't as good as they used to be and, in retrospect, the 1970s looms as the last golden age. But there are still discoveries to be made, still filmmakers around the world capable of challenging our complacency and surprising us. And the great thing about cinema is that it survives.

When I get bored with the new releases I can always retreat to my home cinema and watch, on the big screen, films from the past – *Singin' in the Rain*, *The Night of the Hunter*, *The Grapes of Wrath*, *Red River*, *The General* and so many other movies that I visit again and again. In that sense, the excitement I experienced as a child when I was taken by my grandmother to see my first movies in Andover lives with me still.

Chapter Eighteen

The 2007 Cannes Film Festival closed with a comedy from Canada. *L'Age des Tenebres* (*The Age of Ignorance*) is a satire on contemporary life made by Quebec filmmaker Denys Arcand, the director of *Jesus of Montreal*, *The Decline of the American Empire* and *The Barbarian Invasions*. In one scene in the film the protagonist, a hapless public servant whose role in life is to answer questions from members of the public on behalf of the government, is visited by a young Muslim woman. She tells him that her husband has been arrested, and that no reason has been given for the arrest. 'He's not a terrorist,' she claims, and goes on to say that she's not allowed to see him and doesn't know what to do. After some hesitation, the public servant attempts to comfort her. 'Just remember, it's worse in Australia,' he says.

The line gets a laugh, but for me it was a very bitter moment. It's sad to think that the country to which I now belong, the country which has my loyalty, the country which has been good to me, now has a tarnished international reputation. The last few years have seen Australia change in dramatic ways. I think we've been encouraged by our political leaders to become less tolerant, less humane, more greedy, more selfish. The ideals of mateship, and the fair go – ideals which attracted me so much when I first arrived in Australia – are still celebrated by our leaders, but in an increasingly hypocritical way. The sentiments now have a hollow ring to them.

The treatment of refugees has been of particular concern to many decent citizens of this country, and I have some first-hand knowledge of this. I know an Iraqi who suffered cruel and unusual punishment because of federal government policies. Hassan is a lovely, sensitive man, a devout Shiite Muslim from Karbala who worked as an accountant there and who was happily married with several children. After the First Gulf War, when George Bush Sr advised the people of Iraq to stand up against the dictator Saddam Hussein, Hassan was wounded, imprisoned and lost two of his children, who were killed by Saddam's soldiers. He managed to escape prison and fled with his wife and remaining family to Syria, but when he heard that Iraqis there were being rounded up he was desperate. There was no question of 'joining a queue' (as Immigration Ministers have consistently and misleadingly told us such unfortunates should do), because to show himself at the Australian Embassy in Damascus was to court arrest and maybe murder by Iraqi secret-service spies.

Hassan was desperate, and so he paid money to a people-smuggler, said goodbye to his wife and children, and set off into the unknown. After terrible privations, and a voyage in a crowded, leaky boat, he was picked up by immigration officials at Ashmore Reef and flown to the detention centre in Woomera. Here he was told to write to his wife to let her know where he was, which he did. Weeks later the officials returned with his letter, which had never been sent. It had simply been used to verify his identity. He spent the next four and a half years in detention, first in Woomera and then in Villawood in Sydney, during which time he lost touch with his wife and family. His life, and the lives of all the members of his family, were in ruins. After those endless four and a half years in what amounts to a prison, he was finally released, thanks to the lobbying of good, decent Australians, among them my wife, and the help of a Government minister (unconnected with the Immigration portfolio) who showed an understanding – a decency – that some of his colleagues did not. Hassan is now reunited with his family and living and working in Sydney. He recently became an Australian citizen. But none of this mitigates the tremendous wrong that was done to him, and to a great many like him.

I was raised in a conservative English middle-class family. My parents always voted Tory, as had, I assume, their parents before them. As I child I was cautioned about ever going into a Co-Op shop, because, my mother told me, they were run by the Labour Party, which was tantamount to being run by the Devil himself. In my early twenties I even attended a garden party where the guest of honour was Prime Minister Harold Macmillan, and I was pleased to exchange small talk with the Conservative leader. But despite the conservatism of my parents, they always expressed a tolerance towards others, and my mother's voluntary Red Cross activities were indicative of her humanity and care for those less fortunate.

When I arrived in Australia I was surprised to find that, in those days, voting in elections was obligatory not only for Australian citizens but also for residents. In my first federal election, which took place only a few weeks after my arrival in 1963, I voted for the Liberal/Country Party coalition, mainly because Prime Minister Robert Menzies was a familiar figure and seemed comfortingly British, but also because the Leader of the Opposition, Arthur Calwell, seemed to me not to be a very charismatic character.

Although I was not a regular churchgoer at all, Margaret, my first wife, and I attended Sunday services at an Anglican church on Sydney's North Shore soon after we arrived. I was quite shocked when the minister, in his sermon, started talking about the upcoming election and urged the congregation to vote for the local Coalition candidate. I had never experienced this kind of politicking in any English church, and the unwelcome crossover between church and state completely put me off churchgoing in this country. More than that, the experience made me question any faith I might have had, and in the end I decided that I was really an agnostic or, perhaps, as Grandfather Wells would have said, a non-fogian. Ever since that Sunday morning in 1963 I have only attended church for weddings and funerals. In recent years, the strident political interference of some church leaders has only confirmed my attitude towards religion.

My experiences at a British public school had opened my eyes to the 'born to rule' snobbishness of the Establishment, and I loathed that side of British conservatism and all that it stood for. But I still saw myself as a middle-class Englishman for whom the working class – Labour voters – were the enemy.

I think that my attitude only began to change when I started travelling overseas for the Sydney Film Festival. My visits to Eastern Bloc countries such as Poland, Czechoslovakia and Hungary offered experiences quite at odds with the official rhetoric of the time. The people I met in these countries were not obsessed with the destruction of the West – the vast majority of them weren't even Communists, and they loathed the deadening influence the Soviet Union had on a way of life which, before World War II, had been cosmopolitan and sophisticated.

Then there was the Vietnam War. Britain had chosen not to take part, but Australia was 'all the way with LBJ', to quote Prime Minister Harold Holt, and our troops were fighting and dying in that country alongside American forces. The draft had been imposed; young men were forced to fight, and many were killed. As news of atrocities committed by American forces, such as the My Lai massacre, became public at the end of the 1960s and opposition to the war increased, I became more and more convinced that Australia's presence in Vietnam was a grave mistake. When President Nixon ordered the invasion of Cambodia, and a few days later four unarmed students were shot dead by National Guardsmen at Kent State University in Ohio, I was not alone in becoming convinced that we had our priorities all wrong.

The winds of change were blowing through Australia and I became a supporter of Labor Party leader Gough Whitlam. I was overseas when he was elected in 1972, but when I returned home a month later I was thrilled at the change in direction Australia had taken. I was also away at the time of the Dismissal, three years later, but the excitement of the Whitlam legacy, despite the undoubted economic setbacks of the period, lived on. Australia was becoming a more open country: open to ideas, and open to the sense of generosity that comes with growing confidence in one's identity.

Despite the shift in my political allegiance I would, as Sydney Film Festival Director, always invite politicians of all sides to attend our opening night, and one who often accepted was John Howard. Whitlam was a regular attendee (and was always applauded by the Festival audience when he entered the theatre) and so were other Labor figures, including Lionel Murphy; but I always made Coalition figures very welcome, though they were sometimes booed by sections of the audience.

SBS, as envisioned by Malcolm Fraser, was the proud flag-bearer for multiculturalism, a policy which has come under increasing threat over recent years. The changes brought about by Shaun Brown were part of the reason that Margaret Pomeranz and I decided to accept the offer made to us by the ABC to switch channels. At the time, Margaret made some impassioned statements, which I fully endorsed, on the dangers of commercial advertising and public broadcasting, pointing out – correctly, in my view – that 'the dollar starts to drive decision-making'.

Margaret was attacked by Christopher Pearson, a columnist for *The Australian* who had been appointed to the SBS Board by the Howard Government. Pearson, in an op-ed piece published on 24 June 2006, failed to spell Margaret's surname correctly (he called her 'Pomerantz'), and he accused her of being 'an interested bystander' and of making 'ingratiating remarks [which] may appeal to her new employer'. He might have considered that, as a producer at the network since it began, Margaret knew a lot more about multicultural television than he did. Pearson's real target, I think, was Errol Simper, one of *The Australian*'s most respected media commentators, who had regularly attacked the direction in which SBS was heading.

Since moving to the ABC I have often been criticised by newspaper columnists for my views, but one of the most curious criticisms was by another writer for *The Australian*, foreign editor Greg Sheridan. In a column published on 29 April 2006, just after Anzac Day, Sheridan took me to task for my review of the film *Jarhead* on the ABC almost three months earlier. Made by the British director Sam Mendes and based on Anthony Swofford's well-received memoir, *Jarhead* deals with the moulding of raw recruits into the American marines and their assignment to Iraq for the First Gulf War in 1990. In my review on *At the Movies* I mentioned that I was quite shocked by 'the ugly and demeaning training sequences' in the film, scenes in which Mendes seems to be deliberately inviting comparison to Stanley Kubrick's *Full Metal Jacket*. I continued: '[These scenes] raise all kinds of questions about the morality of the way soldiers are trained these days. This is a film . . . about the way men are dehumanised to be turned into today's soldiers.' That was, as I saw it, what the film was about, but in my comments I went a little further. 'No wonder,' I said, 'atrocities come to be committed.' I was thinking, of course, of the horrors of Abu Ghraib prison.

Sheridan pointed out to his readers that 'Australian military training is just as rigorous as US training. Yet beyond the left-wing arts luvvies who dominate the ABC . . . does anyone really believe our soldiers have been dehumanised . . .?' Well, they might. But the interesting point here is that *my* opinion on a film review programme becomes, in Sheridan's column, the *ABC's* opinion. His column is headed: 'ABC out of step on the military' and concludes with the words: '. . . the ABC is wrong.' Such blatant misrepresentations are, unfortunately, all too common in the opinion pieces of our newspapers today. Had I written the same review for *The Australian*, as I easily might have (my colleague, Evan Williams, reviewed it instead), there is no way Sheridan would have stated that '*The Australian* is wrong'.

The significance of these rants is that those of us who want to protect the ABC are more cautious in voicing our opinions. The danger is that those who rant want only *their* voices to be heard; and when those ranters are awarded by the Government (any government, on either side of politics) with appointments to sensitive media boards like the ABC and SBS, then we have good reason to be very worried indeed.

I hope that soon the *real* Aussie qualities will re-emerge. My grandchildren face an uncertain future as climate change and the threat of international terrorism turn us into people more alarmed than alert. The manipulation of people's fears to push through restrictive agendas is a not a new phenomenon, but it is a policy that has, during recent years, seemingly been embraced by the Government and acceded to by the Opposition. I hope and believe that in the years to come Australians will be able to stand up, proudly, in the name of justice, fairness, tolerance, decency and mateship.

Appendix

Films programmed at SFF 1966–1983

1966

Loves of a Blonde (Miloš Forman, Czechoslovakia); *Charulata* (Satyajit Ray, India); *Thomas the Impostor* (Georges Franju, France); *Fires on the Plain* and *Alone on the Pacific* (Kon Ichikawa, Japan); *Sam-Yong* (Shin Sang-okk, Korea); *The Undignified Old Lady* (Rene Allio, France); *The Pawnbroker* (Sidney Lumet, USA); *Sandra* (Luchino Visconti, Italy); *Before the Revolution* (Bernardo Bertolucci, Italy); *Fists in the Pocket* (Marco Bellocchio, Italy); *Walkover* (Jerzy Skolimowski, Poland); *A Girl in Mourning* (Manuel Summers, Spain); *The Fifth Rider is Fear* (Zdenek Brynych, Czechoslovakia); *Les Abysses* (Nico Papatakis, France); *Man Is Not a Bird* (Dušan Makavejev, Yugoslavia); *The Age of Daydreaming* (István Szabó, Hungary); *Cumbite* (Tomas G. Alea, Cuba); *Heat* (Larissa Shepitko, USSR)

1967

Alphaville (Jean-Luc Godard, France); *The Round-Up* (Miklós Jancsó, Hungary); *Love 65* (Bo Widerberg, Sweden); *Au hasard Balthazar* (Robert Bresson, France); *Barrier* (Jerzy Skolimowski, Poland); *Seconds* (John Frankenheimer, USA); *Red Beard* (Akira Kurosawa, Japan); *The Man who Had His Hair Cut Short* (Andre Delvaux, Belgium); *Intimate Lighting* (Ivan Passer, Czechoslovakia); *Dance of the Heron* (Fons Rademakers, Netherlands); *Three* (Alexander Petrovic, Yugoslavia); *Long Live the Republic!* (Karel Kachyna, Czechoslovakia); *Adventure Starts Here* (Jörn Donner, Sweden); *The Eavesdropper* (Leopoldo Torre Nilsson, Argentina); *Shadows of Our Forgotten Ancestors* (Sergei Paradzhanov, USSR); *Seasons of Our Love* (Florestino Vancini, Italy); *La vie de Chateau* (Jean-Paul Rappeneau, France); *Four in the Morning* (Anthony Simmons, UK); *When Tomorrow Dies* (Larry Kent, Canada); *Forgotten Cinema* (Anthony Buckley, Australia)

1968

How I Won the War (Richard Lester, UK); *The Stranger* (Luchino Visconti, Italy); *Pierrot le Fou* (Jean-Luc Godard, France); *The Face of Another* (Hiroshi Teshigahara, Japan); *China is Near* (Marco Bellocchio, Italy); *The Young Törless* (Volker Schlöndorff, W. Germany); *Closely Watched Trains* (Jiri Menzel, Czechoslovakia); *Elvira Madigan* (Bo Widerberg, Sweden); *Le Depart* (Jerzy Skolimowski, Belgium); *Father* (István Szabó, Hungary); *Judex* (Georges Franju, France); *Hunger* (Henning Carlsen, Denmark); *Mouchette* (Robert Bresson, France); *Lenin in Poland* (Sergei Yutkevich, USSR); *Warrendale* (Allan King, Canada); *In the Town of S* (Josef Heifitz, USSR)

1969

If . . . (Lindsay Anderson, UK); *Silence and Cry* (Miklós Jancsó, Hungary); *Switchboard Operator* (Dušan Makavejev, Yugoslavia); *Capricious Summer* (Jiri Menzel, Czechoslovakia); *The Ernie*

Game (Don Owen, Canada); *Herostratus* (Don Levy, UK); *Man without a Map* (Hiroshi Teshigahara, Japan); *2,000 Weeks* (Tim Burstall, Australia); *Report on the Party and the Guests* (Jan Nemec, Czechoslovakia); *The Night They Raided Minsky's* (William Friedkin, USA); *Voice of the Water* (Bert Haanstra, Netherlands); *Black Cat* (Kaneto Shindo, Japan); *No Vietnamese Ever Called Me Nigger* (David Weiss, USA); *Pierre and Paul* (Rene Allio, France); *Days of Matthew* (Witold Leszcynski, Poland); *Cold Days* (Andras Kovacs, Hungary); *Till Monday* (Stanislav Rostotsky, USSR); *Hugo and Josefin* (Kjell Grede, Sweden); *Fando and Lis* (Alejandro Jodorowsky, Mexico); *Monsieur Hawarden* (Harry Kumel, Netherlands)

[Short films programmed in 1969 included works by Peter Weir, Stephen Frears, Fred Schepisi, Walerian Borowczyk and Lindsay Anderson]

1970

Z (Costa-Gavras, France); *The Bed Sitting Room* (Richard Lester, UK); *Everything for Sale* (Andrzej Wajda, Poland); *Antonio das Mortes* (Glauber Rocha, Brazil); *Goto, Island of Love* (Walerian Borowczyk, France); *Lucia* (Humberto Solas, Cuba); *I Love You, I Love You* (Alain Resnais, France); *Innocence Unprotected* (Dušan Makavejev, Yugoslavia); *An Evening on a Train* (Andre Delvaux, Belgium); *My Night with Maud* (Eric Rohmer, France); *Que la Bete meure* (Claude Chabrol, France); *In the Year of the Pig* (Emile de Antonio, USA); *The Adventures of Goopy and Bagha* (Satyajit Ray, India); *Think of a Number* (Palle Kjaerulff-Schmidt, Denmark); *Calcutta* (Louis Malle, France); *Ambush* (Zivojin Pavlovic, Yugoslavia); *Boy* (Nagisa Oshima, Japan); *The Cremator* (Juraj Herz, Czechoslovakia); *The Best Age* (Jarouslav Papousek, Czechoslovakia); *Prologue* (Robin Spry (Canada); *Salesman* (Maysles Bros, USA); *Lady from Constantinople* (Judit Elek, Hungary)

1971

Deep End (Jerzy Skolimowski, W. Germany); *The Conformist* (Bernardo Bertolucci, Italy); *Une femme douce* (Robert Bresson, France); *Tristana* (Luis Buñuel, Spain); *Teorema* (Pier Paolo Pasolini, Italy); *Wanda* (Barbara Loden, USA); *Duet for Cannibals* (Susan Sontag, Sweden); *Wind from the East* (Jean-Luc Godard, Italy/France); *Claire's Knee* (Eric Rohmer, France); *Even Dwarfs Started Small* (Werner Herzog, W. Germany); *Anna* (Jörn Donner, Finland); *The Wild Child and Domicile Conjugale* (François Truffaut, France); *Joe* (John G. Avildsen, USA); *Harry Munter* (Kjell Grede, Sweden); *The Clowns* (Federico Fellini, Italy); *The Sin of Abbe Mouret* (Georges Franju, France); *Punishment Park* (Peter Watkins, USA); *Love Film* (István Szabó, Hungary); *The Fruit of Paradise* (Vera Chytilova, Czechoslovakia); *The Deserters and the Nomads* (Juraj Jakubisko, Czechoslovakia); *Ramparts of Clay* (Jean-Louis Bertuccelli, Algeria); *Dodes'ka-den* (Akira Kurosawa, Japan)

+ Kurosawa retrospective

1972

W.R. Mysteries of the Organism (Dušan Makavejev, Yugoslavia); *A Nest of Gentry* (Andrei Konchalovsky, USSR); *The Garden of the Finzi-Continis* (Vittorio de Sica, Italy); *Four Nights of a Dreamer* (Robert Bresson, France); *The Spider's Stratagem* (Bernardo Bertolucci, Italy); *Adrift* (Jan Kadar, Czechoslovakia); *Blanche* (Walerian Borowczyk, France); *Blushing Charlie* (Vilgot Sjoman, Sweden); *Two English Girls and the Continent* (François Truffaut, France); *Love* (Karoly Makk, Hungary); *Minnie and Moskowitz* (John Cassavetes, USA); *Knockout* (Boro Draskovic, Yugoslavia); *Dear Irene* (Christian Braad Thomsen, Denmark); *Johnny Got his Gun* (Dalton Trumbo, USA); *Family Life* (Krzysztof Zanussi, Poland); *Family Life* (Ken Loach, UK); *The Sudden Fortune of the Poor People of Kombach* (Volker Schlöndorff, W. Germany); *A Safe Place* (Henry Jaglom, USA); *Mathias Kneissl* (Reinhard Hauff,

W. Germany); *How Tasty was my Little Frenchman* (Nelson Pereira Dos Santos, Brazil); *My Uncle Antoine* (Claude Jutra, Canada); *During the Summer* (Ermanno Olmi, Italy); *Valparaiso Valparaiso* (Pascal Aubier, France); *Millhouse, a White Comedy* (Emile de Antonio, USA); *Just Before Nightfall* (Claude Chabrol, France); *Ice* (Robert Kramer, USA); *Shirley Thompson vs. the Aliens* (Jim Sharman, Australia); *Private Collection* (Keith Salvat, Australia); *A City's Child* (Brian Kavanagh, Australia)

1973

O Lucky Man! (Lindsay Anderson, UK); *Performance* (Nicolas Roeg/Donald Cammell, UK); *Fritz the Cat* (Ralph Bakshi, USA); *The Discreet Charm of the Bourgeoisie* and *The Milky Way* (Luis Buñuel, France); *The Bitter Tears of Petra von Kant* and *The Merchant of Four Seasons* (Rainer Werner Fassbinder, W. Germany); *The Valley* (Berbet Schroeder, France); *Double Suicide* (Masahiro Shinoda, Japan); *The Butcher* (Claude Chabrol, France); *Straw Fire* (Volker Schlondorff, W. Germany); *Bleak Moments* (Mike Leigh, UK); *Klara Lust* (Kjell Grede, Sweden); *Leo the Last* (John Boorman, UK); *The Cow* and *The Postman* (Darius Mehrjui, Iran); *Tales of Mystery and Imagination* (Federico Fellini/Louis Malle/ Roger Vadim, France); *Red Psalm* (Miklós Jancsó, Hungary); *Swastika* (Philippe Mora, UK); *State of Siege* (Costa-Gavras, France); *You and Me* (Larissa Shepitko, USSR); *The Treasure* (Lester James Peries, Sri Lanka); *A Slip-up* (Jan Lomnicki, Poland); *I Am Curious Yellow* and *Blue* (Vilgot Sjoman, Sweden); *The Mattei Affair* (Francesco Rosi, Italy); *Emitai* (Ousmane Sembene, Senegal); *Scarecrow* (Jerry Schatzberg, USA); *Rendezvous at Bray* (Andre Delvaux, Belgium); *The True Nature of Bernadette* (Gilles Carle, Canada); *Dear Summer Sister* (Nagisa Oshima, Japan); *Morgiana* (Juraj Herz, Czechoslovakia); *The Salamander* (Alain Tanner, Switzerland); *The Harder they Come* (Perry Henzell, Jamaica)

1974

Andrei Roublev (Andrei Tarkovsky, USSR); *Spirit of the Beehive* (Victor Erice, Spain); *The Cars That Ate Paris* (Peter Weir, Australia); *Zardoz* (John Boorman, UK); *Love in the Afternoon* (Eric Rohmer, France); *Distant Thunder* (Satyajit Ray, India); *The Fear of the Goalkeeper* (Wim Wenders, W. Germany); *The Clockmaker of St. Paul* (Bertrand Tavernier, France); *Mean Streets* (Martin Scorsese, USA); *Red Wedding* (Claude Chabrol, France); *Return from Africa* (Alain Tanner, Switzerland); *The Conversation* (Francis Ford Coppola, USA); *The Wanderers* (Kon Ichikawa, Japan); *The Traitors* (Raymundo Gleyzer, Argentina); *Between Friends* (Don Shebib, Canada); *The Wedding* (Andrzej Wajda, Poland); *Turkish Delight* (Paul Verhoeven, Netherlands); *Pirosmani* (Georgy Shengelaya, USSR); *The Pedestrian* (Maximilian Schell, W. Germany); *The Invitation* (Claude Goretta, Switzerland); *History of Post-War Japan* (Shohei Imamura, Japan); *Rejeanne Padovani* (Denys Arcand, Canada); *Sindbad* (Zoltan Huszarik, Hungary); *Days of Betrayal* (Otakar Vavra, Czechoslovakia); *One Man's War* (Risto Jaarva, Finland); *Chung Kuo: China* (Michelangelo Antonioni, Italy); *Illumination* (Krztsztof Zanussi, Poland); *Belle* (Andre Delvaux, Belgium); *27A* (Esben Storm, Australia); *The Three Musketeers* (Richard Lester, UK)

| Rouben Mamoulian retrospective

1975

Sunday Too Far Away (Ken Hannam, Australia); *California Split* (Robert Altman, USA); *The Phantom of Liberty* (Luis Buñuel, France); *Alice in the Cities* (Wim Wenders, W. Germany); *The Mouth Agape* (Maurice Pialat, France); *25 Fireman's Street* (István Szabó, Hungary); *The Circumstance* (Ermanno Olmi, Italy); *Nada* (Claude Chabrol, France); *Sweet Movie* (Dušan Makavejev, Canada); *The Passenger* (Michelangelo Antonioni, Italy); *Day of the Locust* (John Schlesinger, USA); *Shadowman* (Georges Franju, France); *Still Life* (Sohreb Shahid Saless, Iran); *Himiko* (Masahiro

Shinoda, Japan); *Celine and Julie Go Boating* (Jacques Rivette, France); *The Holy Office* (Arturo Ripstein, Mexico); *The Valiant Ones* (King Hu, Hong Kong); *Shampoo* (Hal Ashby, USA); *Elektreia* (Miklós Jancsó, Hungary); *The Brutalisation of Franz Blum* (Reinhard Hauff, W. Germany); *Snowfall* (Ferenc Kosa, Hungary); *Brother, Can You Spare a Dime?* (Philippe Mora, UK); *Les Ordres* (Michel Brault, Canada); *Cousin Angelica* (Carlos Saura, Spain); *The Sandglass* (Wojciech J. Has, Poland); *Not as Bad as All That* (Claude Goretta, Switzerland); *A Village Performance of Hamlet* (Krsto Papic, Yugoslavia); Allonsonfan (Paolo & Vittorio Taviani); *Occasional Work of a Female Slave* (Alexander Kluge, W. Germany)

+ Australian retrospective

1976

Seven Beauties (Lina Wertmuller, Italy); *The Devil's Playground* (Fred Schepisi, Australia); *Une Partie de Plaisir* (Claude Chabrol, France); *Land of Promise* (Andrzej Wajda, Poland); *The Travelling Players* (Theo Angelopoulos, Greece); *The Middle Man* (Satyajit Ray, India); *L'innocente* (Luchino Visconti, Italy); *Mad Dog Morgan* (Philippe Mora, Australia); *Illustrious Corpses* (Francesco Rosi, Italy); *The Balance* (Krzysztof Zanussi, Poland); *Kings of the Road* and *Wrong Movement* (Wim Wenders, W. Germany); *Wives* (Anja Breien, Norway); *Triumphal March* (Marco Bellocchio, Italy); *The Judge and the Assassin* (Bertrand Tavernier, France); *Story of Sin* (Walerian Borowczyk, Poland); *The White Wall* (Stig Björkman, Sweden); *The Lost Honor of Katharina Blum* (Volker Schlöndorff, W. Germany); *The Man Who Fell to Earth* (Nicolas Roeg, UK); *Vincent, François, Paul and the Others* (Claude Sautet, France); *Mother Kusters' Trip to Heaven* (Rainer Werner Fassbinder, W. Germany); *Adoption* (Marta Meszaros, Hungary); *Second Wind* (Don Shebib, Canada); *Welfare* (Frederick Wiseman, USA); *Poachers* (Jose-Luis Borau, Spain); *Underground* (Emile de Antonio, USA); *The Stranger and the Fog* (Bahram Beiza'I, Iran);

Xala (Ousmane Sembene, Senegal); *A Lover and His Lass* (Lasse Hallstrom, Sweden); *Touched in the Head* (Jacques Doillon, France); *Action* (Robin Spry, Canada)

1977

One Man (Robin Spry, Canada); *Numero Deux* (Jean-Luc Godard, France); *Mr Klein* (Joseph Losey, France); *In the Realm of the Senses* (Nagisa Oshima, Japan); *The Coup de Grace* (Volker Schlöndorff, W. Germany); *Mado* (Claude Sautet, France); *The Last Woman* (Marco Ferreri, Italy); *Partners* (Don Owen, Canada); *Budapest Tales* (István Szabó, Hungary); *Inside Looking Out* (Paul Cox, Australia); *Allegro non Troppo* (Bruno Bozzetto, Italy); *Daguerrotypes* (Agnes Varda, France); *Jonah Who Will Be 25 in the Year 2000* (Alain Tanner, Switzerland); *The Head of Normande Saint-Onge* (Gilles Carle, Canada); *Raise Ravens* (Carlos Saura, Spain); *Max Havelaar* (Fons Rademakers, Netherlands); *Cantata of Chile* (Humberto Solas, Cuba); *Cottage by a Wood* (Jiri Menzel, Czechoslovakia); *Meat* (Frederick Wiseman, USA); *Chinese Roulette* (Rainer Werner Fassbinder, W. Germany); *Harlan County USA* (Barbara Kopple, USA); *Shirin's Wedding* (Helma Sanders-Brahms, W. Germany); *The Long Vacation of 36* (Jaime Camino, Spain); *Time of Maturity* (Sohrad Shahid Saless, Iran); *When Joseph Returns* (Zsolt Kezdi Kovacs, Hungary); *3 Women* (Robert Altman, USA); *Backroads* (Phillip Noyce, Australia); *Happy Day* (Pantelis Voulgaris, Greece); *Juvenile Liaison* (Nicholas Broomfield, UK); *The Eyes* (Lester James Peries, Sri Lanka); *Man on the Roof* (Bo Widerberg, Sweden); *Edvard Munch* (Peter Watkins, Norway)

1978

Padre Padrone (Paolo & Vittorio Taviani, Italy); *Manthan* (Shyam Benegal, India); *The Old Country where Rimbaud Died* (Jean-Pierre Lefebvre, Canada); *Paradise Place* (Gunnel Lindblom, Sweden); *The Two of Them* (Marta Meszaros,

Hungary); *Games of Love and Loneliness* (Anja Breien, Norway); *Tell Her I Love Her* (Claude Miller, France); *Diary of a Lover* (Sohrab Shahid Saless, W. Germany); *Black and White in Colour* (Jean-Jacques Annaud, Ivory Coast); *The Miracle Tree* (Tengiz Abuladze, USSR); *The Main Actor* (Reinhard Hauff, W. Germany); *Outrageous!* (Richard Benner, Canada); *The Hunters* (Theo Angelopoulos, Greece); *Men Can't Be Raped* (Jörn Donner, Finland); *The American Friend* (Wim Wenders, W. Germany); *To an Unknown God* (Jaime Chavarri, Spain); *Spoiled Children* (Bertrand Tavernier, France); *The Last Supper* (Tomas G. Alea, Cuba); *Providence* (Alain Resnais, France); *The Apple Game* (Vera Chytilova, Czechoslovakia); *The Cycle* (Darius Mehrjui, Iran); *Black Brood* (Manuel Gutierrez Aragon, Spain); *Sleeping Dogs* (Roger Donaldson, New Zealand); *Third Person Plural* (James Ricketson, Australia); *Citizens Band* (Jonathan Demme, USA); *That Obscure Object of Desire* (Luis Buñuel, France); *Elisa My Love* (Carlos Saura, Spain); *The Shout* (Jerzy Skolimowski, UK); *The Chess Players* (Satyajit Ray, India); *Cedda* (Ousmane Sembene, Senegal); *Omar Gatlato* (Merzak Allouache, Algeria); *Filming Othello* (Orson Welles, USA); *The Night the Prowler* (Jim Sharman, Australia); *Tent of Miracles* (Nelson Pereira Dos Santos, Brazil); *Unfinished Piece for a Mechnical Piano* (Nikita Mikhalkov, USSR); *Camouflage* (Krztsztof Zanussi, Poland), *Welcome to L.A.* (Alan Rudolph, USA); *Zero Hour* (Edgar Reitz, W. Germany)

+ American silent cinema retrospective

1979

The Crying Woman (Jacques Doillon, France); *Hullabaloo Over Georgie and Bonnie's Pictures* (James Ivory, UK); *Spiral* (Krzysztof Zanussi, Poland); *My Way Home* (Bill Douglas, UK); *Insiang* (Lino Brocka, Philippines); *Those Magnificent Movie Cranks* (Jiri Menzel, Czechoslovakia); *The Idlers of the Fertile Valley* (Nikos Panayotopoulos, Greece); *The Role* (Shyam

Benegal, India); *In a Year with 13 Moons* and *The Marriage of Maria Braun* (Rainer Werner Fassbinder, W. Germany); *A Simple Story* (Claude Sautet, France); *Legend of the Mountain* (King Hu, Hong Kong); *Stars in the Hair, Tears in the Eyes* (Ivan Nichev, Bulgaria); *Knife in the Head* (Reinhard Hauff, W. Germany); *Ecce Bombo* (Nanni Moretti, Italy); *Bilbao* (Bigas Luna, Spain); *Gates of Heaven* (Errol Morris, USA); *Chez Nous* (Jan Halldoff, Sweden); *The National Shotgun* (Luis G. Berlanga, Spain); *Woman in a Twilight Garden* (Andre Delvaux, Belgium); *Next of Kin* (Anja Breien, Norway); *Blindfolded Eyes* (Carlos Saura, Spain); *Beloved Lover* (Bruno Barreto, Brazil); *The Boon* (Shyam Benegal, India); *A Perfect Couple* (Robert Altman, USA); *Man of Marble* (Andrzej Wajda, Poland); *The Baron* (Anders Refn, Denmark); *Empire of Passion* (Nagisa Oshima, Japan); *Violette Noziere* (Claude Chabrol, France); *Assault on Precinct 13* (John Carpenter, USA); *Dossier 51* (Michel Deville, France); *Blue Collar* (Paul Schrader, USA); *Messidor* (Alain Tanner, Switzerland); *Alexandria Why?* (Youssef Chahine, Egypt); *Nick Carter in Prague* (Oldrich Lipsky, Czechoslovakia); *The Plumber* (Peter Weir, Australia); *The Stud Farm* (Andras Kovacs, Hungary); *In a Wild Moment* (Claude Berri, France); *Movie Movie* (Stanley Donen, USA)

1980

Radio On (Chris Petit, UK); *Mama turns 100* (Carlos Saura, Spain); *Raining in the Mountain* (King Hu, Hong Kong); *Confidence* (István Szabó, Hungary); *Death Watch* (Bertrand Tavernier, France); *Vengeance is Mine* (Shohei Imamura, Japan); *Camera Buff* (Krzysztof Kieslowski, Poland); *The Tin Drum* (Volker Schlöndorff, W. Germany); *Heartland* (Richard Pearce, USA); *The Elephant God* (Satyajit Ray, India); *Christ Stopped at Eboli* (Francesco Rosi, Italy); *The Chain Reaction* (Ian Barry, Australia); *Sentimental Journey* (Michel Deville, France); *The Great Rock 'n' Roll Swindle* (Julian Temple, UK); *Fish Hawk*

(Don Shebib, Canada); *Best Boy* (Ira Wohl, USA); *A Respectable Life* (Stefan Jarl, Sweden); *The Mirror* (Andrei Tarkovsky, USSR); *The Fog* (John Carpenter, USA); *The Survivors* (Tomas G. Alea, Cuba); *Without Anaesthetic* (Andrzej Wajda, Poland); *Junoon* (Shyam Benegal, India); *Love on the Run* (François Truffaut, France); *Germany Pale Mother* (Helma Sanders-Brahms); *Tall Shadows in the Wind* (Bahman Farmanara, Iran); *La Luna* (Bernardo Bertolucci, Italy); *The Herd* (Zeki Okten, Turkey); *Angi Vera* (Pal Gabor, Hungary); *Middle Age Spread* (John Reid, New Zealand); *Shall We Dance First?* (Annette Olsen, Denmark); *Buffet Froid* (Bertrand Blier, France); *The Tempest* (Derek Jarman, UK); *The Last of the Blue Devils* (Bruce Ricker, USA); *On Company Business* (Allan Francovich, USA); *Poto and Cabengo* (Jean-Pierre Gorin, USA)

+ István Szabó retrospective

1981

Eijanaika (Shohei Imamura, Japan); *Health* and *Quintet* (Robert Altman, USA); *The Conductor* (Andrzej Wajda, Poland); *Faster Faster* (Carlos Saura, Spain); *Lightning Over Water* (Wim Wenders/Nicholas Ray, W. Germany); *The Life and Times of Rosie the Riveter* (Connie Field, USA); *Dedicatoria* (Jaime Chavarri, Spain); *Mueda: Memory and Massacre* (Ruy Guerra, Mozambique); *The Falls* (Peter Greenaway, UK); *Grown-Ups* (Mike Leigh, UK); *Pass Your Exams First* (Maurice Pialat, France); *The Cuenca Crime* (Pilar Miro, Spain); *The Beads of One Rosary* (Kazimerz Kutz, Poland); *My American Uncle* (Alain Resnais, France); *The Enemy* (Zeki Okten, Turkey); *A Priceless Day* (Peter Gothar, Hungary); *Land and Sons* (Agust Gudmundsson, Iceland); *Hide and Seek* (Dan Wolman, Israel); *The Grass is Singing* (Michael Raeburn, Zambia); *Bye Bye Brazil* (Carlos Diegues, Brazil); *Alexander the Great* (Theo Angelopoulos, Greece); *Malou* (Jeanine Meerapfel, W. Germany); *Chance* (Feliks Falk, Poland); *The Boat Is Full* (Markus Imhoof, Switzerland); *And Quiet Rolls the Dawn* and *In Search of Famine* (Mrinal Sen, India); *Sitting Ducks* (Henry Jaglom, USA); *The Constant Factor* and *Contract* (Krzysztof Zanussi, Poland); *Slow Attack* (Reinhnard Hauff, W. Germany); *The Black Hand* (Fernando Colomo, Spain)

+ Rare film retrospective

1982

Pixote (Hector Babenco, Brazil); *Moonlighting* (Jerzy Skolimowski, UK); *Americana* (David Carradine, USA); *Broken Sky* (Ingrid Thulin, Sweden); *Veronika Voss* (Rainer Werner Fassbinder, W. Germany); *Muddy River* (Kohei Oguri, Japan); *Blood Wedding* (Carlos Saura, Spain); *The Witness* (Peter Bacso, Hungary); *Cry of the Wounded* (Govind Nihalani, India); *Diva* (Jean-Jacques Beineix, France); *Britannia Hospital* (Lindsay Anderson, UK); *Bad Blood* (Mike Newell, New Zealand); *Garde a Vue* (Claude Miller, France); *A Question of Silence* (Marleen Gorris, Netherlands); *No Mercy No Future* (Helma Sanders-Brahms, W. Germany); *A Strange Affair* (Pierre Granier-Deferre, France); *The Scarecrow* (Sam Pillsbury, New Zealand); *Squizzy Taylor* (Kevin Dobson, Australia); *Looks and Smiles* (Ken Loach, UK); *Light Years Away* (Alain Tanner, Switzerland); *Circle of Deceit* (Volker Schlöndorff, W. Germany); *The Girl with the Red Hair* (Ben Verbong, Netherlands); *Celeste* (Percy Adlon, W. Germany); *The Aviator's Wife* (Eric Rohmer, France); *Burden of Dreams* (Les Blank, USA); *Soldier Girls* (Nick Broomfield/Joan Churchill, USA); *Tender Hours* (Carlos Saura, Spain); *The Atomic Café* (Kevin Rafferty, USA); *Gregory's Girl* (Bill Forsyth, UK); *Farewell to the Island* (Mitsuo Yanagimachi, Japan); *Coup de Torchon* (Bertrand Tavernier, France)

+ Rare horror film retrospective

1983

Forbidden Relations (Zsolt Kezdi-Kovacs, Hungary); *Private Life* (Yuli Raizman, USSR); *Street Kids* (Rob Scott/Leigh Tilson, Australia); *Alsino and the Condor* (Miguel Littin, Nicaragua); *Lucien Brouillard* (Bruno Carriere, Canada); *Another Time Another Place* (Michael Radford, UK); *Return Engagement* (Alan Rudolph, USA); *The Horse* (Ali Ozgenturk, Turkey); *The Night of Varennes* (Ettore Scola, Italy); *The King of Comedy* (Martin Scorsese, USA); *Deliverance* (Satyajit Ray, India); *The Herdsman* (Xie Jin, China); *Irezumi, Spirit of Tattoo* (Yoichi Takabayashi, Japan); *Hero* (Barney Platts-Mills, UK); *Born in Flames* (Lizzie Borden, USA); *The Writing on the Wall* (France, Armand Gatti); *The Three Crowns of the Sailor* (Raul Ruiz, France); *Toute une Nuit* (Chantal Akerman, Belgium); *Too Early, Too Late* (Jean-Marie Straub/Daniele Huillet, France); *A Blow to the Heart* (Gianni Amelio, Italy); *Sans Soleil* (Chris Marker, France); *Stranger Than Paradise* (Jim Jarmusch, USA); *The Draughtsman's Contract* (Peter Greenaway, UK); *The Hatter's Ghosts* (Claude Chabrol, France); *Land of Plenty* (Morten Arnfred, Denmark); *The Taste of Water* (Orlow Seunke, Netherlands); *The Ballad of Gregorio Cortez* (Robert Young, USA); *Rat Trap* (Adoor Gopalakrishnan, India); *Liquid Sky* (Slava Tsukerman, USA); *My Memories of Old Beijing* (Wu Yigong, China); *Daniel takes a Train* (Pal Sandor, Hungary); *Angel* (Neil Jordan, Ireland); *Chicken Ranch* (Nick Broomfield, UK); *In the King of Prussia* (Emile de Antonio, USA); *The Grey Fox* (Philip Borsos, Canada); *Celsa and Cora* (Gary Kildea, Australia); *Demons in the Garden* (Manuel Gutierrez Aragon, Spain); *Danton* (Andrzej Wajda, France); *The State of Things* (Wim Wenders, W. Germany)

+ Peter Greenaway retrospective + Censored films retrospective